AIRLINES
WORLDWIDE

More than 350 Airlines Described and Illustrated in Colour

B I HENGI

Midland Publishing

Airlines Worldwide – 3rd edition
© 2000 NARA-Verlag and Midland Publishing

ISBN 1 85780 103 2

First published in 2000 by
NARA-Verlag, Postfach 1241, D-85388 Allershausen,
Germany, as 'Fluggesellschaften Weltweit' 4th edn.

English language edition published 2000 by
Midland Publishing
24 The Hollow, Earl Shilton
Leicester, LE9 7NA, England.
Telephone: 01455 847 256   Fax: 01455 841 805
E-mail: midlandbooks@compuserve.com

Midland Publishing is an imprint of
Ian Allan Publishing Ltd

Worldwide distribution (except North America):
Midland Counties Publications
Unit 3 Maizefield, Hinckley Fields,
Hinckley, Leics, LE10 1YF, England.
Telephone: 01455 233 747   Fax: 01455 233 737
E-mail: midlandbooks@compuserve.com

North American trade distribution:
Specialty Press Publishers and Wholesalers
11605 Kost Dam Road, North Branch, MN 55056, USA
Telephone: 651 583 3239   Fax: 651 583 2023
Toll free telephone: 800 895 4585

Design concept and layout
© 2000 NARA-Verlag and Midland Publishing

Printed via World Print Ltd, Hong Kong.

Cover and title page illustrations:
Uwe Gleisberg
Josef Krauthäuser collection
Albert Kuhbandner

AIRLINES
WORLDWIDE
More than 300 Airlines Described and Illustrated in Colour

This book is an English-language version of the successful German 'Fluggesellschaften Weltweit', now in its fourth edition, and is the third edition to appear in its English language guise.

Yet again significantly expanded from previous versions , it aims to give an overview and illustrate 351 of the world's leading or more interesting airlines, including smaller national operators, with their history, routes, aircraft fleet and operations.

It cannot set out to be a comprehensive guide to every operator; adding together all the scheduled airlines, holiday and charter and local service operators gives an answer in the region of 5,000, which if included, would clearly result in a very large and extremely expensive publication.

The German edition was compiled by B I Hengi, edited by Josef Krauthäuser and published in Spring 2000. It has been translated, edited and updated by Neil Lewis so that it is as current as possible at press-time in September 2000.

Fleet quantities, and especially details of aircraft on order for future delivery, must be regarded as approximate only. With aircraft being delivered, retired, temporarily stored, loaned to associate operators, or leased between operators every day, it is impossible to be definitive. We have omitted some small aircraft which may be in an airline's fleet for training, communications or other purposes and are not in general passenger service.

Likewise, what are termed as future orders in some circles can range from genuinely firm and fully signed-up contracts, through options, 'rolling options' to such nebulous things as letters of intent for up to 15 years hence! However we have done our best to ensure that the information in these pages is as up-to-date as possible and forms a valid and useful guide to the operations of the airlines described.

Since the last edition was published, there has been a rapid acceleration in airlines' use of codeshares and in the formation and growth of the more structured global alliances, and more information on these is included.

Similarly, the electronic communications media have gained hugely in acceptance and importance, and in this edition, web addresses have been included for most airlines for the first time.

We hope that you will enjoy this book, and welcome your comments for future editions.

Midland Publishing
September 2000

Contents

Airport Abbreviations/Codes

Europe

Aalborg (AAL) Denmark
Aalesund (AES) Norway
Aarhus (AAR) Denmark
Aberdeen (ABZ) Great
  Britain
Adana (ADA) Turkey
Adler/Sochi (AER)
Ajaccio (AJA) France
Akureyri (AEY) Iceland
Alderney ACI) Great
  Britain
Alghero (AHO) Italy
Alicante (ALC) Spain
Almeria (LEI) Spain
Alta (ALF) Norway
Altenrhein (ACH)
  Switzerland
Amsterdam (AMS)
  Netherlands
Ancona (AOI) Italy
Angers (ANE) France
Ankara (ANK) Turkey
Antalya (AYT) Turkey
Antwerp (ANR) Belgium
Arad (ARW) Romania
Archangelsk (ARH) Russia
Arrecife (ACE) Spain
Athens (ATH) Greece
Augsburg (AGB) Germany
Avignon (AVN) France
Banja Luka (BNX) Bosnia
Barcelona (BCN) Spain
Bardufoss (BDU) Norway
Bari (BRI) Italy
Basle/Mullhouse
  (BSL/MLH) Switzerland
Bastia (BIA) France
Belfast (BFS) Great Britain
Belgrade (BEG)
  Yugoslavia
Bergamo (BGY) Italy
Bergen (BGO) Norway
Berlin-Schönefeld (SFX)
  Germany
Berlin-Tegel (TXL)
  Germany
Berlin-Tempelhof (THF)
  Germany
Berne (BRN) Switzerland
Bervelag (BVG) Norway
Biarritz (BIQ) France
Bilbao (BIO) Spain
Billund (BLL) Denmark
Birmingham (BHX) Great
  Britain
Bodo (BOO) Norway
Bodrum (BXN) Turkey
Bologna (BLQ) Italy
Bordeaux (BOD) France

Borlange (BLE) Sweden
Bornholm (RNN) Denmark
Bourgas (BOJ) Bulgaria
Bratislava (BTS) Slovakia
Braunschweig (BWE)
  Germany
Bremen (BRE) Germany
Brest (BES) France
Brindisi (BDS) Italy
Bristol (BRS) Great Britain
Brno (BRQ) Czech
  Republic
Brussels (BRU) Belgium
Bucharest-Otopeni (OTP)
  Romania
Budapest (BUD) Hungary
Caen (CFR) France
Cagliari (CAG) Italy
Cardiff (CWL) Great Britain
Catania (CTA) Italy
Chania (CHQ) Greece
Chisinau (KIV) Moldavia
Clermont-Ferrand (CFE)
  France
Cologne/Bonn (CGN)
  Germany
Copenhagen (CPA)
  Denmark
Corfu (CFU) Greece
Cork (ORK) Ireland
Dalaman (DLM) Turkey
Dijon (DIJ) France
Dinard (DNR) France
Dnepropetrovsk (DNK)
  Ukraine
Dortmund (DTM) Germany
Dresden (DRS) Germany
Dublin (DUB) Ireland
Dubrovnik (DCA) Croatia
Düsseldorf (DUS)
  Germany
East Midlands (EMA)
  Great Britain
Edinburgh (EDI) Great
  Britain
Eindhoven (EIN)
  Netherlands
Elba (EBA) France
Ercan (ECN) Turkey
  Cyprus
Erfurt (ERF) Germany
Erzurum (ERZ) Turkey
Esbjerg (EBJ) Denmark
Faro (FAO) Portugal
Faroes (FAE) Denmark
Florence (FLR) Italy
Frankfurt (FRA) Germany
Friedrichshafen (FDH)
  Germany
Fuerteventura (FUE) Spain
Funchal (FNC) Portugal

Gdansk (GDN) Poland
Geneva (GVA) Switzerland
Genoa (GOA) Italy
Gerona (GRO) Spain
Gibraltar (GIB) Gibraltar
Glasgow (GLA) Great
  Britain
Gothenburg (GOT)
  Sweden
Granada (GRX) Spain
Graz (GRZ) Austria
Guernsey (GCI) Great
  Britain
Hamburg (HAM) Germany
Hammerfest (HFT) Norway
Hanover (HAJ) Germany
Haugesund (HAU) Norway
Helsinki (HEL) Finland
Heraklion (HER) Greece
Hof (HOQ) Germany
Horta (HOR) Portugal
Hudiksvall (HUV) Sweden
Humberside (HUY) Great
  Britain
Ibiza (IBZ) Spain
Innsbruck (INN) Austria
Inverness (INV) Great
  Britain
Isle of Man (IOM) Great
  Britain
Istanbul (IST) Turkey
Ivalo (IVL) Finland
Izmir (ADB) Turkey
Jerez de la Frontera (XRY)
  Spain
Jersey (JER) Great Britain
Jonköpping (JKG)
  Sweden
Kalamata (KLX) Greece
Kaliningrad (KGD) Russia
Katowice (KTW) Poland
Kaunas (KUN) Lithuania
Kefalonia (EFL) Greece
Keflavik (KEF) Iceland
Kharkov (HRK) Ukraine
Kiel (KEL) Germany
Kiev-Borispol (KBP)
  Ukraine
Kirkenes (KKN) Norway
Klagenfurt (KLU) Austria
Kos (KGS) Greece
Krakow (KRK) Poland
Kristianstad (KID) Sweden
Kristiansund (KSU) Norway
La Coruna (LCG) Spain
Lamezia Terme (SUF) Italy
Larnaca (LCA) Cyprus
Las Palmas (LPA) Spain
Le Havre (LEH) France
Leeds/Bradford (LBA)
  Great Britain

Leipzig (LEJ) Germany
Lille (LIL) France
Linköping (LPI) Sweden
Linz (LNZ) Austria
Lisbon (LIS) Portugal
Liverpool (LPL) Great
  Britain
Ljubljana (LJU) Slovenia
London-City Airport (LCY)
  Great Britain
London-Gatwick (LGW)
  Great Britain
London-Heathrow (LHR)
  Great Britain
London-Luton (LTN) Great
  Britain
London-Stansted (STN)
  Great Britain
Londonderry (LDY) Great
  Britain
Lourdes (LDE) France
Lugano (LUG) Switzerland
Luxembourg (LUX)
Lvov (LWO) Ukraine
Lyon (LYS) France
Maastricht (MST)
  Netherlands
Madrid (MAD) Spain
Mahon/Menorca (MAH)
  Spain
Malaga (AGP) Spain
Malmö-Sturup (MMX)
  Sweden
Malta (MLA)
Manchester (MAN) Great
  Britain
Marseilles (MRS) France
Milan-Linate (LIN) Italy
Milan-Malpensa (MXP)
  Italy
Mineralnye Vody (MRV)
  Russia
Minsk (MSQ) Belarus
Montpellier (MPL) France
Moscow-Domodedovo
  (DME) Russia
Moscow-Sheremetyevo
  (SVO) Russia
Moscow-Vnukovo (VKO)
  Russia
Mostar (OMO) Bosnia-
  Herzegovina
Munich FJS (MUC)
  Germany
Münster/Osnabrück
  (FMO) Germany
Murmansk (MMK) Russia
Mykonos (JMK) Greece
Nantes (NTE) France
Naples (NAP) Italy
Narvik (NVK) Norway

Newcastle (NCL) Great Britain
Nice (NCE) France
Nimes (FNI) France
Norrköping (NRK) Sweden
Norwich.(NWI) Great Britain
Nuremberg (NUE) Germany
Nuuk (GOH) Greenland
Odense (ODE) Denmark
Odessa (ODS) Ukraine
Ohrid (OHD) Macedonia
Olbia (OLB) Italy
Oslo (OSL) Norway
Ostrava (OSR) Czech Republic
Oulu (OUL) Finland
Paderborn/Lippstadt (PAD) Germany
Palermo (PMO) Italy
Palma de Mallorca (PMI) Spain
Pamplona (PNA) Spain
Paphos (PFO) Greece
Paris-Charles de Gaulle (CDG) France
Paris-Orly (ORY) France
Perpignan (PGF) France
Pisa (PSA) Italy
Ponta Delgada (PDL) Portugal
Porto (OPO) Portugal
Porto Santo (PXO) Portugal
Prague (PRG) Czech Republic
Prestwick (PIK) Great Britain
Pula (PUY) Slovenia
Reggio Calabria (REG) Italy
Rennes (RNS) France
Reus (REU) Spain
Reykjavik (RKV) Iceland
Rhodes (RHO) Greece
Riga (RIX) Lithuania
Rimini (RMI) Italy
Rome-Ciampino (CIA) Italy
Rome-Leonardo da Vinci (FCO) Italy
Rostov (ROV) Russia
Rotterdam (RTM) Netherlands
Rouen (URO) France
Rovaniemi (RVN) Finland
Saarbrücken (SCN) Germany
Salzburg (SZG) Austria
Samos (SMI) Greece

Santa Cruz de la Palma (SPC) Spain
Santa Maria (SMA) Portugal
Santander (SDR) Spain
Santiago de Compostella (SCQ)
Santorini (JTR) Greece
Sarajevo (SJJ) Bosnia-Herzegovina
Seville (SVQ) Spain
Shannon (SNN) Ireland
Shetland-Sumburgh (LSI) Great Britain
Simferopol (SIP) Ukraine
Skiathos (JSI) Greece
Skopje (SKP) Macedonia
Sofia (SOF) Bulgaria
Sonderborg (SGD) Denmark
Southampton (SOU) Great Britain
Southend (SEN) Great Britain
Split (SPU) Croatia
St.Petersburg (LED) Russia
Stavanger (SVG) Norway
Stockholm-Arlanda (ARN) Sweden
Stockholm-Bromma (BMA) Sweden
Stornoway (SYY) Great Britain
Strasbourg (SXB) France
Stuttgart (STR) Germany
Sundsvall (SDL) Sweden
Svolvaer (SVJ) Norway
Tallinn (TLL) Estonia
Tampere (TMP) Finland
Tees-side (MME) Great Britain
Tenerife (TFS) Spain
Thessaloniki (SKG) Greece
Thingeyri (TEY)
Timisoara (TSR)
Tirana (TIA) Albania
Tivat (TIV) Yugoslavia
Toulouse (TLS) France
Trabzon (TZX) Turkey
Trieste (TRS) Italy
Tromso (TOS) Norway
Trondheim (TRD) Norway
Turin (TRN) Italy
Turku (TKU) Finland
Umea (UME) Sweden
Valencia (VLC) Spain
Varna (VAR) Bulgaria
Vasteras (VST)
Venice (VCE) Italy

Verona (VRN) Italy
Vienna (VIE) Austria
Vilniubania (VNO) Lithuania
Visby (VBY) Sweden
Warsaw (WAW) Poland
Westerland (GWT) Germany
Wroclaw (WRO) Poland
Zadar (ZAD) Croatia
Zagreb (ZAG) Croatia
Zakynthos (ZTH) Greece
Zürich (ZRH) Switzerland

North America

Abbotsford (YXX) Canada
Aberdeen (ABR) USA
Abilene (ABI) USA
Adak Island (ADK) USA
Akron (AKC) USA
Alamogordo (ALM) USA
Alamosa (ALS) USA
Albany, NY (ALB) USA
Albuquerque (ABQ) USA
Alexandria (AEX) USA
Allentown (ABE) USA
Amarillo (AMA) USA
Anchorage (ANC) USA
Aniak (ANI) USA
Appleton (ATW) USA
Asheville (AVL) USA
Aspen (ASE) USA
Atlanta (ATL) USA
Atlantic City (AIY) USA
Augusta (AGS) USA
Austin (AUS) USA
Baie Comeau (YBC) Canada
Baker Lake (YBK) Canada
Bakersfield (BFL) USA
Baltimore (BWI) USA
Bangor (BGR) USA
Bar Harbor (BHB) USA
Barrow (BRW) USA
Baton Rouge (BTR) USA
Beaumont/Port Arthur (BPT) USA
Bellingham (BLI) USA
Bermuda (BDA) Bermuda
Bethel (BET) USA
Billings (BIL) USA
Bimini (BIM) Bahamas
Binghampton (BGM) USA
Birmingham (BHM) USA
Blanc Sablon (YBX) Canada
Boise (BOI) USA
Boston (BOS) USA
Bozeman (BZN) USA
Bridgeport (BDR) USA

Brownsville (BRO) USA
Buffalo (BUF) USA
Burbank (BUR) USA
Calgary (YYC) Canada
Casper (CPR) USA
Cedar Rapids (CID) USA
Charleston (CHS) USA
Charlotte (CLT) USA
Charlottsville (CHO) USA
Charlottetown (YYG) Canada
Chattanooga (CHA) USA
Cheyenne (CYS) USA
Chicago-O'Hare (ORD) USA
Chicago-Midway (MDW) USA
Chico (CIC) USA
Churchill (YYQ) Canada
Cincinnati (CVG) USA
Cleveland (CLE) USA
Colorado Springs (COS) USA
Columbia (CAE) USA
Columbus (CMH) USA
Corpus Christi (CRP) USA
Dallas/Fort Worth (DFW) USA
Dallas-Love Field (DAL) USA
Dallas-Meacham Field (FTW) USA
Dawson City (YDA) Canada
Dayton (DAY) USA
Daytona Beach (DAB) USA
Deer Lake (YDF) Canada
Del Rio (DRT) USA
Denver (DEN) USA
Des Moines (DSM) USA
Detroit MetroWayne (DTW) USA
Detroit City (DET) USA
Dillingham (DLG) USA
Duluth (DLH) USA
Durango (DRO) USA
Dutch Harbor (DUT) USA
Edmonton (YEG) Canada
Elko (EKO) USA
El Paso (ELP) USA
Eugene (EUG) USA
Fairbanks (FAI) USA
Fayetteville (FYV) USA
Flagstaff (FLG) USA
Fort Lauderdale (FLL) USA
Fort Myers (RSW) USA
Fredericton (YFC) Canada
Freeport (FPO) Bahamas
Fresno (FAT) USA
Gander (YQX) Canada

Georgetown (GGT) Bahamas
Goose Bay (YYR) Canada
Grand Canyon (GCN) USA
Great Falls (GTF) USA
Great Harbor Cay (GHC) USA
Green Bay (GRB) USA
Greensboro/High Point (GSO) USA
Greenville (GSP) USA
Gulfport/Biloxi (GPT) USA
Halifax (YHZ) Canada
Hamilton (YHM) Canada
Hana (HNM) USA
Harlingen (HRL) USA
Harrisburg (MDT) USA
Hartford (BDL) USA
Hay River (YHY) Canada
Helena (HLN) USA
Hilo (ITO) USA
Honolulu (HNL) USA
Houston-Hobby (HOU) USA
Houston-George Bush Intl. (IAH) USA
Huntsville (HSV) USA
Indianapolis (IND) USA
Inuvik (YEV) Canada
Iqalit-Frobisher (YFB) Canada
Jackson (JAN) USA
Jacksonville (JAX) USA
Juneau (JNU) USA
Kahului (OGG) USA
Kalamazoo (AZO) USA
Kalaupapa (LUP) USA
Kansas City (MCI) USA
Kauai Isl.-Lihue (LIH) USA
Kelowna (YLW) Canada
Ketchikan (KTN) USA
Key West (EYW) USA
Knoxville (TYS) USA
Kodiak (ADQ) USA
Kona (KOA) USA
Kotzebue (OTZ) USA
Kuujjuaq-Ft.Chimo (YVP) Canada
Lafayette (LFT) USA
Lake Charles (LCH) USA
Laredo (LRD) USA
Las Vegas (LAS) USA
Lexington (LEX) USA
Little Rock (LIT) USA
London (YXU) Canada
Long Beach (LGB) USA
Long Island Mc Arthur (ISP) USA
Los Angeles (LAX) USA
Louisville (SDF) USA
Macon (MCN) USA

Madison (MSN) USA
Manchester (MHT) USA
Marsh Harbor (MHH) USA
Memphis (MEM) USA
Miami (MIA) USA
Midland/Odessa (MAF) USA
Milwaukee (MKE) USA
Minot (MOT) USA
Minneapolis/St.Paul (MSP) USA
Missoula (MSO) USA
Mobile (MOB) USA
Monroe (MLU) USA
Monterey (MRY) USA
Montgomery (MGM) USA
Montreal-Dorval (YUL) Canada
Montreal-Mirabel (YMX)
Myrtle Beach (MYR) USA
Nashville (BNA) USA
Nassau (NAS) Bahamas
Natashquan (YNA) Canada
New Bern (EWN) USA
New Orleans (MSY) USA
New York-Kennedy (JFK) USA
New York-La Guardia (LGA) USA
New York-Newark (EWR) USA
Nome (OME) USA
Norfolk (ORF) USA
Norman Wells (YVQ) Canada
Oakland (OAK) USA
Oklahoma City (OKC) USA
Omaha (OMA) USA
Ontario (ONT) USA
Orlando (MCO) USA
Oshkosh (OSH) USA
Ottawa (YOW) Canada
Palm Springs (PSP) USA
Pensacola (PNS) USA
Peoria (PIA) USA
Philadelphia (PHL) USA
Phoenix (PHX) USA
Pittsburgh (PIT) USA
Pocatello (PIH) USA
Portland (PDX) USA
Prince Albert (YPA) Canada
Prince George (YXS) Canada
Prince Rupert (YPR) Canada
Quebec (YQB) Canada
Raleigh/Durham (RDU) USA
Rapid City (RAP) USA

Regina (YQR) Canada
Reno (RNO) USA
Repulse Bay (YUT) Canada
Resolute Bay (YRB) Canada
Richmond (RIC) USA
Rockford (RFD) USA
Sacramento (SMF) USA
Saint John (YSJ) Canada
St. Johns (YYT) Canada
St.Louis (STL) USA
Salt Lake City (SLC) USA
San Antonio (SAT) USA
San Diego (SAN) USA
San Francisco (SFO) USA
San Jose (SJC) USA
Santa Ana John Wayne (SNA) USA
Santa Barbara (SBA) USA
Santa Fe (SAF) USA
Saskatoon (YXE) Canada
Sault Sainte Marie (SSM) USA
Savannah (SAV) USA
Schefferville (YKL) Canada
Seattle/Tacoma (SEA) USA
Seattle-Boeing Field (BFI) USA
Sept-Iles (YZV) Canada
Sioux City (SUX) USA
Sioux Falls (FSD) USA
Sioux Lookout (YXL) Canada
South Bend (SBN) USA
Spokane (GEG) USA
Sudbury (YSB) Canada
Sun Valley (SUN) USA
Syracuse (SYR) USA
Tallahassee (TLH) USA
Tampa/St.Petersburg (TPA) USA
Thunder Bay (YQT) Canada
Toledo (TOL) USA
Toronto (YYZ) Canada
Toronto-Island (YTZ) Canada
Tri-Cities (TRI) USA
Tucson (TUS) USA
Tulsa (TUL) USA
Valdez (VDZ) USA
Vancouver (YVR) Canada
Victoria (YYJ) Canada
Waco (ACT) USA
Washington-Dulles Intl. (IAD) USA
Washington-Ronald Reagan Natl. (DCA) USA

West Palm Beach (PBI) USA
West Yellowstone (WYS) USA
White Horse (YXY) Canada
Wichita (ICT) USA
Windsor (YQG) Canada
Winnipeg (YWG) Canada
Winston-Salem (INT) USA
Yakutat (YAK) Canada
Yellowknife (YZF) Canada
Yuma (YUM) USA

South America/Caribbean

Acapulco (ACA) Mexico
Aguascalientes (AGU) Mexico
Altamira (ATM), Brazil
Anguilla (AXA) Leeward Islands
Antigua (ANU) Leeward Islands
Antofagasta (ANF) Chile
Aracaju (AJU) Brazil
Aracatuba (ARU) Brazil
Araguaina (AUX) Brazil
Arauca (AUC) Columbia
Arequipa (AQP) Peru
Arica (ARI) Chile
Armenia (AXM) Columbia
Aruba (AUA) Neth Antilles
Asuncion (ASU) Paraguay
Bahia Blanca (BHI) Argentina
Bahia Solano (BSC) Columbia
Balmaceda (BBA) Chile
Barbados (BGI) Barbados
Barbuda (BBQ) Leeward Islands
Barcelona (BLA) Venezuela
Barquisemeto (BRM) Venezuela
Barranquilla (BAQ) Columbia
Belem (BEL) Brazil
Belize City (BZE) Belize
Belo Horizonte Intl. (CNF) Brazil
Belo Horizonte-Pampulha (PLU)
Boa Vista (BVB) Brazil
Bogota (BOG) Columbia
Bonaire (BON) Neth Antilles
Brasilia (BSB) Brazil
Bucaramanga (BGA) Columbia

8

Buenos Aires-J.Newbery (AEP)
Buenos Aires-Pistarini (EZE) Argentina
Cajamarca (CJA) Peru
Calama (CJC) Chile
Cali (CLO) Columbia
Camaguey (CMW) Cuba
Campo Grande (CGR) Brazil
Cancun (CUN) Mexico
Caracas (CCS) Venezuela
Cartagena (CTG) Columbia
Cayenne (CAY) French Guyana
Cayman Brac (CYB) Cayman Island
Chetumal (CTM) Mexico
Chihuahua (CUU) Mexico
Ciudad Bolivar (CBL) Venezuela
Ciudad Del Carmen (CME) Mexico
Ciudad Juarez (CJS) Mexico
Ciudad Obregon (CEN) Mexico
Ciudad Victoria (CVM) Mexico
Cochabamba (CBB) Bolivia
Colima (CLQ) Mexico
Comodoro Rivadavia (CRD) Argentina
Concepcion (CCP) Chile
Cordoba (COR) Argentina
Corumba (CMG) Brazil
Cozumel (CZM) Mexico
Cuiaba (CGB) Brazil
Culiacan (CUL) Mexico
Curacao (CUR) Neth Antilles
Curitiba (CWB) Brazil
Cuzco (CUZ) Peru
Dominica (DOM)
Durango (DGO) Mexico
Easter Island (IPC) Chile
Flores (FRS) Guatemala
Florianopolis (FLN) Brazil
Fort de France (FDF) Martinique
Fortaleza (FOR) Brazil
Georgetown (GEO) Guyana
Grand Cayman (GCM) Cayman Island
Grand Turk (GDT) Turks & Caicos
Grenada (GND) Grenada
Guadalajara (GDL) Mexico

Guatemala City (GUA) Guatemala
Guayaquil (GYE) Ecuador
Guaymas (GYM) Mexico
Havana (HAV) Cuba
Hermosillo (HMO) Mexico
Holguin (HOG) Cuba
Huanuco (HUU) Peru
Huatulco (HUX) Mexico
Iquassu (IGU) Brazil
Iquique (IQQ) Chile
Ixtapa/Zihuatanejo (ZIH) Mexico
Kingston (KIN) Jamaica
La Ceiba (LCE) Honduras
La Paz (LPB) Bolivia
La Paz (LAP) Mexico
La Serena (LSC) Chile
Leon/Guanajuato (BJX) Mexico
Lima (LIM) Peru
Managua (MGA) Nicaragua
Manaus (MAO) Brazil
Manizales (MZL) Columbia
Manzanillo (ZLO) Mexico
Mar del Plata (MDQ) Argentina
Maracaibo (MAR) Venezuela
Matamoros (MAM) Mexico
Mayaguez (MAZ) Puerto Rico
Mazatlan (MZT) Mexico
Medellin (MDE) Columbia
Mendoza (MDZ) Argentina
Merida (MRD) Venezuela
Mexicali (MXL) Mexico
Mexico City (MEX) Mexico
Montego Bay (MBJ) Jamaica
Monteria (MTR) Columbia
Monterrey (MTY) Mexico
Montevideo (MVD) Uruguay
Morelia (MLN) Mexico
Mount Pleasant (MPN) Falkland Islands
Natal (NAT) Brazil
Neuquen (NQN) Argentina
Nuevo Laredo (NLD) Mexico
Oaxaca (OAX) Mexico
Panama City (PTY) Panama
Paramaribo (PBM) Surinam
Pointe à Pitre (PTP) Guadeloupe
Porlamar (PMV) Venezuela
Port au Prince (PAP) Haiti

Port Elizabeth (BQU) Grenada
Port of Spain (POS) Trinidad-Tobago
Porto Alegre (POA) Brazil
Puerto Escondido (PXM) Mexico
Puerto Montt (PMC) Chile
Puerto Ordaz (PZO) Venezuela
Puerto Plata (POP) Dom. Rep.
Puerto Vallarta (PVR) Mexico
Punta Arenas (PUQ) Chile
Punta Cana (PUJ) Dom. Rep.
Punta del Este (PDP) Uruguay
Quito (UIO) Ecuador
Recife (REC) Brazil
Rio de Janeiro (GIG) Brazil
Rio Gallegos (RGL) Argentina
Rio Grande (RGA) Argentina
Riohacha (RCH) Columbia
Rosario (ROS) Argentina
Salvador (SSA) Brazil
San Andres (ADZ) Columbia
San Carlos de Bariloche (BRC)
San Jose (SJO) Costa Rica
San Juan (SJU) Puerto Rico
San Pedro Sula (SAP) Honduras
San Salvador (SAL) El Salvador
Santa Cruz (SRZ) Bolivia
Santiago (SCL) Chile
Santiago (SCU) Cuba
Santo Domingo (SDQ) Dom. Rep.
Santos Dumont (SDU) Brazil
Sao Paulo-Congonhas (CGH) Brazil
Sao Paulo-Guarulhos (GRU) Brazil
St.Croix (STX) US Virgin Islands
St.Eustatius (EUX) Neth Antilles
St.Kitts (SKB) St. Kitts/Nevis
St.Lucia (SLU) St. Lucia
St.Maarten (SXM) Neth Antilles

St.Thomas (STT) US Virgin Islands
Tampico (TAM) Mexico
Tapachula (TAP) Mexico
Tegucigalpa (TGU) Honduras
Temuco (ZCO) Chile
Tijuana (TIJ) Mexico
Torreon (TRC) Mexico
Tortola (EIS) British Virgin Islands
Trujillo (TRU) Peru
Tuxtla Gutierrez (TGZ) Mexico
Union Island (UNI) Grenada
Ushuaia (USH) Argentina
Valencia (VLN) Venezuela
Valledupar (VUP) Columbia
Varadero (VRA) Cuba
Veracruz (VER) Mexico
Villahermosa (VSA) Mexico
Villavicencio (VVC) Columbia
Virgin Gorda (VIJ) British Virgin Islands
Vitoria (VIX) Brazil
Zacatecas (ZCL) Mexico

Middle East - Asia - Australia - Pacific

Abha (AHB) Saudi Arabia
Abu Dhabi (AUH)
Adelaide (ADL) Australia
Aden (ADL) Yemen
Agartala (IXA) India
Agra (AGR) India
Ahmedabad (AMD) India
Ahwaz (AWZ) Iran
Airok (AIC) Marshall Islands
Aitape (ATP) New Guinea
Akita (AXT) Japan
Aktau (SCO) Kazakstan
Al Ain (AAN) UAE
Al Baha (ABT) Saudi Arabia
Al Fujairah (FJR) UAE
Al Ghaydah (AAY) Yemen
Albury (ABX) Australia
Aleppo (ALP) Syria
Alexandria (ALY) Egypt
Alice Springs (ASP) Australia
Almaty (ALA) Kazakstan
Alor Setar (AOR) Malaysia
Alotau (GUR) Papua New Guinea

9

Altai (LTI) Mongolia
Amami o Shima (ASJ)
  Japan
Ambon (AMQ) Indonesia
Amman (AMM) Jordan
Amritsar (ATQ) India
Aomori (AOJ) Japan
Apia (APW) Samoa
Arar (RAE) Saudi Arabia
Armindale (ARM) Australia
Asahikawa (AKJ) Japan
Ashkhabad (ASB)
  Turkmenistan
Astana (TSE) Kazakstan
Auckland (AKL) New
  Zealand
Aurangabad (IXU) India
Ayers Rock (AYQ) Australia
Bacolod (BCD) Philippines
Bagdogra (IXB) India
Baghdad (SDA) Iraq
Bahrain (BAH)
Baku (BAK) Azerbaijan
Balikpapan (BPN)
  Indonesia
Ballina (BNK) Australia
Bandar Abbas (BND) Iran
Bandar Seri Begawan
  (BWN) Brunei
Bandung (BDO) Indonesia
Bangalore (BLR) India
Bangkok (BKK) Thailand
Banjarmasin (BDJ)
  Indonesia
Batam (BTH) Indonesia
Beijing (BJS) China
Beirut (BEI) Lebanon
Bhopal (BHO) India
Biak (BIK) Indonesia
Bintulu (BTU) Malaysia
Bishkek (FRU) Kyrgyzstan
Bora Bora (BOB) Tahiti
Brisbane (BNE) Australia
Broken Hill (BHQ)
  Australia
Broome (BME) Australia
Bundaberg (BDB)
  Australia
Bushehr (BUZ) Iran
Cairns (CNS) Australia
Calcutta (CCU) India
Calicut (CCJ) India
Canberra (CBR) Australia
Cebu (CEB) Philippines
Changchun (CGQ) China
Changzhou (CZX) China
Cheju (CJU) South Korea
Chengdu (CTU) China
Chennai (MAA) India
Chiang Mai (CNX)
  Thailand

Chiayi (CYI) Taiwan
Chinju (HIN) South Korea
Chittagong (CGP)
  Bangladesh
Chongqing (CKG) China
Christchurch (CHC) New
  Zealand
Cochin (COK) India
Cocos Island (CCK)
  Cocos Islands
Coffs Harbour (CFS)
  Australia
Colombo (CMB) Srilanka
Da Nang (DAD) Vietnam
Dacca (DAC) Bangladesh
Dalian (DLC) China
Damascus (DAM) Syria
Darwin (DRW) Australia
Davao (DVO) Philippines
Delhi (DEL) India
Denpasar (DPS) Indonesia
Dhahran (DHA) Saudi
  Arabia
Doha (DOH) UAE
Dubai (DXB) UAE
Dunedin (DUD) New
  Zealand
Dushanbe (DYU)
  Tajikistan
Espiritu Santo (SON)
  Vanuatu
Faisalabad (LYP) Pakistan
Fukuoka (FUK) Japan
Fukushima (FKS) Japan
Fuzhou (FOC) China
Gan Island (GAN)
  Maldives
Gassim (ELQ) Saudi
  Arabia
Gaza (GZA) Palestine
Gladstone (GLT) Australia
Goa (GOI) India
Gold Coast (OOL)
  Australia
Goroka (GKA) Papua-New
  Guinea
Guam (GUM)
Guangzhou (CAN) China
Guilin (KWL) China
Haikou (HAK) China
Haiphong (HPH) Vietnam
Hamilton (HLZ) New
  Zealand
Hangzhou (HGH) China
Hanoi (HAN) Vietnam
Harbin (HRB) China
Hat Yai (HDY) Thailand
Hiroshima (HIJ) Japan
Ho Chi Minh City (SGN)
  Vietnam
Hobart (HBA) Australia

Honiara (HIR) Solomon
  Islands
Hong Kong (HKG) China
Hualien (HUN) Taiwan
Hyderabad (HYD) India
Invercargill (IVC) New
  Zealand
Ipoh (IPH) Malaysia
Irkutsk (IKT) Russia
Isfahan (IFN) Iran
Ishigaki (ISG) Japan
Islamabad (ISB) Pakistan
Jakarta-Halim (HLP)
  Indonesia
Jakarta-Soekarno (CGK)
  Indonesia
Jeddah (JED) Saudi
  Arabia
Jinan (TNA) China
Johnston Island (JON)
Johur Bahru (JHB)
  Malaysia
Jokjakarta (JOG)
  Indonesia
Kabul (KBL) Afghanistan
Kagoshima (KOJ) Japan
Kalgoorlie (KGI) Australia
Kaoshiung (KHH) Taiwan
Karachi (KHI) Pakistan
Kathmandu (KTM) Nepal
Khabarovsk (KHV) Russia
Komatsu (KMQ) Japan
Kota Bharu (KBR)
  Malaysia
Kota Kinabalu (BKI)
  Malaysia
Krasnoyarsk (KJA) Russia
Kuala Lumpur (KUL)
  Malaysia
Kuching (KCH) Malaysia
Kunming (KMG) China
Kuwait (KWI)
Kwajalein (KWA) Marshall
  Islands
Lae (LAE) Papua-New
  Guinea
Lahore (LHE) Pakistan
Langkawi (LGK) Malaysia
Lanzhou (LHW) China
Longreach (LRE) Australia
Luang Prabang (LPQ)
  Laos
Macau (MFM) China
Magadan (GDX) Russia
Majuro (MAJ) Marshall
  Islands
Makung (MZG) Taiwan
Male (MLE) Maldives
Mandalay (MDL) Myanmar
Manila (MNL) Philippines
Mashad (MHD) Iran
Matsuyama (MYJ) Japan

Medan (MES) Indonesia
Medina (MED) Saudi
  Arabia
Melbourne (MEL) Australia
Miri (MYY) Malaysia
Miyazaki (KMI) Japan
Moorea (MOZ) Tahiti
Mount Hagen (HGU)
  Papua New Guinea
Mount Isa (ISA) Australia
Mumbai (BOM) India
Muscat (MCT) Oman
Nadi (NAN) Fiji
Nagasaki (NGS) Japan
Nagoya (NGO) Japan
Nanjing (NKG) China
Nauru (INU)
Nelson (NSN) New
  Zealand
Newcastle (NTL) Australia
Niigata (KIJ) Japan
Norfolk Island (NLK)
  Australia
Norilsk (NSK) Russia
Noumea (NOU) New
  Caledonia
Novosibirsk (OVB) Russia
Okinawa (OKA) Japan
Osaka (OSA) Japan
Pago Pago (PPG) Samoa
Palembang (PLM)
  Indonesia
Papetee (PPT) Tahiti
Penang (PEN) Malaysia
Perth (PER) Australia
Phnom Penh (PNH)
  Cambodia
Phuket (HKT) Thailand
Port Maquarie (PQQ)
  Australia
Port Moresby (POM)
  Papua-New Guinea
Port Vila (VLI) Vanuatu
Pusan (PUS) South Korea
Pyongyang (FNJ) North
  Korea
Qingdao (TAO) China
Queenstown (ZQN) New
  Zealand
Rabaul (RAB) Papua-New
  Guinea
Rarotonga (RAR) C ook
  Islands
Riyadh (RUH) Saudi
  Arabia
Riyan Mukalla (RIY)
  Yemen
Rotorua (ROT) New
  Zealand
Sanaa (SAH) Yemen
Sandakan (SDK) Malaysia

Sapporo (SPK) Japan
Semipalatinsk (PLX) Russia
Sendai (SDJ) Japan
Seoul (SEL) South Korea
Shanghai (SHA) China
Sharjah (SHJ) UAE
Shenyang (SHE) China
Shiraz (SYZ) Iran
Sibu (SBW) Malaysia
Singapore (SIN)
Srinagar (SXR) India
Sung Shan (TSA) Taiwan
Surabaya (SUB) Indonesia
Suva (SUV) Fiji
Sydney (SYD) Australia
Tabuk (TUU) Saudi Arabia
Tacloban (TAC)
  Philippines
Taegu (TAE) South Korea
Taif (TIF) Saudi Arabia
Taipei Intl. (TPE) Taiwan
Tarawa (TRW) Kiribati
Tashkent (TAS)
  Uzbekistan
Teheran (THR) Iran
Tel Aviv (TLV) Israel
Tianjin (TSN) China
Tiflis (TBS) Georgia
Tokyo-Haneda (HND)
  Japan
Tokyo-Narita (NRT) Japan
Tongatapu (TBU) Tonga
Townsville (TSV) Australia
Trivandrum (TRV) India
Truk (TKK) Caroline Island
Ufa (UFA) Russia
Ujung Pandang (UPG)
  Indonesia
Ulaanbataar (ULN)
  Mongolia
Ulan Ude (UUD) Russia
Ulsan (USN) South Korea
Urumqi (URC) China
Varanasi (VNS) India
Vientiane (VTE) Laos
Vladivostok (VVO) Russia
Wagga Wagga (WGA)
  Australia
Wellington (WLG) New
  Zealand
Wenzhou (WNZ) China
Whangarei (WER) New
  Zealand
Wuhan (WUH) China
Xiamen (XMN) China
Xian (SIA) China
Yangon (RGN) Myanmar
Yantai (YNT) China
Yerevan (EVN) Armenia
Zamboanga (ZAM)
  Philippines

Zhengzhou (CGO) China
Zhuhai (ZUH) China

Africa

Abidjan (ABJ) Ivory Coast
Abu Simbel (ABS) Egypt
Abuja (ABV) Nigeria
Accra (ACC) Ghana
Addis Ababa (ADD)
  Ethiopia
Adrar (AZR) Algeria
Agadir (AGA) Morocco
Al Hoceima (AHU)
  Morocco
Alexander Bay (ALJ)
  South Africa
Alexandria (ALY) Egypt
Algiers (ALG) Algeria
Annaba (AAE) Algeria
Antalaha (ANM)
  Madagascar
Antananarivo (TNR)
  Madagascar
Antsiranana (DIE)
  Madagascar
Asmara (ASM) Eritrea
Aswan (ASW) Egypt
Bamako (BKO) Mali
Bangui (BGF) Central
  African Republic
Banjul (BJL) Gambia
Bechar (CBH) Algeria
Beira (BEW) Mozambique
Bejaia (BJA) Algeria
Benghazi (BEN) Libya
Benguela (BUG) Angola
Berbera (BBO) Somalia
Bissao (BXO) Guinea-
  Bissau
Blantyre (BLZ) Malawi
Bloemfontain (BFN) South
  Africa
Boa Vista (BVC) Cape
  Verde
Bouake (BYK) Ivory Coast
Brazzaville (BZV) Congo
Bujumbura (BJM) Burundi
Buka (BUA) Papua-New
  Guinea
Bukoba (BKZ) Tanzania
Bulawayo (BUQ)
  Zimbabwe
Cabinda (CAB) Angola
Cairo (CAI) Egypt
Capetown (CPT) South
  Africa
Casablanca (CMN)
  Morocco
Conakry (CKY) Guinea
Constantine (CZL) Algeria

Cotonou (COO) Benin
Dakar (DKR) Senegal
Dar-Es-Salaam (DAR)
  Tanzania
Diredawa (DIR) Ethiopia
Djerba (DJE) Tunisia
Djibouti (JIB)
Douala (DLA) Cameroon
Durban (DUR) South Africa
East London (ELS) South
  Africa
El Qued (ELU) Algeria
Entebbe (EBB) Uganda
Franceville (MVB) Gabon
Freetown (FNA) Sierra
  Leone
Gabarone (GBE)
  Botswana
Garoua (GOU) Cameroon
Harare (HRE) Zimbabwe
Hurghada (HRG) Egypt
Johannesburg (JNB)
  South Africa
Juba (JUB) Sudan
Kananga (KGA) Congo
Kano (KAN) Nigeria
Kariba (KAB) Zimbabwe
Keetmannshoop (KMP)
  South Africa
Khartoum (KRT) Sudan
Kigali (KGL) Rwanda
Kilimanjaro (JRO)
  Tanzania
Kinshasa (FIH) Congo
Kisumu (KIS) Kenya
Korhogo (HGO) Ivory
  Coast
Lagos (LOS) Nigeria
Libreville (LBV) Gabon
Lilongwe (LLW) Malawi
Livingstone (LVI) Zambia
Lome (LFW) Togo
Luanda (LAD) Angola
Lüderitz (LUD) Namibia
Lusaka (LUN) Zambia
Mahe (SEZ) Seychelles
Majunga (MJN)
  Madagascar
Malindi (MYD) Kenya
Maputo (MPM)
  Mozambique
Marrakech (RAK) Morocco
Maseru (MSU) Lesotho
Maun (MUB) Botswana
Mauritius (MRU)
Mogadishu (MGQ)
  Somalia
Mombasa (MBA) Kenya
Monastir (MIR) Tunisia
Monrovia-Roberts (ROB)
  Liberia

Monrovia-Spriggs Payne
  (MLW)
Moroni (YVA) Comores
Nairobi (NBO) Kenya
Ndjamena (NDJ) Chad
Niamey (NIM) Niger
Nouakchott (NKC)
  Mauritania
Oran (ORN) Algeria
Ougadougou (OUA)
  Burkina Faso
Oujda (OUD) Morocco
Port Elizabeth (PLZ) South
  Africa
Port Gentil (POG) Gabon
Port Harcourt (PHC)
  Nigeria
Praia (RAI) Cape Verde
Pretoria (PRY) South
  Africa
Rabat (RBA) Morocco
Rodrigues Island (RRG)
  Mauritius
Sal (SID) Cape Verde
Sao Tomé (TMS) Sao
  Tomé
St.Denis (RUN) Réunion-
  France
Sun City (NTY) South
  Africa
Tamanrasset (TMR)
  Algeria
Tamatave (TMM)
  Madagascar
Tanger (TNG) Morocco
Tripoli (TIP) Libya
Umtata (UTT) South Africa
Victoria Falls (VFA)
  Zimbabwe
Walvis Bay (WVB) Namibia
Windhoek (WDH) Namibia
Yaounde (YAO) Cameroon
Zanzibar (ZNZ) Tanzania

SKYTEAM ALLIANCE

The Skyteam alliance was launched in New York on 22nd June 2000 and formalises arrangements which had been in place since June 1999 when Delta Airlines and Air France announced their global partnership, but with the addition of Korean and Aeromexico. It is intended that Skyteam will expand to 8-10 members over its first four years. Indeeed CSA is scheduled to join from 1st April 2001, and Aeroflot Russian Airlines, which already co-operates with member airlines, has also signalled its intention to become a member. The combined network of the alliance currently offers about 6,400 daily flights to about 450 destinations in 98 countries, using nearly 1,000 aircraft. It has more non-stop destinations between Europe and the United States than any other grouping.

Airline	Joined	Pax (million)
Air France	September 1999	37.0
Delta Airlines	September 1999	105.5
Aeromexico	September 1999	8.7
Korean Air	August 2000	23.8

Boeing 737-400 VP-BAH (Dennis Wehrmann/Hamburg)

Boeing 757-200 N636DL (Dennis Wehrmann/Ft. Lauderdale)

Boeing 777 HL-7531 (Albert Kuhbandner/Zürich)

ONEWORLD

The oneworld alliance was formed in September 1998, led by British Airways and American Airlines, who at that time were still hopeful of regulatory approval for a full merger, though the prospect of this has since receded, and British Airways has been in discussion with other airlines, notably KLM, with a view to merger with them. The current members are:

Airline	Joined	Pax (million)
American Airlines	September 1998	95.0
British Airways	September 1998	36.6
Cathay Pacific	September 1998	10.5
Finnair	September 1999	6.1
Iberia	September 1999	21.9
LAN Chile	June 2000	4.0
Qantas	September 1998	19.0
Aer Lingus	June 2000	6.3

Airlines who might be candidates to join in this alliance in future are:

Aerolineas Argentinas
Avianca
Japan Airlines
Grupo TACA
TAM
Malaysian (discussing a share acqusition with Qantas August 2000)

(Boeing) Mc Donnell Douglas MD-11 N1762B (Josef Krauthäuser/Miami)

Boeing 757-200 G-BIKC (Martin Bach/London LHR)

Airbus A320 EC-GRH (Dennis Wehrmann/Hamburg)

QUALIFLYER GROUP

The nucleus of the Qualiflyer Group is in central Europe where there had been a longstanding co-operation between Swissair and Austrian Airlines. Swissair's parent, the SAir Group, has over the past few years been very active in acquiring shareholdings in other airlines, notably within the European Community, of which Switzerland is not a member. Though Austrian Airlines defected to the Star Alliance, which it joined in March 2000, the Qualiflyer Group, which was established in March 1998, is made up of the following, most of which are SAir owned or partially-owned:

Airline	Joined	Pax (million)
Air Europe	May 1999	1.2
Air Littoral	May 2000	1.2
AOM	March 1998	3.6
Crossair	March 1998	3.8
Sabena	March 1998	10.0
Swissair	March 1998	13.3
TAP - Air Portugal	March 1998	4.8
THY - Turkish Airlines	March 1998	10.1
LOT Polish Airlines	January 2000	2.8
Portugalia	January 2000	0.8
Volare	January 2000	0.7

SAA - South African Airways may be a candidate to join in the future.

Airbus A319 CS-TTG in TAP-Air Portugal 'Qualiflyer Group' colours (Dennis Wehrmann/Amsterdam)

Airbus A321 OO-SUC in Sabena 'Qualiflyer Group' colours (Uwe Gleisberg/Munich)

Airbus A321 HB-IOH in Swissair 'Qualiflyer Group' colours (Author's collection)

STAR ALLIANCE

Star is currently the largest of the alliances, both in terms of its number of members and its total passenger numbers and revenue. It was formed on 14th May 1997 by Lufthansa, Air Canada, Thai International, SAS and United to 'provide an integrated worldwide transport network' and has now grown to include 13 airlines, operating over 2,100 aircraft to over 800 destinations in over 130 countries, and with an annual passenger total approaching 300 million.

Airline	Joined	Pax (million)
Air Canada	May 1997	15.2
Air New Zealand	October 1999	6.4
ANA - All Nippon Airways	October 1999	49.4
Ansett Australia	March 1999	13.4
Austrian Airlines	March 2000	3.5
British Midland	July 2000	6.5
Lufthansa	May 1997	41.9
Mexicana	July 2000	7.1
SAS - Scandinavian	May 1997	22.0
Singapore Airlines	April 2000	13.5
Thai Airways International	May 1997	16.6
United Airlines	May 1997	87.2
Varig	October 1997	10.0

Lauda Air and Tyrolean Airways are also members by virtue of being members of the Austrian Airlines group.

Airbus A340-200 D-AIBA in Lufthansa 'Star Alliance' colours (Albert Kuhbandner/Munich)

Boeing 767-300 JA8290 ANA 'Star Alliance' colours (Josef Krauthäuser collection)

Boeing 767-300 N653UA in United Airlines 'Star Alliance' colours (Albert Kuhbandner/Munich)

KLM/NORTHWEST

KLM and Northwest Airlines have been co-operating closely since 1989, and Northwest and Continental have been working together more recently. During 1999 KLM agreed to merge with Alitalia, and these four airlines were to form the nucleus of the Wings alliance, with the possible later entry of any or all of Braathens, Kenya Airways and JAS - Japan Air System. However, the KLM/Alitalia co-operation was broken off in short order during 2000, and so there remain three airlines in what may still develop into a significant further global alliance in time.

Airline	Pax (million)
KLM	15.7
Northwest Airlines	56.1
Continental Airlines	45.5

(Boeing) Mc Donnell Douglas DC-10-30 N273NN in a special alliance colour scheme (Albert Kuhbandner/Amsterdam)

Boeing 757-200 N29124 (Josef Krauthäuser/Fort Lauderdale)

Airbus A320-200 VP-BVB (Josef Krauthäuser/Miami)

ACES COLOMBIA

Calle 49, No.50-21 Piso 34, Ed del Cafe,
Medellin 6503, Columbia, Tel. 4-56-053,
Fax. 4-2511677, www.acescolombia.com

Three- / Two- letter code	IATA No.	Reg'n prefix	ICAO callsign
AES / VX	137	HK	Aces

The private Aerolineas Centrales de Colombia - ACES -was originally set up in August 1971 and was in the ownership of the United Coffee Growers' Association. Regional services were begun on 1st February 1972 from its base at Medellin to Bogota and Manizales, using a Saunders ST-27 (a development of the de Havilland Heron). From September 1976 services were added to smaller airports, using the de Havilland DHC-6 Twin Otter. In order to build up a wider network, it was felt necessary to acquire jet aircraft. Boeing 727-100s were acquired from Eastern Air Lines and flew for

ACES from 1981. The ST-27 continued in use until 1987, when it was replaced by the Fokker F.27. By this time, the route network extended to over 20 domestic destinations and would be built up even further. In 1991 a wide-ranging fleet renewal was initiated; ATR 42s gradually replaced the F.27s and the older examples of the Boeing 727-100 were exchanged for newer-build aircraft. With the inauguration of a scheduled service to Miami on 1st July 1992, an international destination was served for the first time. The build-up of this route saw the employment of further Boeing 727-200s, which were leased in

1994 and 1995. ACES was given the task of carrying letters and packages by the postal authorities, and charter flights were operated to many destinations in the Caribbean. From the beginning of 1998 further fleet renewal was instituted, and the first Airbus A320, with a revised colour scheme, arrived as a replacement for the Boeing 727s.

Routes

Apartado, Armenia, Bahia Solana, Barrancabermeja, Barranquilla, Bogota, Bucaramanga, Cali, Cartagena, Condoto, Cucuta, Ipiales, Lima, Manizales, Medellin, Miami, Monteria, Nuqui, Ocana, Otu, Panama City, Puerto Plata, Punta Cana, Quito, San Juan, Santo Domingo

Fleet

7 Airbus A320
6 ATR 42
4 Boeing 727-200
9 De Havilland DHC-6 Twin Otter

Ordered

4 Airbus A320
3 ATR 42-500

Canadair Regional Jet S5-AAF (Lutz Schönfeld/Berlin SXF)

ADRIA AIRWAYS

Kuzmiceva 7, 1001 Ljubljana, Slovenia
Tel. 61-313366 , Fax. 61-323356,
www.adria.si

Three- / Two- letter code	IATA No.	Reg'n prefix	ICAO callsign
ADR / JP	165	S5	Adria

Adria Airways was founded in 1960 in Yugoslavia, and began mostly charter operations in March of the following year, the initial fleet consisting of four Douglas DC-6Bs which were obtained from KLM. During 1969 the airline became a part of the activities of the Interexport trading company, resulting in a swift change of name to Inex Adria Airways. In 1970, using new Douglas DC-9-32 aircraft, the first scheduled services were flown from Ljubljana to Belgrade. From 1985 Inex flew also for the first time to Munich, this being in the form of scheduled services to Ljubljana. Alongside these schedules charter flights were also undertaken for various tour operators. With the delivery of the first of three Airbus A320s during 1989 the company changed the colour scheme of its aircraft and reverted to its original name. All of the shares were now in the hands of the government. Civil unrest in Yugoslavia forced a halt to operations from October 1991 until January 1992. During 1992 Adria became the flag carrier of the newly independent state of Slovenia, after it had separated from Yugoslavia. A part-privatisation of the company followed in 1996 and the first Canadair Regional Jets were brought into service during 1998.

The fleet was optimised for the lower demand, which entailed the phasing out of the DC-9s and Dash 7s which had been in use. Likewise, the route network was redefined.

Routes

Amsterdam, Barcelona, Berlin, Brussels,Copenhagen, Dublin, Dubrovnik, Frankfurt, Ljubljana, London, Manchester, Maribor, Moscow, Munich, Paris, Sarajevo, Split, Tel Aviv, Vienna and Zürich as scheduled services, Charter flights from many european airports to destinations in Croatia and Slovenia, and emigrant workers' flights.

Fleet

3 Airbus A320
4 Canadair Regional Jet 200LR

Boeing 737-548 EI-CDF (Josef Krauthäuser/Düsseldorf)

AER LINGUS

P.O.Box 180, Dublin Airport, Ireland
Tel. 1-8862222, Fax. 1-8863832,
www.aerlingus.ie

Three- / Two- letter code	IATA No.	Reg'n prefix	ICAO callsign
EIN / EI	053	EI	Shamrock

On 22nd May 1936 Aer Lingus Teoranta was set up for regional and european services, and in 1947 Aerlinte Eireann Teoranta for international routes. From 1960, the two were closely integrated as the state-owned Aer Lingus - Irish International Airlines. Flights began using a de Havilland DH.84, from Baldonnel airfield near Dublin to Bristol on 27th May 1936. Soon there were flights to London, Liverpool and to the Isle of Man. During the war, only the Shannon-Dublin-Liverpool route was flown, with a single DC-3. In 1947 the purchase of seven Vickers Vikings signalled a new beginning, but

these were sold in 1948 and DC-3s became the backbone of the fleet. Vickers Viscounts arrived in 1954, Fokker Friendships from 1958 and services were developed to many european destinations; from 1965 the BAC One-Eleven was used. For the transatlantic services, beginning with New York in 1958, Lockheed Constellations were flown, with Boeing 720s taking over from 1960 and the Boeing 747 from 1971. In the mid 1980s Aer Lingus entered a time of crisis; overcapacity had to be eliminated, and a re-organisation had to take place which also entailed a fleet renewal. Boeing 737-200s, later replaced by newer

models, formed the mainstay of the fleet, and Shorts 360s and Fokker 50s were ordered for Aer Lingus Commuter, formed in 1984 for traffic between Ireland and UK regional airports. Aer Lingus Commuter now uses principally BAe 146s, first acquired in 1995, when Saab 340s were disposed of. In March 1994 the first of the airline's new Airbus A330-300s flew to New York for the first time, ousting the 747s, and another Airbus product, the A321 started to replace the 737s from mid 1998; A320s are also on order for 2001/02. Aer Lingus joined the 'oneworld' alliance from June 2000.

Routes

Amsterdam, Belfast, Birmingham, Boston, Brussels, Chicago, Copenhagen, Cork, Dublin, Düsseldorf, Edinburgh, Frankfurt, Galway, Glasgow, Jersey, Kerry County, Knock, Leeds/Bradford, London-Heathrow/-Stansted, Los Angeles, Madrid, Milan, Manchester, Munich, New York, Newcastle, Paris, Rennes, Rome, Shannon, Sligo and Zürich. In addition, seasonal charters to about 15 destinations.

Fleet		Ordered
6 Airbus A321	6 Boeing 737-400	6 Airbus A320
7 Airbus A330	9 Boeing 737-500	
10 BAe 146	4 Fokker 50	

McDonnell Douglas DC-9-32 XA-SYD (Josef Krauthäuser/Los Angeles LAX)

AERO CALIFORNIA

Aquiles Serdan No.1995, La Paz, Baja California 23000, Mexico, Tel. 112-26655, Fax. 112-53993, www.americanair.com/servinfo/aerocal.htm

Three- / Two- letter code	IATA No.	Reg'n prefix	ICAO callsign
SER / JR	078	XA	Aerocalifornia

The company was founded in 1960 and operated as an air taxi concern with several Cessnas and Beech 18s. Until the 1980s the indestructible Douglas DC-3 was also part of the fleet, which was expanded from 1982 by the acquisition of a Douglas DC-9-15. Aero California was at first only active in its own neighbourhood, Baja California, and flew charters, but also scheduled services between La Paz, Tijuana and Hermosillo. These schedules were carried out using a Convair 340; further routes were added over the years. At the end of the 1980s it was decided to undertake a careful

expansion and more DC-9s were acquired, enabling the propeller-driven types to be gradually phased out. At the beginning of 1990 a scheduled service was inaugurated to Los Angeles in the USA. Since 1995, when the last of the Cessnas and Beech 18s were retired, the fleet has been all-jet. As well as scheduled services, Aero California also offers charter services to the country's tourism centres. Outside Mexico, Los Angeles is the most important hub; several flights each day connect LAX with destinations in Baja California and other Mexican provinces, as well as the capital, Mexico City. A close co-operation

with American Airlines has existed for some years.

Routes

Augascalientes, Chihuahua, Ciudad Juarez, Ciudad Obregon, Ciudad Victoria, Colima, Culiacan, Durango, Guadalajara, Hermosillo, La Paz, Leon, Loreto, Los Angeles, Los Mochis, Manzanillo, Matamoros, Mazatlan, Mexico City, Monterey, Puebla, San Jose Cabo, San Luis Potosi, Tampico, Tepic, Tijuana, Torreon, Tucson.

Fleet

12 Douglas DC-9-10
 9 Douglas DC-9-30

Boeing 727-22 OB-1570 (Romano German/Cuzco)

AERO CONTINENTE

Avenue Jose Pardo 651, Lima, Peru
Tel. 14-2424260, Fax. 14-4445014,
www.aerocontinente.com.pe

Three- / Two- letter code	IATA No.	Reg'n prefix	ICAO callsign
ACQ / N6	929	OB	Aero Continente

Aero Continente S.A. was founded on 4th January 1992 in Tarapoto by the Gonzales family. The San Martin regional government gave tax concessions to companies being established in the region. Initially the airline aimed to look after the air transport needs of a government oil support company, whose depots were often in out-of-the-way locations which could only realistically be serviced by air. The first aircraft was a Boeing 737-200, and operations were begun with this on 25th May 1992. Following the deregulation of air transport in Peru at the end of 1992 Aero Continente expanded its services and for the first time offered scheduled services. The fleet was expanded with two more 737s and a 727 and the company's base moved to the Peruvian capital, Lima. Here the company was also able to carry out maintenance in its own hangar. The company continued to develop positively and more aircraft were needed. Further 727s, a Fokker F.28, Antonov An 24 and even Lockheed TriStars were brought into the fleet over the years. Aero Continente was especially able to benefit from the failures of other companies in finding opportunities to expand its own operations. Service to Miami was commenced in 1999 with a leased Boeing 757, this being replaced during the early part of 2000 with two Boeing 767s.

Routes

Arequipa, Ayacucho, Cajamarca, Chiclayo, Cuzco, Iquitos, Juliaca, Lima, Miami, Piura, Pucallpa, Puerto Maldonado, Tacna, Talara, Tarapoto, Trujillo, Tumbes.

Fleet

8 Boeing 727
8 Boeing 737-200
2 Boeing 767-200
1 Fokker F.28
2 Fokker F.27

Boeing 767-300ER EI-CKD (Uwe Gleisberg/Munich)

AEROFLOT

Leningradsky Prospect 37a, 125167 Moscow, Russia, Tel. 70957529071,
Fax. 70957529071, www.aeroflot.org

Three- / Two- letter code	IATA No.	Reg'n prefix	ICAO callsign
AFL / SU	555	RA	Aeroflot

Aeroflot was formed in 1923 as Dobrolet, becoming Aeroflot in 1932, and evolving into the world's largest air transport undertaking. In line with the political status in the former Soviet Union, the development of air transport took a different direction from that in the West. Until 1991, Aeroflot dominated in all aspects of aviation activity, but then with the political changes in the Soviet Union, everything altered. The former Aeroflot directorates were now independent, and many established their own companies. Likewise the newly-independent countries set up their own airlines, taking over former Aeroflot aircraft.

During the course of 1993, a new Aeroflot, comparable to western airlines, emerged, taking on the name of Aeroflot-Russian International Airlines (ARIA). All non-airline services were delegated to independent companies. Only a small part of the former fleet was taken over, and for the first time western aircraft were used, with the lease of five Airbus A310-300s. These were delivered to Aeroflot from July 1992 especially for routes to Japan and South East Asia. Whereas previously services had been operated based on other criteria, now the motivation was only that of successful business. That

held true also for aircraft procurement, and from 1996 other western types, much more efficient than their former Soviet counterparts were acquired; these included Boeing 737s, 767s, 777s and the DC-10. During 1997 Aeroflot was partially privatised, with 51% of the shares remaining with the government, the rest being spread among about 15,000 employees. In mid-2000, the shareholders agreed to drop 'International' from the title in view of increasing success in domestic markets, so the airline is now known as Aeroflot - Russian Airlines. It hopes to join the SkyTeam global alliance by 2003.

Routes

Aeroflot flies to about 135 destinations in nearly 100 countries in Europe, America, Asia and Africa.

Fleet

		Ordered
10 Airbus A310-300	17 Ilyushin IL-86	20 Ilyushin 96-300
6 Boeing 767-300ER	6 Ilyushin IL-96-300	Ilyushin IL-114
2 Boeing 777-200ER	1 McDonnell Douglas DC-10-30F	Tupolev Tu-204
10 Boeing 737-400	12 Tupolev Tu-134	(no quantities quoted)
22 Ilyushin IL-62M	30 Tupolev Tu-154	
13 Ilyushin IL-76		

McDonnell Douglas MD-88 LV-VBY (Author's collection/Buenos Aires AEP)

AEROLINEAS ARGENTINAS

Bouchard 547, 1063 Buenos Aires, Argentina
Tel. 01-3173000, Fax. 01-3173585,
www.aerolineas.com.ar

Three- / Two- letter code	IATA No.	Reg'n prefix	ICAO callsign
ARG / AR	044	LV	Argentina

Aerolineas Argentinas was created as the new national airline by the amalgamation of four smaller companies, Aeroposta, ALFA, FAMA and Zonda in May 1949 at the instigation of the Argentinian transport ministry. The four component airlines brought in their fleets of aircraft such as Douglas DC-3s and DC-4s which were used on internal services and from March 1950 also to New York. In 1959 the de Havilland Comet 4B made its debut on international routes, until in 1966 the first of a total of ten Boeing 707s was delivered. Boeing 747s took over the New York route for the first time in 1976 and from 1977

were also used for services to Europe. For the short and medium length routes, Boeing 727s and 737s, and the Fokker F.28 were brought into use. At the beginning of the 1990s these were supplemented with MD-80s and three Airbus A310s were used for a short while for US services. In 1993, Iberia acquired a 20% shareholding in the company, increased to 83% in 1995. The balance was held by employees and the government. During the Summer of 1996 a hub was set up at Miami, from where Boeing 727s would fly connecting flights to Canada and the Caribbean. The Airbus A340 was introduced in 1999 for long-haul

services. During 1998 Iberia, which was having financial difficulties, was obliged to reduce its shareholding to 10%, at which point American Airlines took a holding of 8.5%. However, by Autumn 2000 Aerolineas Argentinas was close to bankruptcy, and a plan was being advanced whereby the employees would take control of 85% of the shares in an effort to stave this off. ARG works closely with Aeroflot, Aerosur, American Airlines, Iberia, Malaysian and Qantas through various alliances.

Routes

Acapulco, Asuncion, Auckland, Bogota, Buenos Aires, Cancun, Caracas, Catamarca, Comodoro Rivadavia, Cordoba, Florianopolis, Frankfurt, Guayaquil, Havana, Iguacu, La Paz, Lima, London, Madrid, Mendoza, Mexico City, Miami, Montreal, Montevideo, New York, Panama, Paris, Porto Alegre, Punta Cana, Punta del Este, Rio de Janeiro, Rio Gallegos, Rio Grande, Rome, Santiago, Sao Paulo, Sydney.

Fleet

6 Airbus A340
7 Boeing 747-200

21 Boeing 737-200
7 McDonnell Douglas MD-80

Airbus A321-231 D-ALAG (Albert Kuhbandner/Munich)

AERO LLOYD

Lessingstrasse 7-9, 61440 Oberursel, Germany.
Tel. 06171-625347, Fax. 06171-6549,
www.aerolloyd.de

Three- / Two- letter code	IATA No.	Reg'n prefix	ICAO callsign
AEF / YP	633	D	Aero Lloyd

Aero Lloyd Flugreisen GmbH is a private airline, set up on 20th December 1980, and which started operations in March 1981 with three SE 210 Caravelle 10Rs. The name harks back to the pioneering time of civil aviation in Germany in the 1920s. At first, charter flights were operated to popular destinations in the Mediterranean. The tour operator Air Charter Market also contributed to the utilisation of the aircraft, and has been a shareholder in the airline over the years. From May to July 1982 a DC-9-32 was in service. The company entered an expansion phase from 1986, when the first MD-80 was introduced. Over the years up to 22 MD-82/83/87s were used. In addition to charter flights, these have been used on scheduled services, which Aero Lloyd began from Summer 1988. As well as internal German services, there were routes to London, Paris and Zürich. However, Aero Lloyd withdrew from the scheduled market in 1992, after Lufthansa had taken a holding in the airline. The final DC-9-32 left the fleet at the end of 1993 and a pointer to the future given with the order from Airbus of the A320. The capital structure of the company was also changed, the majority now being held by a bank. The first new Airbus A320, in a new, modern colour scheme, arrived in January 1996 at Aero Lloyd's main Frankfurt base; the airline has a second base at Munich. The changeover to a homogeneous Airbus fleet is in progress, with the first of the A321s being delivered in 1998, and the process is expected to be completed by the end of 2000. Whereas in earlier years the airline concentrated on flying from Germany only, this situation is now changing so that more and more flights are being conducted from neighbouring countries.

Routes

Alicante, Almeria, Antalya, Araxos, Arrecife, Bergen, Brindisi, Calvi, Catania, Corfu, Dubrovnik, Faro, Fuerteventura, Funchal, Gerona, Heraklion, Hurgada, Ibiza, Jerez, Cairo,Kalamata, Karpathos, Kavala, Kos, Lamezia Terme, Lakselv, Larnaca, Las Palmas, Lourdes, Luxor, Mahon, Malaga, Monastir, Murcia, Mykonos, Mytilene, Naples, Olbia, Palermo, Palma de Mallorca, Paphos, Preveza, Reuss, Reykjavik, Rhodes, Samos, Santorini, Sharm el Sheik, Skiathos, Split, Tel Aviv, Tenerife, Thessaloniki, Zakynthos.

Fleet		Ordered
7 Airbus A320-200	7 McDonnell Douglas MD-82/83	3 Airbus A321
8 Airbus A321-200		

Boeing 767-3Y0ER XA-RKI (Pascal Mainzer/Paris CDG)

AEROMEXICO

Paseo de la Reforma 445, 06500 Mexico City
Mexico, Tel. 1334000, Fax. 1334619,
www.aeromexico.com

Three- / Two- letter code	IATA No.	Reg'n prefix	ICAO callsign
AMX / AM	139	XA	Aeromexico

The current Aerovias de Mexico, commonly known as Aeromexico, has been active since 1st October 1988. Its predecessor of the same name, which had its origins going back to 1934, was declared bankrupt by its owners, the Mexican government, at the beginning of 1988 and was compelled to cease operations. A consortium of Mexican business interests acquired control and services re-started to thirty domestic destinations and five cities in the United States. A fleet renewal programme brought the airline back up to acceptable international standards and passenger figures improved steadily. Aeromexico is a shareholder in the country's other national airline, Mexicana and in 1990 also acquired Servicos Aereos Litoral. The company is privately owned, with 25% of the shares held by the Mexican pilots union. The apparently permanent state of business crisis in Mexico has its effects on the airline's operations; in 1995 routes to Europe were cut back and all the DC-10s sold. At home, increasingly unprofitable domestic routes also had to be abandoned. A financial restructuring in 1995 brought the company back on course. There are alliances with Aerocaribe, Aerolitoral, Aeromar, Air France, Delta Air Lines, Mexicana and United Airlines. During 1998 services to Europe were recommenced with Madrid and Paris and the fleet was augmented with several Boeing 757s, 767s and MD-80s.

Routes

Acapulco, Aguascalientes, Atlanta, Campeche, Cancun, Chihuahua, Ciudad Juarez, Ciudad Obregon, Colima, Culiacan, Dallas/Fort Worth, Durango, El Paso, Guadalajara, Guaymas, Guerro Negro, Hermosilio, Houston, Ixtapa, La Paz, Leon, Lima, Loreto, Los Angeles, Los Mochis, Madrid, Manzanillo, Matamoros, Mazatlan, Merida, Mexicali, Mexico City, Miami, Monclovia, Monterrey, Morella, New Orleans, Orlando, Paris, Phoenix, Puerto Vallarta, Queretaro, Reynosa, San Antonio, San Diego, San Jose Cabo, Santiago, Sao Paulo, Tampico, Tijuana, Tucson, Veracruz, Villahermosa.

Fleet

8 Boeing 757-200	2 Boeing 767-300 (ER)	38 McDonnell Douglas MD-82/87/88
4 Boeing 767-200 (ER)	17 McDonnell Douglas DC-9-31/32	

McDonnell Douglas DC-9-51 YV-20C (Stefan Schlick/Barbados)

AEROPOSTAL

Ancxo Torre Polar, Plaza Venezuela,
Caracas 1050, Venezuela, Tel. 2-708-6200,
Fax. 2-708-6067, www.aeropostal.com

Three- / Two- letter code	IATA No.	Reg'n prefix	ICAO callsign
LAV / VH	152	YV	Aeropostal

Still under French influence, the Compagnie Générale Aeropostal was founded in 1930. It was a part of the South American network which the French had built up in several countries on the continent. Following the takeover of the company by the national government, the name was changed to Linea Aeropostal Venezolana. At first only regional destinations were served, but from 1953 the leap across the Atlantic was made. Lisbon, Madrid and Rome were served via Bermuda and the Azores. During 1957 Aeropostal grew by taking over TACA of Venezuela and further expanded its operations to cover the whole of Venezuela, using Douglas DC-3s, Martin 2-0-2s and for the overseas routes Lockheed L-1049 Constellations. After the founding of the national airline VIASA in 1960, all route licences for services outside the country were handed over to VIASA. Aeropostal held 45% of the capital of the new airline and also provided staff. HS-748s and from 1968 Douglas DC-9s were used for the domestic services. More DC-9s were added right up until 1994, when the company filed for bankruptcy. The financial difficulties faced by Venezuela were a negative influence on the fortunes of all the country's airlines and in Aeropostal's case were to be resolved by a privatisation. The sale to Alas de Venezuela was completed at the end of 1996 and by February 1997 the new, privatised company was flying under the old name. Again DC-9s formed the major part of the fleet, with several leased Airbus A320 and in addition two Airbus A310s were used, as the company profited from the bankruptcy of VIASA.

Routes

Aruba, Barbados, Barcelona, Barquisemeto, Bogota, Caracas, Curacao, Havana, Lima, Manaus, Maracaibo, Maturin, Miami, Panama City, Porlamar, Port of Spain, Puerto Ordaz, San Antonio, Santo Domingo, Valencia.

Fleet

2 Airbus A320
10 McDonnell Douglas DC-9-30/50

Airbus A310-304 TU-TAZ (Dennis Wehrmann/Hamburg)

AIR AFRIQUE

3, Ave. Joseph Anoma, 01BP3927 Abidjan,
Ivory Coast, Tel. 225-203000,
Fax. 225-203005, www.air-afrique.co.za

Three- / Two- letter code	IATA No.	Reg'n prefix	ICAO callsign
RKA / RK	092	TU	Airafric

This multinational airline was established on 28th March 1961 in co-operation with Air France, UTA and the former French colonies of Benin, Burkina-Faso, Central African Republic, Chad, Congo, Ivory Coast. Mauritania, Niger, Senegal, Cameroon and Gabon. The latter two countries withdrew in the early 1970s, while Togo joined in January 1968. The objective was to create comprehensive internal services within those countries as well as international routes, failing which these relatively poor nations would each have to establish their own airline. Using Douglas DC-4s and DC-6s, operations began, and in the first year a Lockheed L-1049 Constellation operated a Paris service. On 5th January 1972 Air Afrique received its first jet, a DC-8 from UTA. In 1973 came the delivery of an initial DC-10-30, the first widebody for the young airline, whose crews came from all the participating nations. The larger Boeing 747 which was used from 1980 to 1984 showed itself to be not profitable nor flexible enough and the airline turned to Airbus for their equipment. The Airbus A310 proved to be the ideal aircraft for Air Afrique's needs, especially with the opening of new routes in Southern Africa. An increase in passenger numbers and freight carryings was seen from 1992, and this improvement made possible the acquisition in 1995 of the Airbus A300-600 as a replacement for the DC-10 on high-density routes. In 1998 Air Afrique became financially troubled and temporarily suspended its international routes, as it was unable to pay its leasing costs. Several of the A310s were returned to their lessors. A restructuring and possible part-privatisation are planned for 2000.

Routes

Abidjan, Abu Dhabi, Accra, Athens, Bamako, Bangui, Banjul, Bordeaux, Brazzaville, Casablanca, Conakry, Cotonou, Dakar, Douala, Freetown, Geneva, Jeddah, Johannesburg, Lagos, Libreville, Lisbon, Lome, Malabo, Marseilles, Ndjamena, New York, Niamey, Nouakchott, Ouagadougou, Paris, Pointe Noire, Rome.

Fleet

2 Airbus A300B4
2 Airbus A300-600
2 Airbus A310
2 Boeing 707-300F

3 Boeing 737-300

Airbus A321-131 TC-ALL (Dennis Wehrmann/Hamburg)

AIR ALFA HAVA YOLLARI

Fatith Gad 21, Güneseli 34540 Istanbul, Turkey
Tel. 212-6303348, Fax. 212-6575870,
www.airalfa.com.tr

Three- / Two- letter code	IATA No.	Reg'n prefix	ICAO callsign
LFA / H7	770	TC	Alfa

Air Alfa Hava Yollari was founded in 1992 and charter flights were operated using Boeing 727-200s from Spring 1994. The principal destinations were in Belgium, Germany and France , all of which are home to millions of expatriate Turks and have always been a good, though very competitive, market for all Turkish companies. During 1994 the airline's first Airbus A300 was acquired and business was concentrated more on the numerous tourists who had booked their holidays on Turkey's beaches. By 1996 the fleet had grown to five examples. Kombassan Holdings, a company involved in various businesses and based in the Anatolian town of Konya, took over the airline in 1996, in order to make better use of its own tourist activities. One of the Boeing 727s was replaced with a leased Boeing 757, but this was only used briefly on a seasonal basis. The small fleet was again increased with newer aircraft, and equipped with factory-fresh Airbus A321s. Thus Air Alfa's fleet is comparable with those of the established charter operators, and it has its own maintenance facility at its home airport of Istanbul. By 2001 the last of the Airbus A300s is expected to be replaced by more A320s and A321s.

Routes

Air Alfa flies regular charters from airports in Belgium, France, Germany, the Netherlands and Italy to destinations on the Turkish Mediterranean.

Fleet

2 Airbus A300B4
2 Airbus A300-600
3 Airbus A321

Boeing 767-306 7T-VJG (Albert Kuhbandner/Paris CDG)

AIR ALGERIE

1, Place Maurice Audin, Algiers,
Democratic Republic of Algeria
Tel. 664822, Fax. 610553

Three- / Two- letter code	IATA No.	Reg'n prefix	ICAO callsign
DAH / AH	124	7T	Air Algerie

The Compagnie Générale de Transport Aérien was created in 1946 while Algeria was still under French rule. It was merged with the Compagnie Air Transport to form the present Air Algerie on 22nd May 1953. Douglas DC-4s and Lockheed Constellations were used on routes including to Paris and Marseilles. Air Algerie received its first jet equipment, the SE210 Caravelle in December 1959. In 1972 the airline was nationalised and in 1974 the first Airbus A300B4 was taken over from TEA. After the retirement of the Caravelles, the most prevalent types in the fleet were Boeing 727s and

737s, with the first Airbus A310 arriving in 1984. A period of slow growth and fleet renewal took place, marked in 1990 by the delivery of the first Boeing 767, and since then not too much has changed, though some of the older 737s are being replaced now by the new generation models of the same type. Air Algerie undertakes government flying, for instance agricultural work, for which a large number of helicopters and smaller fixed wing aircraft are available. For numerous transport tasks, including services to desert locations, Air Algerie flies the civilianised version of the military

Lockheed Hercules freighter. Alliances are being developed with Royal Air Maroc and Tunis Air, the airlines of Algeria's neighbouring countries.

Routes

Adrar, Agades, Algiers, Alicante, Amman, Bamako, Barcelona, Batna, Bechar, Bejaja, Berlin, Biskra, Bordj Badji Mokhtar, Brussels, Cairo, Casablanca, Constantine, Dakar, Damascus, Djanet, El Golela, El Oued, Forli, Frankfurt, Geneva, Ghardaia, Hassi Messaoud, Illizi, In Amenas, In Salah, Istanbul, Jijef, Lille, London, Lyon, Madrid, Marseilles, Mascara, Moscow, Niamey, Nice, Nouakchott, Oran, Ouagadougou, Ouargla, Paris, Prague, Rome, Sharjah, Tamanrasset, Tbessa, Tiaret, Timimoun, Tindouf, Touggourt, Toulouse, Tunis.

Fleet		Ordered
2 Airbus A310-200	3 Boeing 767-300	3 Boeing 737-600
15 Boeing 737-200	7 Fokker F.27	7 Boeing 737-800
11 Boeing 727-200	2 Lockheed -L382 Hercules	

McDonnell Douglas MD-82 PJ-SEH (Hans-Willi Mertens/Miami)

AIR ALM

Hato Airport, Willemstad, Curacao,
Netherlands Antilles
Tel. 388888, Fax. 338300, www.airalm.com

Three- / Two- letter code	IATA No.	Reg'n prefix	ICAO callsign
ALM / LM	119	PJ	Antillean

Antilliaanse Luchtvaart Maatschappij NV, commonly known simply as ALM, was set up in 1964 in order to take over from KLM in the Caribbean. Operations were begun on 1st August 1964, using three Convair 340s on routes from Curacao. During 1969 96% of the shares in the airline were taken over by the government of the Netherlands Antilles. Windward Island Airways International NV was bought during 1974, with their route network and aircraft passing into the ownership of ALM. Two MD-82s were added to the fleet in October 1982, as a replacement for the DC-9-15s; a third was added in 1991. For the short island-hopping routes the de Havilland DHC-8 is well-suited, and this type was added to the fleet from 1992. Changes in the legal framework of the airline at the beginning of 1999 also brought about a change of name, with 'Air' being added in front of the old ALM. KLM and United Airlines are Air ALM's most important partners.

Routes

Aruba, Atlanta, Bonaire, Caracas, Curacao, Kingston, Maracaibo, Miami, Port-au-Prince, Port of Spain, San Juan, Santo Domingo, St. Maarten, Valencia.

Fleet

3 McDonnell Douglas MD-82
4 De Havilland DHC-8-300

McDonnell Douglas MD-90-30 P4-MDG (Dennis Wehrmann/Miami)

AIR ARUBA

P.O. Box 1017, Oranjestad, Aruba, Netherlands Antilles, Tel. 8-30005, Fax. 8-25867, www.interknowledge.com/air-aruba

Three- / Two- letter code	IATA No.	Reg'n prefix	ICAO callsign
ARU / FQ	276	P4	Aruba

The regional area administration of Aruba set up Air Aruba in September 1986. Initially it functioned as a ground-handling agency. With assistance from Air Holland and KLM however, it started flights to the neighbouring islands in 1988, using NAMC YS-11s. A leased Boeing 757 was also used on a seasonal basis, this being replaced by the larger Boeing 767 during 1991. Air Aruba is active today in the business of providing scheduled flights and charters and has at times served european destinations including Amsterdam and Cologne. Since the Boeing 767 was not really being used profitably, the European routes were abandoned in 1995 in favour of a co-operation agreement with KLM, in which ALM and Avianca are also participants. Since then, the airline has concentrated above all on the United States and regional markets. The fleet, which is mostly leased in, has principally consisted of DC-9s and MD-80s, but now includes three MD-90s acquired in late 1998. Aserca of Venezuela acquired 70% of the shares in 1998, the balance being held by the government.

Routes

Baltimore, Bogota, Bonaire, Caracas, Curacao, Las Piedras, Maracaibo, Medellin, Miami, New York, Newark, Philadelphia, Sao Paulo, St. Maarten, San José, Tampa.

Fleet

1 McDonnell Douglas DC-9-32
2 McDonnell Douglas MD-88
3 McDonnell Douglas MD-90

Boeing 747-200 TF-ABG (Author's collection)

AIR ATLANTA ICELANDIC

P.O.Box 80, Mosfellsbaer, Iceland
Tel. 5667700, Fax. 5667766,
www.airatlanta.is

Three- / Two- letter code	IATA No.	Reg'n prefix	ICAO callsign
ABD / CC		TF	Atlanta

On 10th January 1986 Captain Arngrimur Johannsson and his wife founded Air Atlanta Icelandic as a specialist wet-lease operator, viz the provision of aircraft inclusive of crews and other services. The first contract was for the use of a Boeing 707 for Caribbean Airways, flying the route from London to Barbados. In August 1988 a second Boeing 707 was brought into use, this time on behalf of Air Afrique. Under this leasing arrangement, Islamic pilgrims were flown for the first time to Saudi Arabia for the Hadj, a lucrative business where the company became well-established. In May 1991 came the first widebody,

a Lockheed L-1011 TriStar and two years later the first three Boeing 747s were entered on the Icelandic register. These were employed for several years by Saudia, now Saudi Arabian Airlines. Air Atlanta also started operating its own charter series from 1993 and the fleet continued to expand. Boeing 737-200Fs were brought into use for freight work, and a Boeing 737-300 was used in June 1995 to open up a scheduled service from Iceland to Berlin. The British and African markets proved to be especially profitable for Air Atlanta. The TriStars were used particularly on behalf of British tour operators. The

TF- registered aircraft were seen however over the years in the service of many companies including Air India, Tunis Air, Caledonian or Monarch. During 1999 several of the TriStars and the Boeing 737 were taken out of service and further second-hand Boeing 747-100/200/300s acquired . In the medium term, it is expected that the remaining L-1011s will be replaced by the Boeing 767.

Routes

As a wet-lease specialist, Air Atlanta's aircraft are to be seen operating schedules or charters for other airlines. On its own account, the company operates only some charter series from Iceland to the Mediterranean.

Fleet

3 Boeing 747-100
3 Boeing 747-200
5 Boeing 747-300
4 Lockheed L-1011

Fokker 50 YL-BAR (Dennis Wehrmann/Hamburg)

AIR BALTIC

Riga Airport, Riga LV1053, Latvia
Tel. 207379, Fax. 207659,
www.airbaltic.lv

Three- / Two- letter code	IATA No.	Reg'n prefix	ICAO callsign
BTI / BT	657	YL	Air Baltic

Baltic International was founded in 1992 by Texan businessmen and Latavio-Latvian Airlines. The independent subsidiary company carries out flights into neighbouring western countries. Alongside Tupolev Tu-134s, a DC-9 was also introduced into the fleet on a loan basis in 1993, but this was substituted by a Boeing 727 from 1995. As the company was not developing satisfactorily, a radical cure was decided upon and in September 1995 Baltic International was merged with Latvian Airlines to create a new national airline Air Baltic. The Latvian government owned the majority, 51% of the capital, with the rest shared by Baltic International USA, SAS and two investment firms. Using a Saab SF 340 a fresh start was made and in Spring 1996 three Avro RJ 70s were received. The Latvian government also promised that the airline would be allowed to take over the routes of Latavio, but the legal processes in this country are not the quickest, and so the dissolution of Latavio did not come about until 1998. In January 1999 SAS took over the shareholding of Baltic International USA. During this year also, three Fokker 50s were introduced to replace the Saab 340s and the route network was harmonised with SAS and other partners including Estonian Air and Lufthansa.

Routes

From Riga to Copenhagen, Frankfurt, Hamburg, Helsinki, Kiev, London, Minsk, Moscow, Munich, Stockholm, Tallinn, Vilnius and Warsaw.

Fleet

3 Avro RJ 70
3 Fokker 50

De Havilland DHC-8-102 C-GABH (Jörg Thiel/Calgary)

AIR BC

5520 Miller Rd. Richmond BC, V7B 1A6,
Canada, Tel. 604 273 2464, Fax. 604 244 2676,
www.aircanada.ca

Three- / Two- letter code	IATA No.	Reg'n prefix	ICAO callsign
ABL / ZX	742	C	Aircoach

Air BC (BC being the abbreviation for British Columbia) emerged in 1980 from the amalgamation of various smaller airlines on Canada's west coast, including Canadian Air Transit, Flight Operation, Gulf Air Aviation, Haida Airlines, Island Airlines, Ominecca Air, Pacific Coastal Airlines, Trans Provincial Airlines and West Coast Air Services. As well as operating services on its own account, the new airline also flew feeder services for Canadian Pacific Airlines (CP Air). The first Dash 7 arrived in 1983 and the first Dash 8 in 1986. In 1988 it was decided to enter into a co-operation agreement with Air Canada and the first jets, BAe 146s, were ordered. As an Air Canada Connector airline, the fleet was painted in a colour scheme reflecting that of the national carrier. Eventually Air BC became a 100% subsidiary of Air Canada and operated a dense feeder network from the three central hubs at Calgary, Edmonton and Vancouver. In addition, there were seasonal charter operations to popular salmon fishing locations in the north of British Columbia. Following Air Canada's acquisition of Canadian Airlines in early 2000, some restructuring of Air Canada's regional support services was to be anticipated; it appears that Air BC will continue in independent operation, though under a common operating certificate with Air Canada's other feeder airlines, Canadian Regional, Air Nova and Air Ontario.

Routes

Air BC serves, under Air Canada flight numbers, over 30 destinations in Western Canada, and to Portland and Seattle in the USA. It also flies charters.

Fleet

5 BAe 146-200
9 De Havilland DHC-8-100
6 De Havilland DHC-8-300

Boeing 737-46B OO-ILJ (Josef Krauthäuser/Munich)

AIR BELGIUM

Vilvoordelaan 192, 1930 Zaventem, Belgium
Tel. 7160510, Fax. 7160511

Three- / Two- letter code	IATA No.	Reg'n prefix	ICAO callsign
ABB / AJ		OO	Air Belgium

Abelag Airways, the progenitor of Air Belgium, was set up in May 1979. It commenced operations a month later, initially using a leased Boeing 737-200. For marketing reasons, the name was changed in 1980 to the more memorable Air Belgium; the airline wanted to fly holiday passengers from France and Germany, as well as from Belgium. In 1988 the airline took delivery of their own first Boeing 737-400, and this was followed in 1989 by a Boeing 757. As well as being deployed on the airline's own programme of charter flights, aircraft are leased out seasonally according to demand. At the beginning of the

1996 summer season a further Boeing 737-300 was added, but the year proved to be one of heavy losses, which led to the owners, Sun International, looking for a buyer for their ailing airline. In February 1998 it was sold to the British-based Airtours group. Thus Air Belgium now flies for the group and flies many sub-charters for Airtours and Premiair, the Danish component of the group. Aircraft are moved around between group airlines from time to time to meet changing demand patterns, and with the delivery of Airbus A321s for the 1999 summer season, a standardisation of aircraft within the group to

A320/321s and Boeing 757s is in progress. However, it was announced in the Autumn of 2000 that Airtours plan to close Air Belgium down from 1st November 2000, but a management buyout before then is a possibility, with assistance from Sabena, whose subsidiary Sobelair had a 35% holding in Air Belgium until 1999 and still has some rights to the name.

Routes

Air Belgium flies for various tour operators to the Mediterranean area and the Canary Isles.

Fleet

2 Airbus A320
1 Boeing 737-400

Boeing 737-86J D-ABAN (Josef Krauthäuser/ Paderborn-Lippstadt)

AIR BERLIN

Flughafen Tegel, 13405 Berlin, Germany,
Tel. 030-41012781, Fax. 030-4132003,
www.airberlin.de

Three- / Two- letter code	IATA No.	Reg'n prefix	ICAO callsign
BER / AB	745	D	Air Berlin

Air Berlin USA was set up in July 1978 as a wholly-owned subsidiary of the American company Leico. The first charter flights took off from Berlin in April 1979, using a fleet of US-registered Boeing 707s. Until the reunification of Germany on 3rd October 1990, only airlines belonging to the victorious nations from the Second World War were allowed to fly to Berlin. Air Berlin offered charter flights with specific departure times between Berlin and Florida. However, this service, with a stopover in Brussels, was only operated from October 1980 until October 1981. From that time, Air Berlin flew a single Boeing 737-300.

A 167-seater Boeing 737-400 came into service from April 1990, and this variant became the sole type in the growing fleet for several years. After reunification Air Berlin became more active in charter work, and in April 1991 a German company, Air Berlin GmbH & Co Luftverkehr KG was set up to take over the business. Thus registered under German law, it was not restricted to Berlin departures only. From 1994 to1996 the fleet was quickly expanded to meet new needs, and early delivery positions were secured for the for the 'new generation' Boeing 737-800 model. The delivery of the first of these in May 1998 also marked a change in

the livery of Air Berlin's aircraft. 1998 also marked the introduction of the so-called 'shuttle flights', at first to Majorca. Air Berlin's aim is for continuing growth both in the size of the aircraft fleet, and in passenger numbers, which passed 3 million for the first time in 1999.

Routes

Charter flights from 14 German airports to Agadir, Alicante, Almeria, Antalya, Arrecife, Athens, Corfu, Dalaman, Djerba, Faro, Fuerteventura, Funchal, Heraklion, Hurghada, Ibiza, Jerez, Kos, Larnaca, Las Palmas, Luxor, Mahon, Malaga, Monastir, Palma de Mallorca, Paphos, Rhodes, Samos, Santa Cruz, Tenerife, Thessaloniki, Zakynthos.

Fleet	Ordered
14 Boeing 737-800 4 Boeing 737-400	6 Boeing 737-800

McDonnell Douglas DC-8-61 N845AX (Josef Krauthäuser/Seattle)

AIRBORNE EXPRESS (ABX AIR)

Airborne Air Park, 145 Hunter Drive, Wilmington Ohio, 45177 USA, Tel. 937-3825591, Fax: 937-3822452, www.airborne-express.com

Three- / Two- letter code	IATA No.	Reg'n prefix	ICAO callsign
ABX / GB	832	N	Abex

Airborne Freight began business at the end of the 1940s, importing flowers from Hawaii. These were flown principally into California, where they were sold. Midwest Air Charter of Elyria, Ohio specialised during the 1970s in courier flights for banks and for Airborne Freight Corp, using small aircraft such as the Aerostar, Beech 18, Piper Aztec and Lear Jet, to which five SE.210 Caravelles were added in 1978. A year later Airborne took over Midwest and thus acquired its own flight division. Airborne Express was granted FAA certification in April 1980 and expanded quickly. Alongside the Caravelle the NAMC

YS-11 was introduced as a fast turboprop. From its own airport at Wilmington Airpark, where it has one of the largest package sorting facilities in the USA, more and more destinations in the USA were being served. DC-9s replaced the ageing Caravelles and quickly became the prevalent type in the fleet. In 1983 43000 tonnes of freight were forwarded. Longer distance routes and increasing amounts of freight led to the introduction to service in 1984 of the Douglas DC-8. The Airbus consortium offered a freighter version of the A300 as a replacement for the older aircraft in the fleet, but it was decided to adopt

the Boeing 767-200 freighter conversion instead. The first of these came into service during the second half of 1997, and further examples are being added.

Routes

Scheduled freight services to over 140 destinations within the USA. Canada and the Caribbean are also served.

Fleet

12 Boeing 767-200
35 McDonnell Douglas DC-8-61/62/63/63F
60 McDonnell Douglas DC-9-10/30/40

ATR 42 A2-ABB (Bastian Hilker/Johannesburg)

AIR BOTSWANA

P.O.Box 92, Gabarone, Botswana
Tel. 352812, Fax. 374802,
www.mbendi.co.za/orgs/cbjc

Three- / Two- letter code	IATA No.	Reg'n prefix	ICAO callsign
BOT / BP	636	A2	Botswana

Air Botswana was set up as the national airline by a presidential decree of July 1972 . After Botswana National Airways (1966-1969) and Botswana Airways (1969-1972), Air Botswana took over operations on 1st August 1972 with Fokker F.27s and Britten-Norman Islanders. A fleet renewal programme began in 1988, with the replacement of the F.27s by new ATR 42s. At the end of 1989 Air Botswana received its first jet, a BAe 146-100. There is close co-operation with Air Zimbabwe and for several routes a joint venture agreement is in place. In a dramatic incident in October 1999, the airline's whole fleet of three ATR 42s was destroyed, when the pilot of one of these aircraft committed suicide by crashing his aircraft onto the other two which were on the ground. Services were maintained using leased aircraft, with three replacement ATR 42-500s being delivered as replacements before the end of 1999.

Routes

Domestic routes from Gabarone to Francistown, Maun, Maputo, Maseru. Internationally to Harare, Johannesburg, Luanda, Nairobi, Victoria Falls, Windhoek and Lusaka.

Fleet

3 ATR 42-500
1 BAe 146-100

Dornier Do 228 F-ODYC (Frank Litaudon/Noumea)

AIR CALÉDONIE

BP 212 Aerodrome de Magenta, Nouméa,
New Caledonia (Nouvelle-Calédonie)
Tel. 252339, Fax. 254869, www.air-caledonie.nc

Three- / Two- letter code	IATA No.	Reg'n prefix	ICAO callsign
TPC / TY	190	F	Aircal

Air Calédonie started as Société Calédonienne de Transports Aériens (Transpac) on 25th September 1955, and began operations the same month between Nouméa and Lifan. The local government held 76% of the shares in the airline. In 1968 the company adopted the name of Air Calédonie. In addition to its own routes, it also provided flights on behalf of UTA. Various aircraft types were used, including Cessna 310s, Britten-Norman Islanders and de Havilland Twin Otters. During 1983 they carried 135,000 passengers on regional flights, and this had risen by 1989 to over 180,000. From 1987 the fleet was expanded and renewed with the acquisition of the ATR 42 and Dornier 228, with services extending from New Caledonia to the other islands which form the Loyalty group. Air France has a small shareholding of 3% in the airline; the rest is owned by the regional government. Air Calédonie has alliances with Air France, AOM-French Airlines, Qantas Airways and Solomon Airlines, and some flights are conducted as codeshares with these companies.

Routes

Belep, Huailon, Ile des Pins, Kone, Koumac, Lifou, Mare, Nouméa, Ouvea, Poum, Tiga, Tonho.

Fleet

4 ATR 42
1 Dornier Do 228

Airbus-A340-313 C-FTNQ (Martin Bach/London-LHR)

AIR CANADA

Place Air Canada Montreal, Quebec H2Z 1X5,
Canada, Tel. 514-4225000, Fax. 514-4227741,
www.aircanada.ca

Three- / Two- letter code	IATA No.	Reg'n prefix	ICAO callsign
ACA / AC	014	C	Air Canada

The Canadian government set up Trans-Canada Airlines (TCA) on 10th April 1937, and it was administered by Canadian National Railways (CNR). Service began on 1st September between Vancouver and Seattle, with a Lockheed 10A. The build-up of an internal network was TCA's primary concern in the following years. April 1939 saw the first Vancouver-Montreal flight, and shortly afterwards TCA flew from Montreal to New York. During the war, regular service was provided from Canada to Scotland using converted Lancaster bombers. Post-war, in addition to the DC-3, the Lockheed Constellation, Canadair North Star, Bristol 170, Vickers Viscount and Vickers Vanguard were all used during the prop era. On 1st April 1960 the first jet, a DC-8 entered the fleet. During 1964 the name Air Canada was adopted, and in 1967 the DC-9 was added. Air Canada expanded worldwide and introduced its first widebody in 1971 - the Boeing 747. Lockheed TriStars were also added for longer-range services, being replaced by the Boeing 767. During 1988 a partial privatisation took place. The acquisition of the Airbus A320 from the beginning of 1990 continued the fleet renewal and marked the introduction of a new colour scheme. Newest types in the long-range fleet are the Airbus A340, used for Asian routes since 1994, and the A330, which have largely replaced the 747s. Air Canada controls five regional companies: Air BC, Air Ontario, Air Alliance, Air Nova, NWT-Air, and is closely associated with Continental Airlines in the USA. At the end of 1999, Air Canada also gained control of Canadian Airlines, whose takeover was made possible by support of Air Canada's Star Alliance partners. A phase of integration and consolidation is thus in progress, and other Canadian airlines are lining up to compete.

Routes

Intensive route network in Canada, including feeder services provided by partner airlines, USA, Caribbean, to Europe and Asia.

Fleet

35 Airbus A319
34 Airbus A320
 4 Airbus A330
11 Airbus A340
32 Boeing 767-200/300

 3 Boeing 747-200
 3 Boeing 747-400
25 Canadair Regional Jet
24 McDonnell Douglas DC-9-32

Airbus A340-313 B-2385 (Author's collection/Beijing)

AIR CHINA

100621 Capital Intl. Airport, Beijing, People's Republic of China, Tel. 1-4563220, Fax. 1-4563348, www.airchina.com

Three- / Two- letter code	IATA No.	Reg'n prefix	ICAO callsign
CCA / CA	999	B	Air China

Air China International was set up by the Civil Aviation Administration of China (CAAC) in July 1988 as an independent division, responsible for operating international services. Some of the aircraft were painted with Air China titling, but others were loaned from CAAC as required. . New routes were added from the end of 1992 to Vienna, freight services to Los Angeles and in 1993 to Copenhagen. The fleet and route network are continually being expanded. Thus in 1997 Airbus A340 and in 1998 Boeing 777s were acquired to replace older Boeing 747/747SPs. A significant new service approved in mid-1997 following the handover by Britain of Hong Kong to China was a direct service from Hong Kong to London, the first by a mainland Chinese airline, and in direct competition with the established carrier Cathay Pacific. The delivery of the first of the new generation Boeing 737-800s in April 1999 was a significant marker in the renewal of the short and medium-haul fleet, for which Airbus A318s are also on order for delivery between 2004 and 2008. Air China works closely with Ariana, Austrian, Finnair, Korean Airlines and Tarom and likewise, there is a code-share agreement in place with Northwest since May 1998. Along with Lufthansa, the airline also has a shareholding in the Ameco maintenance organisation in Beijing. The Chinese authorities have indicated that they wish to see a consolidation of the country's now diverse airlines into three major groupings, and Air China is one of the three airlines designated to lead one of these groups; acquisitions of other Chinese operators are therefore to be expected.

Routes

Anchorage, Atlanta, Bangkok, Chicago,Copenhagen, Frankfurt, Fukuoka, Hiroshima, Ho Chi Minh City, Hong Kong, Karachi, Kuwait, London, Los Angeles, Milan, Melbourne, Moscow, Osaka, Paris, Rome, San Francisco, Seoul, Singapore, Stockholm, Sydney, Tokyo, Ulaanbaatar, Vancouver, Vienna, Zürich, and in addition over 50 destinations within China.

Fleet

		Ordered
3 Airbus A340-300	14 Boeing 747-400	8 Airbus A318-100
4 BAe 146-100	10 Boeing 767-200/300ER	6 Boeing 737-800
19 Boeing 737-300	5 Boeing 777-200	5 Boeing 777-200
5 Boeing 737-800	4 Yunshuji Y-7	
4 Boeing 747-200		

ATR 72-500 I-ADLN (Josef Krauthäuser/Munich)

AIR DOLOMITI

Via Aquilera 45, 34077 Ronchi dei Legionari, Trieste, Italy, Tel. 481-474479, Fax. 481-477711, www.airdolomiti.it

Three- / Two- letter code	IATA No.	Reg'n prefix	ICAO callsign
DLA / EN	101	I	Dolomiti

Established in January 1988, Air Dolomiti started operations in May 1991 with a de Havilland Canada Dash 8 on the Trieste-Genoa route. Further Italian domestic services were added quickly. From November 1992 Air Dolomiti flew its first international route, from Verona to Munich. Verona developed into a minor hub for the company, with numerous connecting flights. With the acquisition of the ATR 42 from 1994, the Dash 8s left the fleet, and a new colour scheme was adopted. The airline has worked closely with Lufthansa since 1995 in sales and

marketing and is a Lufthansa Partner, with several joint flights. Thus Munich has developed as the most important airport for Air Dolomiti, and passengers from northern Italy have connections here to Lufthansa services. More direct flights were offered and in order to provide these, the ATR 42 fleet was steadily increased in size. In addition, since 1996 the airline has had an alliance with the Swiss airline Crossair, and the Basle-Rome service is operated jointly. Seasonal and charter flights are operated as well as schedules to Italian holiday

regions and to Sardinia. With the introduction of the larger, 64-seater, ATR 72 in 1998, Air Dolomiti not only took the opportunity to upgrade the interior of their aircraft, but also adopted a new colour scheme. More ATR 42-500s, with more powerful and yet quieter engines have also augmented the fleet over the last five years, and a further three are scheduled for delivery in the last quarter of 2000. The airline has its own maintenance facility.

Routes

Ancona, Barcelona, Cagliari, Frankfurt, Genoa, Munich, Olbia, Pisa, Trieste, Turin, Venice, Verona.

Fleet	Ordered
5 ATR 42-300	3 ATR 42-500
7 ATR 42-500	
5 ATR 72-500	

Dornier Do 328-110 HB-AEG (Josef Krauthäuser/Munich)

AIR ENGIADINA/KLM ALPS

Flughafenstrasse 11, 3123 Belp, Switzerland
Tel. 601211, Fax. 601217,
www.airengiadina.ch

Three- / Two- letter code	IATA No.	Reg'n prefix	ICAO callsign
RQX / RQ	834	CH	Engiadina

Air Engiadina was formed on 22nd April 1987. The Engadine region of Switzerland is a little off the beaten track as far as air transport is concerned and would be better served by having its own regional airline. Using a single BAe Jetstream 31, the route from Samedan to Zürich was opened in January 1988, and in 1989 a new service was established between Zürich and Eindhoven, with a Munich route following in 1992. At this time a Dornier 228 was brought into service. With a factory-fresh Dornier 328, the first aircraft of its type delivered into airline service, a Berne-Vienna route was opened.

Routes from Berne to London, and Berne to Amsterdam followed in 1994, and the company base also relocated to Berne, taking over Sunshine Aviation. In order to finance all this, the company's capital was increased to 10.8 million Swiss Francs. From the beginning of the 1995 summer timetable, Berne-Frankfurt was introduced and the service increased to Amsterdam, as well as developing London City Airport; the Summer also saw a series of charters to Elba. Air Engiadina received its fourth Do 328 on 27th October 1995, and at that time the Jetstream was sold. A further Do 328 was added in

Autumn of 1996 and this completed the planned fleet. With the formation in 1998 of Air Alps, together with KLM in Innsbruck, Air Engiadina broadened its business activity and also became a participant in the KLM/Northwest Airlines alliance. In order to make this abundantly clear to the outside world, the whole fleet was repainted during 1999 in KLM Alps colour scheme. However, Air Engiadina remains an independent company.

Routes

Amsterdam, Berne, Budapest, Dublin, Elba, Geneva, London, Marseilles, Munich, Toulouse, Venice.

Fleet

5 Dornier Do 328

Boeing 737-800 EC-HJP (Uwe Gleisberg/Munich)

AIR EUROPA

Gran Via Asima 23, 07009 Palma de Mallorca
Spain, Tel. 178111, Fax. 431500,
www.g-air-europa.es

Three- / Two- letter code	IATA No.	Reg'n prefix	ICAO callsign
AEA / UX	996	E	Air Europa

Air Europa is one of the profitable remainders of the former multi-national organisation Air Europe, and was set up in June 1986 on the island of Majorca. The airline, registered as Air Espana SA, was at formation 75% owned by two Spanish banks and 25% by the British company ILG, until the time of the latter's failure in 1991. It started flights on 21st November 1986 with a Boeing 737-300. The first flight was from London-Gatwick to Palma de Mallorca, which is also Air Europa's base. Air Europe and Air Europa had an identical livery and fleet of Boeing 737s and 757s and aircraft switched between the carriers to meet their needs at different times of the year. After the failure of its British partner, several tour companies and banks took over Air Europa's shares, enabling operations to continue. During 1991 Air Europa acquired three Boeing 757-200s for use on long-range routes. Boeing 767s were used briefly during 1994/5 but these larger aircraft were found to be inflexible in their operation and they were exchanged for more Boeing 757s. Since 1995 Air Europa has found success as a scheduled service operator, initially in competition with Iberia and from 1998 as a franchise partner.

Additionally, the 767 has returned to the fleet, operating long-range routes on behalf of Iberia, to whom several 757s are also leased. The airline's own regional carrier, Air Europa Express was established in 1996, and this operates a fleet of BAe ATP/Jetstream 61s principally to the Balearics. The Boeing 737 has always formed an important part of Air Europa's fleet, and these have been updated over the past year with the delivery of ten of the new generation -800 series.

Routes

Charter flights from Great Britain, Scandinavia and Western Europe to destinations on the Spanish mainland, to the Balearics and Canary Islands. Bangkok, Cancun, Havana, New York and Santo Domingo are amongst several long-distance charter destinations. Schedules to New York and internal Spanish services from Madrid.

Fleet		Ordered
4 Boeing 737-300	2 Boeing 767-200	2 Boeing 767-300
7 Boeing 737-400	3 Boeing 767-300	
10 Boeing 737-800	15 BAe ATP/Jetstream 61	
6 Boeing 757-200		

Boeing 777-2Q8(ER) EI-CRS (Author's collection/Zürich)

AIR EUROPE

Via Carlo 3, 21013 Gallarate, Varese
Italy Tel.331-713801, Fax. 331-713850
www.aireurope.it

Three- / Two- letter code	IATA No.	Reg'n prefix	ICAO callsign
AEL / PE	667	I	Air Europe

This company also has its origins in the British-founded Air Europe operation which was set up in 1978 and which during the 1980s built up a European network of partner airlines. Air Europa Italy SpA began operations in 1988 with a Boeing 757 and following the collapse of the British parent company (ILG) in1991, was taken over by domestic companies and banks. The outward appearance of the airline however remained unaltered. Alitalia took a minority shareholding and placed the Boeing 767 at the airline's disposal. At first Air Europa standardised on this type, building up the fleet, which was used primarily for long-distance tour work, for which Air Europa was Italy's leading player. From 1998 the company took a change of direction, when the Swiss SAir Group took a 49% shareholding. During 1999 the company operated scheduled services for the first time and received new aircraft, Airbus A320s and its first Boeing 777. The delivery of the latter to the airline's base at Milan-Malpensa also highlighted another change; a new corporate identity had been adopted, with changes in the appearance of the aircraft interiors, and the external colour scheme. In July 2000 it was announced that the SAir Group would combine Air Europe with its other Italian airline Volare under a single holding company, the Volare group, and that the Boeing 767 fleet would be replaced by the Airbus A300-200 by 2002. The two airlines will continue as separate brands but the sales and marketing and other managerial functions will be merged. Air Europe has been a member of the Qualiflyer Group since May 1999.

Routes

Scheduled services within Italy, to Havana, Mauritius, and Montego Bay. Charter work to the Caribbean, USA, South East Asia and Africa.

Fleet	Ordered
7 Airbus A320	2 Airbus A320
6 Boeing 767-300	
2 Boeing 777-200	

Boeing 737-247 PK-OCF (Author's collection via EAS)

AIRFAST INDONESIA

Kuningan Plaza, Suite 305 Jl HR Rasuna Said Kav, C11-14 Jakarta, Indonesia, Tel. 6221-5200696, Fax. 6221-5202557, www.airfast.co.id

Three- / Two- letter code	IATA No.	Reg'n prefix	ICAO callsign
AFE	–	PK	Airfast

Set up in 1971 as a joint venture between Indonesia and Australia, with the objective of offering passenger and cargo charters for the oil industry in Southeast Asia, flights started with Douglas DC-3s. As well as serving Indonesia the airline was also active in Malaysia, Papua-New Guinea, South Korea, the Philippines and in the Near East. Fokker F.27s and various light aircraft were used for services to the many small Indonesian islands. From 1982 the company was in private Indonesian ownership and in addition to its original remit, additional tasks such as offshore flights to oil rigs, aerial photography and earth resource survey flights were undertaken. Additionally there were all sorts of other special flights such as aerial logging and other heavy lift jobs with helicopters. The main base is Jakarta, but there are others in Singapore and Kalimantan. The Indonesian business crisis which came during the late 1990s did not seem to affect Airfast unduly; indeed the company benefited in some areas from the fall in competition and the reduced activities of other companies. The passenger services were notably profitable.

Routes

Passenger and freight flights on behalf of companies within Indonesia, to Singapore, Malaysia, the whole of South East Asia and to Australia.

Fleet

1 BAe HS.748
2 Bell 204
4 Bell 206
2 Bell 212
2 Bell 412
5 Boeing 737-200
1 CASA-IPTN 212
3 De Havilland DHC-6 Twin Otter
1 Douglas DC-3
2 Sikorsky S-58T

Boeing 767-328ER F-GHGI (Kai Schmidt/Paris-CDG)

AIR FRANCE

45 rue de Paris, 95747 Roissy, France
Tel. 1-41567800, Fax. 1-41567029,
www.airfrance.fr

Three- / Two- letter code	IATA No.	Reg'n prefix	ICAO callsign
AFR / AF	057	F	Airfrans

On 30th August 1933 Air Orient, Air Union, CIDNA and SGTA merged to form the national airline Air France. By the outbreak of war, Air France had a leading position in Europe and North Africa, and operated to all France's colonies including Indochina. Post-war nationalisation saw Air France make a new start in 1946, initially using mainly French-built types such as the Breguet 763 and SE 161. In 1953 came the first jet, the Comet. More British aircraft, Vickers Viscounts, took over short and medium length routes, while long range routes were served by DC-4s and Lockheed Constellations.

On 26th May 1959 the successful SE 210 Caravelle saw its first service with Air France. Boeing 707s and 747s replaced propeller-driven types on intercontinental routes. From May 1974 the Airbus A300 was used for the first time between Paris and London, and from 21st January 1976 Concorde was licensed for scheduled services. Naturally, the airline has been a strong supporter of Airbus, and though Boeing has a strong representation in the fleet, all of the Airbus products are used in significant numbers. The operations, routes and aircraft of Aéromaritime and UTA were integrated into Air

France in 1992. By the mid 1990s the Air France Group was in deep crisis and restructuring was necessary; this led to a part privatisation. Air France has shareholdings in many other airlines and has alliances with regional airlines operating for Air France as franchise partners. In September 1999 Air France joined Delta Airlines in founding the global Skyteam alliance. The most recent types introduced into the fleet are the Airbus A319 (1997), A321 (1997) and Boeing 777 (1998), with Airbus A318s scheduled for delivery from 2003.

Routes

Air France has a worldwide route serving over 160 destinations, notably in former French colonies and overseas provinces. In Europe all major cities are served, many in association with franchise partners.

Fleet

Fleet		Ordered
5 Aerospatiale/BAe Concorde	20 Airbus A340-200/300	15 Airbus A318
10 Airbus A310	45 Boeing 737-200/300/500	16 Airbus A319
23 Airbus A319	38 Boeing 747-100/200/400	3 Airbus A321
61 Airbus A320-100/200	5 Boeing 767-300ER	4 Airbus A330
13 Airbus A321-100/200	12 Boeing 777-200ER	2 Airbus A340
		6 Boeing 777

Boeing 727-228 TR-LEV (Josef Krauthäuser collection via EAS)

AIR GABON

P.B. 2206, Libreville,
Gabon
Tel. 733018, Fax. 731156

Three- / Two- letter code	IATA No.	Reg'n prefix	ICAO callsign
AGN / GN	185	TR	Golf November

Formed in 1951 as Compagnie Aérienne Gabonaise, the airline began local services from Libreville with Beech and de Havilland aircraft. The airline was a founder member of Air Afrique and was a member of the consortium from 1961 to 1977. Though operating internationally through Air Afrique, Air Gabon always operated domestic services on its own account. In 1974 it acquired its first Fokker F.28, followed by another aircraft of the same type and a Boeing 737 in 1978. After leaving Air Afrique, Air Gabon obtained a Boeing 747-200 in late 1978 for use on scheduled services to Europe. During 1988 the airline underwent a reorganisation, which entailed a tightening up of the route network. A Fokker 100 was taken on in 1990, but traffic growth on its routes meant that in 1993 this would be exchanged for a Boeing 727. A Boeing 767 has also been leased, initially in 1996, to supplement the 747 on long-range routes, which now include London.

Routes

Abidjan, Bamako, Bangui, Bitam, Conakry, Cotonou, Dakar, Douala, Dubai, Fougamou, Franceville, Gamva, Johannesburg, Lagos, Lome, London, Luanda, Malabo, Marseilles, Mekambo, Moanda, Nairobi, Nice, Oyem, Paris, Point Noire, Port Gentil, Rome, Sao Tome.

Fleet

1 Boeing 727-200
2 Boeing 737-200
1 Boeing 747-200
1 Boeing 767-200
1 Fokker F.28

ATR 72-212 F-OGUO (Christopher Witt/San Juan)

AIR GUADELOUPE

Aéroport du Raizet 97110 Abymes,
French-Guadeloupe
Tel. 590-824734, Fax. 590-824748

Three- / Two- letter code	IATA No.	Reg'n prefix	ICAO callsign
FWI / TX	427	F	Air Guadeloupe

Air Guadeloupe was set up by Air France and the local government of the French overseas department in 1970. It started operations with a Fairchild FH227 and de Havilland DHC-6 Twin Otters for a shuttle service between Pointe-à-Pitre and Fort de France and other neighbouring islands. The FH227 was replaced by an ATR 42 in 1987, with a second aircraft of the same type joining the fleet later in that year. After heavy losses in 1992, the airline applied to begin insolvency proceedings, but flights continued to operate. A new company structure was put in place and Air France took on 45% of the shares,

the balance being with the island's government. At the beginning of 1996 the first ATR 72 joined the fleet. Growth was slow but steady, and in 1998 the first jet, a Boeing 737-200, was introduced to the small fleet. The same year was also marked by the introduction of a new colour scheme for the aircraft. The 737 is used principally for longer routes, for example to Miami, and for group charters. Air Guadeloupe owns 100% of Air Martinique on the neighbouring island. The latter also flies the ATR 42 and uses Air Guadeloupe's 737 as and when required. In August 2000, these two airlines were merged, along with two

other small airlines, Air Saint Martin and Air Barthelemy to form Air Caraibes. The new airline has ordered Embraer Regional Jets, with the first two RJ 145s for delivery at the end of 2000.

Routes

Antigua, Barbados, Cayenne, Dominica, Fort de France, Les Saintes, La Desirade, Marie Galante, Pointe-à-Pitre, San Juan, Santo Domingo, Saint Barthelemy, Saint Martin, Saint Thomas, St.Lucia, St.Maarten, St.Vincent and Terre-de-Haute are important destinations in the Caribbean.

Fleet

2 ATR 42
2 ATR 72
1 Boeing 737-200
2 De Havilland DHC-6

8 Fairchild-Dornier Do 228

Boeing 737-300 PH-OZA (Dennis Wehrmann/Hamburg)

AIR HOLLAND CHARTER

Breguetlaan 670, Postbus 75116,
1117 ZR Schiphol, the Netherlands
Tel. 20-3164444, Fax. 20-3164445

Three- / Two- letter code	IATA No.	Reg'n prefix	ICAO callsign
AHR / GG	895	PH	Orange

Air Holland was formed in early 1984 by private companies and was granted its operating licence on 30th July of that year. A Boeing 727-200 started flights on 2nd April 1985, with a second 727 being added in May 1985. Air Holland flew on behalf of tour operators from Amsterdam, Rotterdam, Maastricht and Eindhoven. From 1988 the 727s were replaced by four new, more modern Boeing 757s, with further examples being added in 1989 and 1990. Air Holland not only provided flights for tour operators, but also leased out its aircraft to other airlines. In1992 Air Holland was obliged to suspend operations for financial reasons, but after reorganisation as Air Holland Charter BV, it was able to resume charter flights in 1993. Six years later, in 1999, came a second cessation of operations. Air Holland, which by then was operating a fleet of Boeing 757s and 737-300s, was sold and the Dutch Schreiner group took over the airline, so that by mid-2000 it was again able to take to the skies with a Boeing 757-200. It is planned that two further 757s will be added during late 2000 and early 2001.

Routes

Charter flights principally to the Mediterranean and the Canary Isles.

Fleet

1 Boeing 757-200

Airbus A310-304 VT-EJK (Björn Kannengiesser/Dubai)

AIR INDIA

Air India Building. 218 Backbay Rec. Nairnam Point, Mumbai 40021, India, Tel. 022-2024142, Fax. 022-2024897, www.airindia.com

Three- / Two- letter code	IATA No.	Reg'n prefix	ICAO callsign
AIC / AI	098	VT	Airindia

Air India's history can be traced back to July 1932 when Tata Sons Ltd operated a mail service between Bombay, Madras and Karachi using de Havilland Puss Moths. The name was changed to Tata Airlines in 1938 and to Air India on 29th July 1946, after independence. Regular flights to London via Cairo and Geneva commenced in 1948 with Lockheed Constellations. During 1953 all Indian air services were placed under state control. On 18th February 1960 Air India received its first Boeing 707, which was used to fly via Europe to New York. The first widebody, the Boeing 747 was delivered in 1971, and the type was used on services to London, Frankfurt and New York. Since August 1980 Air India has also been an Airbus operator, with the A300 replacing the Boeing 707s. 1989 was the year when India's flag carrier was restructured, with the aircraft being given a more modern colour scheme. At the end of 1993 Air India received its first Boeing 747-400, but notably in the 'old' colour scheme, as the new one was disliked by customers. Drastic cost-cutting measures at the end of the century led Air India to a reduction in size and the abandonment of several routes, including those to Frankfurt and Rome and to a reduction in the aircraft fleet. The long-awaited part privatisation has been pushed back more and more. Air India has a shareholding in Air Mauritius of just 3%, and is not a member of any of the major alliances. However, the airline co-operates with Air France, Air Mauritius, Malaysia Airlines and SAS.

Routes

Abu Dhabi, Ahmedabad, Amritsar, Bahrain, Bangalore, Bangkok, Chennai, Chicago, Dar-es-Salaam, Delhi, Dharan, Doha, Dubai, Goa, Hong Kong, Jeddah, Kuala Lumpur, Kuwait, London, Mauritius, Moscow, Mumbai, Muscat, Nairobi, New York, Osaka, Paris, Singapore, Sydney and Tokyo.

Fleet

2 Airbus A300B4
8 Airbus A310-300
7 Boeing 747-200
2 Boeing 747-300

9 Boeing 747-400

Airbus A340-312 6Y-JMC (Dennis Wehrmann/Hamburg)

AIR JAMAICA

72-76 Harbour Street, Kingston, Jamaica
Tel. 809-9223460, Fax. 809-9220107,
www.airjamaica.com

Three- / Two- letter code	IATA No.	Reg'n prefix	ICAO callsign
AJM / JM	201	6Y	Juliett Mike

Air Jamaica was established by the government of the island nation (60% share), together with Air Canada (40%) in October 1968. It succeeded an earlier company of the same name established with the help of BOAC and BWIA in 1962 and which had operated a Kingston-New York service with leased aircraft since 1965. Using a DC-9 leased from Air Canada, who provided technical support, the new company started flights to Miami on 1st April 1969 and with a DC-8, likewise from Air Canada, to New York. From 1974 London became the sole European destination in the timetable, but this was discontinued after a few years.

The DC-8 proved too large for the company's needs and in 1983 was replaced by the Airbus A300. These were used for flights to the USA and Canada. Boeing 727s were used for short and medium haul routes in the Caribbean. The long-awaited privatisation finally came about in May 1994, with the government disposing of 75% of the shares. The subsequent reorganisation brought with it a new colour scheme and new aircraft. The London service was re-opened in 1996 using the Airbus A310 and during 1999 turned over to the more modern Airbus A340. Regional services were taken over in 1996 by a newly-established

100% owned subsidiary company. Air Jamaica Express flies Dornier 228s and de Havilland Canada Dash 8s to the island airports. With the delivery of new Airbus A320 and A321s in 1999, the last Boeing 727s were retired, giving Air Jamaica a modern fleet. There are co-operation agreements with Air Canada and Delta Air Lines.

Routes

From Kingston to Atlanta, Baltimore, Barbados, Chicago, Curacao, Fort Lauderdale, Grand Cayman, Havana, London, Los Angeles, Miami, Montego Bay, Nassau, Negril, New York, Ochos Rios, Orlando, Panama City, Philadelphia, Phoenix, Port Antonio, Port of Spain, St. Lucia, Tobago.

Fleet

4 Airbus A310-300
7 Airbus A320-200
2 Airbus A321-200
1 Airbus A340-300

Tupolev Tu-154B UN-85276 (Dennis Wehrmann/Hanover)

AIR KAZAKSTAN

Ul Ogareva 14, Almaty 480079, Kazakstan
Tel. 3272-573157, Fax. 3272-503738,
www.airkaz.com

Three- / Two- letter code	IATA No.	Reg'n prefix	ICAO callsign
KZK / 9Y	452	UN	Air Kazakstan

State-owned Air Kazakstan emerged in 1996 from Kazakstan Airlines, which, likewise state-owned, had become bankrupt and was practically reorganised. Following independence from the former Soviet Union, Aeroflot's regional directorate was dissolved and about 15 new airlines set up, of which Kazakstan Airlines was the largest, and was recognized as the flag carrier of the new state. Numerous activities in both scheduled and charter work made the airline a candidate for its first Western aircraft types. Thus Boeing 757s, Boeing 747SPs and Boeing 767s all came into service, with the hope that passengers from Western Europe would make Almaty a hub for onward flights within Asia. After a few years, both the country and the airline faced financial crisis. Kazakstan Airlines was in practice dissolved, the leasing contracts for Western types terminated, the route network, aircraft fleet and employee numbers all drastically reduced. Consolidation was deemed to be an important aim, in order to prepare the airline for a partial privatisation. During the later part of 1999 Airbus A310s were leased again.

Routes

Aktau, Aktyubinsk, Almaty, Astana, Atyrau, Baku, Bangkok, Beijing, Budapest, Frankfurt, Hanover, Istanbul, Karaganda, Kiev, Kostanay, Mineralnye Vody, Moscow, Novosibirsk, Pavlodar, Petropavlovsk, Samara, Sharjah, St.Petersburg, Tashkent, Tel Aviv, Uralsk.

Fleet

2 Airbus A310-300	7 Ilyushin IL-86
26 Antonov An-24	8 Tupolev Tu-134
2 Boeing 737-200	16 Tupolev Tu-154
3 Ilyushin IL-76TD	

Ilyushin IL-76MD P-913 (Author's collection)

AIR KORYO

Sunan District, Pyongyang,
People's Republic of Korea
Tel. 37917, Fax. 4571

Three- / Two- letter code	IATA No.	Reg'n prefix	ICAO callsign
KCA / JS	120	P	Airkoryo

Air Koryo, formerly Chosonminhang Korean Airways (CAAK) is the state airline of the Democratic Republic of Korea (North Korea). It was formed in 1954 to succeed SOKAO, the joint Aeroflot - North Korean airline established in 1950, which started with Lisunov Li-2s and operated Ilyushin IL-12s and Antonov An-2s. With the founding of CAAK, the Soviet share of the airline and their aircraft were taken over, with IL-14s and later IL-18s coming into service. As the Soviet Union provided massive support to North Korea, only Soviet aircraft types were used; thus the first jet was a Tupolev Tu-154 delivered in 1975, with further

examples following in 1979 and 1982. These were also used on long-range routes, such as to East Berlin or Prague, with intermediate fuel stops being necessary. With the delivery of the Ilyushin IL-62 came an aircraft properly suited to these longer stretches and it was possible to introduce non-stop service from Pyongyang to Moscow. In 1993 came a change, when Chosonminhang became Air Koryo. In addition to passenger services, freight flights are also undertaken, and Air Koryo fulfils other functions on behalf of the state, including responsibility for handling at all the airports in the country. Its main base

is at the airport of the capital, Pyongyang. In the Autumn of 1996 a new scheduled service was initiated to Macau, and from 1998 a weekly service to Osaka in Japan appeared in the timetable. An agreement is in place with DHL International for co-operation in the carriage of documents and freight.

Routes

Regular services to Bangkok, Beijing, Berlin, Macau, Moscow, Osaka, Sofia and Vladivostok. Charter flights to Eastern Europe and the former Soviet Union, regional services to Chongsin, Kaesong, Wonsan, Hamhun, Kilchu, Kanggyae and Sinuiju.

Fleet

8 Antonov An-24
2 Ilyushin IL-18
4 Ilyushin IL-62
3 Ilyushin IL-76MD

2 Tupolev Tu-134B
4 Tupolev Tu-154B

McDonnell Douglas MD-83 F-GRML (Patrick Lutz/Palma de Mallorca)

AIR LIBERTÉ

3, rue du Pont des Hallas, 94656 Rungis Cedex, France, Tel. 49792300, Fax. 49792369, www.air-liberte.fr

Three- / Two- letter code	IATA No.	Reg'n prefix	ICAO callsign
LIB / IJ	718	F	Air Liberté

Air Liberté was set up in July 1987. Flights began in April 1988 with a leased MD-83, especially for Club Aquarius, one of the major tour operators in France. From its base at Paris-Orly, Air Liberté inaugurated a scheduled service to Montreal from 1993, but principally operated passenger services to European and Mediterranean holiday resorts from French cities. With the advent of Club Méditerranée as a shareholder in1994 , the French internal network was expanded, and the takeover of AOM was mooted. Routes from Toulouse to Dakar and London were inaugurated, but in a squabble over slot allocations at

Orly, routes were quickly started and then discontinued. At the beginning of 1996 more domestic services were started to Nice, where a secondary hub was created. In May 1996 Air Liberté took over the whole Paris-Orly network of Euralair, along with three of the company's Boeing 737-200s, and four DC-10s were taken on long-term lease. By 1996, Air Liberté was suffering serious financial difficulties, and to avoid bankruptcy, 70% of the shares were acquired in 1997 by British Airways, who also owned another French airline, TAT. The two French airlines were merged in March 1998 to form a new entity, retaining the Air

Liberté name. Even so, the venture proved to be a poor investment by British Airways, with continuing losses being incurred, and so in 2000, the airline was sold on again, to the SAir Group (owners of Swissair), who are intending to merge it with their other French interests, AOM - French Airlines (see page 100) and Air Littoral to form a new grouping which will have about 30% of the French market. There will be two divisions, one with aircraft of 100 seats and over which will operate as the mainline, and one with the smaller aircraft which will operate regionally from Nice and Montpellier.

Routes

Scheduled services to Annecy, Basle-Mulhouse, Bordeaux, Brest, Carcassonne, Figari, Fort de France, La Rochelle, Lannion, Lille, Lyon, Marseilles, Metz, Nancy, Montpellier, Nantes, Nice, Paris, Perpignan, Pointe-à-Pitre, Poitiers, Rodez, Rouen, Réunion, Strasbourg, Toulon, Toulouse and Tours.

Fleet

2 Boeing 737-300
11 Fokker 100
2 Fokker F.28
9 McDonnell Douglas MD-83

3 McDonnell Douglas DC-10-30

Airbus A320 CS-MAH (Klaus Brandmaier/Madrid)

AIR MACAU

P.O.Box 1910, Macau, China
Tel. 3966888, Fax. 396866,
www.airmacau.com.mo

Three- / Two- letter code	IATA No.	Reg'n prefix	ICAO callsign
AMU / MX	675	B-M	Air Macau

The first Airbus A321 for Air Macau landed on 5th November 1995 at the new airport at Macau, the Portuguese colony on China's doorstep. The official opening of the airport followed on 8th December with the handover of the aircraft to Air Macau. The airline had been formed a year earlier, in October 1994, and belongs to the predominantly Chinese Macon Aviation Services Company (MASC), which in turn is owned by CAAC and local investors. A small part of the capital is also owned by TAP-Air Portugal. Two Airbus A320s and two A321s were ordered from the leasing company ILFC and when they were delivered during 1996 they were put to work on regional routes. At the New Year 1999/2000 China took over control of Macau from Portugal, and granted it a special business zone status, as it had already done with Hong Kong. The registration prefixes of the aircraft were changed from the Portuguese CS- to China's B-, but otherwise the status of Air Macau is unaltered, as an agreement with the Chinese government ensures its place as the flag carrier for Macau until at least 2020.

Routes

Bangkok, Beijing, Chongqing, Fuzhou, Guilin, Haikou, Kaoshiung, Manila, Nanjing, Ningbo, Sanya, Seoul, Shanghai, Taipei, Wuhan, Xiamen and Zhengzhou.

Fleet

3 Airbus A320
5 Airbus A321

Boeing 767-300ER 5R-MVZ (Uwe Gleisberg/Munich)

AIR MADAGASCAR

31 Ave. de l'Independence, BP 437,
Antanaraivo, 101 Madagascar
Tel. 22222, Fax. 25728, www.air-mad.com

Three- / Two- letter code	IATA No.	Reg'n prefix	ICAO callsign
MDG / MD	258	5R	Madair

Air Madagascar was founded in January 1961, a year after the country became independent. It was set up by the government (51%), Air France (40%) and a predecessor company of the same name which had been in existence since 1947. Prior to 1st January 1962 it had been known as Madair. The first service was inaugurated on 20th October 1961 between Tananarive and Paris with a Douglas DC-7C operated on the carrier's behalf by the French carrier TAI. Air France's contribution to the airline was to bring in the domestic flights which it had previously provided along with the corresponding aircraft, DC-3s and DC-4s. The new airline's own first international route was via Djibouti and Marseilles to Paris, using the Boeing 707. In 1979 came the Boeing 747-200SCD, the first and only widebody in the fleet. The delivery of a Boeing 737-300 in 1995 allowed an expansion of regional routes, particularly in the south of Africa. New routes to Europe were also added, for example to Munich. During 1998 Air Madagascar added a Boeing 767-300 for long-range routes; this has been replaced by two further examples of the same type over the past year. Air Madagascar has its headquarters and maintenance base at the airport of the capital, Antananarivo. The airline co-operates closely with Air Mauritius and Air France, the latter having a 3% shareholding.

Routes

Ambanja, Ambatomainty, Ambilobe, Analalava, Antalaha, Antsiranana, Belo, Besalampy, Doany, Farafangana, Fort Dauphin, Johannesburg, Mahanoro, Mahe, Maintirano, Majunga, Mampikony, Manakara, Mananara, Mananjary, Mandritsara, Manja, Mauritius, Morafenobe, Morombe, Morondava, Moroni, Munich, Nairobi, Nossi-Be, Paris, Port Berge, Rome, Sambava, Singapore, Soalala, St. Denis, Ste. Marie, Tambohorano, Tulear, Vatomandry, Vohemar.

Fleet

2 ATR 42	2 Boeing 767-300ER
2 Boeing 737-200	5 De Havilland DHC-6
1 Boeing 737-300	2 HS.748
1 Boeing 747-200	

Boeing 737-33A 7Q-YKP (Jörg D. Zmich/Johannesburg)

AIR MALAWI

4 Robins Road, P.O.Box 84 Blantyre, Malawi
Tel. 265-620811, Fax. 265-620042,
www.africaonline.co.ke/airmalawi/

Three- / Two- letter code	IATA No.	Reg'n prefix	ICAO callsign
AML / QM	167	7Q	Malawi

Air Malawi was founded in 1964 by the government of the new state (formerly Nyasaland) upon achieving independence from Great Britain. Central African Airways was responsible for the operation of flights with the Douglas DC-3 and the management of the airline until 1967, when Air Malawi became self-sufficient. Regional routes were served with the Vickers Viscount, and the first jet equipment was the BAC One-Eleven with which routes from Blantyre to Salisbury (now Harare), Johannesburg and Nairobi were flown from 1972 . A Vickers VC-10 was introduced on 3rd December 1974 for the London service. Vickers Viscounts, HS.748s, Britten-Norman Islanders and Shorts Skyvans were all in use until the early 1990s when more modern aircraft such as the ATR 42 and Boeing 737-300 joined the small fleet of the national carrier. There is close co-operation with Air Tanzania. The main base is at Blantyre-Chileka, where the airline has its own maintenance facility, which also carries out overhauls for other operators.

Routes

Blantyre, Chelinda, Club Makokola, Dar-es-Salaam, Harare, Johannesburg, Karonga, Lilongwe, Lusaka, Mzuzu, Nairobi.

Fleet

1 ATR 42
2 Boeing 737-300
1 Fairchild-Dornier Do 228

Airbus A310-300 F-OIHS (Josef Krauthäuser collection via EAS)

AIR MALDIVES

P.O.Box 2049 Male,
Maldives
Tel. 322438, Fax. 325056

Three- / Two- letter code	IATA No.	Reg'n prefix	ICAO callsign
AMI / L6	900	8Q	Air Maldives

The original Air Maldives was formed in 1974 and began operations in October of that year. The airline served as the flag carrier for the Maldives until May 1977, providing services between Male and Colombo, Sri Lanka with a Convair 440 from the Sri Lankan Air Force, and in addition covering the internal route to Gan. The airline abruptly halted its Convair operations in 1977 and was succeeded in September of that year as national flag carrier by Maldives International Airlines, operating between Male and Trivandrum in India via Colombo from 2nd November 1977. The company had a technical and management agreement with Indian Airlines whose Boeing 737s were used. This arrangement failed to last and another airline was set up by the government in 1984, but was dissolved in 1986. Air Maldives, operated by the National Travel Bureau, once again launched an air service between Male and Gan via Kiddu Island using a Shorts Skyvan. In late 1989 a further re-organisation was successfully completed and two new Dornier 228s joined the fleet. The first large aircraft was an Airbus A300, leased from Malaysian; this was not entirely surprising since a shareholding had been taken in Autumn 1994 by Malaysian Helicopter, which also had holdings in Malaysian Airways and World Airways. Growing tourism led to the addition of services to Dubai, Frankfurt and Zürich, with further growth planned for 2000. To this end Air Maldives added an Airbus A310-300 in mid 1999 and adopted a new colour scheme. However, in April 2000 Air Maldives suspended long-range services for six months, during which time the company is to undergo re-organization.

Routes

Scheduled services to Abu Dhabi, Colombo, Dubai, Frankfurt, Gan, Hanimaadhoo, Kuala Lumpur, Male, Trivandum.

Fleet

1 Airbus A310-300
1 De Havilland DHC-8-200
2 Dornier 228

Boeing 737-3Y5 9H-ABT (Josef Krauthäuser/Düsseldorf)

AIR MALTA

Luqa Airport LQA 05 Malta, Republic of Malta
Tel. 6229990, Fax. 6673241,
www.airmalta.com

Three- / Two- letter code	IATA No.	Reg'n prefix	ICAO callsign
AMC / KM	643	9H	Air Malta

Air Malta is the national airline of the island republic of Malta and has been in existence since 30th March 1973, when it was set up by order of the government. The first service was Malta-Rome from 1st April 1973. Air Malta has only ever used jet aircraft, initially leased British Airways Tridents, followed from 1st April 1974 by independent operations. The route network was built up and regular flights and charters were carried out to London, Amsterdam, Paris, Zürich, Munich, Cairo and Tripoli. Boeing 720s came into service, supplemented from 1978 by Boeing 737-200s, which later took over completely. Spring

1990 saw the arrival of two Airbus A320s, which also carried a new colour scheme introduced by the airline. From September 1994, Avro RJ 70s were added to the fleet, but these were disposed of to Azzurra Air (an Italian company in which Air Malta has a 48% interest) in mid-1998. Air Malta also has shareholdings in Mediterranean Aviation (Med Avia), which operates CASA 212s, and in Malta Air Charter, which links Malta with the small island of Gozo, using Mil Mi-8 helicopters. Boeing 737-300s have been added to the fleet steadily since 1993, and the first two new generation 737-700s are expected

to join the fleet on lease towards the end of 2000.

Routes

Abu Dhabi, Amsterdam, Athens, Bahrain, Barcelona, Beirut, Berlin, Birmingham, Brussels, Budapest, Cairo, Casablanca, Catania, Copenhagen, Damascus, Dubai, Dublin, Düsseldorf, Frankfurt, Geneva, Glasgow, Gothenburg, Gozo, Hamburg, Istanbul, Larnaca, Lisbon, London, Lyon, Milan, Manchester, Marseilles, Moscow, Munich, Oslo, Palermo, Paris, Prague, Rome, Rotterdam, Stockholm, Stuttgart, Tel Aviv, Thessaloniki, Tunis, Vienna and Zürich.

Fleet

2 Airbus A320-200
2 Boeing 737-200
7 Boeing 737-300

4 Boeing 737-400

Dornier Do 228 MI-8504 (Author's collection)

AIR MARSHALL ISLANDS

P.O.Box 1319 Majuro 96960,
Marshall Islands
Tel. 6253731, Fax. 6253730

Three- / Two- letter code	IATA No.	Reg'n prefix	ICAO callsign
MRS / CW	778	V7	Marhallislands

In 1980 an independent state airline was established with the purpose of creating better air connections between the individual islands of the state territory and the main island of Majuro. It was known as the Airline of the Marshall Islands, with the current name being adopted in 1989. The first flights were with GAF Nomads, but these were augmented in 1982 with a single BAe 748. The primary route is from Majuro to Kwajalein, where an American missile base and air force facility is located. The GAF Nomads were replaced by Dornier Do 228s delivered in 1984 and 1985. In the mid-1990s a leased DC-8-62 was used to help build up a tourist infrastructure, concentrating principally on tourists from the USA. However, this service was abandoned after a short while, as the DC-8 was found to be too expensive to operate. The arrival of a Saab 2000 in 1995 marked the introduction of a new generation of regional aircraft to replace the older types. However, as production of the Saab has ceased and it was not totally suited to the needs of the airline, it was decided to switch instead to the Dornier 328, two of which are expected to be delivered during the second half of 2000.

Routes

Ailuk Island, Airok, Auckland, Aur Island, Bikini Atoll, Brisbane, Ebon, Ine Island, Jabot, Jeh, Kwajalein, Liekip Island, Loen, Majkin, Mili Island, Namdrik Island, Tarawa, Woja and Wotje Island.

Fleet	Ordered
1 BAe HS-748	2 Dornier 328
2 Fairchild-Dornier Do 228	
1 Saab 2000	

Fokker F.28 Fellowship 4000 5T-CLG (Josef Krauthäuser collection/Las Palmas)

AIR MAURITANIE

B.P.41, Nouakchott 174,
Islamic Republic of Mauritania
Tel. 522211, Fax. 53815

Three- / Two- letter code	IATA No.	Reg'n prefix	ICAO callsign
MRT / MR	174	5T	Air Mauritania

Mauritania's national carrier was established in September 1962 by the state to take over and expand the small network previously provided by Air France and UAT. Operations started in October 1963 with technical assistance and equipment, including Fokker F.27s, from the Spanish airline Spantax and the airline quickly built up its services, particularly in the important agricultural areas in the south of the country. By the mid-1980s international services were operated to Dakar and Las Palmas in addition to an extensive domestic network.The airline was owned by the government (60%), Air Afrique (20%) and UTA (20%).Two Fokker F.28s were brought into use in 1983, and the small fleet was renewed at the end of 1996 with the delivery of two ATR 42s, but at the end of 1998 these were returned to the lessor on cost grounds and the airline reverted to Fokker F.28 equipment. Flights to Gran Canaria and Casablanca are carried out in partnership with Iberia and Royal Air Maroc. The airline's base is at the international airport in Nouakchott.

Routes

Aioun Atrouss, Atar, Bamako, Banjul, Casablanca, Dakar, Kiffa, Las Palmas, Nema, Nouadhibou, Nouakchott, Selibaby, Tidjikja and Zouerate.

Fleet

1 Fokker F.28

Airbus A340-300 3B-NAT (Uwe Gleisberg/Munich)

AIR MAURITIUS

Rogers House 5, President John Kennedy Street, Port Louis, Mauritius, Tel. 2087700, Fax. 2088331, www.air-mauritius.com

Three- / Two- letter code	IATA No.	Reg'n prefix	ICAO callsign
MAU / MK	239	3B	Airmauritius

Air Mauritius was set up on 14th June 1967, although until 1972 it functioned only as a handling agent. After the independence from Britain of Mauritius, there was a need for a national airline. With help from the government, from Air India, British Airways and additional support from Air France, operations were begun with a Piper PA-31 Navajo. The first destination in August 1972 was the island of Rodrigues, some 600km from the main island. In 1973, in co-operation with Air India and using its aircraft, a service to Bombay was inaugurated. Likewise flights were started to London, using aircraft leased on a daily basis, and with Air France to Paris. Only on 31st October 1977 did a Boeing 707 in Air Mauritius' own colours come into use. In April 1978 Rome was brought into the network, with Durban, Johannesburg, Nairobi and Antananaraivo following in 1981 and Jeddah and Zürich during 1983. A Boeing 747SP was leased from SAA in 1984 to provide non-stop service to Paris. From April 1987 further new destinations were Munich and Singapore. Flights were scheduled for several times weekly, as the popularity of Mauritius as a holiday destination was growing strongly. The Boeing 707s were replaced in 1988 by new Boeing 767s, but the bulk of the long-haul fleet is now made up of Airbus A340s, the first of which entered service in 1994. For shorter routes, ATR 42s are in use, the first of these having been delivered in 1986. Two Airbus A319s are on order for delivery from Autumn 2001. Aircraft are maintained at the airline's own base at Sir Seewoosagur Ramgoolam International Airport.

Routes

Antananavivo, Brussels, Delhi, Durban, Frankfurt, Geneva, Harare, Hong Kong, Jeddah, Johannesburg, Capetown, Kuala Lumpur, London, Mahe, Manchester, Maputo,Melbourne, Mumbai, Munich, Nairobi, Paris, Perth, Rodrigues, Rome, Singapore, St. Denis de la Réunion, Vienna, Zürich.

Fleet

3 ATR 42
5 Airbus A340-300
2 Boeing 767-200ER

Ordered

2 Airbus A319

Tupolev Tu-134A ER-65071 (Frank Fielitz/Frankfurt)

AIR MOLDOVA

Airport, 277026 Chisinau, Moldova
Tel. 0422-524064, Fax. 0422-524040,
www.aeolos.com/moldova.htm

Three- / Two- letter code	IATA No.	Reg'n prefix	ICAO callsign
MLD / 9U	572	ER	Air Moldova

The former Soviet Republic Moldova, bordering on Romania, declared its independence in 1992 and decided that it needed its own national airline. As soon as May 1992 a regular service from Chisinau (otherwise known as Kishinev) to Frankfurt was being operated. Tupolev Tu-134A and Tu-154s formed the fleet, supplemented by Antonov An-24s for regional routes. The airline also operates charter and freight services; the Antonov An-26 is used for these. As a result of considerable national and business difficulties during the late 1990s, the demand for air transport in the region fell. The Tu-154s were sold off, the rest of the fleet reduced and many routes curtailed. However, after a cash injection from German investors Unistar, who have acquired 49% of the shares in Autumn 2000, Air Moldova is in the position of being able to order two Embraer RJ 145s for delivery from 2002. The airline works in co-operation with Balkan Bulgarian Airlines and has also recently concluded a codeshare agreement with Transaero for the Moscow route.

Routes

Antalya, Athens, Bucharest, Bourgas, Frankfurt, Istanbul, Larnaca, Moscow, Paris, Sofia, St.Petersburg, Thessaloniki, Varna, Vienna and Volgograd.

Fleet

8 Antonov An-24/26
10 Tupolev Tu-134A
1 Yakovlev Yak-40

Boeing 747-48E V5-NMA (Josef Krauthäuser collection/Frankfurt)

AIR NAMIBIA

P.O.Box 731, Windhoek 9100, Namibia
Tel. 061-223019, Fax. 061-221910,
www.airnamibia.com.na

Three- / Two- letter code	IATA No.	Reg'n prefix	ICAO callsign
NMB / SW	186	V5	Namibair

Although this airline was set up as early as 1947 it was only after Namibia, the former South West Africa, became independent, that Air Namibia appeared as Nambia's national carrier. After its formation as South West Air Transport, regular flights from Windhoek to Swakopmuk with Douglas DC-3s began in 1948. Oryx Aviation was taken over in 1959 and the name changed to Suidwes Lugdiens. There was a further takeover in the late 1960s - the charter airline Namibair Pty.Ltd. The name of this airline was adopted in 1978 as the airline provided a number of scheduled domestic feeder services to connect with SAA flights at Windhoek. It became the national airline in 1987. On 24th April 1990 Namib Air started regular services to Frankfurt using a Boeing 747SP and in 1993 the name was changed again, to Air Namibia. In this year also, a second Boeing 747SP was acquired from SAA and the network expanded. As well as international services, Air Namibia also provides regional service within southern Africa, for which Boeing 737-200s and Beech 1900s are used, and from mid-1996 new de Havilland DHC-8s, but the latter type proved too expensive to maintain and were dropped from the fleet after only a short time. A replacement was sought for the 747SPs and in 1988 a Boeing 767-300 was leased. This aircraft also was used to introduce a new colour scheme, incorporating the colours of the Namibian national flag. The 767 was however replaced in October 1999 by a Boeing 747-400. Air Namibia co-operates with LAM, LTU and SAA on its international services.

Routes

From Windhoek to Frankfurt, Harare, Johannesburg, Capetown, Keetmanshoop, London, Luanda, Lubango, Lüderitz, Lusaka, Maun, Mokuti Lodge, Mpacha, Ondangwa, Oshakati, Swakopmuk, Victoria Falls and Walvis Bay.

Fleet

3 Beechcraft 1900C
1 Boeing 747-400
2 Boeing 737-200

Boeing 737-400 C2-RN10 (Author's collection)

AIR NAURU

P.O.Box 40 Nauru Intl. Airport, Republic of Nauru
Tel. 444-3168, Fax. 444-3173,
www.airnauru.com.au

Three- / Two- letter code	IATA No.	Reg'n prefix	ICAO callsign
RON / ON	123	C2	Air Nauru

Air Nauru was founded by the government of the Pacific island nation in1970, and inaugurated service on 14th February 1970 with a Dassault Mystère 20 to Brisbane. Further destinations were Honiara and in the following year Majuro in the Marshall Islands and Tarawa on the Gilbert Islands. A Fokker F.28 replaced the Mystère in January 1972 and with this new routes to Japan and Guam were started. Boeing 737s and 727s followed the Fokker F.28 into service in 1976; there followed further expansion until 1984 when there were four Boeing 737s and a Boeing 727 in use. However, the latter was taken out of service in 1985, thus allowing Air Nauru to operate a small homogeneous fleet. Additional routes were opened to Manila, Hong Kong, Auckland, Nadi, Taipei and Truk. Recession and falling passenger numbers led to a reduction in service and a shrinking of the network during the late 1980s. A marketing alliance was concluded with Air New Zealand and Qantas, which allowed the airline to concentrate only on its profitable routes. During 1993 the remaining fleet was exchanged for a single, modern Boeing 737-400, with other aircraft being leased in for short periods to meet demand and overhaul requirements. As well as the scheduled services, charters and freight work are also undertaken.

Routes

Brisbane, Guam, Manila, Melbourne, Nadi, Pohnpei, Suva and Tarawa.

Fleet

1 Boeing 737-400

Boeing 767-204ER ZK-NBJ (Uwe Gleisberg/Sydney)

AIR NEW ZEALAND

Private Bag 92007, Auckland 1020, New Zealand
Tel. 9-3662400, Fax. 9-3662401,
www.airnz.co.nz

Three- / Two- letter code	IATA No.	Reg'n prefix	ICAO callsign
ANZ / NZ	086	ZK	New Zealand

The present-day Air New Zealand goes back to1939, when Tasman Empire Airways Ltd (TEAL) was formed as a joint British (20%), Australian (30%) and New Zealand (50%) company. Short S-30 flying boats were used for regular flights between Australia and Auckland. The flying boats were in use until 1954, and were then replaced by Douglas DC-6 landplanes. In 1961 the New Zealand government assumed full control. TEAL entered the jet era in 1965 with the purchase of three Douglas DC-8s and in that year also the name was changed to Air New Zealand. New routes to the USA were started and the domestic airline NZNAC (formed in 1945) was taken over on 1st April 1978. Larger DC-10s and Boeing 747s were added to the DC-8s, the last of which left the fleet on 1st September 1989. Frankfurt, apart from London the sole European destination, was first served on 31st October 1987. Boeing 747-400s and Boeing 767s were added to the fleet from 1992, though some aircraft have been leased out from time to time. ANZ has developed regional services, operated by fully-owned subsidiaries Mount Cook Airlines, Eagle Aviation and Air Nelson.

During 1996 ANZ acquired 50% of the shares of the Australian airline Ansett, and in the same year the present colour scheme for the aircraft fleet was introduced. After protracted negotiations, ANZ, itself now 25% owned by Singapore Airlines, took over Ansett completely at the end of 1999. Air New Zealand has been a member of the Star Alliance since March 1999.

Routes

Apia, Auckland, Blenheim, Brisbane, Cairns, Christchurch, Dunedin, Frankfurt, Gisborne, Hamilton, Hoktika, Hong Kong, Honolulu, Invercargill, Kaitaia, Kerikeri, London, Los Angeles, Melbourne, Mount Cook, Nadi, Nagoya, Napier-Hastings, Nelson, New Plymouth, Norfolk Island, Noumea, Osaka, Palmerston, Papeete, Perth, Queenstown, Rarotonga, Rotoura, Singapore, Sydney, Taipei, Tauro, Tauranga, TeAnau, Timaru, Tokyo, Tongatapu, Vancouver, Wanganui, Wellington, Westport, Whakatane, Whangerei.

Fleet

7 Boeing 737-200	3 Boeing 767-200ER
11 Boeing 737-300	10 Boeing 767-300ER
9 Boeing 747-400	

NAMC YS-11 JA8668 (Björn Kannengiesser/Nagoya)

AIR NIPPON

3-5-10 Haneda Airport, Otak-ku, Tokyo 144-0041
Japan, Tel. 3-54621911, Fax. 3-54621950,
www.ana.co.jp

Three- / Two- letter code	IATA No.	Reg'n prefix	ICAO callsign
ANK / EL	768	JA	Ank Air

By the direction of the Japanese commerce ministry, the country's three leading airlines, Japan Air Lines, All Nippon Airways and TOA Domestic Airlines, established a regional operator called Nihon Kinkyori Airways Company. The objective of the new airline was to provide a second-level service, connecting the smaller population centres in the north and south of Japan with the business centres in the middle of the country. It was also tasked with connecting smaller and outlying islands with the air transport centres on the main island. De Havilland Twin Otters and NAMC YS-11 turboprops were used and passenger numbers grew quickly, necessitating the lease of Boeing 737-200s. The commercial make-up of the company changed over the years; first the state withdrew, and after several years All Nippon Airways took over the majority of the shares previously shared between the three mainland airlines. The name was changed to Air Nippon and the colour scheme of the aircraft changed to one closely resembling that of ANA. During the 1990s, Boeing 737-500s and Airbus A320s have seen a fleet modernization, which is over time being brought to a state of standarization on the Boeings, though new examples of the new, quiet de Havilland Dash 8Q are being delivered during 2000 for shorter range services. The airline has access to aircraft from its parent company as required and for charter flights.

Routes

Amami O Shima, Aomori, Fukue, Fukuoka, Fukushima, Hachijo Shima, Hakodate, Hiroshima, Iki, Ishigaki, Iwami, Kagoshima, Kochi, Komatsu, Kushiro, Matsuyama, Memanbetsu, Miyake Jima, Miyazaki, Monetsu, Nagasaki, Nagoya, Nakashibetsu, Odate Noshiro, Oita, Okinawa, Okushiri, Osaka, Oshima, Rebun, Rishiri, Saga, Sapporo, Sendai, Taipei, Takamatsu, Tokyo, Toyama, Tsushima, Wakkanai, Yonaga.

Fleet		Ordered
4 Airbus A320	2 De Havilland DHC-6	1 De Havilland DHC-8Q
3 Boeing 737-200	2 De Havilland DHC-8Q	
16 Boeing 737-500	7 NAMC YS-11	

Fokker F.28 Fellowship 1000 P2-ANC (Uwe Gleisberg/Cairns)

AIR NIUGINI

ANG House, Jacksons Airport P.O.B. 7186, 7186 Boroko, Papua-New Guinea. Tel. 259000, Fax. 3273482, www.airnuigini.com.pg

Three- / Two- letter code	IATA No.	Reg'n prefix	ICAO callsign
ANG / PK	656	P2	Niugini

Ansett, Qantas, TAA and the government of Papua New Guinea formed Air Niugini jointly in November 1973. With eight Fokker Friendships and twelve Douglas DC-3s, the new airline took over operations from Ansett and TAA on 1st November 1973, and carried these out in Australian-administered New Guinea until independence, which came about on 16th September 1975. Flights to Sydney and Singapore began in 1975; the international network of flights was extended to Honolulu using Boeing 707s. A leased Airbus A300B4 – a wonderful, exotic colour scheme – replaced the 707 from 1984. Air

Niugini received the first of its own A310s at the beginning of 1989, with a second following late in 1990. DHC-7s were used only on internal routes, with Fokker Fellowships (the first of which arrived in 1977) and the A310s looking after the modest number of international routes.With the introduction of the de Havilland Dash 8 in1997, the older Dash 7s were retired. During 1999 Air Niugini leased an Avro RJ70 as a replacement for one of the older Fokker Fellowships, indicating the beginning of a fleet renewal for regional routes.

Routes

Alotau, Brisbane, Buka, Cairns, Daru, Goroka, Honiara, Hoskins, Kavieng, Kundiawa, Lae, Lihir Island, Madang, Manila, Manus Island, Mount Hagen, Popondetta, Port Moresby, Port Vila, Rabaul, Singapore, Tari, Vanimo, Wapenamanda, Wewak.

Fleet

2 Airbus A310-300
1 Avro RJ70
2 De Havilland DHC-8
7 Fokker F.28

Boeing 737-3M8 F-GKTA (Alireza Azimzadeh/Geneva)

AIR ONE

Via Sardegna 14, 00187 Rome, Italy
Tel. 06-478761, Fax. 06-4885913,
www.flyairone.it

Three- / Two- letter code	IATA No.	Reg'n prefix	ICAO callsign
ADH / AP	867	I	Heron

In Pescara in Italy in 1983 Aliadriatica was established as a flying school and air taxi operation. The majority of the business passed in 1988 to Gruppo Toto, an engineering company. At first the company structure and activities remained unaltered, but with the delivery of a Boeing 737-200 in 1994 Aliadriatica entered the airline charter business. In April of the following year, 1995, a scheduled service licence was granted and services were begun from Rome to Brindisi, Reggio Calabria and Lamezia Terme. When the company was given permission to operate on the attractive route from Rome to Milan in November 1995, it changed not only the colour scheme of the aircraft, but also the airline's name, to Air One. During 1996 Air One took over the flying operations of Fortune Aviation and expanded strongly. An alliance with the Qualiflyer Group of airlines lasted only briefly, and the airline remains independent. An impressive route network has been built up, with over 400 flights daily flown by the fleet which now numbers 12 Boeing 737s; charter business is also being actively undertaken.

Routes

Bari, Bergamo, Brindisi, Crotone, London-Stansted, Milan, Naples, Pescara, Reggio Calabria, Rome, Turin, Venice.

Fleet

3 Boeing 737-200
6 Boeing 737-300
3 Boeing 737-400

Boeing 737-8X2 DQ-FJH (Uwe Gleisberg/Brisbane)

AIR PACIFIC

P.O.Box 9266 Nadi Airport, Fiji
Tel. 720777, Fax. 720512,
www.airpacific.com

Three- / Two- letter code	IATA No.	Reg'n prefix	ICAO callsign
FJI / FJ	260	DQ	Pacific

Fiji's national airline began operations in September 1951 as Fiji Airways, using de Havilland DH 89 Dragon Rapides. With the support of the Australian airline Qantas and in close co-operation with them, the route network was extended. In 1957 Qantas took over Fiji Airways as a subsidiary. In 1959 de Havilland Herons were added to the fleet, before in 1960 Air New Zealand and BOAC each took over a third of the company. The fleet was refreshed in 1967 with HS.748s and Britten-Norman Trislanders.The first jet was introduced in March 1972, a BAC One-Eleven 400. The name of the airline was changed in 1971 to Air Pacific, and by 1972 the governments of Fiji, Kiribati, Tonga, Nauru and some private investors acquired a majority interest. Embraer Bandeirantes were acquired in 1980 for regional services. Increasing passenger demand resulted in the purchase of two ATR 42s in 1988, but these were given up in favour of an all-jet fleet of Boeing 737s, 767s and 747s, Air Pacific having withdrawn from the regional market in1995. During 1998 Qantas took over a further 28.5% of the capital and is now the largest shareholder. In the latter part of 1998, with the introduction of the 'new generation' Boeing 737-700, the airline's colour scheme was also changed. During1999 Air Pacific took delivery of two more 'new generation' 737s, this time -800s and thus has a very modern fleet. Some routes, and a Boeing 737, are operated jointly with Royal Tongan, and other alliances are in place in association with Qantas to American Airlines, Air Vanuatu and Solomon Airlines.

Routes

Apia, Auckland, Brisbane, Christchurch, Honolulu, Los Angeles, Melbourne, Nadi, Suva, Sydney, Tokyo, Tongapatu, Vila, Wellington.

Fleet

1 Boeing 737-700
2 Boeing 737-800
1 Boeing 767-300ER
2 Boeing 747-200

McDonnell Douglas MD-82 B-88899 (Author's collection)

AIR PHILIPPINES

15F Multinational Bancorporation Center, Avala Ave., Makati City 1200, Philippines, www.airphilippines.com

Three- / Two- letter code	IATA No.	Reg'n prefix	ICAO callsign
GAP / 2P	211	RP	Orient Pacific

After the regulation of air transport in the Philippines was liberalised, new airlines were established quickly. In February 1995 , under the leadership of businessman William Gatchalian and with financial participation from the Chinese airline U-Land Airlines and JAS-Japan Air System, Air Philippines was founded. Services were begun with the Boeing 737-200 in February on the Manila-Cebu route. Air Philippines promotes itself as a low-cost/no-frills airline and offers cheap ticket prices, especially compared with the previous airline monopoly situation. Routes within the Philippine islands were quickly built

up and further 737-200s acquired. For operation on less well frequented routes and to smaller airports, several NAMC YS-11s were taken over from JAS. Lacking international services, Air Philippines was not in a position to have foreign currency income when the Philippines was hit by the Asian business crisis, yet the leasing costs on the aircraft had to be paid in hard currency. Thus U-Land came to the rescue with some of their MD-80s and flew some routes on Air Philippines' behalf. By the beginning of 2000 the situation had improved, and tourist traffic was returning to the country. However, a planned

expansion with Boeing 747-400s operating flights to the USA, Japan and Australia has had to be deferred. The airline's base is at Subic Bay.

Routes

Bacolod, Cagayan de Oro, Cebu, Cotabato, Davao, Dumguente, General Santos, Iloilo, Kalibo, Laoag, Legaspi, Manila, Naga, Puerto Princesa, San Jose, Subic Bay, Tacloban, Zamboango.

Fleet

12 Boeing 737-200
 4 NAMC-YS-11
 3 McDonnell Douglas MD-82

Boeing 767-2Q8ER S7-AAS (Author's collection)

AIR SEYCHELLES

P.O.Box 386,Victoria Mahe, Seychelles
Tel. 381000, Fax. 224305,
www.airseychelles.it

Three- / Two- letter code	IATA No.	Reg'n prefix	ICAO callsign
SEY / HM	061	S7	Seychelles

In July 1979 the government of the Seychelles bought the two domestic airlines Air Mahe (formed in 1972) and Inter Island Airways (formed in 1976), in order to create Air Seychelles as the national airline. The routes and aircraft were also taken over. Britten-Norman Islanders and Trislanders were used for services to the individual islands. Tourism was heavily promoted, creating a demand for international services. On 1st November 1983, Air Seychelles began scheduled flights to London and Frankfurt with a weekly DC-10 flight, using an aircraft chartered from British Caledonian Airways. In November 1985 Air Seychelles took delivery of an Airbus A300B4 from Air France and put it to use on services to Amsterdam, Rome and Frankfurt. In 1989 a Boeing 707 temporarily replaced the Airbus, until the arrival of the first Boeing 767-200. A Boeing 757-200 was added in 1993, but the need for extra capacity resulted in its exchange for a larger Boeing 767-300 at the end of 1996. From the main island radiates a dense network of domestic services, flown principally by the Twin Otters. Further careful expansion is planned by Air Seychelles, with the delivery of a second Boeing 767-300 envisaged during the Spring of 2001.

Routes

Dubai, Frankfurt, Johannesburg, London, Mahe Island, Milan, Mauritius, Nairobi, Paris, Praslin Island, Rome, Singapore, Zürich.

Fleet

1 Boeing 767-200ER
1 Boeing 767-300ER
1 Britten-Norman Islander
4 De Havilland DHC-6 Twin Otter

Boeing 737-200 SU-GAN (Frank Fielitz/Frankfurt)

AIR SINAI

12 Kasr el Nil Street,
Cairo, Egypt
Tel. 2-760498, Fax. 2-574711

Three- / Two- letter code	IATA No.	Reg'n prefix	ICAO callsign
ASD / 4D	903	SU	Air Sinai

This company was set up in 1982 by Egyptair, in order to take over the scheduled service network of the former Nefertiti Airlines, which had served several smaller Egyptian cities and towns and operated a schedule to Tel Aviv. For political reasons, Egyptair as the national airline, was not able to operate this route itself. There had been hostilities between Egypt and Israel, and the withdrawal of Israeli troops from the occupied Sinai peninsula. Services were operated to Eilat, Sharm el Sheik, Hurgada, Santa Katharina, and especially to locations of interest to tourists. Fokker F.27s and Boeing 737s were used, with the fleet becoming all-jet with the delivery of a Boeing 737-500 in 1999. In addition to scheduled services, all operated on behalf of Egyptair, Air Sinai also operates charters to Europe and pilgrim flights to Jeddah.

Routes

Al Arish, Hurgada, Cairo, Mesa Matruh, Ras An Nayb, Sharm el Sheik, Tel Aviv.

Fleet

1 Boeing 737-500

ATR 42 F-ODUC (Frank Litaudon/Pago Pago)

AIR TAHITI

BP 314 Boulevard Pomare,
Papeete Tahiti
Tel. 864011, Fax. 864069

Three- / Two- letter code	IATA No.	Reg'n prefix	ICAO callsign
VTA / VT	135	F	Air Tahiti

Air Tahiti, which is partly in private ownership, was formed in 1953 to improve communications between the individual islands which make up the French overseas province. At that time it was called RAI -Reseau Aérien Interinsulaire. On 1st January 1970 the name was changed to Air Polynésie, after the French airline TAI (later to become UTA) had taken overt 62% of the shareholding. For many years the aircraft fleet consisted of Fokker Friendships and Britten-Norman Islanders, as well as Twin Otters. In January 1987, after UTA disposed of its interest in the company, the name was again changed to Air Tahiti. To demonstrate its new-found independence, with the introduction of the ATR 42 during that year, a new colour scheme was adopted. During 1992 and 1993 the larger ATR 72 was also brought into the fleet, and during the later part of the 1990s the older examples of the ATR 42 were replaced by new, more powerful ATR 42-500 models. A close association has been cultivated with Air France, which has a small shareholding in Air Tahiti. Air Tahiti itself has shareholdings in Air Archipels, Air Moorea and in Air Tahiti Nui, which operates an Airbus A340 on long range services.

Routes

Ahe, Anaa, Bora Bora, Fakarava, Gambier, Hao, Hiva Oa, Huahine, Kaukura, Makemo, Mangareva, Manihi, Maupiti, Moorea, Nuku Hiva, Papeete, Raiatea, Rangioroa, Rurutu, Takapoto, Takaroa, Tikehau and Tubuai.

Fleet

4 ATR 42 -300/500
6 ATR 72
2 Dornier 228-200

Boeing 737-2R8C 5H-MRK (Jörg D. Zmich/Johannesburg)

AIR TANZANIA

P.O.Box 543 Dar-es-Salaam, Tanzania
Tel. 051-38300, Fax. 051-46545

Three- / Two- letter code	IATA No.	Reg'n prefix	ICAO callsign
ATC / TC	197	5H	Tanzania

In January 1977, after the break-up of East African Airlines, which had been a joint venture between Kenya, Uganda and Tanzania, there were practically no air services remaining in Tanzania. Thus in March 1977 Air Tanzania was formed by the government and with Fokker F.27s and a Boeing 737 services were begun from Dar-es-Salaam. During 1978 and 1979 a further Boeing 737 and, for regional services, several de Havilland Twin Otters were acquired. The departure points for international flights are Dar-es-Salaam and Kilimanjaro International Airport. A Boeing 767 was used for a short while during 1994/95, but this could not be fully utilised. In 1995 the Twin Otter was also withdrawn from the fleet and the regional network reduced on financial grounds. The procurement of more modern aircraft was also put back, but a Boeing 737-300 was leased in 1999 as a replacement for one of the -200 models. The airline became a participant in the multi-national Air Alliance in 1995; this initially operated a Boeing 747SP on international services. Additionally there is co-operation with Air Malawi, with some routes being flown on a codeshare basis.

Routes

Aden, Dar-es-Salaam, Dubai, Entebbe, Harare, Jeddah, Johannesburg, Kigali, Kigoma, Kilimanjaro, Lilongwe, Lindi, Lusaka, Mombasa, Mtwara, Muscat, Musoma, Mwanza, Nairobi, Zanzibar, Tabora.

Fleet

2 Boeing 737-200
1 Boeing 737-300
2 Fokker F.27-600

Fokker F.27 Friendship 600 TT-AAK (Author's collection)

AIR TCHAD

27 Avenue Charles de Gaulle, BP 168,
N'Djamena, Chad
Tel. 235-515090

Three- / Two- letter code	IATA No.	Reg'n prefix	ICAO callsign
HTT / HT	95	TT	Hotel Tango

Formed on 24th June 1966 by the Chad government (64% shareholding) and UTA as Compagnie Nationale Tchadienne, the new national airline began regional service with the indestructible Douglas DC-3 from Fort Lamy (nowadays called N'Djamena). A Douglas DC-4 was used to fly via Algiers to Paris, thus creating a quick connection to the former French colony. The state of civil war which existed more or less from 1975 in Chad hindered development of the route system, which could only really begin to be built up slowly following a 1982 peace accord between the conflicting factions. In spite of that a Fokker F.27 was bought in 1983, and a further example was received by way of a gift from neighbouring Libya, but was not registered in Chad. As a replacement for the elderly DC-3, a de Havilland DHC-6 Twin Otter came into service. As a result of its takeover of UTA, Air France became a shareholder in Air Tchad and there is co-operation between the two airlines. Today Air France has only a 2% holding, the balance being with the Chad government. Alongside the very modest scheduled services, Air Tchad uses its sole F.27 for charter and relief work.

Routes

Abecher, Bol, Bongor, Mao, Mongo, Moundou, N'Djamena, Pala and Sarh.

Fleet

1 Fokker F.27

Boeing 767-31K ER G-SJMC (Josef Krauthäuser/Las Vegas)

AIRTOURS INTERNATIONAL

Parkway Three, 300 Princess Road, Manchester, M14 7QU, Great Britain, Tel. 161-2326600, Fax. 161-2326610, www.airtours.com

Three- / Two- letter code	IATA No.	Reg'n prefix	ICAO callsign
AIH / VZ	727	G	Kestrel

One of the major British tour operators, Airtours, set up its own in-house airline in Manchester in 1990. It began operations in March 1991 with three MD-83s. The young company expanded quickly and acquired three further MD-83s in late 1991. During the Summer of 1993, Airtours' parent company took over its competitor Aspro Holidays, along with their airline Inter European Airways (formed in 1987) and its fleet consisting of Boeing 737s and 757s. For the 1994 season, the fleet was augmented with Airbus A320s and in addition two Boeing 767-300s were added for long-range services to holiday destinations in the USA and Thailand. The arrival of the 767s also saw the introduction of a new colour scheme. The MD-83s were dropped from the fleet for the 1996 summer season and replaced with further A320s. During this year also, Airtours acquired the Danish travel concern Spies Holding, along with its airline Premiair, and in 1997 the Belgian tour operator Sun International, with its airline Air Belgium, was also added to the group. Having held a partial shareholding, Airtours is since mid-2000 the 100% owner of the German tour operator Frosch Touristik Gruppe, which set up its own airline Fly FTI in 1998, and for whom A320s from the Airtours fleet were flying during 1999 (see page 197). There is significant interchange of aircraft between the airlines in the group, and to facilitate this, the Premiair colour scheme is a clone of the Airtours livery; the Premiair DC-10s are in process of transfer to Airtours for the Winter 2000/2001 season. Four Airbus A330s for use on long range routes were added to the growing fleet during 1999.

Routes

Charter flights from Manchester, Birmingham, Cardiff, London-Gatwick, Glasgow, Liverpool, Newcastle and other cities to popular destinations around the Mediterranean, in the Caribbean, USA, Thailand, Africa, South America and Australia. Winter charter destinations include Geneva, Salzburg and Munich.

Fleet

11 Airbus A320
2 Airbus A321
4 Airbus A330
7 Boeing 757-200

3 Boeing 767-300 ER
1 Douglas DC-10-30

Douglas DC-9-32 N848AT (Dennis Wehrmann/Tampa)

AIR TRAN AIRWAYS

9955 Air Tran Blvd. Orlando, Florida 32827, USA
Tel. 407-2515600, Fax. 407-2515567,
www.airtran.com

Three- / Two- letter code	IATA No.	Reg'n prefix	ICAO callsign
TRS / FL	332	N	Citrus

Air Tran Airways came into being in September 1997 by the merger of Valujet and Airtran. At first the new company was called Air Tran Airlines, but was then retitled. Valujet was set up in 1993 and expanded rapidly in the east and southeast of the USA. Some 20 destinations were served from Atlanta with a fleet of Douglas DC-9s, and Valujet was the launch operator for the then new McDonnell Douglas MD-95 (later to become the Boeing 717). The company's fortunes were badly damaged by a notorious crash in May 1996, after which the airline was grounded by the FAA. Though it emerged later

that the company was not to blame for the accident, the image had been tainted and passengers were choosing to fly with other airlines. The re-started, though limited, services were again suspended voluntarily in June 1996, in order to allow stringent investigation by the FAA. A further re-start was made in November 1996 under new management and with a small fleet of DC-9s. Air Tran Airways was likewise set up in 1993, initially under the name Conquest Sun Airlines. Its base was in Orlando and it served several routes in Florida and the neighbouring states using Boeing 737-200s, changing name to

Air Tran Airways in August 1994. Naturally, on the merger, it was decided to adopt the Air Tran name, and a new colour scheme was adopted with a prominent 'a' on the tailfin. Deliveries of the Boeing 717 began in the second half of 1999, marking the beginning of renewal of the whole fleet, and the retirement of the Boeing 737-200s.

Routes

From its hub at Atlanta to Akron, Bloomington, Boston, Buffalo, Chicago, Dallas/Forth Worth, Dayton, Flint, Fort Lauderdale, Fort Myers, Greensboro/High Point, Hartford, Houston, Jacksonville, Knoxville, Memphis, Miami, Moline, New Orleans, New York, Newport News, Orlando, Philadelphia, Raleigh/Durham, Richmond, Savannah, Tampa, Valparaiso and Washington.

Fleet	Ordered
34 Douglas DC-9-32 16 Boeing 717	34 Boeing 717

Airbus A330-243 C-GGTS (Hans-Willi Mertens/Fort Lauderdale)

AIR TRANSAT

11600 Cargo Road A 1, Montreal Intl. Airport, Mirabel Quebec J7N 1G9, Canada, Tel. 450-476-1011, Fax. 450-4761038, www.airtransat.com

Three- / Two- letter code	IATA No.	Reg'n prefix	ICAO callsign
TSC / TS	649	C	Transat

Set up in December 1986, Air Transat has become Canada's largest charter airline since Nationair ceased flying in 1992. Operations began in early 1987 with Boeing 727-200s. Its base is at Montreal (where the airline has its own maintenance facility), but Air Transat also serves Toronto, Quebec City, Halifax and Vancouver. The airline obtained its first Lockheed L-1011 TriStar in late 1987 for services to the Caribbean. During the summer seasons, Air Transat flies regularly to Europe, and during 1996 the airline took on further TriStars from Air Canada and Cathay Pacific. Boeing 757s have also been steadily added to the fleet since 1992, and the Boeing 727s phased out. New charter routes have also been established, including to Poland and Portugal. The pattern of destinations varies seasonally, with Europe being strong in the Summer, whilst in Winter the Caribbean and South America predominate. During 1999 Air Transat added three Airbus A330s, and this type is expected to replace the ageing TriStars in the medium term. Also during 1999 the colour scheme of the aircraft has been changed; there is now a star on the tailfin, instead of the former 'at' logo. There are scheduled services between Montreal and Paris, and Air Transat is a leading player with flights from Canada to Cuba, a favourite destination for Canadians.

Routes

Caribbean islands such as Cuba and the Dominican Republic, Mexico, USA, Amsterdam, Birmingham, Belfast, Dublin, Glasgow, Frankfurt, London, Manchester, Newcastle, Paris, Rome, Shannon and other charter destinations.

Fleet

3 Airbus A330-200
2 Boeing 737-400
5 Boeing 757-200

14 Lockheed L-1011 TriStar

Douglas DC-8-62F N41CX (Frank Fielitz/Frankfurt)

AIR TRANSPORT INTERNATIONAL

3800 Rodney Parham Road,
Little Rock, ARK.72212, USA
Tel. 501-6153500, Fax. 501-6032093

Three- / Two- letter code	IATA No.	Reg'n prefix	ICAO callsign
ATN / 8C	346	N	Air Transport

This cargo airline was founded in 1978 as US Airways, but changed its name after a few months to Interstate Airlines. Using Lockheed Electras and Boeing 727s it flew as an independent operator from Detroit's Willow Run airport. Numerous routes were flown, especially for the automobile industry, but also for the emerging overnight express parcels concerns. At the beginning of the 1980s the company gained a lucrative contract from UPS and was thus in a position to expand the fleet with Douglas DC-8s. The company headquarters and operating base were moved to Little Rock in Arkansas, though the aircraft were based in various places. There was another change in 1988, when the current name was adopted. With the delivery of more DC-8s, the Electras were removed from the fleet, and fresh opportunities arose. Thus several DC-8s were flown exclusively for Burlington Express, who did not have their own airline operation. Additionally, many overseas charters were flown for the US military, especially to the Gulf region. On 1st October 1994 ATI took over ICX International Cargo Express and integrated their two Douglas DC-8s into their own fleet. There were thus about twenty DC-8-63s and DC-8-71s at the airline's disposal when in 1998 ATI was sold to BAX-Global. Today ATI continues to operate charter and ad hoc flights in its own colours, but the majority of the fleet is in use on behalf of BAX-Global.

Routes

Scheduled freight services on behalf of BAX-Global to about 50 US destinations. Charter and ad hoc freight flights worldwide.

Fleet

16 McDonnell Douglas DC-8-61/63F
10 McDonnell Douglas DC-8-71

Boeing 767-39H ER G-OOAO (Hans-Willi Mertens/Sanford)

AIR 2000

Jetset House, Church Road, Lowfield Heath, Crawley, RH11 0PQ, Great Britain. Tel. 1293-518966, Fax. 1293-524642, www.air2000.com

Three- / Two- letter code	IATA No.	Reg'n prefix	ICAO callsign
AMM / DP	091	G	Jetset

The airline was formed in 1986 by the tour operator Owners Abroad, one of the leading British tour companies, for the purpose of operating intensive charter services outside London. The densely populated region in the north seemed to be perfect and Manchester was selected as the base. Commercial operations commenced with two leased Boeing 757s on 11th April 1987. During 1988, two further Boeing 757s were added, one of which was based in Glasgow. Restrictions imposed by Canadian law prevented the intended formation of a Canadian subsidiary (see Canada 3000). The first flights to Mombasa were carried out in the winter season 1988/89, and after the 757s were equipped to ETOPS standard there were also transatlantic flights to Newark, Boston and Orlando. In October 1990 Air 2000 was granted a scheduled air service licence for flights from the United KIngdom to Cyprus and services were finally launched in late 1993 from Gatwick to Larnaca and Paphos. Following regular additions of Boeing 757s to the fleet, the first two Airbus A320s arrived in April 1992. In 1995, Newcastle and Belfast were added to the operating bases and from 1996 flights were offered from Dublin. In addition to intensive charter flights, Air 2000 is also involved in the wet-leasing business and leases its aircraft, primarily in the quiet Winter periods, to Canada 3000 and other airlines. Air 2000 today belongs to the major tour operator First Choice Holidays, which in 1998 took over rival Unijet along with its airline Leisure International. During 1999 the Leisure fleet of Airbus A320/A321s and Boeing 767s was integrated. From Spring 2000 the Airbus A330 has also been added to the fleet.

Routes

Schedules from Birmingham, Glasgow, London-Gatwick, Manchester to Larnaca and Paphos. Charters from ten British regional airports to the Mediterranean, northern Africa, Canada, Caribbean, Mexico, Kenya, Sri Lanka and Thailand. In Winter charter flights to the Alpine ski centres.

Fleet

5 Airbus A320-200
3 Airbus A321
2 Airbus A330
14 Boeing 757-200

4 Boeing 767-300ER

Boeing 737-3Q8 YJ-AV18 (Christofer Witt collection)

AIR VANUATU

P.O.Box 148,
Port Vila, Vanuatu Tel. 23838, Fax. 23250
www.vanuatutourism.com

Three- / Two- letter code	IATA No.	Reg'n prefix	ICAO callsign
AVN / NF	218	YJ	Air Van

Following independence in 1980, Air Vanuatu was set up as the national airline of this Pacific republic by Ansett Transport Industries and the local government in 1981, using the former New Hebrides Airways as a basis. Ansett held 40% of the shares. Using a leased Boeing 737-200, flights were begun in September 1981 from Vila to Australia, whence about 70% of the passengers come. In November 1987 the government acquired the balance of the shares from Ansett. The airline entered a close co-operation with Australian Airlines, receiving aircraft and maintenance support. In 1989 Auckland and Adelaide were added to the route network. When Australian Airlines was absorbed into Qantas, it was decided to try to become self-sufficient,even though the sole Boeing 737 was provided by Qantas.There is close co-operation with local operator Vanair, with joint connecting flights. Thus in July 1995 an Embraer Bandeirante was acquired for regional services, though this was sold in 1998 in favour of a larger Saab 2000. Air Vanuatu also works with other airlines in the region including Air Caledonie, Air Pacific, Qantas and Solomon Airlines. The base is at the Bauerfield airport, near Port Vila.

Routes

Aneityum, Aniwa, Auckland, Brisbane, Craig Crove, Dillons Bay, Emae, Espiritu Santo, Futuna, Gaua, Honiara, Ipota, Lamap, Lamen Bay, Longana, Lonorore, Maewo, Melbourne, Mota Lava, Nadi, Norsup, Noumea, Olpoi, Paama, Port Vila, Redcliffe, Sara, Sola, South West Bay, Sydney, Tanna, Togoa, Torres, Ulei, Valesdir, Walaha.

Fleet

1 Boeing 737-300
1 Saab 2000

Boeing 737-2N0 Z-WPC (Jörg D. Zmich/Johannesburg)

AIR ZIMBABWE

P.O.Box AP 1, Harare Airport, Harare, Zimbabwe
Tel. 4-575111, Fax. 4-796039,
www.home.earthlink.net/~airzimbabwe/

Three- / Two- letter code	IATA No.	Reg'n prefix	ICAO callsign
AZW / UM	168	Z	Zimbabwe

Air Zimbabwe was established on 1st September 1967 as a statutory body controlled by a board responsible to the Ministry of Transport as Air Rhodesia following the dissolution of the Central African Airways Corporation. CAA had served the three territories of Southern Rhodesia, Nyasaland and Northern Rhodesia for some 21 years. Due to the political situation, it was only possible to fly domestic routes and to neighbouring South Africa, until the present government took power and the airline was renamed Air Zimbabwe Rhodesia in 1978. Douglas DC-3s, Vickers Viscounts and Boeing 707/720s were used. It was only from 1980 that the present Air Zimbabwe was able to develop into an airline with flights to neighbouring countries and to Europe. In 1983 it took over the cargo airline Affretair. Boeing 737-200s were acquired in the second half of the 1980s, and these remain with the airline today. The first Boeing 767s were delivered in 1989 and 1990 and in 1995 two Fokker 50s were acquired for shorter-range routes, but the latter were disposed of after only a couple of years. Also sold off were the older Boeing 707s and the BAe/HS-748, as well as Affretair in order to meet mounting losses. Since 1998 Air Zimbabwe has operated only jets, though by mid-2000 falling passenger demand, rising fuel prices and political unrest forced the storage of a Boeing 737-200 and the BAe 146, and the cancellation of plans to use a Boeing 777 or Airbus 340 which was to have been leased from a Chinese operator for long-range services. There are alliances with Air Botswana, Air Malawi, LAM and Qantas, and the airline's home base is at Harare-International.

Routes

Bulawayo, Capetown, Dar-es-Saalam, Durban, Frankfurt, Harare, Hwange National Park, Johannesburg, Kariba, Larnaca, Lilongwe, London, Luanda, Lusaka, Mauritius, Nairobi, Paris, Victoria Falls.

Fleet

1 BAe 146-200
3 Boeing 737-200
2 Boeing 767-200ER

Boeing 737-4Q8 N762AS (Josef Krauthäuser/Los Angeles-LAX)

ALASKA AIRLINES

P.O.Box 68947, Seattle Washington 98168, USA
Tel.206-433-3200, Fax. 206-433-3379,
www.alaskaair.com

Three- / Two- letter code	IATA No.	Reg'n prefix	ICAO callsign
ASA / AS	027	N	Alaska

Alaska Airlines traces its history back to the formation of McGhee Airways in 1932, which merged with Star Air Service in 1934. This airline then became Alaska Star Airlines in 1943, after the airlines Pollack Flying Service, Mirow Air and Laverny Airways were all taken over. With these purchases, the airline had over 75% of Alaska's air traffic under its control. In 1944 the present name was adopted. In addition to scheduled services, Alaska Airlines was particularly active in the charter business. Alaska's aircraft participated in the Berlin Airlift, and later, in support of the Korean War. The first route from Alaska to Seattle

was inaugurated in 1951. In 1960 Convair 340s and DC-6s were acquired to replace the DC-3s previously used. On 1st February 1968 Alaska Airlines bought Cordova Airlines and on 1st April of that year, Alaska Coastal Airlines. In an allusion to the opening of the large oilfields, the airline's first jet aircraft were also dubbed 'Golden Nugget Jets'. In 1970 charter flights from Fairbanks to Khabarovsk in the USSR were flown for the first time. During the early 1980s the colour scheme was altered; on the tailfin, a smiling Eskimo appeared. Alaska became the first customer to order the new extended-range MD-83,

ordering nine aircraft in 1983. There were further purchases of airlines in 1986: Jet America and Horizon Air, the latter becoming a feeder operator for Alaska. The network was extended to California and Mexico and western Canada served from Seattle. In 1992 direct services to neighbouring Siberia were initiated. In 1996 Alaska made headlines by ordering Boeing 737-400s instead of the MD-90s which had been on option. The latest generation of 737s are now being delivered, with the first -700 arriving in May 1999, and orders in place for the larger 737-900, the first of which should join the fleet in April 2001.

Routes

Anchorage, Aniak, Astoria, Bellingham, Bethel, Billings, Boise, Burbank, Butte, Calgary, Cold Bay, Cordova, Dutch Harbor, Edmonton, Fairbanks, Fresno, Glacier Bay, Helena, Juneau, Ketchikan, Kodiak, Kotzebue, La Paz, Las Vegas, Los Angeles, Los Cabos, Mazatlan, Nome, Oakland, Ontario, Orange County, Palm Springs, Phoenix, Portland, Prudhoe Bay, Puerto Vallarta, Reno, San Diego, San Francisco, San Jose, Seattle, Sitka, Spokane, Valdez, Vancouver and Yakutat are amongst the points served by Alaska Airlines.

Fleet		Ordered
8 Boeing 737-200	12 Boeing 737-700	7 Boeing 737-700
37 Boeing 737-400	36 McDonnell Douglas MD-83	10 Boeing 737-900

McDonnell Douglas MD-11 I-DUPU (Alireza Azimzadeh/Geneva)

ALITALIA

Viale Alessandro Marchetti 111,
00148 Rome, Italy
Tel. 65622020, Fax. 65624733, www.alitalia.it

Three- / Two- letter code	IATA No.	Reg'n prefix	ICAO callsign
AZA / AZ	055	I	Alitalia

Alitalia (Aerolinee Italiane International) was founded on 16th September 1946. The Italian government, BEA and several Italian companies formed the company. Operations began on 5th May 1947 using Fiat 612s, SIAI Marchetti SM 95s and Avro Lancastrians, with the first international flight, to Buenos Aires, taking place in 1948. In 1950 Douglas DC-4s were acquired, and in 1953 Convair 340/440s and DC-6s. The first jet was a DC-8 in 1960. Alitalia's further development was preceded by its merger with LAI in 1957; Alitalia became the national airline in November 1957. Vickers Viscounts and Caravelles were

acquired for short and medium haul, the latter being replaced from August 1967 by DC-9s. The first Boeing 747 was delivered on 13th May 1970, and the DC-10 in February 1973. During the late 1970s Alitalia's aircraft orders caused something of a furore with the manufacturers, as Airbus A300s and DC-10s were ordered in addition to Boeing 727s and 747s; some orders had to be cancelled however. Since then, the trend has been one of fleet standardisation for cost reasons, this policy also being carried through to subsidiary company Avianova. For its intercontinental flights, Alitalia

acquired MD-11s from 1992 onwards, and older DC-9s were replaced by the Airbus A321, the first of which was delivered in March 1994. Another newcomer during 1995 was the Boeing 767. Following the integration of subsidiary company ATI in 1994, Alitalia is one of Europe's largest airlines. Part of the fleet is operated by 'Alitalia Team' with different cost structures as a cost-saving measure. Alitalia Express, a 100%-owned subsidiary, is responsible for regional services. It was planned for Alitalia to merge with the Dutch airline KLM, but this was all broken off abruptly in June 2000.

Routes

Alitalia has a dense network of services to over 120 destinations on all continents; in Europe alone over 40 airports are served.

Fleet

6 Airbus A300B4	6 Boeing 767-300	
7 Airbus A320	90 McDonnell Douglas MD-82	
23 Airbus A321-100	8 McDonnell Douglas MD-11	
10 Boeing 747-200		

Ordered

15 Boeing 747-400
3 Airbus A320

Boeing 767-381 JA8358 (Uwe Gleisberg/Sydney)

ALL NIPPON AIRWAYS

3-2-5, Kasumigaseki Chiyoda-ku Tokyo 100, Japan, Tel. 3-35923035, Fax. 3-35923119, www.ana.co.jp

Three- / Two- letter code	IATA No.	Reg'n prefix	ICAO callsign
ANA / NH	205	J	All Nippon

All Nippon Airways is Japan's largest airline on the basis of number of passengers carried. Formed in December 1952 as Japan Helicopter and Aeroplane Transport Company, scheduled services began in 1953. It merged in 1958 with Far East Airlines to form All Nippon Airways. The most important route at that time was Tokyo-Osaka. The network of routes was continuously expanded using Convair 340s and 440s. In July 1961 two new aircraft types were introduced at the same time, the Fokker F.27 and the Vickers Viscount 828. By taking over three regional airlines, Fujita in 1963, Central Japan in 1965 and

Nagasaki Airlines in 1967, All Nippon grew rapidly. Jet service with Boeing 727s was offered for the first time between Tokyo and Sapporo in 1964. In December 1973 the Lockheed TriStar became the first widebody with the airline. The Boeing 747SR gave ANA - as it also did with other Japanese companies - a jumbo jet with particularly closely-spaced seating, making it possible to carry around 500 passengers on short routes. Continuing fleet renewal brought in the Boeing 767 from mid-1984, the Airbus A320 from 1990 as well as the Boeing 747-400. Overseas routes were opened up relatively late by ANA, from March 1986, the

first destination being Guam. Services to the USA and Australia soon followed with Beijing added in 1987, Seoul in 1988 and London from 1989. Fukuoka, Osaka and Tokyo are ANA's main hubs. There has been impressive re-equipment in progress since 1997, bringing in new Boeing 777s and Airbus A321s, and newer model 747s to replace the old. Since 1998 ANA has been aligned with the Star Alliance, with formal membership from October 2000. It also regularly catches the attention with brightly painted special colour schemes.

Routes

ANA flies over 140 domestic and international routes including to Bangkok, Beijing, Brisbane, Delhi, Denpasar, Frankfurt, Guam, Hong Kong, Honolulu, Kuala Lumpur, London, Los Angeles, Moscow, Mumbai, New York, Paris, Rome, San Francisco, Seoul, Shanghai, Singapore, Sydney, Vienna, Washington, Xiamen and Yangon.

Fleet

		Ordered
25 Airbus A320	17 Boeing 747-200/SR	8 Airbus A321
7 Airbus A321	22 Boeing 747-400	5 Airbus A340
19 Boeing 767-200	25 Boeing 777-200	11 Boeing 777
43 Boeing 767-300		

Boeing 737-2X6C N817AL (Thomas Kim/Honolulu)

ALOHA AIRLINES

P.O.Box 30028 Honolulu 96820, USA
Tel. 808-8364113, Fax. 808-8360303,
www.alohaair.com

Three- / Two- letter code	IATA No.	Reg'n prefix	ICAO callsign
AAH / AQ	327	N	Aloha

Aloha Airlines was set up as Trans Pacific Airlines Ltd on 9th June 1946 and non-scheduled operations began in July of that year. In the first three years of the airline's existence it operated passenger and cargo charters in the Hawaiian islands. In common with many airlines starting out at this time, its first aircraft type was the Douglas DC-3. The first scheduled flight was on 6th June 1949. The company changed its name to Aloha Airlines in November 1958. Fairchild F.27s replaced the DC-3s from June 1959 and in 1963 the larger Vickers Viscounts followed. Altogether Aloha acquired three Viscounts and six F.27s. Its

first jet aircraft was also a British product; on 29th April 1966 Aloha started scheduled flights from Honolulu to Maui with BAC One-Elevens. A step towards standardising the fleet was taken with the purchase of the first Boeing 737s in 1969. Due to the very short flight times between the islands, the 737s have very high utilisation figures. In 1980 Aloha Island Air was created as a subsidiary company operating DHC- 6 Twin Otters. With the delivery of the first of the Boeing 737-400s in early 1993 came a change of colour scheme; since then, the Boeing 737 has been the only type in the fleet. During 1999

Aloha opened a route to the Marshall Islands. Other destinations in the Pacific include Kwajalein and Johnston Island. As a replacement for the older 737-200s, Aloha took delivery at the end of 1999 their first 737-700, and this was used on 28th February 2000 to inaugurate a route to Oakland, California, the airline's first service to mainland America.

Routes

Hana, Hilo, Honolulu, Hoolehua, Johnston Island, Kahului, Kapalua, Kauai, Kona, Kwajalein, Lanai City, Majuro, with frequent daily internal Hawiian services.

Fleet

15 Boeing 737-200
 2 Boeing 737-700

Boeing 727-223 N866AA (Dennis Wehrmann/Tampa)

AMERICAN AIRLINES

P.O.Box 619616 DFW Intl.Airport Dallas, Texas 75261-9616, USA, Tel. 817-9671234, Fax. 817-9674318, www.aa.com

Three- / Two- letter code	IATA No.	Reg'n prefix	ICAO callsign
AAL / AA	001	N	American

American Airlines came into being on 13th May 1934. Before the DC-3, created to the specifications of American, came into use, Curtiss Condors were mainly used. In 1945 AOA, an airline specialising in flights to Europe, was taken over, but sold on to PanAm in 1950 and American concentrated solely on the American market. The airline was one of America's aircraft manufacturers' most important partners in the period that followed: the DC-7, Convair 240 and 990, Lockheed L-188 Electra and DC-10 all emerged from specifications and orders placed by American. The DC-7 was used from November 1953 to start the transcontinental non-stop service from New York to Los Angeles. Six years later, American's first jet, the Boeing 707 took over. BAC One-Eleven 400s and Boeing 727 also featured in the extensive fleet. In 1970 the widebody era began with the Boeing 747, followed by the DC-10 from August 1971. Also in 1971 American took over Trans Caribbean Airways and its extensive network in this region. After deregulation in1978 American grew even larger, taking over AirCal in1987. Numerous routes were acquired from other companies, paving the way for extensive expansion of routes to the Far East, South America and Europe. During 1984 regional services were consolidated under the 'American Eagle' banner (see page 95). An extensive fleet renewal plan has seen the introduction of the Boeing 777 and 737-800 from 1999. In the west of the USA, Reno Air was bought in 1998 and its fleet and routes integrated during 1999. The 1997 plan for a merger with British Airways, so long delayed by political wranglings, now looks unlikely to come to fruition, but close co-operation is maintained and both airlines are leading members of the powerful Oneworld Alliance.

Routes

Over 160 destinations worldwide and in the USA, with major hubs at Dallas/Fort Worth, Chicago, and Miami.

Fleet

35 Airbus A300-600
66 Boeing 727-200
42 Boeing 737-800
102 Boeing 757-200
80 Boeing 767-200/300
29 Boeing 777
75 Fokker 100
5 McDonnell Douglas DC-10-30
9 McDonnell Douglas MD-11
274 McDonnell Douglas MD-80

Ordered

64 Boeing 737-800
7 Boeing 777

ATR 72-212 N410AT (Hans-Willi Mertens/Tampa)

AMERICAN EAGLE

4333 Amon Carter Blvd. MD 5494, Forth Worth, Texas 76155, USA, Tel. 972-4251520, Fax. 972-4251518, www.aa.com

Three- / Two- letter code	IATA No.	Reg'n prefix	ICAO callsign
EGF / AA	-	N	Eagle Flight

On behalf of American Airlines, a franchise system, American Eagle, was set up on 1st November 1984, with the previously independent Metroflight. Smaller airports were to be brought into the hub and spoke system, starting with a hub at Dallas/Fort Worth. 19-seat Swearingen Metros formed the initial fleet. As early as 1st December that year, Chapperal Airlines was brought into the franchise system. Flights operated under American's 'AA' flight numbers and the aircraft were painted in a unified colour scheme, closely resembling that of American. During 1985 AV Air in Raleigh-Durham and Simmons Airlines in Chicago also joined in, and a year later Air Midwest in Nashville and Command Air in New York. At other hubs such as San Jose or San Juan , Wings West or Executive Air carried out these feeder flights. However, the system had its weaknesses, and Air Midwest went into bankruptcy, but was bought out by American's holding company, the AMR Corporation. Likewise, it was necessary to acquire AVAir and Simmons in order not to endanger the whole system. A new hub was set up at Miami by Flagship Airlines with ATR 42s. Wings West and Command Airways were also integrated, to save them from financial disaster. During the mid-1990s American Eagle suffered heavy losses, brought about by the purchase of larger aircraft and poor business conditions. Rationalisation of the fleet was called for and it was concentrated on the Saab 340 and ATR 42/72. The previously independent companies were all brought into AMR ownership with the purchase of Business Express in 1998, making American Eagle Airlines the world's largest regional carrier with over 12 million passengers. In 1999 the first jet was delivered, an Embraer RJ-145, and there are large orders in place for jets to replace the propeller types.

Routes

Over 150 destinations throughout the USA, and in Canada, the Caribbean and the Bahamas are served

Fleet	Ordered
31 ATR 42	25 Canadair RJ 700
43 ATR 72	56 Embraer RJ-135
24 Embraer RJ-135	
50 Embraer RJ-145	
105 Saab SF 340	

Airbus A319-132 N806AW (Dennis Wehrmann/Hamburg-Finkenwerder)

AMERICA WEST AIRLINES

4000 East Sky Harbor Blvd. Phoenix,
Arizona 85034, USA, Tel. 602-6930800,
Fax. 602-6935546, www.americawest.com

Three- / Two- letter code	IATA No.	Reg'n prefix	ICAO callsign
AWE / HP	401	N	Cactus

America West Airlines is one of the younger and more dynamic of the major American airlines, having only been formed after the 1978 deregulation. Formed in February 1981, America West started flights from its Phoenix base on 1st August 1983. In addition to the Phoenix hub, there is another major hub at Las Vegas and a smaller one at Columbus, Ohio. Within only six years, the fleet grew from the initial three Boeing 737s to over 90 aircraft; with the new routes and destinations the number of employees also rose. They all have a stake in America West Airlines in the form of shares. Initially, as the

name suggests, the airline operated only in the west of the USA, but as the years passed the network was expanded to all the states as well as to Canada and Hawaii, the latter with Boeing 747s from November 1989. In 1991, America West was the first US airline to use the Airbus A320. From 27th June 1991, it flew under Chapter 11 bankruptcy protection with a reduced fleet, unprofitable routes were dropped and an economy programme brought in. This was successful, the carrier emerging from Chapter 11 in August 1994. Continental and Mesa Airlines acquired 25% of the shares. The present colour scheme was

introduced in 1996. To replace the ageing fleet of Boeing 737-200s America West decided upon the Airbus A319, the first aircraft being delivered in October 1998; by the end of 2001 all the 737s should be gone. There are also some examples of the even shorter A318 on order for delivery from 2003. There were takeover negotiations with United during 1999, but the outcome was negative, and so AW is concentrating on building up the company with its own resources. There are codeshare arrangements with Continental , British Airways and Mesa Airlines on several routes.

Routes

Over 60 destinations in the USA, Canada and Mexico from main bases at Phoenix and Las Vegas.

Fleet

14 Airbus A319
42 Airbus A320-200
12 Boeing 737-200
47 Boeing 737-300

14 Boeing 757-200

Ordered

15 Airbus A318
10 Airbus A319
13 Airbus A320

Boeing 727-233F N395AJ (Stefan Schlick/Barbados)

AMERIJET INTERNATIONAL

498 SW 34th Street, Fort Lauderdale FL 33315, USA, Tel. 954-3590077, Fax. 954-3597866
www.amerijet.com

Three- / Two- letter code	IATA No.	Reg'n prefix	ICAO callsign
AJT / M6	810	N	Amerijet

Amerijet International was set up in 1974 and initially provided only cargo and express goods flights using Learjets and Cessna 401s. In 1985 the first three Boeing 727s were acquired and further examples of this type followed in 1988 and 1989, enabling charter, sub-charter and ad hoc freight flights to be undertaken. A combi version of this aircraft (Boeing 727-100C) was used when the airline moved into the passenger charter business as well as ambulance and cargo flights. Amerijet flies regular scheduled cargo flights on behalf of DHL and Burlington, both cargo specialists. In 1993 scheduled flights started for the first time to Guyana. As the market for medium range freight aircraft had become thin, in 1996 five former PanAm Boeing 727s which had been stored for years in the Mojave Desert were bought. Some were taken into service with the airline after extensive overhaul at its base; others serve as spares sources. In 1998 operations and the company maintenance base were moved from Miami to nearby Fort Lauderdale. As well as scheduled services, the airline flies a lot of perishable goods, for instance meat, fish, vegetables and flowers and is always ready for worldwide ad hoc charters.

Routes

Antigua, Aruba, Barbados, Belize City, Cancun, Caracas, Curacao, Domenica, Fort de France, Grenada, Guadalajara, Guayana, Maracaibo, Merida, Mexico City, Miami, Port au Prince, Porlamar, Port of Spain, Puerto Plata, San Juan, St. Kitts, St. Lucia, St. Maarten, St.Vincent and Valencia.

Fleet

10 Boeing 727-200 F
2 Cessna 410/501

Boeing 767-277 VH-RMH (Uwe Gleisberg/Sydney)

ANSETT AUSTRALIA

501 Swanston Street Melbourne,Victoria 3000, Australia, Tel. 3-96233333, Fax. 3-96231114, www.ansett.com.au

Three- / Two- letter code	IATA No.	Reg'n prefix	ICAO callsign
AAA / AN	090	VH	Ansett

Reginald Ansett set up his company in 1931, starting with bus and lorry journeys in Victoria. ATI Ltd. (Ansett Transport Industries) was then formed in 1936, with its first flights from Melbourne to Hamilton using a Fokker Universal. After buying various smaller companies, Ansett took over Australian National Airways (ANA) on 4th October 1957. Until 1969 the new company flew under the logo Ansett-ANA. After the merger, aircraft such as the Vickers Viscount and Lockheed L-188 Electra were used. The first jet was the Boeing 727, in use from November 1964, followed in 1967 by the DC-9. In addition to Australia,

Port Moresby, at that time in Australian-administered New Guinea, was a focal point of Ansett's activities. In 1981 Ansett ordered new aircraft such as the Boeing 767 and 737. A completely new type in the fleet from 1988 was the Airbus A320, known with the airline as the Skystar. When Ansett belonged to TNT and News Corporation, all aviation activities were pulled together under the Ansett Holdings banner. Thus formerly independently operated subsidiaries East-West Airlines, Ansett WA and Ansett Express were all merged into Ansett Australia. The airline's first international services were flown in

1993, to Bali and Hong Kong. For the latter a Boeing 747-300 was used, carrying for the first time the new colours currently in use. Ansett is a member of the Star Alliance and late in1999 was completely taken over by fellow-member Air New Zealand, which had held a minority shareholding for some years. Numerous smaller companies such as Aeropelican, Impulse, Kendell, Skywest and Sunshine Express operate as partners in the vast Australian regional market.

Routes

Extensive Australian route network with about 50 points served. Denpasar, Hong Kong, Osaka and Taipei are the first international routes.

Fleet

20 Airbus A320-200
12 BAe 146-200/300
 2 Boeing 747-400
11 Boeing 767-200/300
22 Boeing 737-300

3 Fokker F.28

De Havilland DHC-8-102 ZK-NEZ (Author's collection)

ANSETT NEW ZEALAND

650 Great South Road, Elleslie, Auckland 1130,
New Zealand, Tel. 9-5268300,
Fax. 9-5268406, www.ansett.co.nz

Three- / Two- letter code	IATA No.	Reg'n prefix	ICAO callsign
AAA / ZQ	941	ZK	Ansett

In 1985 in New Zealand, the well-known transport concern Newmans formed its own airline, known as Newmans Air. De Havilland Canada DHC-7s were used on routes between Auckland, Christchurch, Glentander and Wellington. During 1987 an investor group with participation from Ansett Airlines of Australia formed and took over Newmans Air, which was promptly renamed as Ansett New Zealand. Three Boeing 737-200s supplemented the two Dash 7s. With the accelerated rate of growth of the company, new routes were added and soon coverage extended to all the major centres on both of New Zealand's islands. From mid-1989 the Boeing 737-200s were replaced by BAe 146s. These had the advantage of being more flexible in use on the not so well supported routes. During 1996 the News Corporation took over all the shares in the company and provided several de Havilland Canada DHC-8s, for use at the smaller airports with less traffic. As a consequence of the takeover of Ansett Australia by Air New Zealand, Ansett New Zealand was disposed of to Qantas, and so from September 2000 is in the process of transforming itself into Qantas New Zealand, a somewhat strange turn of events in the light of the previous histories of the competing antipodean operators. The airline has its own overhaul and maintenance centre in Christchurch.

Routes

Auckland, Blenheim, Christchurch, Dunedin, Glentaner, Hamilton, Invercargill, Mt. Cook, Nelson, Palmerston North, Queenstown, Rotorua.

Fleet

10 BAe 146
5 De Havilland DHC-8

Boeing 737-53C F-GHUL (B.I.Hengi/Zürich)

AOM – FRENCH AIRLINES

Strategic Orly 108, 13-15 rue du Pont des
Halles, 94526 Rungis Cedex, France
Tel. 1-49791045, Fax. 1-49791011, www.aom.fr

Three- / Two- letter code	IATA No.	Reg'n prefix	ICAO callsign
AOM / IW	646	F	French Lines

On 15th December 1988 Air Outre Mer was set up on the island of Réunion in the Indian Ocean. A service was planned to the French overseas provinces on the basis of scheduled charter flights. Scheduled services with DC-10-30s began on 26th May 1990, initially with three weekly flights from Paris to St.Denis de la Réunion. In the Autumn of 1990 further DC-10-30s were added to the fleet. In addition three Dornier 228s were purchased in November 1990 for a newly-created domestic service on the island of Réunion. In late 1992, AOM was merged with another French airline Minerve, taking over its

aircraft. The future objectives for the new and restructured airline had to be defined, and a new colour scheme was adopted, incorporating the new name AOM French Airlines. In mid-1998 AOM was put up for sale at the instigation of its majority shareholder, Bank Credit Lyonnaise and a group of investors took over 51%. However at the beginning of February 1999 the SAir Group (owners of Swissair and other airlines) acquired 49%, and AOM became a member of the Qualiflyer Group. Two Airbus A340s joined the fleet from mid-1999 for long-range routes as a replacement for older DC-10s. The airline's Swiss owners

have decided to merge it with their other French interests, Air Liberté (see page 60) and Air Littoral to form a new grouping which will have about 30% of the French market. There will be two divisions, one with aircraft of 100 seats and over which will operate as the mainline, and one with the smaller aircraft which will operate regionally from Nice and Montpellier.

Routes

Cayenne, Colombo, Fort de France, Havana, Los Angeles, Lyon, Marseilles, Nassau, Nice, Noumea, Papeete, Paris, Perpignan, Pointe-à-Pitre, Puerto Plata, Punta Cana, St.Denis de la Réunion, St. Maarten, Sydney, Toulon, Varadero, Zürich.

Fleet

 2 Airbus A340-200
 3 Boeing 737-500
12 McDonnell Douglas DC-10-30
10 McDonnell Douglas MD-83

Boeing 727-113C YA-FAU (Author's collection)

ARIANA AFGHAN

P.O.Box 76 Ansari Watt, Kabul,
Afghanistan
Tel. 11 331 2478 Fax. 11 375 5162

Three- / Two- letter code	IATA No.	Reg'n prefix	ICAO callsign
AFG / FG	255	YA	Ariana

Ariana Afghan Airlines Co Ltd. was founded on 27th January 1955 as a new national airline The Indian company Indama Corp. provided the first Douglas DC-3 aircraft and held 49% of the shares. This holding was acquired in 1956 by Pan American World Airways, which expanded the airline considerably. International routes to Delhi and Beirut were quickly put in place, with the Beirut route being extended via Ankara and Prague to Frankfurt. Douglas DC-4s and later, DC-6s were used. In 1963 its operational base was moved to Kabul from Kandahar, and 1967 saw Bakhtar Afghan Airlines formed to begin taking over Ariana's domestic services. In 1968 Ariana took on its first jet aircraft, a Boeing 727, followed by a DC-10-30 in September 1979. Following the invasion of Afghanistan by Soviet troops over Christmas 1979, flight operations collapsed. The DC-10 was sold after suffering damage in a rocket attack and Soviet-built aircraft were added to the fleet. All operations were integrated into Bakhtar, which became the new national carrier, in October 1985, but by February 1988 the name had been changed back to its present form. During the ten years of the war, there were flights only to Moscow and Prague, and occasionally to Berlin-Schönefeld, primarily to transport casualties for treatment. Gradually air transport has been returning to normal, though the political situation is far from stable. Karachi in Pakistan was used as an alternative base for a while, but operations moved back to Kabul from 1998.

Routes

Amritsar, Delhi, Dubai, Jalalabad, Jeddah, Kabul, as well as charter and freight flights without fixed schedules.

Fleet

2 Antonov An-12
3 Antonov An-24
2 Boeing 727-100
1 Boeing 727-200

1 De Havilland DHC-6
1 Tupolev Tu-154M

Boeing 757-236 4X-BAZ (Uwe Gleisberg/Munich)

ARKIA ISRAELI AIRLINES

P.O.Box 39301, Dov Airport,
Tel Aviv 61392, Israel, Tel. 3-6902222,
Fax. 3-6991390, www.arkia.co.il

Three- / Two- letter code	IATA No.	Reg'n prefix	ICAO callsign
AIZ / IZ	238	4X	Arkia

After the foundation in 1948 of the state of Israel and its airline El Al to serve Europe and the USA, there was also a need for an air service to Eilat. The road conditions across the desert to this Israeli outpost, which at that time consisted only of a small settlement and a military post, were dire. El Al and Histradut, the most important trades union, each took 50% of the shares of Eilata, which was set up late in 1948. On 28th February 1950 the airline carried out its official first flight from Tel Aviv to Eilat, using a Curtiss C-46 from El Al, which with two DH.89 Dragon Rapides formed the fleet. The airline's name was changed to Arkia

Israeli Airlines in September 1950, and subsequent expansion called for more and larger aircraft; several DC-3s and Beech 18s replaced the Dragon Rapides during the 1950s. With the opening of the first hotels in Eilat, passenger traffic increased. Handley Page Dart Heralds were acquired and for the first time Arkia flew internationally, to Cyprus. After the Six Day War in 1967 the occupied Sinai peninsula with Sharm-el-Sheik and Santa Katharina were added to the network. Between 1969 and 1974 Arkia took on Vickers Viscounts and in 1972 took a holding in Kanaf-Arkia Airlines, another domestic operator. In 1979

the airline was privatised. Boeing 737-200 were added from 1981 and used on charter flights; domestic schedules were passed to DHC-7s and moved to Dov airport near the city of Tel Aviv. Increasing tourist traffic drove further expansion. Boeing 707s augmented the 737s until 1998, and in 1999 a fleet renewal began with the introduction of ATR 72s and Boeing 757-200s. A revised aircraft colour scheme was introduced with the delivery of the first Boeing 757, and Arkia was among the first to order the new, stretched 757-300. The Dash 7s are to be replaced by the Dash 8-400Q in 2001.

Routes

Domestic schedules to Eilat, Haifa, Tel Aviv, Jerusalem, Rosh Pina and Kiryat Shmona, and to Amman in Jordan. Regular charter flights from many Western European cities to Tel Aviv and Eilat.

Fleet

3 ATR 72-500
4 Boeing 737-200
1 Boeing 757-200
2 Boeing 757-300

8 De Havilland DHC-7

Ordered

1 ATR 72-500

Airbus A310-222 F-OGYW (Albert Kuhbandner/Frankfurt)

ARMENIAN AIRLINES

Zvartnots Airport, 375042 Yerevan, Armenia
Tel. 2-225444, Fax. 2-243152

Three- / Two- letter code	IATA No.	Reg'n prefix	ICAO callsign
RME / R3	956	EK	Armenian

In 1993 the government of this newly independent republic took the initiative and took over the former Aeroflot Directorate in Armenia. The former Soviet republic, where business was once thriving, was at war with the neighbouring republic of Azerbaijan over the Nagorny-Karabakh territory, as a result of which the delivery of raw materials and energy from its neighbour were cut off. Armenia was dependent on these supplies and since the start of hostilities, business and living conditions had declined. Accordingly the development of air services was to be laborious. Even though the Aeroflot Directorate had

carried a meagre two million passengers, the new airline could only manage a third of that number. Nevertheless, the airline does operate profitably, as there are countless expatriate Armenians who use the flights regularly. These expatriates should also provide a source of capital for a planned privatisation. Agreements have been made with KLM and Air France which should support the development of the company, especially as Armenia's capital, Yerevan, is an attractive tourist city. The business situation has not been good during the 1990s, and the hoped-for privatisation has not been

progressed; in fact the fleet and route network have been trimmed. However, the delivery of a leased Airbus A310 in July 1998 was a step in the direction of fleet renewal.

Routes

Adler, Aleppo, Amsterdam, Ashgabat, Athens, Beirut, Dubai, Frankfurt, Istanbul, Kiev, Kharkov, Minsk, Moscow, Novosibirsk, Odessa, Paris, Samara, Simferopol, Sofia, St. Petersburg, Tashkent, Teheran, Volgograd, Yekaterinburg, Yerevan.

Fleet

1 Airbus A310-200
2 Antonov An-24
1 Antonov An-32
2 Ilyushin IL-86

6 Tupolev Tu-134
7 Tupolev Tu-154

Lockheed L-1011 TriStar 200F N307GB (Lutz Schönfeld/Miami)

ARROW AIR

P.O.Box 026062 Miami Airport, Fl 33126, USA
Tel. 305-5260900, Fax. 305-5260933,
www.arrowair.com

Three- / Two- letter code	IATA No.	Reg'n prefix	ICAO callsign
APW / JW	404	N	Big A

Arrow Airways was set up as a charter airline in late 1946 but only flew actively until 1954. However in 1980 the airline was reactivated by its founder George Batchelor and it started cargo charters on 26th May 1981. A number of DC-8s were acquired for long-range charters, contract services for the USAF's Military Airlift Command and later for passenger flights. July 1982 saw the first scheduled flight from Los Angeles to Montego Bay. On 18th December 1982 Arrow also flew from Tampa to London. Arrow Airways became Arrow Air at the beginning of 1993 and two DC-10s were acquired but returned due to a cutback in operations.

Reorganisation in 1984 resulted in domestic American flights being suspended; on the other hand, some new routes to South America were added. In 1985 Arrow Air withdrew completely from the passenger market. On 11th February 1986 the company filed for bankruptcy although cargo charters subsequently restarted using DC-8Fs. Arrow Air made a comeback as a passenger charter airline with Boeing 727s in 1993. Another setback came in the Spring of 1995 when an FAA purge against other operators also grounded Arrow Air on 'safety grounds'.

However the necessary certification and checks were completed quickly and the airline was able to start up again after just a few weeks, now with a freighter-conversion Lockheed TriStar. This type replaced several DC-8s and the Boeing 727s no longer featured in the reduced fleet. Further converted L-1011 TriStars were added in 1996 and 1997. During 1999, another Miami-based cargo operator, Fine Air (see page 191) acquired Arrow Air for US$ 115 million, but the airline continues independent operation.

Routes

Asuncion, Atlanta, Bogota, Caracas, Costa Rica, Guayaquil, Miami, New York, Panama, Quito, San Juan and worldwide charter flights.

Fleet

7 McDonnell Douglas DC-8-62 F
2 McDonnell Douglas DC-8-63 F
3 Lockheed L-1011F

Embraer EMB-120RT Brasilia N260AS (Josef Krauthäuser/Dallas-Fort Worth)

ASA - ATLANTIC SOUTHEAST AIRLINES

100 Hartsfield Central Parkway, Suite 800
Atlanta, GA 30354 USA, Tel. 404-7661400,
Fax. 404-2090162, www.asa-air.com

Three- / Two- letter code	IATA No.	Reg'n prefix	ICAO callsign
ASE / EV	862	N	Asea

Atlantic Southwest Airlines – ASA was founded in March 1979 and in June of that year began its first services from Atlanta. De Havilland Canada DHC-7s, Embraer EMB 110 Bandeirantes and Shorts 360s were used. The company was successful from the outset and grew steadily, so that by 1981 over 150,000 passengers were being carried to around 20 destinations. In order to finance further expansion, the company went to the stock exchange in 1982. Thus provided with additional capital, it was possible to take over a competitor, Southeastern Airlines, on 1st April 1993. In 1984 the important decision was taken to co-operate with Delta Air Lines, not only in unified marketing, but with ASA as a participant in the newly formed Delta Connection feeder system. With the delivery of the newer and faster Embraer 120 Brasilia during 1985 it was possible to phase out the Shorts 360s and the fleet continued to expand. Larger aircraft such as the ATR 42 in 1983 and the BAe 146 in 1985 were introduced from the two hubs at Atlanta and Dallas for longer routes. The BAe 146 was the airline's first jet type and in future this form of power would have the advantage in equipment choice. Thus in 1997 Canadair Regional Jet 200s were added, to replace Brasilias and with the aim in time of achieving a homogeneous fleet structure. Orders have also been placed for the lengthened RJ 700 version, for delivery from 2001. Likewise the ATR 42s have been replaced by the larger ATR 72. Over the years, Delta Air Lines took on more and more shares in ASA-Holdings and by 1999 ASA became a fully-owned, though independently operating, subsidiary, bound into to all Delta's alliances. All of ASA's maintenance is carried out in its own facilities at Dallas and Atlanta.

Routes

From its two major hubs at Atlanta and Dallas a total of about 60 cities and towns in the south-east and midwest of the USA are served .

Fleet	Ordered
19 ATR 72	9 Canadair Regional Jet 200 ·
50 Embraer EMB-120	12 Canadair Regional Jet 700
36 Canadair Regional Jet 200	

McDonnell Douglas DC-9-31 YV-714C (Ralf Lücke/Porlamar)

ASERCA

Avda Bolivar Norte,Piso 8, Valencia 2002
Venezuela, Tel. 41-237111, Fax. 41-220210,
www.asercaairlines.com

Three- / Two- letter code	IATA No.	Reg'n prefix	ICAO callsign
OCA / R7	717	YV	Aserca

Founded in 1991, Aserca-Aerolineas Regional del Centro from Valencia in northern Venezuela acquired two Douglas DC-9s from Midway Airlines with which to begin operations in 1992, initially to the holiday island of Margarita which lies off the north coast. Several Cessna 402s were also in the fleet for air taxi operations. The company was successful and so during 1993 and 1994 acquired more DC-9s and expanded further. As well as the capital Caracas, most of the important towns in Venezuela were soon being offered direct service from the country's second-largest city. During 1998 Aserca received its first MD-90 and took on a 70% shareholding in Air Aruba. By way of fleet renewal, Boeing 737-800s were ordered to replace older DC-9s, with the first two aircraft being delivered in 1999. Though restricted to domestic services in the early years, the route network, with the participation in Air Aruba, now encompasses the Caribbean region.

Routes

Aruba, Barcelona, Barquisemento, Bogota, Caracas, Havana, Las Piedras, Lima, Maracaibo, Maturin, Porlamar, Puerto Ordaz, Punta Cana, San Antonio, Santo Domingo, Valencia.

Fleet

  2 Boeing 737-800
  1 McDonnell Douglas MD-90
11 McDonnell Douglas DC-9-30

Airbus A321-131 HL7589 (Author's collection via Pierre Alain Petit/Seoul)

ASIANA

1 ka Hoehuyn-Dong, Chung Ku, Seoul 100-052, Republic of Korea, Tel. 02-7588351, Fax. 02-7588080, www.asiana.co.kr

Three- / Two- letter code	IATA No.	Reg'n prefix	ICAO callsign
AAR / OZ	988	HL	Asiana

The economic boom of the 1980s in South Korea and the great mobility of the Koreans led to the formation of this airline. It was originally formed by the Kumho Industrial Group as Seoul Air International and started operations in December 1988, initially on domestic routes only. This restriction was soon lifted and international routes opened in 1989, first to Fukuoka in neighbouring Japan. Nagoya and Tokyo followed swiftly as well as other Korean domestic points; these were served with ten Boeing 737-400s. In 1990 routes to Hong Kong and Bangkok were added as well as new aircraft type, the Boeing 767. New routes to Los Angeles, San Francisco and New York from 1992 brought the Boeing 747-400 into the fleet and in December 1994 the first all-cargo jumbo, a Boeing 747-400F was introduced. The investment required was colossal, and for the decade beginning 1996 about 60 new aircraft, from Airbus as well as Boeing, were ordered or on option, with deliveries commencing in 1998. The leap to Europe was made in 1995 with a regular service to Brussels and Vienna, with London added at the end of 1996 and Frankfurt in 1997. The Asian financial downturn of the late 1990s put a damper on growth, with flights to Europe being particularly affected. However, the worst seems to be over and Asiana is again on an expansion path and acquiring new aircraft. The airline's base is at Kimpo Airport in Seoul.

There are codeshare arrangements with Northwest and Qantas and other co-operation with Air China, China Eastern and Turkish Airlines

Routes

Almaty, Anchorage, Bangkok, Beijing, Boston, Brussels, Chejudoo, Chicago, Chinju, Frankfurt, Fukuoka, Guam, Guilin, Harbin, Hiroshima, Ho Chi Minh City, Hong Kong, Kuala Lumpur, Kwangju, Los Angeles, Macau, Manila, Matsuyama, Mokpo, Nagoya, New York, Okinawa, Osaka, Pohang, Pusan, Saipan, San Francisco, Seattle, Sendai, Shanghai, Seoul, Shenzen, Singapore, Sydney, Taegu, Takamatsu, Tokyo, Toyama, Ulsan, Xian, Yosu.

Fleet

		Ordered
3 Airbus A321	12 Boeing 747-400/-400F	10 Airbus A321-200
20 Boeing 737-400		6 Airbus A330
3 Boeing 737-500		3 Boeing 747-400
11 Boeing 767-300		6 Boeing 777

Lockheed L-1011 TriStar N196AT (Josef Krauthäuser/New Orleans)

ATA-AMERICAN TRANS AIR

P.O.Box 51609 Indianapolis, Indiana 46251,
USA, Tel. 317-2474000,
Fax. 317-2407091, www.ata.coma

Three- / Two- letter code	IATA No.	Reg'n prefix	ICAO callsign
AMT / TZ	366	N	Amtran

American Trans Air is the largest charter operator in the United States, though in recent years has moved more into the scheduled service market also. It was founded in 1973 in Indianapolis, Indiana and started flying for Ambassadair Travel Club, using a Boeing 720. In 1981 permission was granted by the Federal Aviation Administration for American Trans Air to operate as a charter airline. Further Boeing 707s were acquired and in 1982 DC-10s and Boeing 727s were added. As there was an acute shortage of second hand DC-10s on the worldwide airliner market, a switch was made to a fleet of Lockheed

L-1011TriStars, and this type along with the 727 replaced the Boeing 707s, the older examples of the 727 being in turn replaced with Boeing 757s from 1992 onwards. A particularly vigorous expansion took place from 1993 to 1995 and a new, bright colour scheme was adopted, along with a change of name to ATA. After a short lull during the second part of the 1990s, expansion resumed and in 1999 the airline Chicago Express, equipped with BAe Jetstream 31s for feeder services, was bought. ATA's first scheduled service destination in Europe was Dublin, from 1998. The airline has a large maintenance

complex at Indianapolis, and a further important hub at Chicago Midway. As well as its new extensive scheduled service network, ATA remains true to its origins and is active with military and civil charter work. For 2001 ATA is planning a fleet renewal with Boeing 757-300s replacing the older TriStars and Boeing 737-800s taking the place of the 727s.

Routes

Cancun, Chicago, Dallas/Fort Worth, Dayton, Denver, Dublin, Fort Lauderdale, Fort Myers, Honolulu, Indianapolis, Las Vegas, Los Angeles, Maui, Milwaukee, Montego Bay, New York, Orlando, Phoenix, San Francisco, San Juan.

Fleet	Ordered
12 Boeing 757-200	3 Boeing 757-200
24 Boeing 727-200	10 Boeing 757-300
19 Lockheed L-1011	32 Boeing 737-800

Tupolev Tu-154 RA-85710 (Björn Kannengiesser/Dubai)

ATLANT-SOYUZ AIRLINES

10/2 Nikolskaya Ul. Moscow 103012, Russia
Tel. 095-2469419, Fax. 095-2468503

Three- / Two- letter code	IATA No.	Reg'n prefix	ICAO callsign
AYZ / 3G	411	RA	Atlant Soyuz

During June 1993 a new joint stock company was registered in Moscow with the name Atlant-Soyuz Airlines. The Ukrainian airline Atlant and other investors were the shareholders. It was planned to operate freight flights, but in addition passenger services from Moscow. The aircraft were taken over from Aeroflot and operations were begun in the same month as the company was formed. Atlant-Soyuz Airlines also established a scheduled service between Chklakovsky and Magadan using Ilyushin IL-62s or Tupolev Tu-154s, and charter flights were made particularly to the shoppers' paradise of the Middle East, for instance to Dubai or Abu Dhabi in the United Arab Emirates. The company's IL-76s are often seen at airports in Western Europe operating freight charters. The Ilyushin IL-96 is also a freight version and was delivered to the airline in 1999.

Routes

Abu Dhabi, Chklakovsky, Dubai, Magadan, Moscow, Simferopol.

Fleet

3 Antonov An-12
1 Antonov An-124
2 Ilyushin IL-18
1 Ilyushin IL-62
14 Ilyushin IL-76
3 Ilyushin IL-86
1 Ilyushin IL-96-300
3 Tupolev Tu-134
7 Tupolev Tu-154

Boeing 747-2212B (SF) N808MC (Josef Krauthäuser/Los Angeles LAX)

ATLAS AIR

538 Commons Drive, Golden, Colorado 80401, USA, Tel. 303-5265050, Fax. 303-5265051, www.atlasair.com

Three- / Two- letter code	IATA No.	Reg'n prefix	ICAO callsign
GTI / 5Y	369	N	Giant

In 1992 Atlas Air was formed in New York by Atlas Holdings, a sister company of Aeronautics Leasing, as a freight-only carrier, and since then has grown rapidly. With a fleet of Boeing 747 freighters Atlas Air operates worldwide. Regular flights operate from New York to Hong Kong via Anchorage and via Khabarovsk in Russia back to New York. As well as its own scheduled services, Atlas Air flies regular freight charters for other well-known airlines including for example Alitalia, British Airways, Cargolux, China Airlines, FedEx, Iberia, KLM, Lufthansa, SAS and Thai, leasing them both crews and aircraft. In

1996 five Boeing 747s were taken over from Fed Ex, but as there are few freighter 747s on the market, pure passenger aircraft have had to be acquired and converted to freighters for the airline. Thus for example the entire 747-200 fleet of Thai International was acquired and converted from 1997. Thus the fleet has grown quickly and the first of 12 new-build 747-400Fs entered service from mid-1998. The airline has indicated that it will be one of the launch customers for the new Airbus A3XX superjumbo, and that it intends to order around 12 of the type. Atlas Air's base is at New York's JFK International Airport; a

further important departure point, especially for services to South America, is Miami.

Routes

Scheduled, charter and ad hoc freight flights. Atlas Air flies on behalf of Alitalia, British Airways, Lufthansa, SAS and other companies.

Fleet

24 Boeing 747-200F
12 Boeing 747-400F

De Havilland DHC-8-314 D-BMUC (Ralf Kaminski/Leipzig)

AUGSBURG AIRWAYS

Flughafenstr. 6, 86169 Augsburg,
Germany
Tel, 0821-270970, Fax. 0821-2709766

Three- / Two- letter code	IATA No.	Reg'n prefix	ICAO callsign
AUB / IQ	614	D	Augsburg Air

From 1979 Interot Air Service maintained a regular charter service on behalf of the Haindl Paper Company and Interot Internationale Spedition. The company aircraft, a Beech 200 Super King Air, was used. From 1986 this casual service was improved to become a scheduled service as required and the necessary licence was granted. A second King Air was added from Autumn 1987 in order to provide service to Hamburg. The demand for these services from Augsburg was good, so that in September 1988 the acquisition of a Beechcraft 1900 Airliner was warranted, with a second following in May 1989.

Interot obtained its licence as a scheduled service operator in December 1989 and this offered new perspectives for the future. A leased de Havilland Canada DHC-8 was put into service on the Düsseldorf route from October 1990; three aircraft of this type were ordered firm. The reunification of Germany brought with it new destinations from Augsburg, and a change of name to Interot Airways. After the opening of the new Munich airport, Augsburg was seen as an alternative to this, and new routes were opened to London and Cologne. From 1st January 1996 the name was changed again to

Augsburg Airways and the aircraft colour scheme was changed. Effective from the Winter 1996/97 timetable, Augsburg Airways became a Lufthansa franchise partner under the Team Lufthansa banner and began flying for the national airline for the first time from Munich and other German regional airports. Some of the aircraft are now painted in Team Lufthansa colours. The airline's base remains at Augsburg however. A changeover of the fleet to the quieter and more powerful Dash-8Q should begin towards the end of 2000; most will operate from Munich on Team Lufthansa routes.

Routes

Augsburg, Berlin, Brussels, Dresden, Düsseldorf, Frankfurt, Hamburg, Cologne, Leipzig, London-City, Munich and other destinations on behalf of Team Lufthansa.

Fleet	Ordered
1 De Havilland DHC-8-100	5 De Havilland DHC-8-400Q
2 De Havilland DHC-8-200Q	
4 De Havilland DHC-8-300	
7 De Havilland DHC-8-300Q	

Shorts 360 G-OAAS (Gerhard Schütz/Jersey)

AURIGNY AIR SERVICES

La Panque Lane, States Airport,Forest, Guernsey Channel Island GY8 ODT, Great Britain, Tel. 1481-66444, Fax. 1481-66446, www.aurigny.com

Three- / Two- letter code	IATA No.	Reg'n prefix	ICAO callsign
AUR / GR	924	G	Ayline

For more than 30 years Aurigny Air Services has been an institution on the British Channel Isles. It was set up on 1st March 1968 and began its inter-island services with two Britten-Norman Islanders between Guernsey, Jersey and Alderney. The small airline developed rapidly in the first couple of years, so that by 1970 eight Islanders were in use. A larger aircraft type was required, and the answer to this problem came also from Britten-Norman, who developed the three-engined Trislander, the first of which was delivered to Aurigny in July 1971.

This unpretentious yet dependable aircraft proved to be ideal and has formed the mainstay of the fleet ever since that time. The route network was extended to northern France and the south of England. In 1987 Aurigny concluded a contract with the British Post Office for the carriage of letters between the islands and to London-Gatwick and East Midlands. Aurigny also undertakes ambulance flights as required. During 1990 the company took delivery of its first turboprop type, a Shorts 360. In July 1999 the airline received the first of two Saab

SF 340s, and if they prove to be suitable they may partially replace the Trislanders They have also been used for an expansion of longer range services, for instance to Manchester, filling a void left by the withdrawal of other airlines from routes between the Channel Islands and the British mainland.

Routes

Alderney, Cherbourg, Dinard, Guernsey, Jersey, London-Gatwick, Manchester, Southampton. Additionally postal flights to Gatwick and East Midlands.

Fleet

9 Britten Norman Trislander
1 Shorts 360
2 Saab SF 340

Airbus A330-223 OE-LAM (Andreas Witek/Graz)

AUSTRIAN AIRLINES

Postfach 50, 1107 Vienna, Austria
Tel. 1-17660, Fax. 1-685505,
www.aua.com

Three- / Two- letter code	IATA No.	Reg'n prefix	ICAO callsign
AUA / OS	257	OE	Austrian

Austrian Airlines was set up on 30th September 1957 and began operations on 31st March 1958 on the Vienna-London route using Vickers Viscounts leased from shareholder Fred Olsen. A short time later, services also began to Frankfurt, Zürich, Paris, Stuttgart and Rome. In February 1960 AUA bought its own Vickers Viscount 837s. In April 1963 the Caravelle entered service. Domestic routes were still being served by the DC-3s, which were however replaced in 1966 by HS.748s. During 1969 AUA underwent a reorganisation with unprofitable routes and the entire domestic network being dropped. The DC-9 was ordered, with the first entering service in 1971. Two attempts to launch long-range services with Boeing 707s, the first in association with Sabena in 1969, were abandoned in 1973. From 1975 DC-9-51s were ordered and AUA was one of the launch customers for the MD-81. From 1988, MD-87s, with extended range, were also added to the fleet. The third attempt at long-range services in 1989 was more successful and began with services to Tokyo and New York, using Airbus A310s. Three new types entered the fleet during 1995: the Fokker 70, Airbus A321 and Airbus A340, all of which displayed a new colour scheme. During 1999 Austrian broke away from its long-term 'Qualiflyer' partner Swissair and joined the Star Alliance from March 2000. Austrian now owns the majority of Lauda Air and Tyrolean Airways. Fleet changes during 1999 were the introduction of the Airbus A330 and the beginning of the replacement of the MD-80s by the Airbus A320 and A321.

Routes

Aleppo, Almaty, Amman, Amsterdam, Ankara, Astana, Athens, Atlanta, Baku, Beijing, Beirut, Berlin, Boston, Bratislava, Brussels, Budapest, Bucharest, Chicago, Cologne, Copenhagen, Damascus, Dubai, Düsseldorf, Frankfurt, Graz, Hamburg, Hanover, Istanbul, Johannesburg, Kiev, Larnaca, Linz, London, Milan, Minsk, Moscow, Munich, New York, Odessa, Osaka, Ostrava, Paris, Prague, Salzburg, Sofia, Stockholm, Stuttgart, Tashkent, Teheran, Tel Aviv, Timisoara, Tokyo, Vienna, Vilnius, Warsaw, Zagreb, Zürich.

Fleet

4 Airbus A310-300
13 Airbus A320
7 Airbus A321-100/200
4 Airbus A330-200

4 Airbus A340-200/300
6 Fokker 70
8 McDonnell Douglas MD-81/82/83
5 McDonnell Douglas MD-87

Ordered

2 Airbus A321-200

Boeing 737-229 CC-CVD (Author's collection)

AVANT AIRLINES

Santa Magdalena 75, L-1 Santiago, Chile
Tel. 56-23370800, Fax. 56-23370875
www.avant.cl

Three- / Two- letter code	IATA No.	Reg'n prefix	ICAO callsign
VAT / OT	246	CC	Avant Airlines

Aero Chile was founded during 1996 by several private investors, and it took over the operating licence of Lineas Aereas Chilensas, which had become bankrupt. Operations began with Boeing 737-200s from Santiago to Chilean domestic destinations, but after only three months, operations were suspended. However, after further financial support had been arranged, a fresh start was made at the end of 1996, taking up the new name of Avant Airlines from January 1997. Even so, in May 1997 Avant Airlines was taken over by the Tur Bus company, thus placing it in a better position to compete with the flag carrier. The fleet was augmented with further Boeing 737-200s, and National Airlines and their aircraft were also taken over, enabling more new routes to be opened up. A single Boeing 727-200 was acquired and is used for charter and freight work. Continental Airlines has become a partner, and there is also close co-operation with Copa Panama, in which Continental Airlines is also a shareholder, and European partners are being sought. A fleet renewal is envisaged for late 2000, and as well as a replacement for the 737-200s, there is also interest in acquiring a smaller aircraft type for operation into smaller airfields for which the 737 is too large. The aircraft are painted in three colour variations of the basic scheme, a pink (as illustrated), a blue and a yellow.

Routes

Antofagasta, Arica, Balmaceda, Calama, Concepcion, Copiapo, Iquique, La Serena, Mendoza, Osorno, Pucon, Puerto Montt, Punta Arenas, Santiago, Temuco, Valdiva.

Fleet

1 Boeing 727-200
8 Boeing 737-200

Boeing 727-281 YV-94C (Dennis Wehrmann/Miami)

AVENSA

Avda. Universidad Torre El Chorro Edif.29,Piso 2/3 Aptdo 943, Caracas 101, Venezuela,Tel. 2-5623022, Fax. 2-5630225, www.avensa.com.ve

Three- / Two- letter code	IATA No.	Reg'n prefix	ICAO callsign
AVE / VE	128	YV	Ave

Aerovias Venezolanas SA – Avensa – was set up on 13th May 1943 by Pan American and a group of Venezuelan businessmen. Freight flight started in December 1943 with Ford Trimotors and Stinson Reliants ferrying much-needed supplies to the growing oil industry in the Carteru part of the country; passenger services started in May 1944 with Lockheed 10As. After the Second World War, Douglas DC-3s were added to the fleet, and in 1953 Convair 340s were ordered and these were used to open a route to Miami from 1955. By 1960 Avensa had developed a substantial domestic route network plus a regional system to Miami, New Orleans, Aruba and Jamaica but in 1961, these international services were merged with those of Aeropostal and transferred to form the basis of VIASA, in which Avensa had a 45% holding. The first jet aircraft, a Caravelle, was received in 1964, as was the Convair 580 turboprop. During 1976 Pan Am sold its shareholding to the Venezuelan government. Boeing 727s were added to the fleet and in 1989 a renewal programme was begun with the arrival of the first Boeing 757s and 737-300s. Financial difficulties led however to the disposal of these new types, and for the 1990s the fleet was composed primarily of a motley mixture of various models of the Boeing 727. When VIASA ceased operations in 1997, Avensa again took up international routes, operating DC-10s to Europe. These services were suspended in early 2000, as a result of Avensa's financial problems and the DC-10s were returned to their lessors, but the routes to Madrid, Rome and Lisbon were expected to recommence in Autumn 2000. The airline's headquarters and maintenance base are at the Caracas airport.

Routes

Barcelona, Barquisemeto, Caracas, Coro, Maracaibo, Merida, Miami, Porlamar, Puerto Ayacucho, Puerto Ordaz, San Antonio, San Fernando de Apure, San Tome.

Fleet

4 Boeing 727-200
6 Boeing 727-100
2 McDonnell Douglas DC-9-51
1 McDonnell Douglas DC-9-31

Boeing 767-259ER N985AN (Albert Kuhbandner/Paris CDG)

AVIANCA COLOMBIA

Av. Eldorado 93-30 Piso 4, Bogota 1, Columbia, Tel. 1-4139511, Fax. 1-4138716
www.avianca.com

Three- / Two- letter code	IATA No.	Reg'n prefix	ICAO callsign
AVA / AV	134	HK	Avianca

Avianca is one of the world's oldest airlines, tracing its history back for 80 years, and claims to be the first airline in the Americas. The Sociedad Colombo-Alemanos de Transportes Aereos (SCADTA) was set up on 5th December 1919 and started flights from the port of Barranquilla on 12th September 1920. Initially Junkers F-13s were used for the route to Puerto Berrio. Destinations in neighbouring Ecuador and Venezuela were served with Junkers W34s. In 1930 Pan American acquired an 80% interest in SCADTA, took over the international flights itself and exchanged the German aircraft types for American ones. On 14th June 1940 SCADTA became Aerovias Nacionales de Colombia (Avianca) and merged with Servicio Aereo Colombiano, which had operated a small network since its foundation in 1933. In 1947 Avianca flew to Miami and two years later to New York also, using Douglas DC-4s. This type was also used to Europe - Paris and Lisbon. On 17th April 1953 Lockheed Constellations were used to begin service to Hamburg and to Frankfurt in the following year. Jet aircraft, Boeing 707s and 720s, were acquired for international routes from 1962. Avianca was the first South American airline to purchase 727s, and the first went into service in April 1966. During 1970 aircraft were painted in the colour scheme still in use now, and from 1971 Zürich was added to the European destinations. The Boeing 747 was delivered in November 1976 and since 1988 the 767 has also been used; likewise older 727s have been replaced with 757s. Avianca has been in Colombian ownership since 1978, and itself owns over 90% of the shares in SAM-Colombia. Its base is at the Eldorado airport at Bogota.

Routes

Aurauca, Armenia, Aruba, Barranquilla, Bogota, Bucaramanga, Buenos Aires, Cali, Caracas, Cartagena, Cucuta, Curacao, Frankfurt, Lima, London, Los Angeles, Madrid, Manizales, Medellin, Mexico City, Miami, New York, Paris, Pasto, Pereira, Popayan, Quito, Rio de Janeiro, San Andres, Santa Marta, Santiago, Sao Paulo, Tumaco, Valledupar.

Fleet

3 Boeing 727-200	13 McDonnell Douglas MD-83
4 Boeing 757-200	
4 Boeing 767-300ER	
10 Fokker 50	

Boeing 737-2H6 N122GU (Hans-Willi Mertens/Miami)

AVIATECA

Avienda Hincapie 12-22, Aeroporto La Aurora,
Guatemala City, Guatemala, Tel. 3318261,
Fax. 3317412, www.flylatinamerica.com

Three- / Two- letter code	IATA No.	Reg'n prefix	ICAO callsign
GUG / GU	240	TG	Aviateca

On 14th March 1945 the airline Empresa Guatemalteca de Aviacion SA (Aviateca) was set up by the government, to take over the operations of PAA-financed Aerovias de Guatemala SA, which had been founded in 1939. DC-3s were used to continue the services, with Douglas DC-6Bs being added in 1961, allowing an expansion of the route network to Miami, New Orleans and other destinations. The first jet was a leased BAC One-Eleven in 1970. In 1974 the airline was renamed as Aerolinas de Guatemala and two Boeing 727s were added to the fleet . From 1989 Aviateca also flew two leased Boeing 737-200s, and further examples were acquired up until 1995. TACA held 30% of the shares and as a result there was co-operation in scheduling and aircraft use. During 1998 the co-operation was intensified, as Aviateca became a member of Gruppo TACA, which is building up a network of airline operations in South and Central America. The aircraft livery was changed accordingly to reflect membership of the group. The airline is also a member of the Latin Pass marketing alliance in which most of the region's airlines participate to try to counterbalance the US airlines. The airline's base is at Guatemala - La Aurora, and there is a subsidiary company, Inter, which operates Cessna Grand Caravans on domestic services.

Routes

Cancun, Dallas/Fort Worth, Flores, Managua, Merida, Mexico City, Miami, New Orleans, Panama, San Jose, San Salvador.

Fleet

5 Boeing 737-200

Tupolev Tu-154B-1 4K-85192 (Author's collection/Moscow)

AZERBAIJAN AIRLINES

Bina Airport, 370109 Baku, Azerbaijan
Tel. 243714, Fax. 254466
www.azal.az

Three- / Two- letter code	IATA No.	Reg'n prefix	ICAO callsign
AHY / J2	771	4K	Azal

In 1992 the government of the new republic of Azerbaijan in Baku brought into being the Azerbaijan Airline Concern, organised in three divisions. Azal Avia is responsible for passenger transport; it is the national flag carrier and flies under the name of Azerbaijan Airlines. The Soviet-built aircraft were taken over from the former Aeroflot division, and some older western aircraft, Boeing 707s and 727s, were also acquired. The Tupolev Tu-134s and 154s will be phased out slowly and preparations have been made for the introduction of the Boeing 757, which were due for delivery from the middle of 2000 especially for use on routes to central Europe. Further development of the company however is dependent on the country's political situation. At the end of the 1990s a re-organisation was carried out, and some of the older An-26s, and several Tu-134s and 154s were retired. International oil companies have been granted licences in the region, and Azerbaijan Airlines is benefiting from the resulting increased traffic. Two Boeing 757-200s were acquired on lease in mid-2000.

Routes

Adana, Aleppo, Aktau, Ankara, Baku, Bishkek, Chelyabinsk, Dubai, Frankfurt, Istanbul, Kiev, London, Moscow, St. Petersburg, Teheran, Tel Aviv, Trabzon, Voronezh, Yekaterinburg.

Fleet

2 Boeing 727-200
2 Boeing 757-200
10 Tupolev Tu-134B
10 Tupolev Tu-154B/M

9 Yakovlev Yak-40

Boeing 737-275 C6-BGL (Josef Krauthäuser/Fort Lauderdale)

BAHAMASAIR

P.O. Box N4881 Nassau, Bahamas,
Tel. 3778451, Fax. 3778550,
www.bahamasair.com

Three- / Two- letter code	IATA No.	Reg'n prefix	ICAO callsign
BHS / UP	111	C6	Bahamas

Bahamasair was established on 18th June 1973, just prior to Bahamian independence from Britain, and immediately took over the domestic routes of Out Island Airways and the domestic routes of Flamingo Airlines to become the national airline. Among the early aircraft used were HS.748s and BAC One-Elevens. Bahamasair's main routes are those from Nassau and Freetown and Miami in Florida, only 45 minutes flying time away. The One-Elevens were replaced from 1976 by three Boeing 737-200s from 1976, and two Boeing 727-200s followed for routes to New York and Boston. There was close co-operation with Eastern Airlines, before the US airline collapsed. Several of the older HS.748s were replaced by more modern de Havilland Canada DHC-8s from 1990, with the last 748 leaving in 1996. The use of jet aircraft, and their maintenance costs, proved to be too expensive, and as a result, in 1992 Bahamasair took all the jets out of service and replaced them with turboprops. However, this move left the significant market to the east of the USA open to its competitors, until in 1995 it was again decided to lease a Boeing 737. During 1997 two further 737s were added, and these operate flights several times a day to Miami, Orlando and Fort Lauderdale.The Shorts 360s were acquired between 1995 and 1997 and are used for shorter range trips within the Bahamas.

Routes

Andros Town, Arthurs Town, Bimini, Crooked Island, Deadmanns Cay, Fort Lauderdale, Freeport, George Town, Governors Harbour, Grand Turk, Inagua, Mangrove Cay, Marsh Harbour, Miami, Nassau, North Eulethera, Orlando, Providenciales, Rock Sound, San Andros, Stella Maris, Treasure Cay, West Palm Beach.

Fleet

3 Boeing 737-200
6 De Havilland DHC-8-300
3 Shorts 360-200

Boeing 737-3Y0 LZ-BOD (Author's Collection)

BALKAN

Vrajdebna Airport Sofia 1540, Bulgaria
Tel. 02661690, Fax. 02723496,
www.balkan.com

Three- / Two- letter code	IATA No.	Reg'n prefix	ICAO callsign
LAZ / LZ	196	LZ	Balkan

The formation of Balkan-Bulgarian Air Transport goes back to 29th June 1947, when BVS-Bulgarske Vazdusne Sobsternic was set up. This airline served only a few domestic destinations up to 1949, when, with 50/50 participation from the Soviet Union, a new company was created - TABSO. The first international service, between Sofia and Budapest was operated on 12th September 1949. Lisunov Li-2s and Ilyushin IL-14s served Paris, Frankfurt and Moscow. During 1954, the Soviet shareholding in TABSO was passed over to the Bulgarian state. The four-turboprop Ilyushin IL-18 came into service in 1962; the type must be familiar to many holidaymakers on the shores of the Black Sea, as it was particularly used for these charters. 1968 saw the change of name to that used today and the acquisition of the first Tupolev Tu-134, with the larger Tu-154 following in 1972. During 1987, to the surprise of many, the fleet was given a modern colour scheme, and in the Autumn of 1990 came the first Western aircraft type, a Boeing 737-500. The fleet and service are being increasingly brought up to Western standards: thus Airbus 320s and Boeing 767s were brought into use for a while, though the well-proven Russian types continue in some numbers. Business difficulties however made it necessary to make large reductions in the fleet and routes and after privatisation in 1999 an Israeli investor group, Zeevi, took over 75% of the shares. The airline's prospects should be improved by the delivery at the end of 1999 and in early 2000 of new Boeing 737-300s, again in a new colour scheme, and for regional services the first ATR 42s are replacing An-24s from mid-2000. It is planned that four more 737s, two each in 2001 and 2002, will replace the last of the Soviet types still used on charter work from Bourgas and Varna.

Routes

Amsterdam, Athens, Berlin, Bourgas, Brussels, Budapest, Cairo, Copenhagen, Dubai, Frankfurt, Helsinki, Istanbul, Kiev, Larnaca, London, Madrid, Milan, Male, Moscow, Paris, Prague, Rome, Stockholm, Tel Aviv, Tripoli, Varna, Warsaw, Vienna, Zürich.

Fleet

4 Antonov An-12	3 Boeing 737-500
6 Antonov An-24B	12 Tupolev Tu-154
3 ATR 42	
2 Boeing 737-300	

ATR 42-202 HS-PGG (Romano Germann/Koh Samui)

BANGKOK AIR

140 Pacific Place Building, Sukhumvit Road,
Bangkok 10110, Thailand, Tel. 2-2538352,
Fax. 2-2534005, www.bkkair.co.th

Three- / Two- letter code	IATA No.	Reg'n prefix	ICAO callsign
BKP / PG	829	HS	Bangkok Air

Set up in 1985 by the owner of Sahakol Air, an air-taxi company which had been formed in 1968 to operate between Bangkok and the tourist resorts of Samui Island and other points, Bangkok Airways started operations with an Embraer Bandeirante in January 1986. A Piper PA-31 Navajo was used also, though the company was still licensed only as an air-taxi operator and flew tourists to smaller resorts. An order for two Saab 340As was announced in September 1986 but did not come to fruition. During 1989 and 1990 however the fleet was augmented with the delivery of the de Havilland DHC-8 and a

scheduled service licence was granted. The Dash 8s were replaced during 1994/95 with two ATR 72s. In addition Shorts 360s were used on services to the smaller island airports. Permission was forthcoming in 1992 for the first international route, to Phnom Penh, and in 1993 for the first time Mandalay in neighbouring Myanmar was served. Further ATR 72s and ATR 42s strengthened the fleet as passenger numbers grew, and Bangkok Air was fortunate in not being badly affected by the Asian business crisis. Two Boeing 717s have been ordered for delivery in November 2000 and March 2001,

with two more planned for 2003 and it has also been agreed that by 2003 the existing ATR fleet will all have been rolled over in favour of 12 new ATR 72-500s. The airline's home base is at Don Muang Domestic Airport in Bangkok.

Routes

Bangkok, Chiangmai, Hua Hin, Koh Samui, Phnom Penh, Phuket, Ranong, Siem Reap, Singapore, Sukhothai, Utapao.

Fleet	Ordered
1 ATR 42	2 Boeing 717
8 ATR 72-200	

McDonnell Douglas DC-8-71F N826BX (Josef Krauthäuser/Fort Lauderdale)

BAX GLOBAL

16808 Armstrong, Irvine, California 92714, USA
Tel. 714-7524000, Fax. 714-8521488,
www.baxworld.com

Three- / Two- letter code	IATA No.	Reg'n prefix	ICAO callsign
BUR / 8W	–	N	–

This undertaking was founded in 1971 as Burlington Air Express and specialises in the express transport of all kinds of freight, and offering customers a complete logistical service. The key to success here is in having one's own delivery organisation. Consideration to having an in-house airline operation had been given for some years, as competitors such as DHL, Federal Express and UPS were already owning their own aircraft. Thus from 1985 Boeing 707s and DC-8-62/63s started to appear in the colours of Burlington Air Express, though in truth the company had shied away from forming its own air operation, and instead was leasing aircraft and crews from Southern Air Transport (707) or Rosenbalm Aviation (DC-8). As well as operating its own schedules, some ad hoc freight flights were carried out. Over the years the size of the fleet grew amd Boeing 727s, and other operators of these aircraft, were introduced. In 1998 the company, which by now had changed its name to BAX-Global, acquired ATI- Air Transport International which already operated several DC-8s for Burlington/BAX. This freight operator continues to operate DC-8s for BAX in their colours, as well as conducting its own operations (see page 86).

Routes

Around 80 destinations are served on a regular basis in the USA, Canada and Mexico.

Fleet

3 Boeing 727-200
7 McDonnell Douglas DC-8-62F/63F
11 McDonnell Douglas DC-8-71F

Ilyushin IL-76TD EW-76836 (Oliver Köstinger/Sharjah)

BELAIR

5 Kortkevicha, 222039 Minsk, Belarus
Tel. 225702, Fax. 225045

Three- / Two- letter code	IATA No.	Reg'n prefix	ICAO callsign
BLI	–	EW	Air Belarus

BELAIR - Belarussian Airlines, as it is also known (though not to be confused with state-owned Belavia - Belarussian Airlines, for details of which please see page 124), was the first private airline set up in Belarus and was founded in 1992. It is based in Minsk and operated regional routes from there using Yakovlev Yak-40s. However its main activity is in operating cargo flights, being the only way for the country to earn money or foreign currency from flying. Thus Belair flies charters for other airlines, including Western companies, to Western Europe and the Middle East, where Sharjah is a very regular destination. Two Tupolev Tu-134s were leased from 1996 for use on passenger charter work.

Routes

Regional routes and charter flights, ad hoc and subcharters.

Fleet

2 Ilyushin IL-76TD
2 Tupolev Tu-134A
1 Yakovlev Yak-40

Tupolev Tu-154B-2 EW-85538 (Dennis Wehrmann/Hanover)

BELAVIA-BELARUSSIAN AIRLINES

Ul. Neminga 14, 220004 Minsk
Belarus
Tel. 2791792, Fax. 2791742

Three- / Two- letter code	IATA No.	Reg'n prefix	ICAO callsign
BRU / B2	628	EW	Belarus Avia

A new national airline for Belarus was formed in November 1993; Belavia took over the aircraft, assets and routes of the former Aeroflot Directorate, as happened in other former Soviet republics, and continued its services. It was only much later that businesslike thinking and practices came to be applied, as financial resources were now much more limited. With many services into western and northern Europe, the airline tried to earn as much foreign currency as possible. The standards of service and reliability of the fleet were important marketing considerations and co-operation with western partners showed success after only a few years. A modernisation of the fleet is planned over time, with new Russian equipment such as the Tupolev Tu-204 and Ilyushin IL-114 being considered as well as western types.

Routes

Adler, Astana, Beijing, Berlin, Chelyabinsk, Frankfurt, Istanbul, Karaganda, Kiev, Krasnodar, Larnaca, London, Minsk, Moscow, Novosibirsk, Prague, Rome, Samara, Shannon, Stockholm, Tashkent, Tbilisi, Tel Aviv, Vienna, Warsaw, Yekaterinburg.

Fleet

 5 Antonov An-24
 3 Antonov An-26B
 9 Tupolev Tu-134
15 Tupolev Tu-154

2 Yakovlev Yak-40

McDonnell Douglas DC-10-30 S2-ACP (Josef Krauthäuser/Amsterdam)

BIMAN BANGLADESH

100 Motijheel Commercial Aera, Dhaka 1000
People's Republic of Bangladesh, Tel. 9560151,
Fax. 863005, www.bangladeshonline.com/biman/

Three- / Two- letter code	IATA No.	Reg'n prefix	ICAO callsign
BBC / BG	997	S2	Bangladesh

After Bangladesh split away from Pakistan, a new state airline was set up on 4th January 1972 to represent the state of Bangladesh (formerly East Pakistan) to the outside world. Flights started on 4th February 1972 with scheduled services to Chittagong and several other domestic points using a Douglas DC-3 leased from the Bangladesh Air Force. The DC-3 was soon replaced by Fokker F.27s. The first international flights were between Dhaka and and Calcutta. From January 1973 scheduled flights to London began, using two leased Boeing 707s. Two Fokker F.28s were added to the fleet in 1981, and the Boeing 707s left the fleet when DC-10-30s arrived from Singapore Airlines in 1983. In August 1990 the first BAe ATP was introduced to update the regional fleet, and in 1996 two Airbus A310s were acquired, principally for use on Asian services. The ATPs and a DC-10 left the fleet in 1998. The intention is that the other DC-10s are to be replaced with either Airbus A340-300s or Boeing 777-200ERs in due course.The government is intending to sell 40% of the shares in Biman to other airlines by the end of 2000 and hope to obtain stronger management and better co-operation in doing so. In order to motivate the employees, they are also to receive 9% of the shares.

Routes

Abu Dhabi, Bahrain, Bangkok, Brussels, Calcutta, Chittagong, Cox's Bazaar, Dhaka, Delhi, Dubai, Doha, Frankfurt, Hong Kong, Jeddah, Jessore, Karachi, Kathmandu, Kuala Lumpur, Kuwait, London, Mumbai, Muscat, New York, Paris, Rajshahi, Riyadh, Rome, Saidpur, Singapore, Tokyo, Yangon.

Fleet

3 Airbus A310-300
2 Fokker F.28
5 McDonnell Douglas DC-10-30

ATR 72-202 EC-EUJ (Stefan Schlick/Arrecife)

BINTER CANARIAS

Aeropuerto de Gran Canaria, P.O.B.50, 35230
Telde, Gran Canaria, Spain, Tel. 928-579601,
Fax. 928-579604, www.irinfo.es/aviacion/binter.html

Three- / Two- letter code	IATA No.	Reg'n prefix	ICAO callsign
IBB / NT	138	EC	Canarias

In January 1988, Iberia, Spain's state airline, set up Binter Canarias in order to reorganise regional Spanish flights to the Canary Isles from mainland Spain, previously operated by Aviaco. The brief hops to the islands were uneconomic for Iberia's jets and so in mid-1988 Binter Canarias started operations with a CASA CN-235. Later in the same year, another aircraft was required, with two more in Spring 1989, followed by the first ATR 42s in the Autumn of that year. However, the latter were only used for a short time before being replaced with the larger ATR 72. For a new route from Tenerife to Funchal on Madeira DC-

9-32 jets were leased from the parent company, and these were also used on other routes. After various reorganisations within the Iberia group, Binter since 1999 is again concentrating on those tasks for which it was set up - flights between the Canary Isles - and uses only ATR 72s.

Routes

Binter Canarias maintains scheduled services within the Canary Isles, thus Lanzarote, Tenerife, Gran Canaria, Fuerteventura and La Palma.

Fleet

10 ATR 72-200
1 ATR 72-500

Boeing 737-230 PK-IJI (Björn Kannengiesser/Jakarta)

BOURAQ AIRLINES

P.O.Box 2965, Jalan Angkasa 1-3,
Jakarta Pusat 10720, Indonesia
Tel. 21-655289, Fax. 21-6298651

Three- / Two- letter code	IATA No.	Reg'n prefix	ICAO callsign
BOU / BO	666	PK	Bouraq

PT Bouraq Indonesian Airlines is a private company founded in the middle of 1970. With three Douglas DC-3s it flew from Jakarta to Banjarmasin, Balikpapan and Surabaya. In the following year it was able to re-equip with turboprops in the form of the NAMC YS-11. Britten-Norman Islanders were used to provide services to destinations well away from the main cities, mostly where only grass strips were available. Later came Fokker Friendships, Dornier Do 28s and HS.748s, and the Vickers Viscount replaced the DC-3s from 1980. The tasks for the airline were many and varied and freight and charter flights were also undertaken, including some to Malaysia, Thailand and to Manila. In 1973 Bouraq founded a subsidiary company Bali Air, which established its own network using aircraft provided by the parent company. As the turboprop fleet was showing its age, the transition to jets is slowly being made. The Boeing 737-200 was used for the first time in 1993, with further examples added in 1994 and 1995. There is a co-operation agreement with Philippine Airlines. The Asian business downturn of the late 1990s brought expansion plans to an abrupt end. Bouraq was obliged to drop some routes and to shrink its fleet , with several aircraft being taken out of service and sold.

Routes

Balikpapan, Bandung, Banjarmasin, Batu Besar, Berau, Denpasar, Jakarta, Manado, Medan, Palembang, Palu, Pangkalpinang, Pontianak, Samarinda, Semarang, Surabaya, Tarakan, Tawau, Ujung Pandang, Yogyakarta.

Fleet

5 BAe HS.748
7 Boeing 737-200

Boeing 737-405 LN-BRI (Florian Morasch/Innsbruck)

BRAATHENS

Okseneyveien 3, 1330 Oslo, Norway
Tel. 67-597000, Fax. 67-591309,
www.braathens.no

Three- / Two- letter code	IATA No.	Reg'n prefix	ICAO callsign
BRA / BU	154	LN	Braathens

Ludvig G Braathen, a Norwegian ship owner, formed his airline, Braathens South America and Far East Air Transport on 26th March 1946 and began operations with Douglas DC-4s. As is apparent from the name, the airline operated charters to South America and Hong Kong. On 5th August 1949 a scheduled service from Oslo via Amsterdam-Cairo-Basra-Karachi-Bombay-Calcutta-Bangkok to Hong Kong was introduced, but the route was taken over by SAS in April 1954. From 1952 a route network was also built up in Norway, at first with de Havilland Herons and from 1958 with Fokker F.27s. The first jet aircraft, Boeing 737s came in 1969; the F.27s and Douglas DC-6s were replaced by Fokker F.28s. During 1984 Braathens took on its first widebody, a Boeing 767, but it was sold again because it was not being well-enough used. The introduction of the new Boeing 737-400/500 models provided Braathens with a very modern and homogeneous fleet, which is kept updated. Each year Braathens carries as many passengers as the entire population of Norway, about 4.5 million. In 1997 KLM acquired a 30% holding in Braathens S.A.F.E. In the later part of 1997 competitor Transwede was bought, and this then operated as Braathens Sweden. A further acquisition in 1998 was Malmö Aviation. With the delivery of the first of the new Boeing 737-700s in April 1998, Braathens adopted a new corporate identity, dropping the old 'S.A.F.E.' suffix. The main bases are at Oslo and Stavanger, where there is also a maintenance facility.

Routes

Alesund, Alicante, Amsterdam, Bergen, Billund, Bodo, Evenes, Gothenburg, Halmstad, Harstadt/Narvik, Haugesund, Jonköping, Kristiansand, Kristiansund, London, Longyearbyen, Lulea, Malaga, Molde, Murmansk, Newcastle, Oslo, Roros, Stavanger, Stockholm, Svalbard, Tromsö, Trondheim, Umea. Charter flights in Europe.

Fleet	Ordered
5 Boeing 737-400	6 Boeing 737-500
24 Boeing 737-500	2 Boeing 737-700
10 Boeing 737-700	

Boeing 757-204 G-BYAT (Dieter Roth/Salzburg)

BRITANNIA AIRWAYS

Luton Airport,Bedfordshire LU2 9ND,
Great Britain, Tel. 1582-424155,
Fax. 1582-458594, www.britanniaairways.com

Three- / Two- letter code	IATA No.	Reg'n prefix	ICAO callsign
BAL / BY	754	G	Britannia

From modest beginnings, Britannia has grown into the largest charter airline in the world. On 1st December 1961 Euravia (London) was set up, and it started operations on 5th May 1962 with an L-1049 Constellation under contract to Universal Sky Tours, then the principal shareholder. When a Bristol Britannia 102 was commissioned on 6th December 1964, the present name for the airline was also adopted. The Thomson Organisation, one of the larger tour operators, took over the company on 26th April 1965, and Boeing 707s were used for charter flights to Hong Kong, Kuala Lumpur and other long-range destinations, but the airline withdrew from long distance work from 1973 to 1985, as the Boeing 737, the sole type in the fleet for many years, was not suited. Boeing 757s and the larger 767, the first of which was delivered in February 1984, restored this capability. In 1988 Orion Airways was bought when Thomson's acquired its parent company, Horizon Travel, and six Boeing 737-300s were integrated. With the delivery of more 757s the number of 737s, which had totalled 34 in 1989, was reduced, until the last one left the fleet in 1994. During 1997 Britannia established a German subsidiary; Britannia Deutschland uses four 767s on long-range tour flights from several German airports. Likewise in Sweden in 1998 tour operator Fritidsresor and its airline Blue Scandinavia were taken over and this now flies as Britannia AB. In order to be able to offer smaller aircraft, Airbus 320s were leased for the 1999 season, and from Spring 2000 the Boeing 737 is back, with the latest model -800s added to the fleet. In May 2000 parent company Thomson accepted a takeover offer from the German concern Preussag at around £1.8 billion; when this is implemented it will result in some realignment of tour airline business.

Routes

Worldwide charter flights from about 25 airports in Great Britain, Germany and Scandinavia to the Caribbean, Australia, New Zealand, USA, within Europe and to Africa.

Fleet		Ordered
3 Boeing 737-800	9 Boeing 767-300ER	2 Boeing 737-800
5 Boeing 757-200 ER		
18 Boeing 757-200		
6 Boeing 767-200ER		

Boeing 757-236 G-BIKR (Dennis Wehrmann/Hanover)

BRITISH AIRWAYS

P.O.Box 365, Harmondsworth, UB7 0GB
Great Britain, Tel. 2087595511,
Fax. 2085620788, www.britishairways.com

Three- / Two- letter code	IATA No.	Reg'n prefix	ICAO callsign
BAW / BA	125	G	Speedbird

British Airways is the result of the amalgamation on 1st April 1972 of BEA and BOAC, after a government decision to bring British aviation interests under state ownership. The predecessors of British Airways can be traced back to the founding of Imperial Airways after the First World War. Until 1974 BEA and BOAC were still apparently operating separately; the merger became visible on the aircraft during 1974. The activities of the new BA were organised into seven divisions, for example BA Helicopters. In 1988 the second largest, privately-owned, airline, British Caledonian was taken over, after British Airways had been partly privatised in 1984. A major re-equipment programme was begun in 1989, with the aim of replacing older aircraft with a more homogeneous fleet. During 1992 and 1993 British Airways often made the headlines. First it acquired a stake in US Air, then in the Australian airline Qantas and in the French airline TAT, in Air Mauritius and set up Deutsche BA. For the symbolic amount of one pound, Gatwick-based airline Dan Air with

its routes and aircraft was taken over. Individual profit centres were created in 1993, and thus came about the regional operations BA-Manchester and BA-Birmingham. In 1995 British Asia Airways was formed for operations to Taiwan. German internal operations including Berlin services were passed over to Deutsche BA. On 11th November 1995 BA received its first Boeing 777, signalling the start of replacement of some of the older examples from the extensive 747 fleet. During this year also BA began building Gatwick up as a second major base. The later part of the 1990s was also noteworthy for BA's moves towards franchised operations for shorter-haul services. Brymon Airways, City Flyer Express (both now fully owned), GB Airways, Maersk, Loganair and Manx Airlines (the latter two now merged as British Regional Airlines) all participate in these arrangements, which have also been extended outside to South Africa, where Comair is a partner. Air Liberté and TAT in France were also acquired and merged, and operated in BA

colours, but proved loss-making and was sold to SAir in 2000. A major agreement with American Airlines was planned to lead to a merger, but regulatory difficulties obstructed this for so long that it is now on ice; however, the co-operation is strong and is the cornerstone of the expanding Oneworld alliance. A spectacular development in mid-1997 was the introduction of the controversial new colours, with tailfins decorated in artworks from various countries; however from mid-1999 all new aircraft are again being painted in the Union Flag variant only. During 1998 BA not only completed its acquisition of franchise partner City Flyer Express, but also set up a low-cost subsidiary Go Fly, based at Stansted. Fleet plans for the future were signalled by large orders for the Airbus 318/319/320, which will more or less replace the 737s and 757s, while Boeings, especially 777s will predominate on long-range routes. During Summer 2000, talks were in progress for a possible merger with KLM, but these were called off in September.

BRITISH AIRWAYS FRANCHISE PARTNERS

British Mediterranean
4 Airbus A320

British Regional Airlines
12 BAe Jetstream 41
10 BAe ATP
3 BAe 146-200
17 Embraer RJ-145

Brymon Airways
18 DHC-8
4 Embraer RJ-145EP

Comair (South Africa)
6 Boeing 737-200
4 Boeing 727-200

GB Airways
1 Airbus A320
4 Boeing 737-300
5 Boeing 737-400

Loganair
5 BN-2B Islander
3 Shorts 360
3 Saab 340B

Maersk Air (GB)
8 Canadair RJ-200
5 Boeing 737-500

Sun Air (Denmark)
6 BAe Jetstream 31
3 BAe ATP

British Regional Airlines EMB-145 G-EMBC
(Albert Kuhbandner/Zürich)

Brymon Airways de Havilland DHC-8-300 G-BRYV
(Albert Kuhbandner/Paris-CDG)

Maersk Air Canadair RJ G-MSKN (Josef Krauthäuser/Munich)

Routes

British Airways flies worldwide to over 160 destinations, or over 255 including those served by franchise partners.

Sun Air BAe Jetstream 31 OY-SVS (Dennis Wehrmann/Billund)

Fleet

		Ordered
10 Airbus A320	11 Boeing 737-200	12 Airbus A318
13 Airbus A319	7 Boeing 737-300	32 Airbus A319
7 AS/BAe Concorde	37 Boeing 737-400	20 Airbus A320
26 Boeing 767-300	5 Boeing 737-500	14 Boeing 777
58 Boeing 747-400	52 Boeing 757-200	
13 Boeing 747-200	35 Boeing 777	

Airbus A321-231 G-MIDF (Martin Bach/London-LHR)

BRITISH MIDLAND

Donington Hall, Castle Donington, Derbyshire
DE74 2SB, Great Britain, Tel. 1332-854000,
Fax. 1332-854662, www.britishmidland.co.uk

Three- / Two- letter code	IATA No.	Reg'n prefix	ICAO callsign
BMA / BD	236	G	Midland

Originally set up as a flying school in 1938, the airline operation was founded in 1947 as Derby Aviation and changed to Derby Airways in 1953, and then British Midland in July 1964. Schedules were flown from Derby, Birmingham and Manchester, using DC-3s, Handley Page Heralds, BAC 1-11s, Vickers Viscounts and Boeing 707s. In 1965 the airline moved base from Derby to the new East Midlands Airport, which is still the main base and maintenance centre. In addition to scheduled services and charters, in the 1970s BMA was also successful with aircraft leasing. Bought in 1968 by an investment group, it became privately owned again in 1978 under present managing director Michael Bishop, and has flourished since then. British Midland is a main shareholder in Manx Airlines and Loganair; the Airlines of Britain Group, formed in 1987 and in which SAS had a 40% stake, acts as holding company for all three airlines. The retirement of the DC-9 fleet came with the delivery of the Fokker 100 in April 1994 and the Fokker 70 a year later, but the desired total of these types could not be met because of Fokker's collapse. Backbone of the fleet was therefore the Boeing 737, flying mainly from Heathrow, where BMA is a major operator, but fleet additions since 1998 have concentrated on the Airbus A320/321. By taking over Aberdeen-based Business Air, British Midland Commuter was created, and this subsidiary now operates a fleet of Embraer 145s, BAe 146s and Saab 340s, partially on behalf of the parent. In 1997 the Airlines of Britain Group was reorganised and renamed British Midland; Lufthansa replaced SAS as a major investor and became an important partner, with British Midland becoming part of the Star Alliance in July 2000. A330s are on order to resume long-distance services from April 2001.

Routes

Aberdeen, Amsterdam, Belfast, Birmingham, Bristol, Brussels, Budapest, Cardiff, Dublin, Edinburgh, Esbjerg, Faro, Glasgow, Guernsey, Humberside, Jersey, Leeds/Bradford, Liverpool, London-Heathrow, Malaga, Munich, Nice, Palma de Mallorca, Paris, Prague, Teesside,Warsaw.

Fleet

4 Airbus A320	12 Boeing 737-500
10 Airbus A321	3 Fokker 70
9 Boeing 737-300	6 Fokker 100
4 Boeing 737-400	

Ordered

6 Airbus A320
1 Airbus A321
4 Airbus A330-200

BAe ATP G-OBWM (Uwe Gleisberg/Munich)

BRITISH WORLD AIRLINES

Viscount House, Southend Airport, Essex SS2 6YL, Great Britain, Tel. 1702-354435, Fax. 1702-331914, www.britishworld.co.uk

Three- / Two- letter code	IATA No.	Reg'n prefix	ICAO callsign
BWL / VF	762	G	Britworld

British United Air Ferries Ltd. was set up at Southend in January 1963, as a result of a merger between Silver City Airways (formed in 1948) and Channel Air Bridge (established as Air Charter in 1954). The airline became well known for its ferry services with Carvair aircraft. Cars were loaded through a large front door, while the passengers also boarded and flew from England to France, Belgium and the Netherlands. Handley Page Heralds were used for charter services, for which larger Vickers Viscounts were also added. In September 1967 the company changed name to British Air Ferries, was purchased by the Keegan family in 1971, and then by Jadepoint in March 1983. During the 1980s it was involved in worldwide aircraft leasing, contract and flight support and tour group charter activities. In the late 1980s there were financial problems and a further change of ownership, but recovered and took on its present name in 1993, with an attractive new colour scheme. The main operating base is at Stansted, but with centres also at Aberdeen and Southend. British World's activities are varied and extensive, and include flying schedules on behalf of other airlines, charter flights, freight services, and North Sea oil support work. For the latter in 1996 two ATR 72s were acquired as replacements for the last Vickers Viscounts in the fleet and used on the Aberdeen-Sumburgh route, but they have now been replaced in turn by BAe ATPs, of which a small fleet is being built up. The BAC One-Elevens are being replaced by Boeing 737-300s, of which the first two arrived during the first half of 2000. In 1998 the company was floated on the London stock exchange.

Routes

Charter flights in Great Britain and Europe. Domestic freight and postal services.

Fleet

5 BAC 1-11-500
6 BAe ATP
3 Boeing 737-300

133

Douglas DC-4 C-GPSH (Romano Germann/Yellowknife)

BUFFALO AIRWAYS

P.O.Box 1479, Hay River,
NW Territories X0E 0R9, Canada,
Tel. 867-8743333, Fax. 867-8743572

Three- / Two- letter code	IATA No.	Reg'n prefix	ICAO callsign
BFL / J4	–	C	Buffalo

This Northern Canadian company was founded in 1959 in Fort Smith. Its principal field of operations is in supply flights in the North West Territories and the Yukon. Several helicopters and smaller aircraft types were used. However the ideal aircraft for most of these varied tasks is the ubiquitous Douglas DC-3, built around 1942, and brought into service here in 1979. At the beginning of the 1980s a regional scheduled service was begun, serving Hay River, Uranium City and Chipewyan. The DC-3s are operated with wheeled undercarriages in Summer and on skis in the Winter, an advantage of one of the few aircraft of this size which can be used to such remote and snow-covered places.Over the course of time, and following the relocation of the company to its present base at Hay River, further DC-3s and the larger DC-4 were added to the fleet, along with another veteran, the Curtiss C-46 Commando. Not surprisingly, Hay River is now a place of pilgrimage for propliner enthusiasts. Aerial firefighting duties are also undertaken, using four specialist Canadair CL-215 fire-bombers, on behalf of the North West Territories government as the first line of defence against forest fires.

Routes

Schedules to Yellowknife, and ad hoc, charter, freight and special flights in the region.

Fleet

```
 2 Curtiss C-46 Commando
10 Douglas DC-3/C-47
 4 Douglas DC-4/C-54
 1 Noorduyn Norseman
 4 Canadair CL-215
```

BAe 146-300 G-UKAC (Jan-Alexander Lück/Hamburg)

BUZZ

Endeavour House, Stansted Essex CM24 1RS
Great Britain, Tel. 1279-660400,
www.buzzaway.com

Three- / Two- letter code	IATA No.	Reg'n prefix	ICAO callsign
BUZ / UK	–	G	Buzz

London's Stansted airport is developing as a centre for low-fare airlines. Following EasyJet, Ryanair and Go, Buzz began its cheap services to the continent on 4th January 2000. Preparations for the launch of the airline had taken barely a year. KLM UK, already based at Stansted, decided to set up its own low-fare operation at the end of 1998. Much of what is on offer is comparable with the other low-fare operators, but some things are different with Buzz. Only major airports are served directly; no secondary or provincial airports. Also it is possible to buy extras from Buzz; for instance to order and pay for meals and drinks during the flights. Eight BAe 146s from KLM UK formed the initial fleet; they were painted in a very striking new colour scheme, whose banana yellow is strongly reminiscent of the former Hughes Air West airline in the USA. At first twelve destinations were served, but this is planned to be up to 20 by mid-2001, by which time the fleet should comprise 15 aircraft. In February 2000 two Boeing 737-300s were added and used on the longer-range routes to Vienna and Helsinki; in both of these cities Buzz is the first low-cost operator to introduce services.

Routes

Berlin, Bordeaux, Düsseldorf, Frankfurt, Hamburg, Helsinki, Jerez de la Frontera, London-Stansted, Lyon, Milan, Marseilles, Montpellier, Paris Charles de Gaulle, Toulouse, Vienna.

Fleet

8 BAe 146-300
2 Boeing 737-300

Boeing 737-8Q8 9Y-GEO (Christofer Witt/ Miami)

BWIA WEST INDIES AIRWAYS

Administration Buildg. Intl. Airport Port of Spain, Trinidad and Tobago, Tel. 809-6693000, Fax. 809-6643540, www.bwee.com

Three- / Two- letter code	IATA No.	Reg'n prefix	ICAO callsign
BWA / BW	106	9Y	West Indian

BWIA began operations on 17th November 1940 with a Lockheed Lodestar between Trinidad and Barbados. Two further Lodestars were added in 1942 and charters were begun for US military personnel. In 1947 BWIA was sold to BSAA, but a new airline with the old 'BWIA' name was set up in 1948. Five Vickers Vikings were used to serve almost all the major Caribbean islands. In June 1949 BSAA was merged into BOAC, thus BWIA became a BOAC subsidiary and took over some routes and aircraft. Four Vickers Viscounts were added in 1955 and in 1960 leased Bristol Britannias were first used to fly to

London via New York. In 1961 the government of Trinidad and Tobago bought back 90% of the shares from BOAC, and the final 10% in 1967. BWIA used Boeing 727s for the first time to Miami in 1965, replacing the Viscounts. On 14th December 1968, Boeing 707s were first used on the New York route; flights to London-Heathrow started in 1975. A merger with Trinidad and Tobago Air Services, brought a change of name to BWIA International. The first Lockheed TriStar arrived in Trinidad on 29th January 1980. In 1994 the company was part-privatised, with the Acker Group and local investors participating; along with this went a

fundamental reorganisation. Routes were dropped, with London the only European destination to survive. Aircraft procurement policy was strange: new Boeing 757s and 767s were ordered, to replace the predominantly MD-83 fleet, but dropped in favour of A340s and A321s; the 340s were cancelled and only the 321s arrived and operated only very briefly from late 1996. Eventually 737-800s were chosen, with deliveries from December 1999. Early in 1999 received two DHC-8s for its new regional division BWee Express and later in the year there were more management changes and a new colour scheme.

Routes

Antigua, Barbados, Caracas, Georgetown, Grenada, Kingston, London, Miami, New York, Port of Spain, St. Kitts, St. Lucia, St. Maarten, Tobago, Toronto.

Fleet	Ordered
4 Boeing 737-800	2 Boeing 737-800
2 De Havilland DHC-8Q	
4 Lockheed L-1011-500	
5 McDonnell Douglas MD-83	

Boeing 737-3Q8 TJ-CBF (Bastian Hilker/Harare)

CAMEROON AIRLINES

BP 4092, Ave. General de Gaulle,
Douala, Cameroon
Tel. 4-24949, Fax. 4-33543

Three- / Two- letter code	IATA No.	Reg'n prefix	ICAO callsign
UYC / UY	604	TJ	Camair

Cameroon Airlines was set up on 26th July 1971 by the Cameroon government in order to be in a position to withdraw from the multinational airline Air Afrique; its interest in the consortium ended on 2nd September 1971. In setting up the new national airline, the privately-owned Air Cameroun and its regional network was also taken over. Operations began in November 1971 with flights between Douala and Yaounde, using Boeing 737s. A Boeing 707 was acquired from Air France for long-distance services and was used to Paris via Rome. In 1982 it was replaced by the airline's sole widebody, a Boeing 747. With its own maintenance and base facilities in Douala, Cameroon Airlines has the necessary infrastructure to look after its own aircraft. New Boeing 737-300s were introduced between August 1997 and October 1998, allowing the older 737-200s to be retired and the fleet thus modernised. Air France now owns just 4% of the capital; the rest remains with the government. There is close co-operation with Nigeria Airways, Air Affretaires Afrique, Air France, Air Gabon and Oman Air.

Routes

Abidjan, Brazzaville, Cotonou, Douala, Garoua, Harare, Jeddah, Johannesburg, Kigali, Kinshasa, Lagos, Libreville, London, Malabo, Maroua, Nairobi, N'Djamena, Ngaoundere, Paris, Yaounde.

Fleet

1 BAe HS.748
3 Boeing 737-300
1 Boeing 747-200

Airbus A330-202 C-GGWB (Dennis Wehrmann/Amsterdam)

CANADA 3000 AIRLINES

27 Fasken Drive, Toronto Ontario M9W 1K6, Canada, Tel. 416-6740257, Fax. 416-6740256, www.canada3000.com

Three- / Two- letter code	IATA No.	Reg'n prefix	ICAO callsign
CMM / 2T	570	C	Elite

Founded in 1988 as Air 2000 Airline Ltd., a subsidiary of the British airline Air 2000, the airline suffered suspension of its licence by the Canadian Ministry of Transport a few days before operations were due to commence. The reason for this was massive objections on the part of other airlines in Canada at foreign ownership. Consequently, local investors took over the British shares and logically enough the name was changed to the present one. Operations started in 1989 using Boeing 757s leased from Air 2000. The airline is based in Toronto, but also operates from Vancouver on the west coast,

Calgary, Edmonton, Montreal and Winnepeg. In addition to regular charter flights, the airline also leases aircraft out seasonally, and in turn takes aircraft from Air 2000 to meet demand. In 1992 over a million passengers were carried for the first time. The first Airbus A320 was delivered on 29th May 1993, giving Canada 3000 a most modern fleet. In 1996 the fleet was again expanded with an Airbus A320 and a Boeing 757. Plans for the new century envisaged the demand for widebodies, and thus Canada 3000 took delivery of its first Airbus A330 for the 1998 summer season. Following the takeover of Canadian

Airlines by Air Canada, Canada 3000 has been granted more scheduled service licences, both domestic and international, and 75% of its operations are now scheduled services. An initial public offering of shares was made in mid-2000 to fund the expansion of domestic routes; it is already Canada's second largest domestic carrier.

Routes

Acapulco, Amsterdam, Anchorage, Antigua, Auckland, Barbados, Belfast, Birmingham, Calgary, Cancun, Costa Rica, Düsseldorf, Edmonton, Fort Lauderdale, Fort Myers, Glasgow, Honolulu, Kona, Las Vegas, Los Angeles, London, Montreal, Munich, Nadi, Orlando, Ottawa, Palm Springs, Phoenix, Rarotonga, St. Johns, Sydney, Toronto, Vancouver, Victoria, Whitehorse, Vienna, Winnepeg.

Fleet

6 Airbus A320-200
6 Boeing 757-200
4 Airbus A330-200

Ordered

4 Airbus A319
2 Airbus A320

Boeing 737-275 C-GTPW (Author's collection)

CANADIAN AIRLINES

Scotia Center 2800, 700-2nd Street SW Calgary, Alberta T2P 2W2 Canada, Tel. 294-2000, Fax. 294-2066, www.cdnair.ca

Three- / Two- letter code	IATA No.	Reg'n prefix	ICAO callsign
CDN / CP	018	C	Canadian

Canadian Airlines International was formally established on 1st January 1988, though it was formed in the previous January and the name came into use in March 1987. Prior to that the former Canadian Pacific Airlines had been taken over by the slightly smaller Pacific Western Airlines, which had already absorbed Eastern Provincial Airways and Nordair during the preceding year. In 1989, in order to strengthen its position against Air Canada, it also took over Canada's largest private airline, Wardair. Canadian received its first Boeing 767 in 1988 and in the later part of 1990 its first Boeing 747-400; the Airbus A320

was also added to the fleet. Following approval by the regulatory authorities in 1995, AMR Corporation, the parent of American Airlines, took a 33% shareholding in Canadian Airlines Corporation, Canadian's parent company which also had holdings in various other Canadian regional operators such as Time Air, Air Atlantic, Ontario Express and Canadian Regional. A separate division of the airline, Canadian North, served the wide expanses of Canada's remote northern areas. During the later part of 1999 there were fierce takeover battles between the major Canadian airlines. Together with its partner

AMR, Canadian tried to acquire a majority in the national carrier Air Canada, but eventually the battle was won by Air Canada with help from its financially strong Star Alliance partners, taking over 82% of the shares in Canadian. During the first part of 2000, there was a redistribution of routes and responsibilities between the two airlines. Canadian continues to operate independently, but its aircraft are being repainted into an Air Canada colour scheme. Codesharing with Delta Airlines is to commence from 1st October 2000.

Routes

Bangkok, Beijing, Boston, Buenos Aires, Chicago, Cleveland, Dallas/Fort Worth, Detroit, Hong Kong, Honolulu, Houston, London, Los Angeles, Manila, Mexico City, Milan, Miami, Monterey, Nagoya, New York, Orlando, Osaka, Portland, Rome, San Francisco, Sao Paulo, Seattle, Taipei, Tokyo. Additionally, further cities in Canada and the USA are served in partnership with American Airlines.

Fleet

13 Airbus A320-200
44 Boeing 737-200
14 Boeing 767-300ER

4 Boeing 747-400
8 McDonnell Douglas DC-10-30

Boeing 747-4R7F LX-KCV (Pascal Mainzer/Luxembourg)

CARGOLUX

Luxembourg Airport P.O.Box 591,
2015 Luxembourg, Tel. 42111,
Fax. 435446, www.cargolux.com

Three- / Two- letter code	IATA No.	Reg'n prefix	ICAO callsign
CLX / CV	172	LX	Cargolux

Cargolux Airlines International SA, Europe's largest scheduled all-cargo airline, was set up on 4th March 1970. The shareholders were Luxair SA, the Icelandic airline Loftleidir and the Swedish shipping concern Salenia AB. Operations began in May 1970 with a Canadair CL-44. Altogether five CL-44s were used, augmented in 1971 by a Douglas DC-8-61. In 1973 the first Boeing 747-200C was acquired. The Salenia and Loftleidir shares were taken over by Luxair in the late 1970s, and then in 1992 Lufthansa took a shareholding in Luxair, and thereby also in Cargolux. However, more than 40% of the shares are owned by various Luxembourg banks. The first Boeing 747-400F in the world, a cargo aircraft of the latest generation, was delivered in November 1993, with a second following at the beginning of 1994 as Cargolux's services to the USA and South-East Asia were strengthened.There is a code-share agreement with China Airlines, with an exchange of freight space on the Taipei-Luxembourg route, and similar codeshares have been put into place with other airlines. During 1997 SAir Logistics, a part of the Swissair group, acquired Lufthansa's shareholding in Cargolux. From 1997 to 1999 the fleet was converted fully to the Boeing 747-400F, making the company one of the most modern freight concerns in the world, and also one of the most profitable.

Routes

Global freight services on scheduled, charter and ad hoc basis.

Fleet	Ordered
11 Boeing 747-400F	1 Boeing 747-400F

Boeing 747-467 B-HOX (Jan-Alexander Lück/Bremen)

CATHAY PACIFIC

Swire House, 9 Connaught Road, Hong Kong, China, Tel. 27475000, Fax. 28106563, www.cathaypacific.com

Three- / Two- letter code	IATA No.	Reg'n prefix	ICAO callsign
CPA / CX	160	B-H	Cathay

Cathay Pacific Airways Ltd. was set up on 24th September 1946 and began by connecting Shanghai via Hong Kong and other intermediate stops to Sydney, using a Douglas DC-3. In 1948 the Swire Group bought its way into the airline, acquiring 45% of the capital (increased to 70% by 1980), and in 1959 the BOAC subsidiary Hong Kong Airways was taken over. From April 1959 the fleet which had included DC-6s from the early 1950s, was updated with Lockheed L-188 Electras, and three years later Convair 880s. These were supplemented by Boeing 707s until the decision was made to acquire the first widebody, the Lockheed TriStar. This type was used to open up new routes in the Middle East. As a British company, Cathay wanted to be able to serve London, and to do this, Boeing 747s were bought, and the first service to London took place on 17th July 1980. In addition to London, Frankfurt was added in 1984, and these quickly converted to non-stop services with the delivery of the new 747-300s, which had longer range. Fleet renewal at Cathay was a continuing process with the Boeing 747-400 (1989), Boeing 777 (1996) and Airbus A330-300 (1995) and Airbus A340 (1996). The airline also introduced a new colour scheme from Autumn 1994. In deference to the changed political situation in Hong Kong, the Swire Group sold part of its Cathay shares to Chinese investors. The airline, always regarded as one of the most successful, was hit by the Asian business crisis and in 1998 made a loss for the first time ever. As a member of the Oneworld alliance the company is however a strong partner in the Far East. Cathay Pacific has shareholdings in Dragon Air (17.8%) and Air Hong Kong (75%).

Routes

Adelaide, Amsterdam, Anchorage, Auckland, Bahrain, Bangkok, Beijing, Brisbane, Cairns, Cebu, Chicago, Colombo, Denpasar, Dubai, Frankfurt, Fukuoka, Ho Chi Minh, Hong Kong, Johannesburg, Kuala Lumpur, London, Los Angeles, Manchester, Manila, Mauritius, Melbourne, Mumbai, Nagoya, New York, Osaka, Paris, Penang, Perth, Rome, San Francisco, Seoul, Sharjah, Singapore, Surabaya, Sydney, Taipei, Tokyo, Toronto,Vancouver and Zürich.

Fleet		Ordered
12 Airbus A330-300	3 Boeing 747-400F	3 Airbus A330-300
14 Airbus A340-300	19 Boeing 747-400	1 Boeing 747-400F
3 Boeing 747-200F	11 Boeing 777-200	

Boeing 737-236 VP-CKX (Hans-Willi Mertens/ Miami)

CAYMAN AIRWAYS

P.O.Box 1101, Georgetown, Grand Cayman,
Cayman Islands, Tel. 9498200,
Fax. 9497607, www.caymanairways.com

Three- / Two- letter code	IATA No.	Reg'n prefix	ICAO callsign
CAY / KX	378	VP-C	Cayman

Cayman Airways Ltd. was formed in July 1968 to take over the business of Cayman Brac Airways Ltd., which in turn had been set up by the Costa Rican airline LACSA. LACSA owned 49% of the shares in Cayman Airways until December 1977 when the airline came under the control of the Cayman government. Operations began to Jamaica and Miami with BAC One-Elevens. Britten-Norman Trislanders were used for the Cayman inter-island services, linking Grand Cayman, Brac and Little Cayman. Boeing 727-200s replaced the One-Elevens, and a Douglas DC-8 which had been in service during the 1970s.

During 1989 the first leased Boeing 737-400s were brought into the fleet to replace the Boeing 727s, but in 1993 operations were scaled down as the 737-400 proved to be too large and expensive. Since that time the airline has concentrated on providing services to Jamaica and to several destinations in the USA and has been using Boeing 737-200s. There is an agreement with United Airlines, which provides technical and administrative support to Cayman Airways.

Routes

Cayman Brac, Grand Cayman, Houston, Kingston, Miami, Montego Bay, Orlando, Tampa.

Fleet

3 Boeing 737-200

McDonnell Douglas DC-9-32 RP-C1536 (Author's collection via Pierre Alain Petit/Manila)

CEBU PACIFIC AIR

30 EDSA Corner Pioneer, Mandalayong City, Metro Manila 5506, Philippines, Tel. 2-6371810, Fax. 2-6379170, www.cebupacific.com.ph

Three- / Two- letter code	IATA No.	Reg'n prefix	ICAO callsign
CPI / 5J	203	RP	Cebu Air

Following deregulation of air transport in the Philippines in 1995, one of the many new start-up airlines which emerged was Cebu Pacific Air. Many investors were tempted to invest in an airline with the chance to enter into competition on lucrative routes which had previously been monopolised by the state. So it was with JG Summit Holding, a concern owned by the Gokongwei family, and Cebu's operations were able to begin in March 1996. Using four McDonnell Douglas DC-9-32s flights were from Manila to Cebu, at high frequency and with low fares, following the pattern seen to be so successful in the United States. After only a year of operation, Cebu Pacific took on three more DC-9-32s and had carried over a million passengers. As well as the primary route, six further destinations were added. However in February 1998 a grounding by order of the government put a stop to further rapid expansion. Following the crash of one of its aircraft, Cebu Pacific Air was being viewed in a poor light, and only after a close examination of its whole flight operation was it able to resume services again at the end of March 1998. As a consequence of the Asian business downturn, expansion was now slower than it had been, yet the fleet has continued to expand, with three more colourfully-painted DC-9-32s being added during 1999, and an order has been placed for Boeing 717s for delivery between 2001 and 2004.

Routes

Bacalod, Cagayan d'Oro, Cebu, Davao, Iloilo, Kalibo, Manila, Port Moresby, Roxas, Tacloban, Zamboango.

Fleet

12 McDonnell Douglas DC-9-32   10 Boeing 717-200

Boeing 727-2S7 N685CA (Stefan Schlick/Puerto Vallarta)

CHAMPION AIR

8009 34th Ave. South Suite 700, Bloomington Minnesota, 55425 USA, Tel. 612-8148700, Fax. 612-8148799, www.championair.com

Three- / Two- letter code	IATA No.	Reg'n prefix	ICAO callsign
CCP / MG	–	N	Champion Air

Champion Air is a successor to the former MGM Grand Air, which was known for its luxuriously outfitted Douglas DC-8s and Boeing 727s. MGM's clientele consisted of stars of entertainment, sport, music and their associates and entourages; the level of luxury and privacy appealed to the very wealthy more than the idea of travelling by regular airlines. However, in 1994, when this type of flying was no longer proving to be profitable, MGM sold a part of its operation to Front Page Tours, which specialised in the transport of sports teams and their fans to events such as the Super Bowl or the Kentucky Derby. The change of name to Champion Air took place at the same time as the takeover of the licence from MGM in 1995. More Boeing 727s were acquired for the planned expansion of the company. When the new company encountered difficulties in 1997, the shares were acquired by Carl Pohland (60%) and Northwest Airlines (40%) and Champion Air was reorganised as a charter company catering for the needs of the general public. The fleet was expanded with more Boeing 727s to carry out its new tasks. The company's headquarters was moved from Salt Lake City to Minneapolis, where the aircraft were maintained by Northwest Airlines.

The airline now works closely with two major tour companies, Adventure Tours in Dallas and MLT Vacations in Minneapolis.

Routes

Aruba, Cancun, Denver, Detroit, Grand Cayman, Kingston, Las Vegas, Oklahoma City, San Jose, St. Louis, Tulsa.

Fleet

11 Boeing 727-200

Airbus A300B4F G-CEXC (Pascal Mainzer/Luxembourg)

CHANNEL EXPRESS

Bldg. 470 Bournemouth Intl. Airport, Christchurch, Dorset BH23 6SE, Great Britain, Tel. 1202-597600, Fax. 1202-573512, www.channel-express.co.uk

Three- / Two- letter code	IATA No.	Reg'n prefix	ICAO callsign
EXS / LS	839	G	Channex

Express Air Service began operations from its home base at Bournemouth in 1978 with a small fleet of Handley Page Heralds. The Channel Islands were provided with their daily needs, and cut flowers formed the return loads. During the summer holiday season, passengers were also carried, though that was not a profitable exercise. Contracts for the carriage of mail made more aircraft necessary, and the fleet grew to eight aircraft. In 1983 the name was changed by the addition of 'Channel'. The whole fleet of Heralds were modified and updated, but in the mid 1990s this process could not be economically sustained on the ageing airframes, and the Fokker F.27 was introduced gradually as a replacement. The last Heralds left the fleet in 1998 after 20 years service for the type. In order to be able to handle other freight contracts, especially express parcels, Lockheed L-188 Electras were introduced. These are able to carry palletised cargo which gives the advantage of reducing loading and turnaround times; the type is also more capacious and has greater range than the F.27. The Electras were used on new international routes. With the delivery of the airline's first Airbus A300B4 freighter in 1997, new possibilities were opened for Channel Express. Long-term contracts with DHL led to the acquisition of more Airbus A300B4 freighters during 1998 and 1999. Channel Express is in the position of being able to react to customers' special needs and also flies ad hoc charters and on a wet-lease basis for other companies.

Routes

Bournemouth, Bristol, Brussels, Coventry, Dublin, East Midlands, Edinburgh, Guernsey, Jersey, Cologne, London-Gatwick, Liverpool, Luton, Newcastle, Nuremberg, Stansted are all served regularly .

Fleet

4 Airbus A300B4 Freighter
7 Fokker F.27
4 Lockheed L-118 Electra

Boeing 747-409 B-163 (Josef Krauthäuser/Los Angeles-LAX)

CHINA AIRLINES

131, Nanking East Rd. Taipei 104, Republic of China, Tel. 02-27152233, Fax. 02-27155754, www.china-airlines.com

Three- / Two- letter code	IATA No.	Reg'n prefix	ICAO callsign
CAL / CI	297	B	Cal

On 16th December 1959 some former members of the Chinese Nationalist Air Force set up CAL. Consolidated PBY Catalina flying boats were initially used for charters. Domestic scheduled services were also operated using Douglas DC-3s and Curtiss C-46s. In 1965 the airline became the official flag carrier of the Republic of China and in December 1966 Lockheed Constellations were used to start a scheduled service to Saigon, primarily to transport members of the US armed forces and cargo to Vietnam. During 1967 services to

Hong Kong and Tokyo were also started, using two new Boeing 727s. 1970 saw the first trans-Pacific flight to San Francisco, via Tokyo and Honolulu. CAL took delivery of its first widebody, a Boeing 747, in 1975, and this was followed from June 1982 by the Airbus A310 for regional services. In 1983 a route to Amsterdam was inaugurated, the only destination in Europe for many years, because of political considerations. MD-11s and Boeing 747-400s were acquired, to replace older aircraft. With Mandarin Airlines and Formosa Air, CAL had powerful

subsidiaries, which were in sharp competition with private enterprises. The airline also has a shareholding in FAT-Far Eastern Air Transport. The current colour scheme for the aircraft was introduced in October 1995. During 1999 Formosa Air was merged with Mandarin and there was a substantial reorganisation within the group. New Boeing 737-800s were introduced from the later part of 1998 and the MD-11s transferred to Mandarin. The airline's base is at the Chiang Kai Chek airport in Taipei.

Routes

Abu Dhabi, Amsterdam, Anchorage, Atlanta, Bangkok, Chicago, Colombo, Dallas/Forth Worth, Delhi, Denpasar, Frankfurt, Fukuoka, Ho Chi Minh City, Hong Kong, Honolulu, Jakarta, Kaohsiung, Kuala Lumpur, London, Los Angeles, Luxembourg, Miami, Nagoya, New York, Okinawa, Penang, Phuket, Rome, San Francisco, Singapore, Sydney, Taipei, Tokyo.

Fleet

4 Airbus A300B4
12 Airbus A300-600
6 Boeing 747-200F
13 Boeing 747-400
10 Boeing 737-800

Ordered

7 Airbus A340-300
4 Airbus A330
5 Boeing 737-800
13 Boeing 747-400F

Boeing 737-39P B-2573 (Björn Kannengiesser/Beijing)

CHINA EASTERN

2550 Hongqiao Rd, Intl. Airport, 200335 Shanghai,
People's Republic of China, Tel. 21-62686268,
Fax. 21-62686039, www.chinaeasternair.com

Three- / Two- letter code	IATA No.	Reg'n prefix	ICAO callsign
CES / MU	781	B	China Eastern

In December 1987 China Eastern Airlines separated from CAAC, which had previously been responsible for all air transport operations, and assumed responsibility for its flights from Shanghai, initially using a fleet of ten MD-82s shared with China Northern Airlines. A flourishing international airline has developed from the former CAAC regional directorate. Using MD-11s delivered during 1992/93, routes were opened to the USA and Europe. Chinese-assembled MD-82s for the backbone of the modern fleet,

augmented by Airbus A310s from 1987. Even during CAAC times the Shanghai district had used western aircraft such as the Shorts 360, DHC-8, Lockheed Hercules and BAe 146, though only in small numbers. With the upsizing of the fleet came an expansion of the network. Hong Kong, Nagoya and Seoul were served with Airbuses, and from 1996 delivery of new Airbus A340-300s allowed the addition of further destinations in Europe, including Munich. On the route from Shanghai to Seoul there is a codeshare arrangement with Asiana; other

partners are Air France and American Airlines. During 1997 the loss-making China General Aviation was taken over. Fokker 100s were replaced by Airbus A320s during 1998/99. Regular freight services are flown to the USA, using the MD-11. China Eastern Airlines has two main bases: Hongqiao airport in Shanghai concentrates on international flights, while domestic services are also flown from Nanchang. The centre for all other operations, which include agricultural aviation and spraying, using Yunshuji Y-5s, is at Hefei.

Routes

Bangkok, Beijing, Changsha, Cheju, Chengdu, Chicago, Dalian, Fukuoka, Fuzhou, Guangzhou, Guilin, Haikou, Hong Kong, Hongzhou, Hefei, Huangyan, Jinan, Jinjiang, Kunming, Los Angeles, Madrid, Munich, Nagasaki, Nagoya, Nanchang, Nanjing, Okayama, Osaka, Paris, Pusan, San Francisco, Seoul, Shanghai, Santou, Shenzen, Singapore, Sydney, Tokyo, Tunxi, Wenzhou, Wuhan, Xiamen, Xian, Yantai, Zhengzhou, Zhoushan.

Fleet

Fleet		Ordered
10 Airbus A300-600	9 McDonnell Douglas-SAIC-MD-90	6 Airbus A320-200
14 Airbus A320-200	6 McDonnell Douglas MD-11	
6 Airbus A340-300	4 Yunshuji Y-7	
6 Boeing 737-300	18 Yunshuji Y-5	
5 McDonnell Douglas-SAIC-MD-82	4 Yakovlev 42	

Airbus A300-622R B-2316 (Björn Kannengiesser/Beijing)

CHINA NORTHERN AIRLINES

Dongtha Airport, Shenyang, Liaoning 110043, People's Republic of China, Tel. 24-8294231, Fax. 24-8294433, www.cna.ln.cninfo.net

Three- / Two- letter code	IATA No.	Reg'n prefix	ICAO callsign
CBF / CJ	782	B	China Northern

This airline from the furthest northern regions of the People's Republic of China was set up in 1988, taking on the mantle of the former CAAC Shenyang administration. Its home base is at the Shenyang-Taoxin airport. Yunshuji Y-7s and MD-82s form the main body of the fleet; indeed China Northern is the largest user of the MD-82 in China. Included in this fleet are MD-82s assembled in China by SAIC under a licence agreement with McDonnell Douglas. As well as scheduled and charter flights, Mil-8 helicopters are used for industrial work and for various other tasks including heavy lifting and the erection of masts. In 1993 two Airbus A300-600s were leased and proved to be successful in service, so that six further examples were ordered, entering service during 1994-95. A further licence-building arrangement was agreed with McDonnell Douglas, this time for the MD-90, and China Northern was the first airline to receive finished examples. In Spring 1996 the airline operated its first international route, from Shenzento the new airport at Macau. Charter flights are now also operated to Japan, Korea and other points in South East Asia. MD-90s are also operated on behalf of partner company Beiya Air.

Routes

Beijing, Changchun, Changhsa, Chengdu, Chongqing, Dalian, Dandong, Fuzhou, Guangzhou, Gulyang, Haikou, Hangzhou, Harbin, Hefei, Hong Kong, Jilin, Jinan, Kunming, Lianyungang, Macau, Nanjing, Niigata, Ningbo, Pyongyang, Qingdao, Sapporo, Seoul, Shanghai, Shantou, Shenyang, Shenzen, Tianjin, Urumqi, Wenzhou, Wuhan, Xiamen, Xian, Yangi, Yantai, Zhengzhou and Zhuhai.

Fleet

6 Airbus A300-600
11 Yunshuji Y-7
25 McDonnell Douglas/SAIC MD-82

11 McDonnell Douglas MD-90

Airbus A320-214 B-2357 (Björn Kannengiesser/Beijing)

CHINA NORTHWEST AIRLINES

Xiguan Airport, Laodong Nanlu, 710082 Xian,
Shanxi, People's Republic of China
Tel. 29-4263029, Fax. 29-4262022

Three- / Two- letter code	IATA No.	Reg'n prefix	ICAO callsign
CNW / WH	783	B	China Northwest

The former CAAC regional directorate of Xian has been flying under the name of China Northwest Airlines since 1989 and has the task of operating regional scheduled and charter flights, as well as the agricultural and forestry work, for which the Yunshuji Y-5 sprayers are used. The fleet which was taken over from CAAC was based in Lanzhou and Xian and still consisted of Soviet-designed aircraft, mainly Tupolev Tu-154s. China Northwest has a modern maintenance centre at the new Xian-Xianyang airport. Conditions were therefore right for a successive replacement of the fleet with aircraft up to Western standards. Thus in 1990/91, BAe 146s were delivered for regional services as a replacement for the Antonov An-24, and in the following year Airbus A300-600s and A310s were brought into service. Further fleet renewal took place with the delivery of the first Airbus A320 in November 1997; these had replaced the Tupolev Tu-154s by the end of 1999. The company has an 80% shareholding in Nanjing Airlines, which operates two Yunshuji Y-7s from Nanjing.

Routes

Beijing, Changsha, Chengdu, Chongqing, Dunhuang, Fukuoka, Fuzhou, Guangzhou, Guilin, Guiyang, Haikou, Hangzhou, Harbin, Hiroshima, Hong Kong, Jiayugan, Kunming, Lanzhou, Lianyungang, Macau, Nagoya, Nanchang, Nanjing, Niigata, Ningbo, Qingdao, Shanghai, Shantou, Shenyang, Shenzen, Urumqui, Wenzhou, Wuhan, Wuyishan, Xian, Xiamen, Xining, Yantai, Yinchuan, Zhanjiang, Zhuhai.

Fleet

3 Airbus A310-200
5 Airbus A300-600
12 Airbus A320

10 BAe 146-100/300
13 Yunshuji Y5

Airbus A320-232 B-2365 (Author's collection/Beijing)

CHINA SOUTHERN AIRLINES

Baiyun Intl.Airport, 510406 Guangzhou, People's Republic of China, Tel. 20-6678901, Fax. 20-6667637, www.cs-air.com

Three- / Two- letter code	IATA No.	Reg'n prefix	ICAO callsign
CSN / CZ	784	B	China Southern

In common with other Chinese airlines, China Southern stems from the 1989 reorganisation of CAAC. Based in Guangzhou, it is now China's second largest international airline, and has grown at a spectacular rate. In a two-year period alone, over $600 million was invested in the fleet and its renewal. Thus from 1990 Boeing 737s, 757s and more recently 767s were being delivered continually. China Southern was the first Chinese company to take delivery of the up-to-the-minute Boeing 777 from 1995, for its long-range routes. During 1996 China Southern also set up its own 'business airline', equipped with LearJets. Twenty Airbus A320s were ordered in 1997, the first Airbuses to be sold directly to a Chinese operator, thus it became possible to retire all the former Soviet-built types and older Boeing 737-200s. In addition to its airline operations, China Southern also undertakes other diverse flying tasks including agricultural aviation and offshore work, and uses various light aircraft and helicopters for these. The airline also has shareholdings in other Chinese airlines: Guangxi Airlines (60%), Guihou Airlines (60%), Shantou Airlines (60%), Xiamen Airlines (60%), Zhuhai Helicopter (100%) and Zhuhai Airlines (100%). China Southern is one of the three airlines which the government has designated to lead new consolidated groups with the air transport industry, and as a first step, it acquired Zhongyuan Airlines (see page 375) in mid-2000, though this will continue in independent operation for the time being. There are alliances and codeshare arrangements with Delta Air Lines and United Airlines.

Routes

Amsterdam, Bangkok, Beihai, Changchun, Changde, Changsha, Changzhou, Chengdu, Chongqing, Dalian, Dandong, Dayong, Fukuoka, Fuzhou, Guangzhou, Guilin, Guiyang, Haikou, Hangzhou, Hanoi, Harbin, Hefei, Ho Chi Minh City, Hong Kong, Jakarta, Jilin, Jinan, Jinjiang, Jinzhou, Jiujiang, Kuala Lumpur, Kunming, Lianyungang, Liuzhou, Los Angeles, Manila, Mudanjiang, Nanchang, Nanjing, Nanning, Nantong, Nanyang, Ningbo, Osaka, Penang, Qingdao, Sanya, Seoul, Shanghai, Shantou, Sharjah, Shasi, Shenyang, Shenzen, Singapore, Surabaya, Taiyuan, Tianjin, Tunxi, Urumqui, Weiha, Wenzhou, Wuhan, Xian, Xiamen, Xuzhou, Yichang, Yiwu, Zhanjiang, Zhengzhou, Zhuhai .

Fleet

20 Airbus A320-200
22 Boeing 737-300
12 Boeing 737-500

18 Boeing 757-200
10 Boeing 777-200

Ordered

2 Boeing 777-200

Boeing 757-2Z0 B-2841 (Romano Germann/Beijing)

CHINA SOUTHWEST AIRLINES

Shuangli Airport, Chengdu 610202, People's Republic of China, Tel. 28-5814466, Fax. 28-5582630, www.cswa.com

Three- / Two- letter code	IATA No.	Reg'n prefix	ICAO callsign
CXN / SZ	785	B	China Southwest

China Southwest was founded in October 1987 to take over the activities of the former CAAC regional administration. Initially the fleet consisted of the inherited types - Antonov 24s, Boeing 707s and Tupolev Tu-154s, but soon no less than 20 Boeing 737-300s and various propeller-driven types were serving over 30 destinations from Chengdu-Shuangliu airport . Other hubs were at Chongqing and Guiyang. The fleet grew quickly as did the network, including more and more international destinations. Hong Kong, Bangkok, Kathmandu and Singapore were all served from 1989. Particularly noteworthy was the route over 'the roof of the world' from Chengdu to Lhasa in Tibet. Freight operations were carried out using the former CAAC Boeing 707s, though the number of this type in service reduced as new Boeing 757s were delivered from 1992 onwards. This fast-growing company, which carries over six million passengers each year, has its maintenance base at the airport at Chengdu and is building up its staff and experience as Boeing specialists. However, the airline is not quite an all-Boeing operator, having taken delivery of Airbus A340s from December 1998.

Routes

Bangkok, Beihai, Beijing, Changsa, Chengdu, Chongqing, Dalian, Fuzhou, Guangzhou, Guiyang, Guilin, Haikou, Hangzhou, Hefei, Hong Kong, Kunming, Lhasa, Lanzhou, Longdongbao, Luoyang, Nanchang, Nanjing, Nanning, Ningbo, Qingdoa, Shanghai, Shantou, Shenzen, Singapore, Urumqi, Wenzhou, Wuhan, Xian, Xiamen, Xichang, Xining, Xuzhou, Yantai, Yichang, Zhanjiang, Zhangjiajie, Zhengzou.

Fleet

3 Airbus A340-300
20 Boeing 737-300
3 Boeing 737-800

13 Boeing 757-200
3 Yunshuji Y-12

Boeing 757-200 B-2851 (Author's collection via EAS/Beijing)

CHINA XINJIANG AIRLINES

Diwobao Intl. Airport, Urumqi, Xinjiang 830016,
People's Republic of China
Tel. 991-3801703, Fax. 991-3711084

Three- / Two- letter code	IATA No.	Reg'n prefix	ICAO callsign
CXJ / XO	651	B	Xinjiang

Xinjiang Airlines was founded in 1985, its forbear being the CAAC Xinjiang regional administration. It is owned 50% each by CAAC and the regional government of Xinjiang. This far western region of China borders on Kyrgyzstan, Mongolia and India, and many places are not quickly accessible other than by air. Thus it is no surprise that for such routes the de Havilland Canada DHC-6 Twin Otter was introduced into service from February 1985. Xinjiang Airlines acquired a further Western type, the Boeing 737-300, during 1993 and 1994; these were used for international services to Islamabad and Hong Kong. For the high-frequency scheduled service to Beijing, three 350-seat Ilyushin IL-86 widebodies were acquired at the end of 1993, and at that time the name of the airline was also changed to China Xinjiang Airlines. The fleet has been regularly updated: from August 1997 the Twin Otters were replaced with the larger ATR 72, and Boeing 757s, first delivered in April 1998, have replaced the older Russian types. Three of the new generation Boeing 737-700s are on order, with delivery expected from March 2001. The airline's principal operating and maintenance base is at Urumqi.

Routes

Aksu, Almaty, Beijing, Changsha, Chengdu, Chongqing, Dalian, Fuyun, Guangzhou, Guilin, Harbin, Hong Kong, Hotan, Islamabad, Jinan, Karamy, Kashi, Korla, Kunming, Kuqa, Lanzhou, Moscow, Novosibirsk, Qiemo, Qingdao, Shanghai, Shenyang, Shenzen, Tianjin, Xian, Xiamen, Yinning, Zhengzhou.

Fleet

Fleet		Ordered
5 ATR 72-500	5 Tupolev Tu-154M	3 Boeing 737-700
3 Boeing 737-300		
6 Boeing 757-200		
3 Ilyushin IL-86		

Boeing 767-3W0ER B-2568 (Author's collection/Beijing)

CHINA YUNNAN AIRLINES

Wujiabao Airport, Kunming,
Yunnan 650200, People's Republic of China
Tel. 871-7112999, Fax: 871-7151509

Three- / Two- letter code	IATA No.	Reg'n prefix	ICAO callsign
CYH / 3Q	592	B	Yunnan

Like almost all Chinese airline companies, Yunnan has its origins in CAAC, in this case the Yunnan regional administration. It became independent in July 1992 and began a daily Boeing 737-300 service from its base at Kunming-Wujiabao to Beijing and Shanghai. From 1993, international flights were introduced to Bangkok and Singapore. Until mid-1996 the fleet had consisted of Boeing 737-300s only, but was then expanded by the addition of two 263-seat Boeing 767-300s in order to accommodate steeply rising passenger numbers. The 767s took over on popular routes including those to Beijing and Bangkok. The latest model of the 737, the -700 came into service with China Yunnan at the beginning of 1999. Thus the airline remains all-Boeing equipped.

Routes

Bangkok, Baoshan, Beihai, Beijing, Changchun,Changsha, Chengdu, Dali City, Dalian, Fuzhou, Guangzhou, Guilin, Guiyang, Haikou, Hangzhou,Harbin, Hefei, Jinan, Kuala Lumpur, Kunming, Lijiang, Luxi, Macau, Shanghai, Shenzen, Singapore, Wuhan, Xian, Xiamen, Xuzhou, Yibin, Yichang, Zhanjiang, Zhengzhou, Zhuhai.

Fleet

14 Boeing 737-300
 4 Boeing 737-700
 3 Boeing 767-300ER

ATR 42-300 OY-CID (Josef Krauthäuser/Nuremberg)

CIMBER AIR

Sonderborg Airport, 6400 Sonderborg, Denmark, Tel. 74-422277, Fax. 74-426511, www.cimber.com

Three- / Two- letter code	IATA No.	Reg'n prefix	ICAO callsign
CIM / QI	647	OY	Cimber

Cimber Air was founded by Ingolf Nielsen in 1950 when he took over Sonderjyllands Flyvelskab and remains largely in the hands of the Nielsen family. At first air taxi operations were carried out, often from the airline's Sonderborg base to Copenhagen. At the end of 1963 Cimber Air was awarded a schedules service licence for this route. Nord 262s were brought into use and the radius of service was extended to Germany with flights to Hamburg and Kiel. During 1971 SAS, Maersk and Cimber Air together formed a new company called Danair, which took on all of their domestic services. More Nord 262s and from 1975 VFW 614s were brought into use; Cimber Air was the launch customer for the latter type. The limited opportunities in the Danish market led Cimber Air to look abroad for work; the airline flew services on behalf of Saudi Arabian Airlines and for DLT, the precursor of today's current Lufthansa Cityline. In order to do this a German subsidiary company was founded in Kiel. Fokker F.27s and F.28s were used on the various routes, until in 1989 the ATR 42, an optimal aircraft for the company's needs, became available. This type, and the larger ATR 72, now form the entire fleet, though Canadair CRJs are being added from the second part of 2000. The co-operation with Lufthansa was built up especially around the time of German reunification at the beginning of the 1990s and today Cimber Air is a member of the Team Lufthansa operation, with some aircraft flown in Team Lufthansa colours. In order to facilitate further expansion, SAS took a shareholding during 1998. Through its co-operation with Lufthansa and SAS, Cimber Air benefits from numerous activities of the Star Alliance.

Routes

Aalborg, Aarhus, Berlin, Bremen, Brussels, Cologne/Bonn, Copenhagen, Dublin, Esbjerg, Frankfurt, Helsinki, Karup, Kiel, Luxembourg, Montpellier, Nice, Nuremberg, Sonderborg, Vienna.

Fleet	Ordered
12 ATR 42-300/500 3 ATR 72-500	4 Canadair CRJ

Boeing 767-33A OO-CTR (Lutz Schönfeld/Berlin-SXF)

CITY BIRD

Building 117D, Airport B-1820 Melsbroek, Belgium Tel. 2-7525252, Fax. 2-7525210, www.citybird.com

Three- / Two- letter code	IATA No.	Reg'n prefix	ICAO callsign
CTB / H2	–	OO	Dreamflight

Following his sale of Euro Belgian Airlines to Richard Branson's Virgin Express, Victor Hasson of the City Hotel Group already had plans to re-enter the airline business. A non-compete clause in the sale agreement precluded him from European operations, but did not prevent him from operating to the Caribbean and the USA. So in August 1996 the City Hotel Group set up City Bird and ordered three MD-11s from McDonnell Douglas. Operations began on 27th March 1997 with the first MD-11. Miami, Orlando and several destinations in the Caribbean were on the agenda for this low-cost airline. From the outset there was a good understanding with the national carrier Sabena, who took a 3% holding in City Bird. Further MD-11s were received in 1998, but they were used on behalf of Sabena. As well as charter flights for various tour operators, the leasing of aircraft or the use of aircraft on behalf of other airlines has been a lucrative activity. During 1999 City Bird took delivery of two Airbus A300 freighters, which were flown on behalf of CAL-Cargo Airlines and Air France. Two Boeing 767s also came into use and a contract was signed with Lignes Congolaises for the provision of a service from Kinshasa to Brussels, though its implementation was fraught with political difficulties. The airline intends to acquire more freighter aircraft to expand this side of its business, and it has also entered the European charter market from Spring 2000, using Boeing 737-400s on an interim basis until new 737-800s are delivered.

Routes

Miami and Orlando are served on a scheduled basis from Brussels. Charter and freight flights worldwide.

Fleet	Ordered
2 Airbus A300F	2 Boeing 737-800
3 (Boeing) McDonnell Douglas MD-11	2 Boeing 747-400F
2 Boeing 767-300ER	
3 Boeing 737-400	

Canadair Regional Jet 100ER N920CA (Dennis Wehrmann/Miami)

COMAIR

P.O.Box 75021, Cincinnati Intl. Airport,
Ohio 45275, USA, Tel. 606-5252550,
Fax. 606-7672278, www.comair.com

Three- / Two- letter code	IATA No.	Reg'n prefix	ICAO callsign
COM / OH	886	N	Comair

Comair began regional services in March 1977 with a Piper Navajo between Cincinnati and Cleveland. The larger Embraer EMB-110 Bandeirante came into service from 1981, with more destinations being added. The addition of Shorts 360s, Swearingen Metros and in 1984 Saab 340s were indicative of the expansion to meet increasing demand. At the beginning of 1984 some 30 points were being served from Cincinnati and the airline was already a major regional carrier. In September 1984 Comair became a partner in the newly-created 'Delta Connection' system, under which marketing banner Delta brought together the feeder and regional services which had previously been operated by individual airlines under their own identities. Delta took a 20% shareholding in Comair. In 1989 Comair Holdings Inc. was formed to bring together the by now substantial activities of the group. From 1988 the Embraer 120 Brasilia, a fast turboprop, was introduced; Comair was a launch customer. Likewise it was a substantial launch customer for the Canadair Regional Jet, which began deliveries in 1993 and was the airline's first jet. In October 1999 Delta Air Lines took over all the shares in Comair. More Canadair Jets continue to be acquired and the propeller-driven types phased out, so that by 2002 the airline will have an all-jet, indeed an all-CRJ, fleet. Comair will also be one of the first users of the new lengthened Canadair Regional Jet 700 model when deliveries begin from the middle of 2001.

Routes

From major hubs at Cincinnati and Orlando to 85 destinations in 28 US states, as well as points in Canada and the Bahamas.

Fleet

98 Canadair Regional Jet 100
24 Embraer EMB-120 Brasilia

Ordered

12 Canadair Regional Jet 100
20 Canadair Regional Jet 700

Boeing 757-330 D-ABOG (Dennis Wehrmann/Hamburg)

CONDOR FLUGDIENST

Am Grünen Weg 3, 65440 Kelsterbach, Germany, Tel. 06107-939 0, Fax. 06107-939520, www.condor.de

Three- / Two- letter code	IATA No.	Reg'n prefix	ICAO callsign
CFG / DE	881	D	Condor

Condor is the traditional charter subsidiary of German flag-carrier Lufthansa. Set up in 1955 as Deutsche Flugdienst GmbH, German Federal Railways, two shipping companies and Lufthansa were the shareholders in DF. The first aircraft were Vickers Vikings. After considerable initial successes, it suffered a setback in 1959 and was completely taken over by Lufthansa with state aid, thus avoiding bankruptcy. In 1961 Lufthansa bought the Condor Luftreederei (formed in 1957) from the Oetker group and merged it with DF to form the new Condor Flugdienst GmbH. Vickers Viscounts were bought in 1961 and two Fokker F.27s in 1963; in 1965 the first Boeing 727 entered service. By 1968 Condor had an all-jet fleet, and added examples of the Boeing 747-200 in 1971 and 1972; these were used to open new routes to the USA and Bangkok. During the late 1970s, the first oil crisis resulted in excess capacity being reduced; the smaller DC-10-30 replaced the 747s on long-range routes. Boeing 737-300s and Airbus A310s were used from 1987, and from 1989 the Boeing 757 was added as a 727 replacement. To meet increased demand, and additionally to operate scheduled flights for Lufthansa for a while, the fleet was increased. In 1995 Condor took shareholdings in various tour operators, to ensure getting their business for its flights. In 1997 Condor Berlin, a low-cost subsidiary was founded, operating Airbus A320s. Condor was the launch customer for the lengthened Boeing 757-300, with the first delivery at the beginning of 1999, when the DC-10s were retired. Their aircraft also have a new colour scheme in yellow and white. Condor holds 40% of Sun Express and participates in the frequent flyer programme of Lufthansa/Star Alliance.

Routes

From various German cities to the USA, the Caribbean, Middle and Far East, India, Nepal and the traditional Mediterranean holiday resorts, the Canary Isles, Northern Africa, Cape Verde, Mauritius, Seychelles and Kenya.

Fleet

18 Boeing 757-200
12 Boeing 757-300
 9 Boeing 767-300ER

Boeing 777-224 N78002 (Josef Krauthäuser/Los Angeles-LAX)

CONTINENTAL AIRLINES

1600 Smith Street, Houston Texas 77002, USA
Tel. 713-324-5000, Fax. 713-24-2087,
www.continental.com

Three- / Two- letter code	IATA No.	Reg'n prefix	ICAO callsign
COA / CO	005	N	Continental

Continental can trace its history back to July 1934 as the southwest division of Varney Speed Lines; it changed name to Varney Air Transport on 17th December 1934 and in 1937 to Continental Air Lines. A network was established using various Lockheed aircraft, mainly in the western USA. Post-war, Convair 240s, DC-6s and DC-7Bs and Vickers Viscounts were used. Pioneer Airlines was taken over in 1954. Boeing 707s began 'Golden Jet' flights on 8th June 1959. The first 747 entered service on 18th May 1970, with the DC-10 following two years later. In October 1981 Texas International acquired a stake

in Continental, and the two merged in October 1982, using the Continental name. 1983 brought enormous financial problems and entry to Chapter 11 bankruptcy protection. Aircraft and routes were dropped and it emerged from Chapter 11 in 1986. In February 1987, the parent company bought PeoplExpress, New York Air and Frontier and all were merged into Continental, but not without difficulty, as Chapter 11 was again used from December 1990 to May 1993. With a new colour scheme, the airline was ready to move on to the next crisis; in 1994 a low-cost division was set up 'Continental

Light' but after losing millions it was abandoned. In the late 1990s a major re-equipment programme was begun with the introduction of the Boeing 777 and 737-800, to replace the DC-10s and Boeing 727s. Boeing 757s and 767s were also added and by 2003 the whole fleet will have been renewed by Boeing alone. Continental Micronesia is a separate division for Pacific island services. Northwest Airlines has a 14% holding in Continental, and naturally there is co-operation, as there is with Avant Air, Copa and in Europe with KLM and Alitalia.

Routes

Continental has an intensive internal US network based on Cleveland, Houston and Newark and flies to about 140 destinations; additionally about 90 international destinations are served.

Fleet

Fleet		Ordered
131 Boeing 737-300/500	16 Boeing 777-200	15 Boeing 737-900
50 Boeing 737-700	74 McDonnell Douglas MD-80	9 Boeing 767-200
28 Boeing 737-800	34 McDonnell Douglas DC-10-10/30	26 Boeing 767-400
41 Boeing 757-200		
1 Boeing 767-200		

Embraer RJ-145LR N14953 (Josef Krauthäuser/Gulfport-Biloxi)

CONTINENTAL EXPRESS

1600 Smith Street, Houston Texas, 77002 USA,
Tel. 713-3242639, Fax. 713-3244914, www.
continental.com/corporate/corporate_03_01.asp

Three- / Two- letter code	IATA No.	Reg'n prefix	ICAO callsign
BTA / CO	565	N	Jetlink

In 1956 Vercoa Air Service was founded and later renamed as Britt Airways. Its network in the US midwest served many smaller towns, centred on its base at Terre Haute, Indiana. Beech 99s, Swearingen Metros,Fairchild F.27s and FH-227s and later BAC One-Elevens were used. Flights were also operated on behalf of Allegheny and Piedmont on newly created commuter routes. The airline was taken over in 1986 by PeoplExpress, but PeoplExpress in turn was taken over by the Texas Air

Corporation in 1987. Britt Airways was then sold off, but continued to operate as an independent undertaking and was one of the companies which then operated feeder flights for Continental Airlines. From January 1989 these were brought under the banner of Continental Express and over time the aircraft were updated; in place of the Metros came Embraer EMB-120 Brasilias. After the airline was taken over by Continental in the early 1990s, ATR 42s and Beech 1900s were introduced. As launch

customer for the Embraer Regional Jets, Continental Express received its first RJ-145s as soon as late 1996, becoming the first operator to bring them into scheduled service, from the beginning of 1997. Delivery of the first of the smaller RJ 135s followed in late 1999. In the long term Continental Express will switch all its operations over to jets. The main hubs for Continental Express are Cleveland, Denver, Newark and Houston.

Routes

Abilene, Akron, Albany, Alexandria, Allentown, Amarillo, Atlanta, Baltimore, Baton-Rouge, Birmingham, Boston, Brownsville, Buffalo, Burlington, Charleston, Charlotte, Chicago, Cincinnati, Cleveland, Colorado Springs, Columbus, Corpus Christi, Dallas/Fort Worth, Dayton, Denver, Detroit, El Paso, Erie, Flint, Fort Wayne, Grand Rapids, Greenville, Gulfport/Biloxi, Harlingen, Harrisburg, Hartford, Houston, Huntsville, Indianapolis, Jacksonville, Kalamazoo, Kansas City, Knoxville, Lake Charles, Lansing, Laredo, Little Rock, Louisville, Lubbock, Memphis, Midland/Odessa, Milwaukee, Minneapolis,Mobile, Monroe, Nashville, New York, Oklahoma City, Omaha, Ottawa, Philadelphia, Pittsburgh, St.Louis, Syracuse, Tampico, Toledo, Toronto, Vail, Waco, Washington, Wichita.

Fleet		Ordered
36 ATR 42	10 Embraer RJ-135	16 Embraer RJ-135
2 ATR 72	63 Embraer RJ-145	20 Embraer RJ-145
21 Embraer EMB 120	20 Beech 1900D	

Boeing 737-71Q HP-1370CMP (Josef Krauthäuser/Miami)

COPA PANAMA

Apartado Postal 1572, Panama City 1, Panama
Tel. 2272522, Fax. 2271952,
www.copaair.com

Three- / Two- letter code	IATA No.	Reg'n prefix	ICAO callsign
CMP / CM	230	HP	Copa

The Compania Panamena de Aviacion SA – COPA – was formed on 21st June 1944. As was the case with many other South and Central American airlines, Pan American Airways (holding 32% of the shares) was behind the formation, in association with business people from Panama. Scheduled services to neighbouring countries commenced on 15th August 1947 with Douglas DC-3s. A Convair 240 was added to the fleet in 1952. Until the time when jet aircraft were introduced, an HS.748 and Lockheed L-188 Electra were in service with COPA. During 1971 Pan American sold its shareholding in the airline to the Panamanian government. Domestic services were discontinued from 1981, but international services were expanded, with Mexico City being added from 1991 and Cali, Montego Bay and Puerto Rico in 1992. In 1995 service to the Dominican Republic was added. An event of significance in the airline's recent development took place in 1998 when Continental Airlines acquired 49% of the capital, setting the scene for a close commercial co-operation. A fleet renewal was begun with the delivery of the first Boeing 737-700 in May 1999. With the introduction of the new type, a new colour scheme which has strong similarities to that of Continental, was adopted. There is also co-operation with Avant Airlines of Chile.

Routes

Barranquilla, Bogota, Cali, Caracas, Cartagena, Guatemala City, Guayaquil, Havana, Kingston, Lima, Managua, Medellin, Mexico City, Miami, Montego Bay, Panama City, Port au Prince, Quito, San Jose, San Juan, San Pedro Sula, San Salvador, Santiago, Santo Domingo.

Fleet	Ordered
11 Boeing 737-200 3 Boeing 737-700	4 Boeing 737-700

Boeing 747-312 F-GSUN (Alireza Azimzadeh/Geneva)

CORSAIR

24 rue Saarinen, Silic 221, 94528 Rungis Silic Cedex, France, Tel. 1-49794979, Fax. 1-49794968, www.corsair-int.com

Three- / Two- letter code	IATA No.	Reg'n prefix	ICAO callsign
CRL / SS	–	F	Corsair

Formed in 1981 as Corse-Air International, the airline started operations on 1st July 1981 and acquired four SE.210 Caravelles. Charters were operated from Paris and Ajaccio, within Europe and to Northern Africa. A characteristic feature of the fleet was a striking head with a headband painted on the tailfins of the aircraft. The first Boeing 737s were taken on in 1987, marking the start of a fleet replacement programme and during 1990 the first Boeing 747 was added. After a leading French tour operator, Nouvelles Frontières, took a stake in the airline in 1991, the airline's name was changed to its present form, and a new colour scheme was adopted for the aircraft. Traffic rights were obtained for a greater range of destinations, including flights to the French overseas territories, and Corsair developed into one of the larger charter operators. More long range routes continued to be added from 1994 to 1997, and in 1999 the first new Airbus A330 was introduced, the first new generation aircraft to replace the Boeing 747SPs on these long-range services. A further A330 was added at the beginning of 2000. Two Boeing 737-400s are operated on charter work exclusively for Nouvelles Frontières.

Routes

Abidjan, Ajaccio, Amman, Athens, Bamako, Bangkok, Barcelona, Bari, Bastia, Calvi, Cairo, Cayenne, Cotonou, Dakar, Djerba, Dublin, Faro, Fort de France, Funchal, Havana, Heraklion, Hurghada, Istanbul, Larnaca, Lisbon, Los Angeles, Luxor, Malaga, Male, Marrakesh, Mombasa, Montreal, New York, Noumea, Oslo, Palma de Mallorca, Papeete, Pont a Pitre, Porto, Rome, San Francisco, St.Denis, St. Louis, St. Martin, Tenerife, Venice.

Fleet		Ordered
2 Airbus A330-200	2 Boeing 747-200	2 Airbus A330-200
1 Boeing 737-300	3 Boeing 747-300	
2 Boeing 737-400	1 Boeing 747SP	

Airbus A320-200 9A-CTJ (Uwe Gleisberg/Munich)

CROATIA AIRLINES

Savska Cesta 41, 1000 Zagreb, Croatia
Tel. 1-6160066, Fax. 1-6176845,
www.ctn.tel.hr/ctn

Three- / Two- letter code	IATA No.	Reg'n prefix	ICAO callsign
CTN / OU	831	9A	Croatia

After the break-up of Yugoslavia, the Republic of Croatia was formed in the north of the country, with Zagreb as its capital. The national airline formed in 1989 was initially called Zagal-Zagreb Airlines and used Cessna and Piper light aircraft, but it took on the present name in 1990. The scheduled services formerly operated by JAT were taken over, using DC-9s from Adria Airways and operations commenced on 5th May 1991 between Zagreb and Split. As a result of the United Nations embargo and continued fighting, the airspace over the country was closed from September 1990 until 1st April 1992. After it was re-opened, Croatian Airlines expanded its operations, using Boeing 737-200s. From 1993, ATR 42s also came into use for internal and short-range international flights. With the opening of airports at Mostar and Sarajevo in Summer 1996, these points were also served. A fleet renewal with factory-fresh Airbus A320s and A319s began in 1997, allowing the older Boeing 737s to be retired, and giving Croatia one of the youngest fleets in Europe. In addition to scheduled services, there are also special flights for expatriate Croatian workers, as well as holiday charters for the Adriatic tourist market, which is coming back to life, partially by the efforts of the airline's own tour company which has been formed for this purpose. There are co-operation agreements with Air France, Alitalia, CSA, Iberia, Lufthansa and THY-Turkish Airlines.

Routes

Amsterdam, Berlin, Bol, Brussels, Dubrovnik, Düsseldorf, Frankfurt, Istanbul, London, Madrid, Milan, Manchester, Mostar, Moscow, Munich, Osijek, Paris, Prague, Pula, Rome, Sarajevo, Skopje, Split, Stockholm, Tel Aviv, Vienna, Zadar, Zagreb and Zürich.

Fleet

4 Airbus A319-100
3 Airbus A320-200
3 ATR 42-300

Boeing 737-4Y0 SX-BGH (Uwe Gleisberg/Munich)

CRONUS AIRLINES

500 Vougliamensis, 17456 Alimos, Greece
Tel. 1-9956400, Fax. 1-9956405,
www.cronus.gr

Three- / Two- letter code	IATA No.	Reg'n prefix	ICAO callsign
CUS / X5	198	SX	Cronus

This private scheduled-service airline was formed in 1994 by the Manetas industrial family, with Boeing 737-300 operations from Thessaloniki beginning in April 1995 to destinations including Düsseldorf, Frankfurt, Cologne, Munich and Stuttgart. It was intentional that at first, services were concentrated on German cities, with operations also added from Athens. With the delivery of a second Boeing 737-300, Cronus was able to add service to London from July 1997. From December 1998 Greek domestic services from Athens to Heraklion and Rhodes, were added. The fleet was expanded, to match the growing network but the airline remains loyal to the Boeing 737, with the first -400 model added in April 1998, and a new generation -700 on order for delivery in July 2001. Chania and Rome were added from Summer 1999 for the first time. As well as scheduled services, the airline operates charter flights from many European cities. The company's base is in Athens, where with the opening of the new airport, the airline has hopes for further expansion.

Routes

Athens, Chania, Cologne/Bonn, Düsseldorf, Frankfurt, Heraklion, Kavala, London, Munich, Paris, Rhodes, Rome, Stuttgart and Thessaloniki are served regularly. Numerous charter flights from other airports to Greece.

Fleet	Ordered
5 Boeing 737-300	1 Boeing 737-700
2 Boeing 737-400	

Avro RJ 100 HB-IXQ (Jan-Alexander Lück/Hamburg)

CROSSAIR

Postfach, 4002 Basle-Flughafen, Switzerland
Tel. 61-3252525, Fax. 61-3253554,
www.crossair.ch

Three- / Two- letter code	IATA No.	Reg'n prefix	ICAO callsign
CRX / LX	724	HB	Crossair

On 2nd July 1979 Crossair, using a Swearingen Metro II, began service from Zürich to Nuremberg. A non-scheduled predecessor, Business Flyers Basle, had been in existence since 14th February 1975. When scheduled services were started, the name Crossair was adopted, and is now well-known beyond the borders of the Swiss Confederacy. Under the leadership of their President, Moritz Suter, Crossair made great contributions to European regional services, with pioneering ideas for its Saab 340 regional aircraft, for which the airline was a launch customer with an order for ten in October 1980. Within Switzerland, Crossair opened up new services over the years from Basle, Berne and Lugano. The airline's achievements were recognised with many awards, for instance 'Commuter Airline of the Year'. In 1990 over a million passengers were carried for the first time, and the Fokker 50 and the first jet, the BAe 146, were introduced. By now 70% owned by the Swissair Group, on behalf of whom many services were operated, the airline was also the launch customer for the Saab 2000, which was introduced after some delivery delays in 1994. As a result of a reorganisation within the Swissair group, Crossair took over some MD-80s from 1997, using them for both scheduled and charter services. Future fleet policy has been affected by the withdrawal of Saab from regional aircraft manufacture, and it is Embraer who have won favour with Crossair. The first RJ-145 was delivered in March 2000 (marking also the introduction of a new colour scheme for the airline) and there are large orders in place for more 145s, and the larger 170s and 190s for delivery from December 2002 and June 2004 respectively.

Routes

Ajaccio, Amsterdam, Athens, Baku, Barcelona, Basle, Berlin, Berne, Birmingham, Bremen, Brussels, Copenhagen, Dresden, Düsseldorf, Edinburgh, Florence, Frankfurt, Geneva, Genoa, Gerona, Graz, Guernsey, Hamburg, Hanover, Helsinki, Ibiza, Jersey, Klagenfurt, Krakow, Leipzig, Linz, Lisbon, London, Lugano, Luxembourg, Lyon, Madrid, Malaga, Manchester, Milan, Marseilles, Munich, Münster, Naples, Nice, Nuremberg, Paris, Prague, Rome, Salzburg, Sevilla, Sion, Skopje, Sofia, Stockholm, Stuttgart, Toulouse, Tunis,Valencia, Venice, Warsaw, Vienna, Zagreb, Zürich.

Fleet		Ordered
20 Avro RJ 85/100	34 Saab 2000	19 Embraer RJ-145
6 Embraer RJ-145	12 (Boeing)McDonnell Douglas MD-82/83	30 Embraer RJ-170
12 Saab SF-340 B		30 Embraer RJ-190

ATR 42-400 OK-AFE (Nikolaus Gruber/Prague)

CSA - CZECH AIRLINES

Ruzyne Airport 16008 Prague, Czech Republic,
Tel 2-20111111, Fax. 2-20562266,
www.csa.cz

Three- / Two- letter code	IATA No.	Reg'n prefix	ICAO callsign
CSA / OK	064	OK	CSA Lines

CSA was founded on 6th October 1923 and flew its first service from Prague to Bratislava with a Hansa Brandenburg Aero A-14. In the mid-1930s the exclusively domestic service was expanded internationally with a Prague-Bratislava-Vienna-Zagreb route, and connections to Romania and the USSR followed. By the mid-1930s CSA was one of the leading European airlines. However, closure was enforced by the war from 1938 to 1946. A new start was made in 1947 with the Douglas DC-3, but following political change in 1948 came the influx of Soviet technology, and CSA flew Ilyushin

IL-12s and -14s, and from 9th December 1957, the Tupolev Tu-104A, with which service to Jakarta was introduced.The IL-12s were replaced by Ilyushin IL-18s and a schedule to Havana initiated for political reasons. For long-range routes the Ilyushin IL-62 was acquired in 1969 and in 1970 New York and Montreal were first served. The Tu-134A was employed for many years on European routes, but gradually replaced from April 1988 with Tu-154Ms. The major political change during 1989 made it possible for the first time in 40 years to order Western aircraft. Airbus

A310-300s were thus delivered in 1990 to replace the IL-62s. Since then the fleet has been constantly renewed and upgraded, with ATR 72s added from 1992, ATR 42s from March 1996, Boeing 737-500s from March 1997 and 737-400s from April 1998. Following the division of the former Czechoslovakia into two republics, a change of name (from 26th March 1995) and a new colour scheme were introduced. By the end of the 1990s the last of the Tupolevs had been retired. It is planned that CSA will join the Sky Team alliance from 1st April 2001, and be partly privatised by 2002.

Routes

Abu Dhabi, Al In, Amsterdam, Athens, Bahrain, Bangkok, Barcelona, Beirut, Belgrade, Berlin, Bologna, Bratislava, Brno, Brussels, Bucharest, Cairo, Copenhagen, Damascus, Dubai, Dublin, Düsseldorf, Frankfurt, Geneva, Gothenburg, Hamburg, Hanover, Helsinki, Istanbul, Karlovy Vary, Kiev, Kosice, Larnaca, London, Madrid, Milan, Manchester, Montreal, Munich, New York, Nice, Oslo, Paris, Poprad/Tatry, Prague, Riga, Rome, Sofia, Split, St. Petersburg, Stockholm, Stuttgart, Tel Aviv, Toronto, Warsaw, Vienna, Zagreb, Zürich.

Fleet

2 Airbus A310-300
4 ATR 42-300/400
4 ATR 72-200

7 Boeing 737-400
10 Boeing 737-500

Ilyushin IL-62M CU-T1283 (Romano Germann/Havana)

CUBANA DE AVIACION

23-64 Vedado Havana 4, Republic of Cuba
Tel. 334949, Fax. 334056,
www.cubana.cu

Three- / Two- letter code	IATA No.	Reg'n prefix	ICAO callsign
CUB / CU	136	CU	Cubana

Staunchly socialist Cuba has had its doors open for tourists for several years, ever since tourism was recognised as a valuable source of foreign currency. Thus Cubana Ilyushin IL-62s have been seen from time to time at European airports. Empresa Consolidada Cubana de Aviacion was set up on 27th June 1961 by the new Cuban government, taking over and reorganising its predecessor Compania Cubana de Aviacion SA and merging in several smaller airlines. At that time the inherited fleet consisted of British and American built aircraft such as Constellations, Britannias and Viscounts, but after the imposition of a trade embargo by the USA, Soviet types were brought into use, with IL-14s, IL-18s, An-12s and An-24s arriving between 1961 and 1967. In 1974 Cubana's first jet, an IL-62, arrived and went into service in November between Havana and Madrid. Following the collapse of the Warsaw Pact, services were increased to non-communist countries, some flown with wet-leased DC-10s. The acquisition of six Fokker F.27s from Aviaco in 1994 was another sign of the easing of relations, and was also marked by the introduction of a new colour scheme. From November 1998, Airbus A320s were added, and the total of Soviet built types has been steadily declining. In the medium term, Cubana has need for more new aircraft, as the average age of the fleet and its heavy demand for maintenance militates against keeping the older types flying.

Routes

Baracoa, Barcelona, Bayamo, Bogota, Buenos Aires, Camaguey, Cancun, Caracas, Cayo Largo, Ciego de Avila, Cienfuegos, Cordoba, Fort de France, Guantanamo, Guatemala City, Havana, Holguin, Kingston, Las Tunas, Lisbon, Madrid, Mendoza, Mexico City, Montego Bay, Montevideo, Montreal, Nassau, Nueva Gerona, Paris, Punta Cana, Santiago, Santiago de Cuba, Santo Domingo, Sao Paulo, Varadero.

Fleet

2 Airbus A320-200	4 Fokker F.27
5 Antonov An-24	5 Ilyushin IL-62
2 Yakovlev Yak-42	1 Ilyushin IL-76

Airbus A320-231 5B-DAT (Dieter Roth/Salzburg)

CYPRUS AIRWAYS

PO Box 21903, CY-1514 Nicosia, Cyprus
Tel. 2-663054, Fax. 2-663167
www.cyprusair.com.cy

Three- / Two- letter code	IATA No.	Reg'n prefix	ICAO callsign
CYP / CY	048	5B	Cyprus

Cyprus Airways was set up on 24th September 1947 by British European Airways, Cypriot business interests and the government. BEA Douglas DC-3s were used to start operations to Athens on 6th October 1947. Other routes were added to Haifa, Istanbul, Rome, Beirut and Cairo. The airline took delivery of the first of its own DC-3s in April 1948 and was thus able to operate its own services. During 1950 BOAC took over 23% of the shares, though these were sold in 1959 to the Cypriot government. Vickers Viscounts opened the London route in the 1950s after BEA, on behalf of Cyprus Airways, began the world's first sustained turboprop passenger service on 18th April 1953 when a Viscount flew from Heathrow to Nicosia. Cyprus gained independence in August 1960 and BEA signed a deal with Cyprus Airways in 1961 to operate its services, initially for a five year period, with BEA aircraft. The arrangement finally ended in 1969, in which year Cyprus took delivery of its first jets, two Hawker-Siddeley Tridents bought from BEA in November. In July 1974 Cyprus Airways had to cease operations, as Turkish troops occupied Nicosia airport and a Trident was destroyed in fighting. However, on 8th February 1975 the first Boeing 707 took off from the new base at Larnaca in the south of Cyprus. BAC One-Elevens were acquired from 1978 to 1980 and in 1984 came the first Airbus A310, with the first A320 following in mid-1989. A subsidiary company, Eurocypria Airlines, was founded in 1990, using A320s for charter work. A new colour scheme was introduced in 1991 and is still in use. For several years now Cyprus Airways has operated an almost unchanged network; further expansion does not seem to be on the agenda.

Routes

Amman, Amsterdam, Athens, Bahrain, Beirut, Berlin, Birmingham, Brussels, Damascus, Dresden, Dubai, Frankfurt, Hamburg, Heraklion, Jeddah, Kuwait, Larnaca, London, Milan, Manchester, Moscow, Munich, Paris, Riyadh, Rome, Salzburg, Tel Aviv, Thessaloniki, Vienna and Zürich.

Fleet

8 Airbus A320
4 Airbus A310-200

(Boeing) McDonnell Douglas MD-11 N804DE (Dennis Wehrmann/Frankfurt)

DELTA AIR LINES

Hartsfield Atlanta Airport, Georgia 30320-6001, USA, Tel. 404-7152600, Fax. 404-7155876, www.delta-air.com

Three- / Two- letter code	IATA No.	Reg'n prefix	ICAO callsign
DAL / DA	006	N	Delta

Delta Air Lines is not only one of the largest airlines in the USA, but also one of the oldest, tracing its history back to Huff Daland setting up in 1924 at Monroe, LA to spray cotton fields in the Mississippi Delta. The name Delta Air Services was taken in 1928. A Travelair was used on the first scheduled passenger service on 17th June 1929 from Dallas to Jackson. The company was sold to the Aviation Corporation in 1930 and became Delta Air Corporation. By 1940 the fleet consisted of ten Lockheed Electras and five DC-3s. In 1953 Delta merged with Chicago & Southern Airlines, Northeast Airlines was taken over in 1972 and

finally Western Airlines was acquired in 1987; thus the network and fleet were continually expanded. In 1959 DC-8s, in 1960 Convair 880s and in 1965 DC-9s were brought into service, with Delta being a launch customer in each case. Widebodies, Boeing 747s from 1970-1977, and DC-10s from 1972-1975 were also used before the airline settled on the Lockheed TriStar. During 1978 began transatlantic service, to London, with Frankfurt added a year later. In November 1991, the ailing Pan Am was bought and all its routes and aircraft integrated. Delta Express, a low-cost division serving about 20 destinations, was

established in October 1996. In Spring 1997 Delta signed an exclusive 20-year fleet acquisition plan with Boeing, and as a result, two new types, the 737-800 and 777 were added from 1998 to replace the older 737-200s and Lockheed TriStars. It is also a launch customer for the Boeing 767-400. A further acquisition at the beginning of 1999 was ASA-Atlantic Southwest Airlines, which provides feeder services as 'Delta Connection'. There had been close co-operation with Swissair, but this was dropped in 1999 and a new venture with Air France forms the initial building block for the 'SkyTeam' global alliance.

Routes

Delta has over 2600 flights daily to about 250 destinations worldwide. Delta Express serves about 20 points and Delta Shuttle links New York, Boston and Washington hourly. Principal hubs are Atlanta, Dallas/Fort Worth and Cincinnati.

Fleet

		Ordered
102 Boeing 727-200	7 Boeing 777-200	86 Boeing 737-800
45 Boeing 737-200	20 Lockheed L-1011	6 Boeing 757-200
26 Boeing 737-300	15 McDonnell Douglas MD-11	3 Boeing 767-300
26 Boeing 737-800	120 McDonnell Douglas MD-88	21 Boeing 767-400ER
113 Boeing 757-200	16 McDonnell Douglas MD-90	6 Boeing 777-200
15 Boeing 767-200		
83 Boeing 767-300/300ER		

Boeing 737-3L9 D-ADBI (Josef Krauthäuser/Munich)

DEUTSCHE BA

Wartungsallee 13, 85356 München-Flughafen, Germany, Tel. 089-97591 500, Fax. 089-97591 503, www.deutsche-ba.de

Three- / Two- letter code	IATA No.	Reg'n prefix	ICAO callsign
BAG / DI	944	D	Speedway

Delta Air of Friedrichshafen was set up by the Scholpp transport group in Stuttgart in March 1978 and started flights between Friedrichshafen and Stuttgart with a DHC-6 Twin Otter in April 1978, as well as from Friedrichshafen to Zürich. In 1982 a Swearingen Metro III was added to the fleet. A second Metro III was added in 1984 as well as a Dornier 228, which was used on the route from Friedrichshafen to Oberpfaffenhofen. In 1985 Delta Air was converted into a private limited company, with the involvement of the Swiss airline Crossair. In May 1987 it was given the status of a scheduled airline and from that time flew some routes with Saab 340s, added to the fleet in 1986, on behalf of Lufthansa. In March 1992 three German banks bought 51% of the shares and British Airways the remaining 49% stake in Delta, and the name was changed to Deutsche BA on 5th May 1992. The new airline used not only Saab 340s, but also Boeing 737-300s, introducing the Saab 2000 and Fokker 100 from 1995. During 1992 and 1993 scheduled services were inaugurated amongst others to Moscow and Ankara. The company headquarters were moved to Munich from 1st January 1995, and in 1997 the regional operations were sold and the company withdrew from the operation of propeller-driven types, the fleet being standardised on the Boeing 737-300 alone (though it was announced in mid-2000 that a switch would be made to Airbus A320s, from around 2004, following the lead of its parent company). A new colour scheme was introduced, following the British Airways' example of artistic and colourful tail adornment. As a subsidiary of BA, Deutsche BA is a member of the Oneworld alliance, and it codeshares with US Airways, TAP Air Portugal, Lot, Finnair and Iberia.

Routes

Barcelona, Berlin, Cologne/Bonn, Düsseldorf, Hamburg, London-Gatwick, Munich, Stuttgart, charter flights principally to the Mediterranean holiday spots.

Fleet

18 Boeing 737-300

McDonnell Douglas DC-8-73F N802DH (Patrick Lutz/San Francisco)

DHL AIRWAYS

P.O.Box 75122, Cincinnati Ohio 45275, USA
Tel. 606-2832232, Fax. 606-5251998,
www.dhl.com

Three- / Two- letter code	IATA No.	Reg'n prefix	ICAO callsign
DHL / ER	423	N	Dahl

DHL Airways is an enterprise of the internationally represented DHL Worldwide Express, which was founded in 1969. The DHL name stems from the first letters of the surnames of the three founders. Initially its task was the carriage of courier packages between California and Hawaii, carried on scheduled flights, and then on other routes within the USA. In time, as the volume of business grew, the company started to use its own smaller aircraft such as the Swearingen Metro II or Cessna 402 on selected domestic routes. At the beginning of the 1980s business had grown so much that packages were carried on their own aircraft only and within the USA there were 12 hubs and 76 so-called gateways, where freight could be accepted - not only small and express packages. DHL now has 14 international hubs worldwide. Boeing 727s have formed the bulk of the fleet, with DC-8s for long-range routes, and even a helicopter for service in New York. Other operators fly on behalf of DHL, for example European Air Transport of Belgium, for various European services. For the expanding Asia market DHL has a Chinese partner in Sinotrans and similarly there are regional partners in several other countries. With the delivery of the first Airbus A300B4 in April 1999 DHL both initiated fleet renewal and added capacity.

Routes

Scheduled freight services within the USA and internationally to over 140 destinations on all continents.

Fleet

```
 7 Airbus A300B4F
 1 Bell 206-L1 Longranger
20 Boeing 727-100/200
 7 McDonnell Douglas DC-8-73F
```

McDonnell Douglas MD-81 LV-WTY (Author's collection/Buenos Aires-AEP)

DINAR LINEAS AEREAS

San Martin 320, Buenos Aires, Argentina
Tel. 11-43271111, Fax. 11-43253899

Three- / Two- letter code	IATA No.	Reg'n prefix	ICAO callsign
RDN / D7	429	LV	AeroDinar

The private bus operator TAC expanded its sphere of business in 1991, by founding its own airline Dinar Lineas Aereas. Services began in 1992 using a Fokker F.28, initially concentrating on charter flights to tourist destinations within Argentina. Following the acquisition of a further Fokker F.28 and additionally two Boeing 737-200s in 1993, Dinar offered scheduled services for the first time. From the Jorge Newbery airport at the national capital Buenos Aires, it flew to Mar del Plata and Cordoba. Further Argentinian domestic destinations followed, and the fleet was further expanded with Douglas DC-9-41s. During the high season, Dinar regularly leases in aircraft from other operators, notably from Europe. An increasing number of charter flights are being undertaken to neighbouring Brazil and Chile, and to the Caribbean. During 1998 a Boeing 757 was added, while the Boeing 737-200s and one of the Fokker F.28s were withdrawn. Such a small and yet varied fleet is expensive to maintain and so rationalisation of the fleet was a logical move. Thus the fleet now consists entirely of DC-9 variants, the DC-9-34 having been added in January 2000.

Routes

Buenos Aires, Comodoro Rivadavia, Cordoba, Jujuy, Mar del Plata, Mendoza, Puerto Madryn, Rio Gallegos, Salta, Santiago del Estero, Tacuman.

Fleet

1 Douglas DC-9-34
3 Douglas DC-9-41
1 McDonnell Douglas MD-81

Tupolev Tu-154B-2 RA-85400 (Ralf Lücke/Düsseldorf)

DONAVIA

Sholokova Prospekt 272, Rostov-na-Donu,
Russia
Tel. 8632-525079, Fax. 8632-520567

Three- / Two- letter code	IATA No.	Reg'n prefix	ICAO callsign
DNV / D9	733	RA	Donavia

Following the break-up of the Soviet Union, the former national airline Aeroflot was also divided into many individual companies, with new airlines being created from the majority of the former Aeroflot directorates. All had the same objective - economic change and the path from central direction to a style of market economy. Only a few of the new airlines in Russia managed to make this U-turn in the way they operate. Donavia was established as a joint stock company in 1993 by the employees of the former Aeroflot directorate in Rostov on Don. The employees owned 51% of the shares, with the balance held by the state. Partly in co-operation with the new Aeroflot, Donavia succeeded in establishing a well-ordered scheduled service network, using aircraft, principally Tupolev Tu-154s, which had been inherited from Aeroflot. The routes are largely domestic, though there are several international services. Donavia is also successful in freight and charter business, especially to the Gulf and Middle East.

Routes

Dubai, Düsseldorf, Irkutsk, Istanbul, Khabarovsk, Krasnoyarsk, Larnaca, Moscow, Omsk, Rostov, St. Petersburg, Tashkent, Tel Aviv, Tyumen, Vladivostok, Yekaterinburg, Yerevan.

Fleet

5 Antonov An-12BP
8 Tupolev Tu-134A
13 Tupolev Tu-154

Airbus A330-342 (Martin Bach/Hong Kong)

DRAGONAIR

22F. Devon House, Taikoo Place 979 Kings Rd, Quarry Bay, Hong Kong, Tel. 25901328, Fax. 25901333, www.dragonair.com

Three- / Two- letter code	IATA No.	Reg'n prefix	ICAO callsign
HDA / KA	043	B-H	Dragonair

Dragonair began its activities in 1985, mainly to serve destinations in the People's Republic of China from Hong Kong. The airline, a wholly-owned subsidiary of Hong Kong Macau International Investments, started operations with two Boeing 737-200s, though during the first year the aircraft were often grounded as a result of strong opposition from Cathay Pacific. However over the next few years some scheduled routes were awarded to Dragonair and several more Boeing 737s were leased as the network was expanded. From 1989 destinations other than in the People's Republic of China were served and a charter division established. It was also in 1989 that China International Trust and Investment and the Swire Group, owners of Cathay Pacific, acquired most of the shares in Dragonair. In mid-1990 a Lockheed L-1011 TriStar was acquired from Cathay Pacific. When the first Airbus A320 was delivered in late 1992, a new aircraft colour scheme was adopted. Four Airbus A330s were introduced in 1995/96 as replacements for the TriStars, and these have been augmented by the delivery of further Airbus types, giving the airline a modern fleet. In 1998 and 1999 Airbus A321s were also leased, to add further services to Chinese destinations following the return of Hong Kong to Chinese sovereignty and the opening of the new Hong Kong airport.

Routes

Beijing, Changsa, Chengdu, Chongqing, Dalian, Fuzhou, Guillin, Haikou,Hangzhou, Hiroshima, Hong Kong, Kaohsiung, Kota Kinabalu, Kunming, Nanjing, Phnom Penh, Phuket, Qingdao, Sendai, Shanghai, Wuhan, Xian, Xiamen.

Fleet	Ordered
8 Airbus A320-200	5 Airbus A320
3 Airbus A321-200	1 Airbus A330
6 Airbus A330-300	

BAe 146-100 A5-RGD (Josef Krauthäuser/Bangkok)

DRUK AIR

P.O.Box 209 Thimpu, Kingdom of Bhutan
Tel 22825, Fax. 22775,
www.drukair.com

Three- / Two- letter code	IATA No.	Reg'n prefix	ICAO callsign
DRK / KB	787	A5	Royal Bhutan

Druk Air was established as the national airline on 1st April 1981 by decree of the King of Bhutan. After the infrastructure for air traffic had been prepared – it was necessary to build an airport near to the capital – a Dornier 228 began services with a flight to Calcutta on 12th February 1983. In mid-1983 a second aircraft of the same type was acquired. Charters were flown on behalf of the Indian domestic carrier, Vayudoot, on routes in eastern India. When a BAe 146 was delivered, the young airline entered the jet age; the new type allowed an expansion of the network and the addition of service to more distant destinations. The first new route was to Bangkok, where passengers from Europe change aircraft to fly to Bhutan with Druk Air. The BAe 146 is also at the disposal of the King of Bhutan for his personal use. With the delivery of a further BAe 146 in December 1992 the Dorniers were sold and the fleet became all-jet. During the tourist season from May to October Druk Air operates special 'Sky Kingdom' flights, which show off the tiny Kingdom of Bhutan from a fantastic perspective, flying amongst the Himalayan peaks and offering unique panoramas. Outside the tourist season, one of the BAe 146s is sometimes leased out .

Routes

Bangkok, Dacca, Delhi, Calcutta, Kathmandu, Paro, Yangon.

Fleet

2 BAe 146-100

Boeing 737-300 G-EZYA (Dennis Wehrmann/Geneva)

EASYJET AIRLINE

Luton Intl. Airport, Luton LU2 9LS
Great Britain, Tel. 1582445566,
Fax. 1582443355, www.easyjet.com

Three- / Two- letter code	IATA No.	Reg'n prefix	ICAO callsign
EZY / U2	–	G	Easy

In October 1995 Stelios Haji-Ioannou, a member of the Greek shipping line family, set up this new airline in London. EasyJet was the first British airline to follow the low-cost model which had been proved in the United States. The airline began services from London-Luton to Glasgow three times daily, only a month after its formation. Using two leased Boeing 737-200s and foreign cockpit crews, EasyJet was initially without its own operators certificate. Two weeks later, services were begun to Edinburgh. After some start-up difficulties, new services were added, but there was a shortage of aircraft in the fleet to

accomplish all this and the company had to take time to stabilise the situation before proceeding. New Boeing 737-300s in 148-seat configuration were ordered and introduced from 1996, with deliveries on a monthly basis. Amsterdam became the first foreign destination from Spring 1996. During 1997 the airline was granted its own operating licence and created a second hub at Liverpool. A majority of the shares in TEA Switzerland was acquired, and this airline renamed as EasyJet Switzerland; it too operates Boeing 737-300s and there is some interchange of aircraft, and naturally,

a close co-operation. New model Boeing 737-700s are on order for EasyJet, with deliveries scheduled to commence in October 2000.

Routes

Aberdeen, Amsterdam, Athens, Barcelona, Belfast, Edinburgh, Geneva, Glasgow, Inverness, Liverpool, London-Luton, Madrid, Malaga, Nice, Palma de Mallorca, Zürich.

Fleet	Ordered
16 Boeing 737-300	15 Boeing 737-700

Boeing 727-287 HC-BVT (Josef Krauthäuser collection)

ECUATORIANA DE AVIACION

Colon Y Reina Victoria Edf. CP 505 Quito
Ecuador, Tel. 2-563003, Fax. 2-563920,
www.ecuatoriana.com.ar

Three- / Two- letter code	IATA No.	Reg'n prefix	ICAO callsign
EEA / EU	341	HC	Ecuatoriana

Empresa Ecuatoriana de Aviacion was formed in 1974 as a new national airline for Ecuador. It was supervised by the government. Two Boeing 720Bs and four Douglas DC-6s were taken over from the predecessor airline CEA, in which the state also had a financial holding, and it was thus simple to transfer the traffic rights and licences to Ecuatoriana. More jet aircraft, Boeing 707s, replaced the old DC-6s from 1976 and the Boeing 720Bs were sold in 1989, in order to provide the funds for the acquisition of a DC-10, which came from Swissair in 1990, in a new livery for the airline. Ecuatoriana had already been noteworthy for the artistic and colourful schemes applied to its 720s. Because of business difficulties, the state wanted to privatise the company from 1991, but no investor could be found, and equally, the costs of supporting the airline were simply too high. Thus, in 1993 all flights were suspended and the route licences sold. Likewise, those aircraft which were not leased, were put up for sale. However, with help from the Brazilian airline VASP, which had shareholdings in various airlines throughout South America, a reorganisation and fresh start was made in 1998 as Ecuatoriana de Aviacion. VASP holds 51% of the shares and provides the aircraft. The airline is based at Quito.

Routes

Buenos Aires, Cancun, Guayaquil, Manaus, Mexico City, New York, Panama City, Quito, Santiago, Sao Paulo.

Fleet

1 Airbus A310-300
2 Boeing 727-200
1 McDonnell Douglas DC-10-30

Airbus A320-200 HB-IHY (B. I. Hengi/Zürich)

EDELWEISS AIR

Postfach, 8055 Zürich-Flughafen, Switzerland
Tel. 1-8165060, Fax. 1-8165061,
www.edelweiss.ch

Three- / Two- letter code	IATA No.	Reg'n prefix	ICAO callsign
EDW –	–	HB	Edelweiss

On 19th October 1995 a new charter company was set up in the Zürich area, with the Kuoni travel company and the Greek airline Venus as the shareholders. It was set up as a joint stock company and could therefore take on further participants; the capital was raised to 3.5 million Swiss francs on the acquisition of aircraft in December 1995. At the end of January 1996 the first McDonnell Douglas MD-83 arrived, with the second following at the end of March. In the words of the officials at Kuoni Reisen AG, the main shareholder after the departure of Venus, Edelweiss tries to be an airline which offers a very Swiss atmosphere. The attractive colour scheme corresponds with the name and features a stylised version of the Swiss national flower. Beginning in the 1996 summer season, flights were operated to the traditional Mediterranean holiday resorts and to European cities. Good service and punctuality led to success, and a further MD-83 was acquired. From February 1999 the fleet was changed over to factory-fresh Airbus A320s, with three aircraft being delivered by June 1999. Edelweiss plans to enter the long-distance tour market, and has on order an Airbus A330 for delivery in November 2000.

Routes

Antalya, Catania, Corfu, Djerba, Eilat, Faro, Fuerteventura, Geneva, Heraklion, Hurghada, Ibiza, Kos, Lanzarote, Larnaca, La Palma, Las Palmas, London, Mahon, Malaga, Monastir, Mykonos, Naples, Olbia, Palermo, Palma de Mallorca, Rhodes, Santorini, Sharm el Sheik, Tenerife, Vienna, Zürich.

Fleet	Ordered
3 Airbus A320	1 Airbus A330

Boeing 777-200ER SU-GBS (Uwe Gleisberg/Munich)

EGYPT AIR

International Airport, Cairo, Egypt
Tel. 2-2454400, Fax. 2-3901557,
www.egyptair.com.eg

Three- / Two- letter code	IATA No.	Reg'n prefix	ICAO callsign
MSR / MS	077	SU	Egyptair

Misr Airwork was founded on 7th June 1932 and services began in July 1933 with de Havilland Dragons. In 1949 the then wholly Egyptian-owned operation was renamed Misrair. Following a political union between Egypt and Syria in February 1958, Misrair was renamed United Arab Airlines and in December 1958, Syrian Airways was merged into UAA. However, in September 1961, Syria withdrew from the amalgamation. UAA used Comet 4Bs and Vickers Viscounts. Egypt carried on the airline alone under the UAA name, but in 1964

Misrair was revived as a domestic airline, and then was brought together with UAA on 10th October 1971 to form the new Egypt Air. For political reasons UAA/Egypt Air flew Soviet types in the 1960s and 1970s, including An-24s, IL-18s, IL-62s and Tu-154s. In April 1975 the airline switched over to Airbus A300s and Boeing 737s. Boeing 707s followed for longer-range work, and later 747s as well. An extensive fleet replacement began with Boeing 767s and Airbus A300-600s in 1989. In 1991 Airbus A320s followed for short and medium-range routes.

Late in 1996 the Airbus A340 was introduced as an eventual replacement for the Boeing 747, and the introduction of the 340 also brought a new colour scheme for the airline. Also for long-distance flights, the Boeing 777 was added from 1997, completing the fleet renewal. However, at the turn of the century the process was begun again, with Egypt Air becoming a launch customer for the Airbus A318, and for the very long-range Airbus A340-600, deliveries of both of which are planned to commence in March 2003.

Routes

Abu Dhabi, Abu Simbel, Addis Ababa, Aden, Alexandria, Algiers, Amman, Amsterdam, Aswan, Athens, Bahrain, Bangkok, Barcelona, Beirut, Berlin, Brussels, Budapest, Cairo, Casablanca, Copenhagen, Damascus, Dubai, Düsseldorf, Frankfurt, Geneva, Hamburg, Hurghada, Istanbul, Jeddah, Kuwait, Larnaca, London, Los Angeles, Luxor, Manchester, Moscow, Mumbai, Munich, New York, Osaka, Paris, Rome, Sanaa, Sharjah, Singapore, Sydney, Tokyo, Vienna, Zürich.

Fleet		Ordered
9 Airbus A300-600	5 Boeing 737-500	5 Airbus A318
2 Airbus A300F	2 Boeing 747-300	2 Airbus A340-600
7 Airbus A320-200	1 Boeing 767-300ER	
4 Airbus A321-200	3 Boeing 777-200ER	
3 Airbus A340-200		

Boeing 737-800 4X-EKB (Uwe Gleisberg/Munich)

EL AL ISRAEL AIRLINES

P.O.Box 41 Ben Gurion Airport 70100 Tel Aviv, Israel, Tel. 3-9716111, Fax. 3-9716040, www.elal.co.il

Three- / Two- letter code	IATA No.	Reg'n prefix	ICAO callsign
ELY / LY	114	4X	ElAl

El Al took the initiative after the founding of the State of Israel and started building up services with aircraft belonging to the Israel Air Force. These were and are vital to Israel, which is surrounded by potential enemies. The aircraft used after the airline was formally established on 15th November 1948 were Curtiss C-46 Commandos and Douglas DC-4s (C-54s). Operations began on 31st July 1949 with services to Switzerland and Paris, with London added later in the year. A regular service to New York was established as soon as 1950 using

Lockheed Constellations. Bristol Britannias were acquired in 1957 and the change to jets began in 1960, initially with leased Boeing 707s; indeed 707s and 720s were to be the backbone of the fleet for many years. In 1971 the first Boeing 747 arrived; in 1983 767s replaced 707s, followed in 1987 by 757s. During the mid-1980s El Al was restructured as the danger of economic collapse was threatening, and with a view to eventual privatisation. Following Israel's peace treaty with the PLO and further easing of tension in the

Middle East, El Al was in a position to expand its regional services. New Boeing 747-400s were introduced during 1994 and 1995, lowering the average age of the fleet. With the delivery of new Boeing 737-700s and -800s in 1999 a new colour scheme was adopted by the airline; Boeing 777s are also on order for delivery from early in 2001. Some aircraft are loaned to another Israeli airline, Arkia on a seasonal basis and Boeing 747 freighters operate for CAL Cargo Airlines.

Routes

Amman, Amsterdam, Athens, Baltimore, Bangkok, Barcelona, Beijing, Berlin, Brussels, Budapest, Bucharest, Cairo, Chicago, Copenhagen, Delhi, Detroit, Düsseldorf, Eilat, Frankfurt, Geneva, Graz, Hanover, Helsinki, Hong Kong, Istanbul, Johannesburg, Kiev, Larnaca, London, Los Angeles, Luxembourg, Madrid, Milan, Malaga, Manchester, Marseilles, Miami, Minsk, Montreal, Moscow, Mumbai, Munich, Nairobi, New York, Odessa, Orlando, Ovda, Paphos, Paris, Prague, Rome, St. Petersburg, Stockholm, Tel Aviv, Toronto, Warsaw, Vienna, Zürich.

Fleet

Fleet		Ordered
4 Boeing 747-400	9 Boeing 757-200	3 Boeing 777
5 Boeing 747-200	2 Boeing 737-700	
2 Boeing 747-200F	3 Boeing 737-800	
6 Boeing 767-200		

Boeing 777-31H A6-EMM (Josef Krauthäuser collection via EAS/Dubai)

EMIRATES

P.O.Box 686, Dubai, United Arab Emirates, Tel. 4-2951111, Fax. 4-2952001, www.ekgroup.com

Three- / Two- letter code	IATA No.	Reg'n prefix	ICAO callsign
UAE / EK	176	A6	Emirates

This independent state airline was formed in 1985 with political and financial support of the council of the seven independent emirates and the reigning head of government, the Emir of Dubai. The first aircraft, a Boeing 727 and Airbus A300, were leased from Pakistan International Airlines, who also gave assistance with establishing the airline under a management agreement. The first service was on 25th October 1985 to Karachi in Pakistan, and India was also served from the outset. In 1986 Dacca, Colombo and Cairo were added, with the first European

routes starting from 1987, to London, Frankfurt and Istanbul. Newly-delivered Airbus A310s were used here, with further examples being added in 1988 and 1990. The larger Airbus A300-600 was ordered however, and the last two Boeing 727s withdrawn from the fleet in 1995. Emirates has seen purposeful expansion, but always with caution in new markets. In 1996 a new service to Melbourne was added, using the new Boeing 777, first delivered tin June 1996. Emirates operates a very modern fleet, consisting only of widebody aircraft.

Six Airbus A340-500s are on order for delivery from October 2002, and the airline was the first to order the new Airbus A3XX super jumbo, with five firm and five options. There is a codeshare agreement with SriLankan Airlines, in which company Emirates has a 25% shareholding,and other co-operation and codeshares with United Airlines, Thai Airways International, British Airways and South African Airways.

Routes

Abu Dhabi, Amman, Amsterdam, Athens, Bahrain, Baku, Bangkok, Beirut, Cairo, Colombo, Damascus, Dammam, Dar-es-Salaam, Delhi, Dacca, Doha, Dubai, Entebbe/Kampala, Frankfurt, Hong Kong, Islamabad, Istanbul, Jakarta, Jeddah, Johannesburg, Karachi, Kuala Lumpur, Kuwait, Lahore, Larnaca, London, Male, Malta, Manila, Manchester, Melbourne, Mumbai, Munich, Muscat, Nairobi, Nice, Paris, Peshawar, Riyadh, Rome, Sanaa, Shiraz, Singapore, Sydney, Teheran, Zürich.

Fleet	Ordered
8 Airbus A310-300	10 Airbus A330
5 Airbus A300-600	6 Airbus A340-500
9 Airbus A330-200	5 Airbus A3XX
11 Boeing 777	2 Boeing 777-300

De Havilland Canada DHC-8 N882EA (Josef Krauthäuser/Anchorage)

ERA AVIATION

6160 Carl Brady Drive, Anchorage, Alaska
99502-1801, USA, Tel. 907-2484422,
Fax. 907-2668383, www.era-aviation.com

Three- / Two- letter code	IATA No.	Reg'n prefix	ICAO callsign
ERH / 7H	808	N	Erah

ERA Aviation is an important undertaking, known not only for its extensive operations in Alaska, but also for its wide-ranging activities in support of exploration and oil production in the Gulf of Mexico. Founded in 1948, ERA was taken over in 1967 by the Houston, Texas-based Rowan Companies, who are active in the oil and natural gas production business. ERA is organised into several divisions, for instance ERA Helicopters Alaska Division, or the Gulf Coast Division. Then there was Jet Alaska, later known as ERA Jet Alaska, which mainly flew ad hoc and freight charters, but also passengers, mostly Alaska Pipeline building workers. In 1983 scheduled services were also being operated, and ERA's individual activities were brought together. Using DHC-6 Twin Otters, DHC-7s and Convair 580s ERA Aviation flew on behalf of Alaska Airlines from Anchorage and Bethel. The DHC-7s were replaced by the de Havilland Canada DHC-8, with the first being delivered in 1990. The Convair 580 is especially suited to Alaskan operations, and more examples have been acquired. ERA flies under Alaska Airlines flight numbers, but operates its aircraft in its own colour scheme. Two Douglas DC-3s are used for special flights and appear in ERA Classic Airlines colours.

Routes

Anchorage, Bethel, Chefornak, Chevak, Cordova, Eek, Goodnews Bay, Homer, Hooper Bay, Iliamna, Kenai, Kipnuk, Kodiak, Kongiganak, Mekoryuk, Mountain Village, Newtok, Nightmute, Pilot Station, Platinium,Quinhagak, Scammon Bay, St. Marys, Toksook Bay, Tuntutuliak, Tununak, Valdez, Whitehorse.

Fleet

12 De Havilland DHC-6 Twin Otter
 2 De Havilland DHC-8
 6 Convair 580
 2 Douglas DC-3

Boeing 737-500 ES-ABE (Albert Kuhbandner/Salzburg)

ESTONIAN AIR

2 Lennujaama Str. Tallinn 11101, Estonia
Tel. 6401100, Fax. 6312740,
www.estonian-air.ee

Three- / Two- letter code	IATA No.	Reg'n prefix	ICAO callsign
ELL / OV	960	ES	Estonian

Estonian Air was set up by the government of the newly independent state of Estonia on 1st December 1991 and declared to be the country's flag carrier. The first scheduled service, to Helsinki, started in the same month using Tupolev Tu-134s inherited along with Yak-40s and An-12s from Aeroflot. Further routes, especially within Scandinavia, were established in quick succession. In 1995 the state privatisation commission permitted conversion into a public company. 34% of the capital remained with the government; the rest is with private investors led by the Danish airline Maersk Air, who now give considerable management assistance. The first step after privatisation was the disposal of several Tupolev Tu-134s and the acquisition of two Boeing 737-500s decorated in a new, modern colour scheme, along with an expansion of the route network. The main base is in the Estonian capital of Tallinn, where the airline also has maintenance facilities. As well as scheduled services, seasonal charters are conducted throughout Europe. There are co-operation agreements with Air Botnia, Finnair and SAS. Estonian Air now operates only Western-built aircraft, the last Yak-40s having been replaced on regional routes in 1998 by two Fokker 50s supplied by Maersk. From the same source during the Spring of 2001 are to come two Canadair Regional Jets.

Routes

Amsterdam, Copenhagen, Frankfurt, Hamburg, Helsinki, Kiev, London, Minsk, Moscow, Oslo, Riga, Stockholm, Tallinn, Vilnius.

Fleet	Ordered
3 Boeing 737-500	2 Canadair Regional Jet 200LR
2 Fokker 50	

Boeing 757-260 ET-AKF (Bastian Hilker/Harare)

ETHIOPIAN AIRLINES

P.O.Box 1755, Bole Airport, Addis Ababa
Ethiopia, Tel. 1-612222,
Fax. 1-611474, www.ethiopianairlines.com

Three- / Two- letter code	IATA No.	Reg'n prefix	ICAO callsign
ETH / ET	071	ET	Ethiopian

Ethiopian Airlines was set up on 26th December 1945 by proclamation of the emperor at the time, Haile Selassie, to develop international services and to establish connections from the capital to communities in isolated, mountainous regions, where little or no surface transport existed. Scheduled flights started on 8th April 1946 with five Douglas DC-3s. The first service was between Addis Ababa and Cairo. A management contract was concluded with the American airline TWA assuring long-term support; this lasted until 1970. Douglas DC-6Bs were used to

operate regular flights to the first European destination, Frankfurt, from June 1958, followed by Athens, Rome, Paris and London. Boeing 720 jets were introduced from 1962, followed by further 707s and 720s. The first Boeing 727 arrived in December 1981 and Boeing 767s replaced the 707s and 720s from 1984. The DC-3s were augmented with Twin Otters, and phased out with the delivery of ATR 42s from 1989. From 1993, new Boeing 757s replaced the 727s. After some years of relative stagnation, partially brought about by the country's poor economic position and the war with

Eritrea, the company acquired some Fokker 50s from September 1996 onwards and a Boeing 767-300ER, which was used at the beginning of 1998 to open up services to New York and Washington. During 1999 a further Boeing 767-300ER was leased.

Routes

Over 40 domestic points. International services to Abidjan, Abu Dhabi, Accra, Athens, Bahrain, Bamako, Bangkok, Beijing, Beirut, Dakar, Dar-es-Salaam, Delhi, Djibouti, Dubai, Entebbe, Frankfurt, Harare, Jeddah, Johannesburg, Karachi, Khartoum, Kigali, Kilimanjaro, Kinshasa, Kuwait, Lagos, Lilongwe, Lome, London, Luanda, Lusaka, Mumbai, Muscat, Nairobi, Ndjamena, New York, Niamey, Ostend, Riyadh, Rome, Sanaa, Tel Aviv, Washington.

Fleet

2 Boeing 737-200
5 Boeing 757-200
2 Boeing 767-200
2 Boeing 767-300ER

1 De Havilland DHC-5
3 De Havilland DHC-6
5 Fokker 50
2 Lockheed L-100-30 Hercules

Airbus A320-231 5B-DBC (Josef Krauthäuser/Salzburg)

EUROCYPRIA AIRLINES

P.O.Box 40970, CY-6308 Larnaca
Cyprus Tel. 4-658000, Fax. 4-658008
www.cyprusair.com.cy

Three- / Two- letter code	IATA No.	Reg'n prefix	ICAO callsign
ECA / UI		5B	Eurocypria

On 12th June 1991,Cyprus Airways set up a subsidiary company called Eurocypria Airlines. The objective of the new airline was to offer attractive charter prices to tour operators for holidays on Cyprus, and to make the island tempting for new types of holidaymaker. Until then, Cyprus had attracted overwhelmingly English tourists because of the former links and the historical sights and beauty of the island, but few of the beach-loving tourists from other parts of Europe. More and more tourists discovered Cyprus during and after the Gulf War. The new airline began operations in March 1992 using Airbus A320s seconded from the parent company Cyprus Airways. The fleet of three 174-seat Airbus A320s has remained unaltered throughout the years, and they fly all over Europe, including to some of the smaller airports.The destinations in Cyprus are Larnaca and Paphos, both in the Greek sector of the divided island.

Routes

Charter flights from about 30 European airports to Larnaca and Paphos.

Fleet

3 Airbus A320-200

Airbus A319-112 D-AKNF (Dieter Roth/Munich)

EUROWINGS

Flugplatz 21, 44319 Dortmund, Germany
Tel. 0231-92450, Fax. 0231-9245102,
www.eurowings.de

Three- / Two- letter code	IATA No.	Reg'n prefix	ICAO callsign
EWG / EW	104	D	Eurowings

Eurowings stems from the amalgamation from 1st January 1993 of NFD-Nürnberger Flugdienst and RFG-Regional Fluggesellschaft. The majority shareholder, Albrecht Knauf, had proposed a concentration and work-sharing by the two companies, and the logical result was a combined operation. At the same time a new colour scheme was introduced for the combined fleet. NFD and RFG both had extensive regional networks from Dortmund and Nuremberg, using ATRs, Fairchild Metros and Dornier 228s. A BAe 146-200 QT was also used as a pure freighter on behalf of TNT, but the adaptable characteristics of this aircraft meant that it could also be used for passengers from 1995; it was used for busier scheduled routes and for charter work. EWG entered the tour market strongly from Autumn 1995 with the formation of its own tour company Eurowings Flug. Two A319s were ordered from Airbus for this purpose, and were used for the first time during the 1997/98 season. As well as operating its own scheduled services with a fleet now made up mainly of BAe 146s and ATR 42s and 72s, Eurowings flies on behalf of other companies on a codeshare basis. There are co-operation agreements with Air France, KLM and Northwest Airlines, offering passengers good connections to these companies' international routes in Amsterdam and Paris. More Airbus A319s were added during 1998 and 1999 , and used mainly for charter work. The airline is not only principally based at Dortmund, but also at Nuremberg, where there are extensive overhaul and maintenance facilities. Lufthansa acquired a 25% shareholding in September 2000.

Routes

Amsterdam, Berlin, Bremen, Brussels, Cologne/Bonn, Dortmund, Dresden, Düsseldorf, Hamburg, Hanover, Krakow, Leipzig, London, Milan, Munich, Münster/Osnabrück, Nuremberg, Paderborn/Lippstadt, Palma de Mallorca, Paris, Poznan, Rome, Saarbrücken, Stockholm, Stuttgart, Vienna, Wroclaw, Zürich. Charter flights to the Mediterranean, Northern Africa and Canary Islands.

Fleet

6 Airbus A319	10 BAe 146-200
17 ATR 42	
10 ATR 72	

Boeing 747-45E B-16402 (Josef Krauthäuser/Los Angeles-LAX)

EVA AIR

376 Hsin-nan Road, Sec. 1 Luchu, Taoyuan
Hsien 338, Republic of China, Tel. 3-3515151,
Fax. 3-3510005, www.evaair.com.tw

Three- / Two- letter code	IATA No.	Reg'n prefix	ICAO callsign
EVA / BR	695	B	Evaair

In March 1989 Evergreen, the largest container shipping line in the world, set up its own airline. However, state-imposed conditions, quarrels concerning the airline's name (confusion with the names of other companies) and the non-immediate availability of new aircraft prevented the new airline from starting operations straightaway. Finally, EVA Air, provided with US$ 370 million, started flights on 1st July 1991. It used Boeing 767-300ERs on routes to Bangkok, Manila, Hong Kong and Seoul. Vienna was served from November 1991 and London from April 1993. There are also important connections to the USA, with the first trans-Pacific service starting from Taipei to Los Angeles in December 1992. Fast-growing EVA Air has become one of the top Taiwanese airlines and has acquired stakes in Makung Airlines and Great China Airlines, thus adding a regional dimension to its network. The first MD-11was delivered in Autumn 1994, and the fleet of Boeing 747-400s has also been built up. The first MD-11 freighter service took place in October 1995 from Taiwan to Amsterdam. New routes to Brisbane, Paris and San Francisco were also added. In 1996 there was a further acquisition of a Taiwanese domestic carrier, Taiwan Airlines which flies several Britten-Norman Islanders and Dornier 228s and operates non-scheduled flights, with seasonal services to Far Eastern holiday centres. Makung Airlines and Taiwan Airlines were merged to form Uni-Air and in 1998 took over the whole of EVA's regional services. EVA is also a shareholder in Air Macau, and has alliances with Air Canada, Air New Zealand, ANA, American Airlines, Ansett and Uni-Air.

Routes

Amsterdam, Anchorage, Atlanta, Bangkok, Brisbane, Brussels, Chicago, Dubai, Fukuoka, Ho Chi Minh City, Hong Kong, Jakarta, Kaoshing, Kuala Lumpur, Los Angeles, London, Macau, Manila, Maldives, Mumbai, New York, Osaka, Paris, Penang, San Francisco, Seattle, Seoul, Sharjah, Singapore, Surabaya, Sydney, Taipei, Vancouver, Vienna.

Fleet / Ordered

Fleet		Ordered
15 Boeing 747-400	12 (Boeing) McDonnell Douglas MD-11	2 Boeing 747-400F
1 Boeing 747-400F		
4 Boeing 767-200		
4 Boeing 767-300ER		

Boeing 747-132 N481EV (Josef Krauthäuser/Los Angeles-LAX)

EVERGREEN INTERNATIONAL AIRLINES

3850 Three Mile Lane, McMinnville,
OR 97128-9496, USA, Tel. 503-4720011,
Fax. 503-4344221, www.evergreenaviation.com

Three- / Two- letter code	IATA No.	Reg'n prefix	ICAO callsign
EIA / EZ	494	N	Evergreen

Evergreen International Airlines is a division of Evergreen Aviation. This holding company also owns one of the largest helicopter companies in the USA, Evergreen Helicopters, as well as the famous Marana Airpark in Arizona, where large numbers of transport aircraft are parked when temporarily out of use. Here Evergreen also has an extensive maintenance facility and performs storage and overhaul work on most airliner types. The airline was set up on 28th November 1975 when Evergreen Helicopters acquired the operators' certificate from Johnson Airlines of Missoula. Operating as Johnson International, the company was founded in 1924 and was awarded one of the first supplemental certificates in 1957. Evergreen operates a domestic American cargo service on behalf of UPS and other companies but also has its own services to China and Hong Kong. In addition, aircraft are wet leased (i.e. inclusive of crew) to other operators. In 1995 the fleet was slimmed down and the Boeing 727s which had been in use were sold to a customer for re-engining. Evergreen operates scheduled and ad hoc charter flights, both freight and passenger, and undertakes troop transportation for the United States Army.

Routes

Scheduled freight flights within the USA, and to Hong Kong, China and Australia. Worldwide freight charters.

Fleet

12 Boeing 747-100/200
10 McDonnell Douglas DC-9-15/30

Boeing 727-2M7 N721RW (Gerhard Schütz/Munich)

EXPRESS ONE INTERNATIONAL

3890 West Northwest Highway, Suite 700,
Dallas TX 75220, USA
Tel. 214-9022500, Fax. 214-3501399a

Three- / Two- letter code	IATA No.	Reg'n prefix	ICAO callsign
LHN / EO	–	N	Longhorn

This airline began life in 1975 as Jet East International with air taxi services from Dallas Love Field Airport, using Beech King Airs and Lear Jets. The move to 'airline' operation came in 1980. It flew five Boeing 727s on behalf of UPS, the well-known 'parcel flyer'. In 1989 the name was changed to Express One, and it had contracts with Emery and DHL, also package freight carriers. It used five further Boeing 727s for passenger charter work, adding DC-9s to these in 1991/92. Express One made it across the Atlantic for the first time in July 1993, using leased DC-10s for charter flights to Frankfurt. In June 1995 all aircraft were voluntarily grounded after the Federal Aviation Administration had expressed safety concerns during a routine inspection. At the same time the company sought Chapter 11 bankruptcy protection to enable a restructuring to take place. The company recommenced operations with a reduced fleet and concentrated on freight work, until Chapter 11 protection could be lifted. Express One is active from its hub at Indianapolis for the US Postal Service and other Boeing 727s are used on behalf of DHL, and painted in their colours.

Routes

US domestic freight flights on behalf of DHL and the US Postal Service. Charter flights to the Florida resorts, Mexico and the Caribbean.

Fleet

27 Boeing 727-200F

Boeing 757-200 B-27007 (Josef Krauthäuser collection)

FAR EASTERN AIR TRANSPORT – FAT

No.5 Alley 123, Lane 405, Tun Hwa North Road
Taipei 105, Republic of China,
www.fat.co.tw

Three- / Two- letter code	IATA No.	Reg'n prefix	ICAO callsign
FEA / EF	265	B	

Far Eastern Air Transport Corporation – FAT was established in Spring 1957 by former military pilots and several business people. Operations began in July 1957 using Douglas DC-3s and Beech 18s, and for a long time only domestic services were flown. Handley Page Heralds, Vickers Viscounts and as the first jet type, Caravelles were used. Using the Vickers Viscount, the first international services were flown to Hong Kong and Saigon. During the Vietnam War many special flights were also operated from Saigon to Taipei. Boeing 737-100s joined the fleet as replacements for the Viscounts, with more modern Boeing 737-200s following a couple of years later. At the beginning of the 1990s the fleet was converted to McDonnell Douglas MD-80s and the larger Boeing 757. FAT is today the largest regional airline in Taiwan and as well as scheduled services, it flies charters. China Airlines holds 10% of the shares in what is still a private company. The main operating and maintenance base is at the Sung San Airport at Taipei.

Routes

Chiayi, Hualien, Kaoshiung, Kinmen, Koror, Kota Kinabalu, Makung, Phuket, Subic Bay, Tainan, Taipei, Taitung.

Fleet

7 Boeing 757-200
8 McDonnell Douglas MD-82/83

(Boeing) McDonnell Douglas MD-11 N601FE (Frank Fielitz/Frankfurt)

FEDEX

P.O.Box 727, Memphis TN 38134-2424, USA
Tel. 901-3693600, Fax. 901-3323772,
www.fedex.com

Three- / Two- letter code	IATA No.	Reg'n prefix	ICAO callsign
FDX / FX	023	N	Fedex

Frederick W Smith set up Federal Express in June 1971 and it began operations on 17th April 1973 using Dassault Falcon 20s; up to 60 were used. In it was floated on the stock exchange and became a joint stock company. The FedEx system revolutionised the entire cargo market and has since seen many imitators. Shipments are distributed from a central hub in Memphis with US regional sorting centres, using the hub and spoke distribution system which FedEx invented. After air cargo deregulation in November 1977, FedEx was also able to operate larger aircraft. They bought Boeing 727s in large numbers, and later DC-10s and Boeing 747s as well. During 1989 the Flying Tiger Line, which had been established and well-known for many years, was bought and its DC-8s and 747s integrated. Although only express shipments were forwarded at the beginning, other cargo is now transported. 1995 was a year of particular innovation, when FedEx opened its own hub at the former US military base at Subic Bay in the Philippines and in July started Asia One, the first overnight delivery service in Asia; from Subic the whole Asian region is accessible to FedEx. A second change in 1995 was the introduction of a new corporate identity with the adoption of the former colloquial acronym of FedEx as its official name. New Airbus A310 freighters carried the new colour scheme. Many A310s and A300s, DC-10s and MD-11s have been acquired from other airlines and converted to freighters, and older Boeing 747-200Fs sold off by the world's largest airfreight carrier. Numerous smaller companies operate feeder services from smaller cities and towns on behalf of FedEx with Cessna Caravans, Fokker F.27s or Shorts 360s; the massive order for Ayres Loadmasters is to re-equip this part of the operation.

Routes

Federal Express serves over 130 US cities and worldwide over 180 countries. Hubs are in Memphis, Miami, Brussels, Paris and Hong Kong.

Fleet

		Ordered
36 Airbus A300-605F	92 McDonnell Douglas DC-10	250 Ayres LM200 Loadmaster
41 Airbus A310	30 (Boeing) McDonnell Douglas MD-11	28 (Boeing) McDonnell Douglas MD-11
155 Boeing 727-100/200	11 Shorts 360	
250 Cessna Caravan		
30 Fokker F.27		

Lockheed L-1011 TriStar 200F N260FA (Hans-Willi Mertens/Miami)

FINE AIRLINES

P.O.Box 523726, Miami,FL.33152, USA
Tel. 305-8716606, Fax. 305-8714232,
www.fineair.com

Three- / Two- letter code	IATA No.	Reg'n prefix	ICAO callsign
FBF / FB	340	N	Fine Air

Frank and Barry Fine set up their eponymous freight company at the beginning of 1992 and began in November of the same year with flights to South America from their Miami base. More than half of the total air traffic from the USA to Central and South America, is concentrated at this airport and so it is no surprise that this is the market on which Fine Air chose to concentrate, though there are other centres of operation at Atlanta and Houston. Douglas DC-8-50/60s fitted with hushkits were the ideal aircraft for the task and so the company acquired more than 15 of the type. Some however were leased and operated by other companies. A network of routes to South America and the Caribbean was built up and flown on a regular basis. The sole Lockheed TriStar was acquired in June 1997. On 4th September 1997 Fine Air voluntarily suspended operations, in order to address possible maintenance and safety shortcomings. However, services were fully restored on 28th October 1997. In April 1999 Fine Air acquired its competitor Arrow Air, including its aircraft and routes. As both companies are based at Miami, operations are combined. However, Arrow Air continues to maintain its own identity to the outside world.

Routes

Atlanta, Bogota, Caracas, Guatemala City, Guayaquil, Houston, Maraceibo, Managua, Miami, Panama City, Puerto Plata, Quito, San Jose, San Juan, Santo Domingo, San Pedro Sula, San Salvador.

Fleet

1 Lockheed L-1011 TriStar 200
7 Douglas DC-8-50
2 Douglas DC-8-60

Airbus A319-112 OH-LVA (Albert Kuhbandner/Munich)

FINNAIR

PL 15, 01053 Finnair Vantaa, Finland
Tel. 9-81881, Fax. 9-8184401,
www.finnair.fi

Three- / Two- letter code	IATA No.	Reg'n prefix	ICAO callsign
FIN / AY	105	OH	Finnair

Finnair was set up on 9th October 1923 as Aero OY, the German company Junkers holding 50% of the shares. The first flight was from Helsinki to Tallinn on 20th March 1924 with a Junkers F-13. Until 1936, when airports were built in Finland, seaplanes were used. Flights to Berlin and Paris were added, but operations had to cease on 21st September 1944 until Spring 1945 when eight Douglas C-47s were bought from the USAAF. The first services were to Stockholm and Copenhagen. Convair 340s and 440s replaced the C-47s and a new service to Moscow in 1956 was followed by Frankfurt, Cologne,

Basle and Geneva in 1957. The Caravelle was introduced at Finnair in 1960, marking the beginning of the changeover to jets. Kar Air, a private Finnish airline founded in 1957, was taken over in 1962. Douglas DC-8s were ordered for new long range services to the USA, with the first being delivered in 1969; these were also used on charters to the Mediterranean. In 1968 the name Finnair was adopted as the sole valid designation for the airline. DC-10-30s were delivered from 4th February 1975 and used primarily for flights to the American west coast, Tokyo and New York. For medium-range services Caravelles

were replaced by DC-9s. The first MD-11 was acquired in December 1990. On economic grounds, Kar Air, which had operated independently, was integrated in 1993. Likewise, Finnaviation which had operated Saab 340s on domestic services, was integrated in 1996. The first Boeing 757 was received in 1997 at which point a new colour scheme was adopted . Major fleet renewal began in 1999 with Airbus A321s from January and A319s from September, with A320s to follow from early 2001; the DC-9 variants will be retired as they arrive. Since September 1999 Finnair has been a partner in the Oneworld alliance.

Routes

Finnair serves about 60 destinations, including most important centres in Europe, plus flights to the USA and the Far East.

Fleet

3 Airbus A319
4 Airbus A321
9 ATR 72
5 Boeing 757-200
4 (Boeing) McDonnell Douglas MD-11

10 McDonnell Douglas MD-82
12 McDonnell Douglas MD-83
2 McDonnell Douglas MD-87
7 McDonnell Douglas DC-9-51
2 Saab SF 340

Ordered

2 Airbus A319
4 Airbus A320

Boeing 727-233 C-GXFA (Dennis Wehrmann/Miami)

FIRST AIR

Carp Airport, 3257 Carp Road, Carp Ontario
KOA ILO, Canada, Tel. 613-8393340,
Fax. 613-8395690, www.firstair.com

Three- / Two- letter code	IATA No.	Reg'n prefix	ICAO callsign
FAB / 7F	245	C	First

Bradley Air Services is Canada's largest independent regional carrier and provides scheduled charter and cargo flights from various points in Canada; the scheduled flights use the marketing name First Air. Having originally started out as Bradley Flying School in 1946, Bradley Air Services was set up in 1954 and started flight operations with Douglas DC-3s the same year. The first scheduled services were flown in the 1970s by DC-3s, followed from 1978 onwards by HS.748s, a type extremely well suited to operation in the extreme climatic conditions found where the company flies. Jets, in the form of the Boeing 727 arrived in 1986, being used initially on the Frobisher Bay to Ottawa services. The operating profile is quite unusual; principally carrying freight in the far north of Canada and on to Greenland, and even on occasion into Europe, but with the possibility of carrying passengers on some sectors. For this reason the aircraft are configured in combi versions. The main base is Ottawa, where the company has maintenance facilities, but there is a further base at Yellowknife, which is also the home of a subsidiary company, Ptarmigan Airways. Since 1995 First Air has been a part of the Makivik Corporation. During 1999, First Air took over Northwest Territorial Airways and their three Yellowknife-based Boeing 737-200s.

Routes

Broughton Island, Cambridge Bay, Cape Dorset, Clyde River, Edmonton, Fort Simpson, Gjoa Haven, Hall Beach, Hay River, Holman Island, Igloolik, Inukjuak, Iqaluit, Kangerlussaq, Kimmirut/Lake Harbour, Kugluktuk Coppermine, Kuujjuarapik, La Grande, Montreal, Nanisivik, Ottawa, Pangnirtung, Pelly Bay, Pond Inlet, Puvirnituq, Resolute Bay, Sanikiluaq, Taloyoak, Umiujaq, Whitehorse, Yellowknife.

Fleet

1 Beech 99 Airliner
8 BAe HS-748
6 Boeing 727-200C/F
3 Boeing 737-200

8 De Havilland DHC-6
1 Grumman Gulfstream 1C
1 Lockheed L-100-30 Hercules

Boeing 737-33A OK-FUN (Author's collection)

FISCHER AIR

P O Box 15, Ruzyne Airport, 16008 Prague 6
Czech Republic, Tel. 2-20116170,
Fax. 2-20115439, www.fischer.cz

Three- / Two- letter code	IATA No.	Reg'n prefix	ICAO callsign
FFR / 8F	–	OK	Fischer

Vaclav Fischer had led and built up a successful tour company for some years in Germany. As a result of the political changes and restoration of democracy and a free market in Czechoslovakia in the early 1990s, the Czech exile sold his German business and set out to repeat his success in his former homeland. Because there was strong demand for travel to Western countries, the business flourished. It was however difficult for tour operators to find sufficient aircraft capacity, as the state airline CSA was fully occupied looking after the needs of its own in-house tour company. Thus, without further ado, in 1996 Fischer set up his own airline. Using a leased 148-seat Boeing 737-300, operations began on 27th April 1997, full of optimism for the summer season. The first flight was from Prague to Palma de Mallorca. A further 737-300 was delivered in the same year to Prague, Fischer Air's base airport. Fischer co-operates with CSA and operates the Prague to Malta route as a codeshare. Since the airline otherwise flies exclusively for its own tour company, expansion has been careful. A third Boeing 737-300 was added to the fleet in March 1999.

Routes

Malta is served from Prague on a scheduled basis. Charter flights to the Mediterranean area, Northern Africa, Canary Islands and Middle East.

Fleet

3 Boeing 737-300

Fokker F.28 Mk4000 VH-EWC (Uwe Gleisberg/Brisbane)

FLIGHT WEST AIRLINES

P.O.Box 1126, Eagle Farm, Brisbane, Queensland 4009, Australia, Tel. 7-32121212, Fax. 7-32121299, www.fltwest.com.au

Three- / Two- letter code	IATA No.	Reg'n prefix	ICAO callsign
FWQ / YC	060	VH	Flight West

This relatively young airline was founded in 1987, and started flying on 1st June with three leased Beech Super King Airs. Brisbane and Townsville in Queensland were initially the main centres of operation. Dennis Buchanan, well known in aviation circles in Australia, set up the company to fill the vacuum left when Australia Airlines abandoned services in northern Queensland. Air Queensland also gave up some of its routes and Flight West was able to take these on too. More aircraft seating 5 to 11 passengers were added; however, the delivery of the first Embraer EMB 110 Bandeirante marked an upsizing of aircraft size and the addition of longer routes. Flight West Airlines continued to expand rapidly. DHC-6 Twin Otters and further EMB 110s augmented the fleet in 1989 for special flights to the mines at Mont Selva. During 1990 a hangar and overhaul complex was built at Brisbane Airport; the Embraer EMB-120 Brasilia, now the largest aircraft in the fleet, was based here. Following an extended pilots' strike in Australia, Flight West took over the route network and de Havilland DHC-8s from Talair. Particular emphasis has been placed on working with regional bodies on the development of tourism in Northern Queensland. Correspondingly routes have been added, and some dropped and more Brasilias have strengthened the fleet. Flight West took on its first jet in March 1997, with Fokker F.28s. A service to Sydney was introduced, and for the first time the airline ventured abroad, to neighbouring Papua New Guinea. The larger Fokker 100s were added in the first half of 1999. There is co-operation with Ansett Australia and Flight West Airlines has benefited from taking over some routes from Ansett.

Routes

Bamaga, Barcaldine, Bedourie, Birdsville, Blackall, Boulia, Brisbane, Bundaberg, Cairns, Charleville, Cloncurry, Emerald, Gladstone, Hervey Bay, Hughenden, Julia Creek, Longreach, Mackay, Mount Isa, Norfolk Island, Proserpine, Quilpie, Richmond, Rockhampton, Roma, Sydney, Thangool, Townsville, Windorah, Winton.

Fleet

4 BAe Jetstream 32
6 Embraer EMB-120 Brasilia
3 Fokker F.28-4000
2 Fokker 100

Boeing 737-2L9 N270FL (Josef Krauthäuser collection)

FRONTIER AIRLINES

12015 East 46th Avenue, Denver,
Colorado 80239-3116, USA, Tel. 303-3717400,
Fax. 303-3717007, www.flyfrontier.com

Three- / Two- letter code	IATA No.	Reg'n prefix	ICAO callsign
FFT / F9	422	N	Frontierflight

Shortly after the opening of Denver's new airport Continental Airlines reduced its services there by 80%. To fill this vacuum local investors and business people created a new airline with the historic name of 'Frontier'. The first Frontier Airlines was formed, also in Denver, in 1948 and was active until 1986 when deregulation in the US airline industry led to the creation of mega-carriers, taking over the smaller companies; thus Frontier was absorbed into Continental and the name disappeared from the skies. So on 5th July 1994 the new Frontier, operating two leased Boeing 737-200s, began service

from Denver again, with service to Bismarck and Fargo. Two more Boeing 737s were leased in August 1994 and the network expanded. The tailfins of Frontier's 737s, which have gone on to include -300s as well as the original -200s, are decorated with attractive animal motifs. There is a marketing alliance with Continental Airlines, and to allow for future expansion the issue of further shares is planned, but it is a condition that no shareholder may own more than 10% of the shares. Thus Vanguard Airlines has an 8% stake. At the beginning of 2000 a bold step was taken for the future, with the placing of orders for Airbus

A318s and A319s. The 114-seat 318s are to commence delivery from 2003, while the 132-seat 319s will be delivered earlier, starting from May 2001. In the meantime further Boeing 737-300s are expected to be leased to continue the airline's expansion.

Routes

Albuquerque, Atlanta, Baltimore, Bloomington/Normal, Boston, Boulder, Chicago, Dallas/Fort Worth, Denver, El Paso, Fargo, Las Vegas, Los Angeles, Minneapolis/St. Paul, Omaha, Orlando, Phoenix, Portland, Salt Lake City, San Diego, San Francisco, Seattle.

Fleet	Ordered
7 Boeing 737-200	6 Airbus A318
16 Boeing 737-300	21 Airbus A319

Airbus A320-321 D-ACAF (Josef Krauthäuser/Munich)

FTI-FLUGGESELLSCHAFT

Lohstr. 26 85445 Schwaig, Germany
Tel. 089-25255130, Fax. 089-25255131,
www.fti.de

Three- / Two- letter code	IATA No.	Reg'n prefix	ICAO callsign
FTI –	–	D	Frogline

The German tour market has seen a concentration of business over the last few years into a few large operators, parts of large groups. Each of these groups has its own airline and so it is difficult for other operators to purchase capacity with these airlines. The Munich-based tour operator FTI has seen such growth in recent years that its need for airline seats has outstripped the ability of the German airline market to provide them. Additionally, FTI wanted to retain independence of operation, and at first it supported the formation of the German arm of Britannia Airways, with whom it flew an extensive programme. The

British tour company Airtours however acquired 29% of FTI during 1998 and thus the pieces were in place for the formation of FTI's in-house airline for short and medium-haul work. Airtours of course runs its own airline of the same name and is in head-on competition with Britannia, so FTI's former association was terminated. In October 1998 FTI-Fluggesellschaft mbH was formed in Munich. Under the marketing name Fly FTI it began operations on 1st May 1999 with a flight from Munich to Lamezia Terme. Airbus A320s were used, a type which is already well established in the Airtours fleet.

The colour scheme is near identical to that of Airtours and Premiair, with the addition of the 'Fly FTI' titling on the forward fuselage. The first season was successfully completed with three A320s and the company is looking to grow. In the early part of 2000 three more Airbus A320s were added, and thoughts turned towards the acquisition of longer range and widebody types. However in mid-2000 Airtours acquired the balance of the shares in FTI, and to stem losses announced that it would reduce operations from sixteen German airports to only six.

Routes

Fly FTI flies from many German airports to the well-known holiday resorts in the Mediterranean, the Canary Isles, Northern Africa and Gambia.

Fleet	Ordered
6 Airbus A320-200	3 Airbus A320

Boeing 737-86N EC-HHG (Stefan Schlick/Arrecife)

FUTURA INTERNATIONAL AIRWAYS

Gran Via Asima 17, Poligono Son Castello,
07009 Palma de Mallorca, Spain
Tel. 971-432053, Fax. 971-202014

Three- / Two- letter code	IATA No.	Reg'n prefix	ICAO callsign
FUA / FH	–	EC	Futura

Futura International Airways was set up in 1989 as a joint venture between the Irish airline Aer Lingus (initially with a 25%, later 85% shareholding) and Spanish investors. Based at Palma, its objective was to provide package tours from Ireland to Spain. In February 1990, flights started from Dublin to Palma de Mallorca with two Boeing 737-300s leased from Guinness-Peat Aviation. Services from other airports including Basle, Düsseldorf, Manchester, Munich and Vienna followed quickly. Larger Boeing 737-400s were acquired during 1991 and 1992. With the opening up of markets in the former Warsaw Pact states, Futura was able to take a slice of this business, and thus flies tourists from Hungary, Ukraine and Russia to Spain. During 1995 more Boeing 737-400s were added, with the -300s being traded in. Around 1.3 million passengers flew with Futura during that year. The expansion and development of the airline continued to the end of the century, with the first of six new generation Boeing 737-800s being added in November 1999. This delivery also marked the introduction of a new subdued dark blue colour scheme in place of the former bright red and yellow.

Routes

Charter flights from Ireland, Israel, Great Britain, Germany, Austria, Ukraine, Hungary, Czech Republic, and Switzerland to Spain, especially Mallorca and the Canary Isles.

Fleet

10 Boeing 737-400
 6 Boeing 737-800

Airbus A330-341 PK-GPA (Uwe Gleisberg/Perth)

GARUDA INDONESIA

Jalan Merdeka Selastan 13, Jakarta 10110,
Indonesia. Tel. 21-3801901,
Fax. 21-3806652, www.garuda.co.id

Three- / Two- letter code	IATA No.	Reg'n prefix	ICAO callsign
GIA / GA	126	PK	Indonesia

26th January 1949 is the official date when Garuda was founded. On this day, a DC-3 flew from Calcutta to Rangoon registered under the name of 'Indonesian Airways'. It was the first civil aircraft of the new Republic of Indonesia, but could not fly in Indonesia for political reasons. It was only after the official declaration of independence at the end of 1949 that the airline was also installed by the government in Indonesia; however, at first, it needed assistance which came from KLM. The airline was nationalised in 1954. In addition to DC-3s, Convair 240/340s were used, plus Lockheed L-188 Electras from 1961. In 1963, de Kroonduif, an airline in the Indonesian part of New Guinea, was taken over. Convair CV990s were Garuda's first jets, and were used for a service to Amsterdam. They were replaced from 1968 by DC-8s. Sydney was served for the first time in 1969, via Bali, and DC-9s were also bought in that year, with some Fokker F.27s for domestic services. These were however, taken out of service in 1971 and sold, as F.28s were delivered. The first widebody was the DC-10-30, leased from KLM from 1973. Boeing 747s entered service in 1980, and were used to Frankfurt and London, with the first new MD-11 added in 1992. There are codeshare agreements with KLM, China Airlines and Iberia and the airline has a shareholding in Merpati. The Asian business crisis of the late 1990s hit Garuda hard, and there was a drastic reduction in staff, routes and aircraft. All the MD-11s and Airbus A300s were taken out of service and capacity almost halved. In the early part of 2000, the situation has stabilised somewhat, but the tourist industry has been badly affected. New Boeing 777s are on order for delivery from April 2002.

Routes

Adelaide, Amsterdam, Auckland, Balikpapan, Banda Aceh, Bangkok, Banjarmasin, Batam, Biak, Brisbane, Cairns, Dammam, Darwin, Denpasar, Frankfurt, Hong Kong, Jakarta, Jayapura, Jeddah, Kuala Lumpur, London, Manado, Mataram, Medan, Melbourne, Nagoya, Osaka, Padang, Palembang, Pekanbaru, Pontianak, Perth, Riyadh, Semarang, Singapore, Solo City, Surabaya, Sydney, Tokyo, Ujung Pandang, Yogyakarta.

Fleet		Ordered
2 Airbus A300B4F	4 Boeing 747-200	3 Airbus A330-300
6 Airbus A330-300	3 Boeing 747-400	6 Boeing 777-200ER
8 Boeing 737-300	5 McDonnell Douglas DC-10-30	
7 Boeing 737-400	5 Fokker F.28	
5 Boeing 737-500		

Boeing 737-75B D-AGEO (Ralf Kaminsky/Leipzig)

GERMANIA

Flughafen Tegel, Gebäude 23, 13405 Berlin, Germany Tel. 030-41013610, Fax. 030-41013615 www.germaniaairline.de

Three- / Two- letter code	IATA No.	Reg'n prefix	ICAO callsign
GMI / ST		D	Germania

In 1986, exactly tens years after it had been set up, the SAT (Special Air Transport) airline changed its name to Germania. Operations had begun with a Fokker F.27, but switched to jets from September 1978 with three former LTU Caravelle 10Rs. As well as the Caravelles, the airline owned two Boeing 727s, but these were only flown in Germania's colours after the airline had been renamed. The Caravelles were replaced from 1989 onwards and the first Boeing 737-300s were acquired. Germania flew sub-charters for other airlines and for tour operators; some aircraft were flown in DFD colours.

Germania is particularly active out of Berlin, including scheduled services from Berlin to Heringsdorf/Baltic Sea. Six further Boeing 737-300s were brought into use from the Spring of 1992, at which point the colour scheme was also modified. The airline was taken over by the Hetzel travel company in 1995. Several aircraft have been leased to Condor and fly for that airline, but with Germania crews. Germania was one of the first to order the new generation Boeing 737-700 for its future equipment, and so in 1998 it received early deliveries, with the whole fleet having now been switched over to the latest model.

Several aircraft fly as 'logojets' on behalf of LTU and other tour operators.

Routes

Charter flights from German airports principally to the Mediterranean, Northern Africa, Canary Isles, Turkey, and Madeira.

Fleet

14 Boeing 737-700

McDonnell Douglas DC-10-30 OO-PHN (Josef Krauthäuser/Düsseldorf)

GHANA AIRWAYS

Ghana Airways Ave 9., P.O.Box 1636 Accra, Ghana, Tel. 21-773321, Fax. 21-777078, www.ghana-airways.com

Three- / Two- letter code	IATA No.	Reg'n prefix	ICAO callsign
GHA / GH	237	9G	Ghana

With the support of BOAC, the government of Ghana set up its national airline on 4th July 1958, with the government having a 60% stake and BOAC 40%, to take over the operations of West African Airways Corporation in the British colony formerly known as the Gold Coast. Only 12 days later, on 16th July, a scheduled service to London began, using Boeing 377 Stratocruisers leased from BOAC. Domestic services were taken over from WAAC on 1st October 1958. The Stratocruisers were later replaced by Bristol Britannias. On 14th February 1961 Ghana took over sole control of the airline.

Soviet-built Ilyushin IL-18s were acquired as part of a further expansion, but these proved to be not very economical in use and all eight aircraft were returned to the manufacturer after a period. Ghana Airways' first jet was a Vickers VC-10, and for short-range routes which had previously been flown by Douglas DC-3s, HS.748s were acquired. In 1983 the Douglas DC-10 was acquired for long-range routes, and regional services were flown with Fokker F.28s and Douglas DC-9s, but the F.28s were replaced by F.27s. In the long term, it is intended to expand regional services and to serve more points in

Europe; a further DC-10 was added in 1999. A new service from Accra to Baltimore/Washington was opened in July 2000. The main base is at the international airport at Accra-Kotoka, and there are co-operation agreements in force with MEA, Nigeria Airways and SAA.

Routes

Abidjan, Accra, Bamako, Baltimore/Washington, Banjul, Beirut, Conakry, Cotonou, Dakar, Douala, Dubai, Düsseldorf, Freetown, Harare, Johannesburg, Kuassi, Lagos, Lome, London, Monrovia, New York, Ouagadougou, Rome.

Fleet

1 Fokker F.27
3 McDonnell Douglas DC-10-30
3 McDonnell Douglas DC-9-51

Boeing 737-3Y0 G-IGOG (Uwe Gleisberg/Munich)

GO FLY

Enterprise House, Stansted, Essex CM24 1SB
Great Britain, Tel. 1279-666333,
Fax. 1279-681763, www.go-fly.com

Three- / Two- letter code	IATA No.	Reg'n prefix	ICAO callsign
GOE / GO	-	G	Goflight

Seeing the continued growth of the new low-cost/low-fare airlines EasyJet at Luton and Ryanair at Stansted, British Airways decided to weigh in with some competition. Not that Stansted was an important airport for British Airways, whose operations are concentrated on London's Heathrow and Gatwick airports, but it was felt necessary to counter the long-term competition for European passengers from the lucrative market in the South East of Britain. Additional competition for this business at Stansted was also to come from buzz, the low-fare operation of KLM, established here at the beginning of 2000. Go Fly was established by British Airways in 1997, but it did not start operations until 22nd May 1998. Boeing 737-300s were leased and this has been the sole type to be used. Milan and Copenhagen were the first destinations, and were served with multiple daily flights. As more 737-300s were added, so the number of destinations increased, with Munich included. In this case, Go was met with low-price competition from Lufthansa, even though the German airline had not flown to Stansted until then. The established airlines obviously had something to fear from the low-cost/low-fare operations. Go expanded steadily and by its second year had 14 Boeing 737-300s in use. Aircraft are painted with different coloured undersides, and with various different slogans on the forward fuselage, for instance 'go now', 'go often'.

Routes

Barcelona, Bilbao, Bologna,Copenhagen, Edinburgh, Faro, Lisbon, London-Stansted, Lyon, Madrid, Milan, Malaga, Prague, Reykjavik, Rome, Venice, Zürich.

Fleet

14 Boeing 737-300

Boeing 757-236 OY-GRL (Dennis Wehrmann/Hamburg)

GROENLANDSFLY

Nuuk Airport, POB 1012, 3900 Greenland
Denmark, Tel. 299-343434, Fax. 299-327288,
www.greenland-guide.dk/gla

Three- / Two- letter code	IATA No.	Reg'n prefix	ICAO callsign
GRL / GL	631	OY	Greenlandair

Groenlandsfly was founded in 1960 to ensure air services to the Arctic island of Greenland, a province of Denmark, much larger than its motherland, yet sparsely populated. Shares in the company were taken by the government, Royal Greenland Trading, Kryolit Mining Co. and the state airline SAS. Initially a Douglas DC-4 was used for reconnaissance of the ice fields, and this was also available for transport tasks as required. For other tasks, PBY Catalinas were leased, as there were few airfields on Greenland and these could take to the water to reach some settlements. Godthaab (now known as Nuuk) and Sondre Stromfjord were the only made-up airfields, also used for military purposes by NATO. The use of a number of helicopters appeared to be a suitable answer for the needs of some settlements.Though more costly to operate than fixed-wing aircraft, they are not dependent on airfields. Also especially suited were the de Havilland Canada DHC-6 Twin Otter and DHC-7 with their exceptional take-off and landing abilities; they could use short runways which may have loose gravel, or be covered in ice during Winter. Groenlandsfly's tasks cannot be compared with those of conventional airlines. In addition to numerous smaller helicopters, 25-seat Sikorsky S.61s form part of the fleet and are an important asset for passenger transport. Ambulance, rescue and reconnaissance flights are all important duties of the airline. During 1998 a Boeing 757 was acquired and is the largest aircraft in the fleet and is used for holiday flights to Greenland, but also from Greenland to the USA, Canada and to Europe.

Routes

Aasiaat, Alluitsup Paa, Copenhagen, Groennedaal, Ilulissat, Kangerlussuaq, Kulusuk, Maniitsoq, Nanortalik, Narsaq, Narsasuaq, Neerlerit Inaat, Nuuk, Paamiut, Pituffik, Qaarsut, Qaqortoq, Qasigiannguit, Qeqertarsuaq, Reykjavik, Sisimiut, Upernavik, Uummannaq are served on a scheduled basis. Charter flights to the USA, as far as Florida, to Canada and the Mediterranean.

Fleet

1 Boeing 757-200
2 De Havilland DHC-6 Twin Otter
6 De Havilland DHC-7 Dash 7

4 Sikorsky S.61N

Boeing 767-3P6 A4O-GJ in special colours marking the 50th anniversary of the airline's foundation (Author's collection)

GULF AIR

P.O.Box 138 Manama, Bahrain
Tel. 322200, Fax. 330466,
www.gulfairco.com

Three- / Two- letter code	IATA No.	Reg'n prefix	ICAO callsign
GFA / GF	072	A4O	Gulfair

Gulf Air is the national carrier of the Gulf state co-operation of Bahrain, Qatar, the United Arab Emirates and Oman. The airline was set up as Gulf Aviation on 24th March 1950, with regional flights starting on 5th July 1950 with Avro Ansons. De Havilland Dove and Heron aircraft followed and DC-3s and Fokker F.27s were added, partly under British sponsorship. These were replaced from 1969 onwards with BAC One-Elevens. 1970 saw the start of regular flights to London with leased Vickers VC-10s. On 1st April 1974 the four states took over Gulf Aviation, giving the airline a new legal status and the present name of Gulf Air. Boeing 737s replaced the One-Elevens from 1977. For longer-range flights, Gulf Air used Lockheed L-1011 TriStars starting in 1976. Fleet renewal and expansion began with the arrival of the first Boeing 767-300ERs as replacements for the TriStars. As a result of the Gulf War, the renewal programme was halted, but re-started in 1993 with the delivery of the Airbus A320, with the last of the Boeing 737-200s being taken out of service during 1994/95. At the same time the long-range Airbus A340 was introduced, with the last of the TriStars leaving the fleet by the later part of 1996. Because member states have formed their own airline operations, Gulf Air has suffered from overcapacity, with the result that some aircraft have been leased out to other airlines, though new aircraft acquisition continues, with the Airbus A330 being added from June 1999. To mark the airline's 50th anniversary in 2000, a Boeing 767 was painted in a special colour scheme, and examples of the Avro Anson and de Havilland Dove were also flown from the UK to Bahrain to represent the original equipment types as part of the celebrations.

Routes

Abu Dhabi, AlAin, Al-Fujairah, Amman, Athens, Bahrain, Bangkok, Beirut, Cairo, Casablanca, Chennai, Colombo, Damascus, Dammam, Dar-es-Salaam, Delhi, Dharan, Doha, Dubai, Entebbe, Frankfurt, Hong Kong, Istanbul, Jakarta, Jeddah, Karachi, Kathmandu, Khartoum, Kuala Lumpur, Kuwait, Lahore, Larnaca, London, Malta, Manila, Melbourne, Mumbai, Muscat, Nairobi, Paris, Peshawar, Rome, Riyadh, Sanaa, Sharjah, Shiraz, Singapore, Sydney, Teheran, Zanzibar.

Fleet		Ordered
13 Airbus A320-200	10 Boeing 767-300	4 Airbus A320
6 Airbus A330-300		6 Airbus A330
5 Airbus A340-300		1 Airbus A340

Beech 1900C Airliner N197GA (Hans-Willi Mertens/Fort Myers)

GULFSTREAM INTERNATIONAL AIRL.

1815 Griffin Road, Dania Florida 33004, USA
Tel. 305-8710727, Fax. 305-8714800,
www.gulfstreamair.com

Three- / Two- letter code	IATA No.	Reg'n prefix	ICAO callsign
GFT / 3M	449	N	Gulf Flight

As a former Eastern Air Lines captain,Thomas L Cooper had many years of experience in the business to draw on when he founded his own small non-scheduled airline in 1990. Using a Cessna 402 he offered air taxi services between Miami and Haiti. As the Haitian political situation became more and more unstable during 1991/92, and with the government making attacks against the population, Cooper moved his operations to the Bahamas. The signing of a codeshare agreement with United Airlines in May 1994 opened up new possibilities and called for larger

equipment. Beech 1900s were thus brought into use for United's feeder service. A similar agreement was negotiated with Continental Airlines and the route network and aircraft fleet doubled in only a few years. Shorts 360s were added to the fleet from 1996 and one of these aircraft, painted in a special Sandals Clubs colour scheme, was flown exclusively on behalf of the club. Cooper founded G-Holdings as an umbrella company, as other activities such as aircraft ground handling were undertaken. In 1998 Continental took a shareholding in Gulfstream International, and in

August 1998 G-Holdings took over the Fort Lauderdale-based Paradise Island Air, along with its fleet of de Havilland Canada DHC-7s.

Routes

Beef Island, Fort Lauderdale, Fort Myers, Freeport, Gainesville, Jacksonville, Key West, Marsh Harbor, Miami, Nassau, North Eleuthera, Orlando, San Juan, St. Croix, St.Kitts, St. Maarten, St. Thomas, Tallahassee, Tampa, Treasure Key, Virgin Gorda, West Palm Beach.

Fleet

30 Beech 1900 Airliner
 5 De Havilland DHC-7

Airbus A310-204 D-AHLX (Ralf Kaminsky/Leipzig)

HAPAG LLOYD FLUG

Postfach 420240, 30662 Hannover,
Germany, Tel. 0511-97270,
Fax. 0511-9727494, www.hapag-lloyd.com

Three- / Two- letter code	IATA No.	Reg'n prefix	ICAO callsign
HLF / HF	617	D	Hapaglloyd

The well-known German shipping company Hapag-Lloyd set up the airline with its traditional name in July 1972. Flights started in March of the following year with three Boeing 727-100s acquired from All Nippon Airlines and the 727 fleet had increased to eight aircraft by 1979. After lengthy negotiations Bavaria-Germanair was taken over in late 1978. This takeover provided Hapag-Lloyd with various BAC One-Eleven and Airbus A300B4 aircraft. While the latter were integrated, the One Elevens were sold and new Boeing 737-200s ordered. A renewal of the fleet and its adaptation to future needs was decided in 1987. A total of six Airbus A330B4s were exchanged for Airbus A310s, and Boeing 737-400s were ordered, the first of which arrived at Hapag's Hanover base in Autumn 1990. With the introduction of the A310, the company was for the first time in a position to offer flights to the USA and the Caribbean. Hapag-Lloyd was the first to order the new Boeing 737-800 and from early 1999 had the first of these new aircraft at its disposal; now the airline has the most modern of the German charter fleets. Services are flown from all German airports, principally for the tour operator TUI, which is also a shareholder in Hapag-Lloyd. There is a partnership with the British airline JMC, also a part of the larger concern and a common fleet policy will be pursued, especially for long-range routes.

Routes

Charter flights, principally from Germany, to the Mediterranean, the Canary Isles, Afric, Middle East, Far East and Caribbean.

Fleet	Ordered
4 Airbus A310-200	8 Boeing 737-800
3 Airbus A310-300	
8 Boeing 737-400	
16 Boeing 737-800	

McDonnell Douglas DC-9-51 N649HA (Thomas Kim/Honolulu)

HAWAIIAN AIR

P.O.Box 3008 Int.Airport Honolulu, 96820 Hawaii, USA, Tel. 808-8353700, Fax. 808-8353690, www.hawaiianair.com

Three- / Two- letter code	IATA No.	Reg'n prefix	ICAO callsign
HAL / HA	173	N	Hawaiian

Hawaiian Air was founded in Honolulu on 30th January 1929 as Inter Island Airways by the Inter Island Steam Navigation Company. Flights started on 11th November 1929 between Honolulu and Hilo with Sikorsky S-36 amphibians, later replaced by larger Sikorsky S-43s. In 1941 the current name was introduced and operations changed over to Douglas DC-3s. Strong expansion in the tourist business and route additions led to the acquisition of larger aircraft such as the Convair 340 in 1952 and the Douglas DC-6 from 1958. In 1967 the airline moved over to jet equipment with the introduction of the Douglas DC-9-30. For charter flights to the American mainland, the Pacific and Europe, DC-8s were added to the fleet in 1983, followed in 1987 by Lockheed TriStars. As a result of financial problems, Hawaiian Air entered Chapter 11 bankruptcy protection in 1993, and sought new financial partners, with the whole company being reorganised. Initially DHC-7s were sold, DC-8s taken out of service, the TriStars exchanged for Douglas DC-10s and many routes dropped, but in September 1994 things had improved so that Chapter 11 protection could be left behind. A marketing agreement was agreed with American Airlines and there is close co-operation. Once the market had stabilised, more aircraft were acquired and flights to Papeete and Samoa offered. During 1999 new routes from Los Angeles to Maui and Kona were added; only Honolulu had been served with direct flights from the mainland before. Further DC-10-30s were added to the fleet and some shares were bought back by the company. During 2001, the entire DC-9 fleet is scheduled for replacement by new Boeing 717s .

Routes

Hilo, Honolulu, Hoolehua, Kahului, Kauai, Kona, Lanai City, Las Vegas, Los Angeles, Pago Pago, Papeete, Portland, San Francisco, Seattle.

Fleet	Ordered
15 McDonnell Douglas DC-9-51	13 Boeing 717
11 McDonnell Douglas DC-10-10	
4 McDonnell Douglas DC-10-30	

Airbus A300B4F G-HLAA (Josef Krauthäuser/Frankfurt)

HEAVYLIFT CARGO AIRLINES

Stansted Airport, Essex CM24 1QW, Great Britain
Tel. 1279 680611, Fax. 1279 680615,
www.azfreight.com./h-lift

Three- / Two- letter code	IATA No.	Reg'n prefix	ICAO callsign
HLA / NP	–	G	Heavylift

Heavylift's origins go back to Transmeridian Air Cargo, one of the forerunners of British Cargo Airlines. The Trafalgar Group took over 90% of the shares in Transmeridian in 1977 and merged it in 1979 with IAS Cargo to form British Cargo Airlines. In a time of business recession there was not room for too many specialist cargo airlines. The merged fleet was made up of Boeing 707s, Douglas DC-8s (IAS) and CL-44s (TMAC). When the Royal Air Force decided to retire its large, specialised transport, the Shorts Belfast, British Cargo Airlines took them on and converted them for civil freight use. The first Belfast

was received in March 1980, and took the opportunity at that time to change its name to TAC-Heavylift. The company expanded slowly and transported all sorts of freight, especially for the aviation industry. Helicopters for Westland, jet engines for Rolls-Royce and fuselages for Fokker F.27s and F.28s for Fokker were all carried. In total, five Belfasts saw service with Heavylift, and Lockheed-130 Hercules also came into service for North Sea oil support work. From 1991 Heavylift developed an association with the Ukrainian Volga-Dnepr Airlines in a joint venture project. Antonov An-124

and Ilyushin IL-76 transports were made available to Heavylift as required. In 1997 Heavylift put its first Airbus A300B4 freighter into service; this was a converted passenger aircraft. The Airbuses are used on scheduled freight services on behalf of KLM and other airlines.

Routes

Heavylift is available for ad hoc and charter freight flights, and operates regular services between Athens, Frankfurt, Cologne/Bonn, Istanbul and Stockholm.

Fleet

4 Airbus A300B4F
2 Shorts SC-5 Belfast

De Havilland DHC-8-102 N830PH (Josef Krauthäuser/Seattle-SEA)

HORIZON AIR

P.O.Box 48309 Seattle,Washington 98148
USA, Tel. 206-4333200, Fax 206-4314696
www.horizonair.com

Three- / Two- letter code	IATA No.	Reg'n prefix	ICAO callsign
QXE / QX	481	N	Horizon Air

Horizon Air, part of the Alaska Air Group, has its origins in May 1981 when its first route was opened from Seattle to Yakima. With the purchase of Air Oregon, a small airline from the north west of the USA, in mid 1982, the way was set for Horizon to grow to become one of the largest regional operators in the USA. Swearingen-Fairchild Metros and Fokker F.27s came into service. In 1984 Horizon Industries went to the stock exchange in order to acquire the capital necessary for the further expansion of the airline. Following the acquisition of Transwestern Airlines the pace of expansion quickened. Within three years the passenger total quadrupled from 185,000 in the first year to well over half a million in 1984. Further growth came from the operation of feeder flights on behalf of both Northwest Airlines and Alaska Airlines. The first jet, a Fokker F.28, came into service in 1985 and as it was found to be well suited, more were acquired. In 1986 Alaska Group took over the majority shareholding, but left Horizon to operate as an independent company. More modern DHC-8s and Dornier Do 328s replaced the F.27s and Metros during the mid-1990s, but while the Do 228s did not come up to expectations with Horizon and were removed from the fleet, the number of DHC-8s grew steadily. Further re-equipment is expected with orders in place for the DHC-8-Q400 for delivery from late 2000, and the longer version of the Canadair Regional Jet, the 700, from July 2002. There are alliances which bring the benefit of marketing activities and bookings with Alaska Airlines, Northwest Airlines, TWA, Continental Airlines and KLM. The main base and central hub is Seattle, with further hubs in Boise, Portland and Spokane.

Routes

Arcata, Bellingham, Billings, Boise, Bozeman, Butte, Calgary, Edmonton, Eugene, Fresno,Great Falls, Helena, Idaho Falls, Kalispell, Kelowna, Klamath Falls, Lewiston, Medford, Missoula, Moses Lake, North Bend, Pasco, Pendleton, Pocatello, Port Angeles, Portland, Pullman, Redding, Redmont, Sacramento, San Jose, Seattle, Spokane, Sun Valley, Vancouver, Victoria, Walla Walla, Wenatchee, Yakima.

Fleet

12 De Havilland DHC-8-100
28 De Havilland DHC-8-200
21 Fokker F.28-4000

Ordered

15 De Havilland DHC-8-Q400
25 Canadair Regional Jet-700

Airbus A340-313 EC-GJT (Uwe Gleisberg/Madrid)

IBERIA

130 Calle Velazquez, 28006 Madrid, Spain
Tel. 91-5878787, Fax. 91-5857329,
www.iberia.com

Three- / Two- letter code	IATA No.	Reg'n prefix	ICAO callsign
IBE / IB	075	EC	Iberia

The present-day Iberia was formed in 1940 by the merger of several companies. After the Spanish Civil War, German influence was still quite considerable, with Lufthansa holding 49% of the shares. In 1944 the Spanish government took over all the shares and ordered DC-3s to replace the Junkers Ju 52s. Iberia, as a pioneering European airline after the war, opened up important routes to Buenos Aires (1946), Caracas and San Juan (1949), Havana, New York and Mexico (1954), Bogota (1958), Santiago and further destinations in early 1960.

South America is thus traditionally one of its most important markets. DC-4s and Lockheed Constellations were used, and the first jet was the DC-8 in 1961. The Caravelle was acquired from 1962 for short and medium-haul flights; these were passed on to subsidiary Aviaco from 1967 and DC-9s acquired. The first widebody, the Boeing 747 arrived in October 1970; in 1972 Boeing 727s were bought and a year later DC-10-30. A large scale fleet renewal programme marked the 1990s. MD-87s, Boeing 757s and A320s replaced older DC-9s and 727s.

Iberia also took shareholdings in other airlines including VIASA, Aerolineas Argentinas, Viva, Aviaco, Ladeco and Royal Air Maroc. In 1996 the Airbus A340 was introduced to replace DC-10s on long-range services. During 1999, Aviaco was integrated as a result of stronger domestic competition. More new aircraft introduced to replace Boeing 727s from 1999 were the Airbus A321 and in 2000 the A319, but the fleet remains a very varied mixture. Iberia became a member of the Oneworld alliance in September 1999.

Routes

Domestic network with over 30 destinations centred on Madrid and Barcelona. Scheduled services to the USA, Caribbean, South and Central America, Middle East, Africa and many cities in Europe.

Fleet

		Ordered
6 Airbus A300B4	5 Boeing 757-200	7 Airbus A319
38 Airbus A320-200	2 Boeing 767-300ER	27 Airbus A320
3 Airbus A319	7 McDonnell Douglas DC-10-30	14 Airbus A321
2 Airbus A321	2 McDonnell Douglas DC-8-62F	3 Airbus A340-300
12 Airbus A340-300	25 McDonnell Douglas DC-9-30	4 Boeing 757-200
28 Boeing 727-200	24 McDonnell Douglas MD-87	
3 Boeing 737-300	13 McDonnell Douglas MD-88	
9 Boeing 747-200		

Boeing 757-208 TF-FIH (Josef Krauthäuser/Frankfurt)

ICELANDAIR

Reykjavik Airport, 101 Reykjavik, Iceland
Tel. 5050300, Fax. 5050391,
www.icelandair.is

Three- / Two- letter code	IATA No.	Reg'n prefix	ICAO callsign
ICE / FI	108	TF	Iceair

Icelandair, or Flugfelag Islands HF, was formed on the north coast of Iceland as Flugfelag Akureyar on 3rd June 1937 and began service to Reykjavik with a Waco YKS. In 1940 the headquarters of the airline was moved to the capital, Reykjavik and a Beech 18, two Dragon Rapides and another Waco YKS were bought. After the end of the Second World War, a scheduled service from Iceland via Prestwick to Copenhagen was set up for the first time in 1946. In April 1948 Flugfelag took delivery of its first Douglas DC-4, using it for a second route to London, with services to Germany being added from 1955. In 1965 the present title was adopted and Fokker F.27s brought into service; two years later came the first Boeing 727. Icelandair was set up in its present form on 20th July 1973 as the holding company for a merger of Flugfelag Islands and Loftleidir Icelandic Airlines, formed on 10th March 1944. Initially Icelandair flew domestic and European services and Loftleidir continued in its transatlantic role, in close co-operation, but from 1st October 1979 services were fully merged under the Icelandair name. In 1988, 836,000 passengers were carried. From 1989 the former Loftleidir DC-8s were replaced by Boeing 757s, and the rest of the fleet has been steadily renewed, principally with Boeing 737s. For regional services the Fokker F.27s were replaced with Fokker 50s. More Boeing 757s are on order, including the stretched -300 for service entry in 2001; one of the current 757s is a freighter, operated by Icelandair Cargo. During 1999 a new colour scheme was adopted.

Routes

Icelandic domestic services to some 10 destinations. International routes from Reykjavik to Amsterdam, Baltimore, Barcelona, Boston, Chicago, Cologne, Copenhagen, Faroe Islands, Frankfurt, Glasgow, Gothenburg, Halifax, Hamburg, Helsinki, London, Milan, Minneapolis, Munich, New York, Orlando, Oslo, Palma de Mallorca, Paris, Salzburg, Stockholm and Zürich.

Fleet	Ordered
9 Boeing 757-200ER	2 Boeing 757-300
4 Boeing 737-400	
3 Fokker 50	

Beech 1900D (Author's collection)

IMPULSE AIRLINES

11th Street, Kingsford Smith Airport, Sydney NSW 2020, Australia, Tel. 2-93175400, Fax. 2-93173327, www.impulseairlines.com.au

Three- / Two- letter code	IATA No.	Reg'n prefix	ICAO callsign
OOA / VQ	253	VH	Impulse

During the 1980s Oxley Airlines operated several routes in the south of Queensland and in the north of New South Wales; this private commuter company used Piper Chieftains. Departure point for their flights was Port Macquarie and there were daily services to Brisbane, Casino, Coffs Harbour, Coolangatta/ Gold Coast, Lismore and Taree. For the Impulse Transportation Group, Oxley Airlines represented a desirable addition to their activities, and so they acquired Oxley in December 1992, renaming it as Impulse Airlines. Larger aircraft in the form of 19-seater Beech 1900s were acquired and the company

developed positively. More routes were added, and consequently more Beech 1900s. On some routes Impulse flew in co-operation with Ansett Airlines. When Tamair ceased operations in 1998, Impulse was able to take over its most important route from Tamworth to Sydney. Expansion continues, and several of the aircraft are painted in very eye-catching and colourful schemes. An ambitious new venture from June 2000 was the acquisition of factory-fresh Boeing 717s for use on low-cost/low-fare services in competition with the mighty Qantas.

Routes

Armindale, Bamaga, Brisbane, Cairns, Canberra, Cloncurry, Coffs Harbour, Coolangatta, Cooma, Dubbo, Glenn Innes, Inverell, Kempsey, Mackay, Melbourne, Mount Isa, Newcastle, Perth, Port Macquarie, Rockhampton, Sydney, Tamworth, Townsville, Wollongong.

Fleet	Ordered
12 Beech 1900D 2 Boeing 717	2 Boeing 717

Airbus A320-231 VT-ESL (Uwe Gleisberg/Kuala Lumpur)

INDIAN AIRLINES

113 Gurdwara Rakabganj Road, New Delhi 110001, India, Tel. 11-3718951, Fax. 11-3711014, www.nic.in/indian-airlines

Three- / Two- letter code	IATA No.	Reg'n prefix	ICAO callsign
IAC / IC	058	VT	Indair

Indian Airlines Corporation was set up on 28th May 1953 by central government in Delhi and on 1st August 1953 formally acquired the routes and assets of eight independent airlines - Airways (India), Bharat Airways, Himalayan Aviation, Kalinga Airlines, Indian National Airways, Deccan Airways, Air India and Air Services of India. They were all nationalised and combined to form Air India and Indian Airlines, with Indian Airlines being responsible for regional services. The airline's first flights were on 1st August 1953 and it used DC-4s, Vickers Vikings and DC-3s. In 1957 these aircraft were partly replaced by Vickers Viscounts, and by the Fokker F.27 from May 1961 onwards. The airline's first jet was the Caravelle, acquired in February 1964. HS.748s manufactured under licence in India were also used, as were Airbus A300s, the first widebody for Indian. When the latest generation of aircraft, the Airbus A320, was introduced from the end of 1989, some operational problems arose which had an effect on flights and on passenger numbers. Indian Airlines' flights were divided on a regional basis, from Delhi, Calcutta, Madras and Mumbai (formerly Bombay). The airline was partially privatised in 1994, with a further offer of sale of shares in 1998 but the government retains 49% and has a strong influence. The regional carrier Vayudoot formed with Air India in 1981 and its Dornier 228s were integrated into Indian Airlines during 1996. There are co-operation agreements with Air France, Air India and Srilankan.

Routes

Over 50 points in India are served regularly, and there are international services to Al-Fujairah, Bahrain, Bangkok, Colombo, Dacca, Doha, Karachi, Kathmandu, Kuala Lumpur, Male, Muscat, Ras al Khaimah, Sharjah, Singapore, and Yangon.

Fleet

11 Airbus A300B4
30 Airbus A320-200
 3 Fairchild-Dornier 228

Airbus A300B2-203 EP-IBV (Author's collection)

IRAN AIR

P.O.Box 13185-775, Mehrabad Airport,
Teheran, Islamic Republic of Iran
Tel. 979111, Fax. 6003248 www.iranair.com

Three- / Two- letter code	IATA No.	Reg'n prefix	ICAO callsign
IRA / IR	096	EP	Iranair

Iran Air came into existence in February 1962 as the result of the fusion of Iranian Airways and Persian Air Service, by order of the government of the day, and took over the routes and aircraft of both airlines. Iran Air had been established as a private company in 1944 and was known as Iranair. Persian, also in private hands, had begun freight services in 1955 with Avro Yorks. In 1965 Iran Air acquired Boeing 727s and used them to open new routes to London and Frankfurt. In March 1976 a Boeing 747SP began scheduled services to New York. The first Airbus A300s were brought into use during 1978, mainly on the much travelled routes to neighbouring countries. Political developments in the early 1980s following the Ayatollah Khomeini's rise to power in 1979, with the departure of the Shah, and the war lasting several years with neighbouring Iraq brought many changes. Prior to 1979 Iran Air had been one of the world's fastest growing airlines scheduling over 100 weekly international departures from Teheran to nearly 30 destinations, but by the mid-1980s the departures had reduced to less than 30 a week. However, from 1989 restructuring became possible and fleet modernisation began in September 1990 with the delivery of the first Fokker 100 for regional services. Further modernisation has fallen foul of the United States instigated economic embargo however, which extended even to civil aircraft. In 1992, in co-operation with Tajikistan Airlines, a subsidiary company, Iran Air Tours was set up and this operates a fleet of Tupolev Tu-154s. In 1998 a co-operation agreement was forged with Malaysia Airlines.

Routes

Abu Dhabi, Ahwaz, Almaty, Amsterdam, Ardabil, Ashgabat, Bahrain, Baku, Bandar Abbas, Bandar Lengeh, Beijing, Buskihr, Cha-Bahar, Copenhagen, Damascus, Dacca, Delhi, Doha, Dubai, Entebbe, Frankfurt, Geneva, Gothenburg, Hamburg, Isfahan, Istanbul, Jeddah, Karachi, Kerrnan, Kormanshar, Kuala Lumpur, Kuwait, Larnaca, London, Mashad, Moscow, Mumbai, Nairobi, Paris, Rome, Sary, Sharjah, Shiraz, Stockholm, Tabriz, Tashkent, Teheran, Tokyo, Vienna, Yazd, Zahedan.

Fleet

5 Airbus A300B2	3 Boeing 747-200
2 Airbus A300-600	1 Boeing 747-100
4 Boeing 737-200	4 Boeing 747SP
6 Boeing 727-200	6 Fokker 100
4 Boeing 707-300	

Boeing 727-228 EP-ASB (Josef Krauthäuser collection via EAS)

IRAN ASEMAN AIRLINES

P.O.Box 141748 Mehrabad Airport
Teheran 13145-1476, Islamic Republic of Iran
Tel. 21-6484198, Fax. 21-6404318

Three- / Two- letter code	IATA No.	Reg'n prefix	ICAO callsign
IRC / EP	–	EP	Aseman

Following the revolution in Iran, in 1980 Iran Asseman Airlines was formed by state order from the merger of various smaller air taxi companies. Air Taxi founded in 1958, Air Service in 1962, Pars Air which had been in existence since 1969, and Hoor Asseman, all with their light aircraft formed the nucleus of the new company, which soon was using Fokker F.28s. The continuing war between Iran and Iraq was for a while a hindrance to the further development of the company, which operated only domestic services. There were no scheduled routes however, but overwhelmingly charter and contract work for companies and state enterprises and institutions which had need of air services. During 1993 and 1994 there was a wholesale reorganisation, which led to the acquisition of further Fokker F.28s and ATR 42s and ATR 72s. In addition the airline equipped itself with four Boeing 727s. Iran Aseman Airlines, as it is now known, having dropped one of the 's's from its original name, has built up an extensive domestic network in Iran, and flies in addition, to the neighbouring countries in the Arabian peninsula. As well as Teheran, Shiraz is an important hub for the airline. During 1999 the company's fleet was brought up to date with the delivery of the latest, more powerful model ATR 72-500.

Routes

Ahwaz, Birjand, Chah Bahar, Fasa, Gonbad, Hamadan, Isfahan, Kerman, Keramshah, Khorramabad, Lar, Mashad, Ramsar, Shiraz, Tabas, Tabriz, Teheran, Zahedan.

Fleet

1 ATR 42
6 ATR 72
4 Boeing 727-200
2 Britten-Norman Islander
6 Fokker F.28

Boeing 737-4Y0 TC-AZA (Dennis Wehrmann/Hanover)

ISTANBUL AIRLINES

Firuzköy Yolu 26, Avcilar, Istanbul 34850, Turkey
Tel. 212-5092100, Fax. 212-5938742

Three- / Two- letter code	IATA No.	Reg'n prefix	ICAO callsign
IST / IL	393	TC	Istanbul

Istanbul Airlines (or Istanbul Hava Yollari) was set up in December 1985 by Turkish and West German interests in order to meet the increased demand for aircraft seats to Turkey. Flights started on 14th March 1986 with SE.210 Caravelles; two BAC One-Elevens were also leased for a while from TAROM. The first Boeing 737s were introduced in November 1988, and this type was used to establish scheduled services, providing improved connections from Istanbul to other Turkish centres. The company developed very quickly and further Boeing 737-400s were bought. In order to meet demand in the charter business, Boeing 727s were also added, replacing the Caravelles. During 1995 Istanbul Airlines took on two Boeing 757-200s. As well as operating its schedules and charters, Istanbul Airlines also entered the freight business, using a Boeing 727 freighter, though the passenger versions of the 727 were phased out during 1997 and 1998 with the delivery of further Boeing 737-400s. In 1999 there was a change of fleet strategy and the Boeing 757s were returned to their lessor, being replaced by the first two examples of the new Boeing 737-800. Clearly the airline has been experiencing financial problems during the Summer season of 2000, with operations drastically reduced.

Routes

Adana, Amsterdam, Ankara, Antalya, Basle, Berlin, Bremen, Brussels, Cologne/Bonn, Düsseldorf, Ercan, Erzurum, Frankfurt, Gaziantep, Hamburg, Hanover, Istanbul, Izmir, Leipzig, Linz, London, Manchester, Munich, Münster/Osnabrück, Nuremberg, Paris, Salzburg, Stuttgart, Trabzon, Van, Warsaw, Vienna.

Fleet	Ordered
1 Boeing 727-200	12 Boeing 737-800
4 Boeing 737-400	
1 Boeing 737-800	

Boeing 737-446 JA 8991 (Josef Krauthäuser collection)

JAL EXPRESS

4-11 Higashi-Shinagawa, 2-chome Sinagawa-ku,
Tokyo 1040, Japan
Tel. 6-68577378, Fax. 6-68577384

Three- / Two- letter code	IATA No.	Reg'n prefix	ICAO callsign
JEX / JC	–	JA	Janex

Domestic air services have a particular significance in densely populated Japan. Over the last few years new, smaller airlines have established niche markets in competition with the former dominant carriers ANA/All Nippon, Japan Airlines and JAS. On several routes there have been strongly competitive battles, partly based on ticket prices. The established airlines had high operating costs which led ANA to pass over the operation of several flights to its subsidiary Air Nippon. Similarly, in April 1997, Japan Airlines was moved to set up its own low cost airline known as JAL-Express. Initially it used two Boeing 737-400s leased from the parent company, and began operations on 1st July 1998. The first route was Osaka-Miyazaki and this was flown several times daily. With the delivery of further 737-400s, operations were expanded, so that Kagoshima was also served from Osaka, again several times a day. JAL Express has the long term aim of creating an intensive domestic network, following the model established by similar low-cost/low-fare airlines in the United States and in Europe.

Routes

Kagoshima, Kumamoto, Miyazaki, Nagasaki, Oita, Osaka, Sapporo, Sendai.

Fleet

6 Boeing 737-400

Saab SF 340B JA8887 (Josef Krauthäuser collection via EAS)

JAPAN AIR COMMUTER

822 Fumoto, Mizobecho, Airagun
Kagoshimaken 899-6495, Japan
Tel. 995-582151, Fax. 995-583904

Three- / Two- letter code	IATA No.	Reg'n prefix	ICAO callsign
JAC / 3X	–	JA	Commuter

This new regional airline was formed on 1st July 1983 with participation from the provincial government of Kagoshima and TOA Domestic Airlines, with 40% and 60% of the shareholdings respectively. The Dornier 228-200 was selected as the aircraft equipment and two of the type were ordered. JAC began operations on 10th December 1983. The company developed slowly, with a further Dornier 228 being added to the fleet in 1988. At the end of the 1980s TOA Domestic changed its name to JAS-Japan Air System and restructured its services. Japan Air Commuted was the beneficiary of the handover of several routes and was obliged to acquire larger aircraft with which to operate them; NAMC-YS-11s thus supplemented the Dornier 228s. Early in 1992 JAC took delivery of its first Saab SF 340, thus increasing capacity, and from that time, one or two aircraft a year have been added. JAC operates a feeder service to the two hubs at Kagoshima and Osaka and thus delivers passengers to connect to further JAS flights.

Routes

Amammi O Shima, Fukuoka, Izumo, Hiroshima, Kagoshima, Kigaiga-shima, Komatsu, Matsumoto, Matsuyama, Miyazaki, Nagasaki, Nagoya, Okayama, Okino Erabu, Osaka, Takamatsu, Tanegashima, Tokushima, Toyooka, Yakushima, Yoronjima.

Fleet

12 NAMC YS-11
11 Saab SF 340B

(Boeing) McDonnell Douglas MD-11 JA8586 (Josef Krauthäuser/Frankfurt)

JAPAN AIRLINES

Jal Building, Higashi Shinagawa 2-4-11
Shinagawaku, Tokyo 140, Japan
Tel. 3-54603121, Fax. 3-54603936, www.jal.co.jp

Three- / Two- letter code	IATA No.	Reg'n prefix	ICAO callsign
JAL / JL	131	JA	Japanair

JAL was set up on 1st August 1951 as Japanese Air Lines when civil aviation was reactivated in Japan after the Second World War. The first flight was from Tokyo-Haneda to Osaka with a leased Martin 202 on 25th October 1951. A year later the first flight with a DC-4 owned by the airline took place. In 1953 the DC-6 was introduced and 2nd February 1954 saw the first international flight from Tokyo to San Francisco; in August 1960 the DC-8 was introduced for this route. In the following year the Tokyo-London polar route and Paris/ Copenhagen to Tokyo were opened with DC-8s. Convair 880s were introduced in 1962 and used for the first time to Frankfurt via South East Asia. In 1967 a round-the-world flight was established; the first flights over Siberia to Europe were in March 1970, saving several hours over the previous polar route. In the same year, on 1st July 1970, the Boeing 747 was introduced, at first on Pacific routes. The Douglas DC-10-40 was specially designed for JAL and used from the mid-1970s. New destinations were Zürich in 1979 and Düsseldorf from 1985, and there was expansion to the USA in the 1980s. The first Boeing 767 was brought into the fleet during 1987, and the airline privatised during the following year. The MD-11 was introduced from 1993, the Boeing 737-400 from 1995 and the Boeing 777 from 1996. JAL has shareholdings in the following airlines: Japan Asia, JALexpress, JALways, JAS, Japan Trans Ocean and DHL. There is co-operation with numerous other carriers, especially through JAL's membership of the Oneworld Alliance.

Routes

Amsterdam, Anchorage, Atlanta, Bangkok, Beijing, Brisbane, Chicago, Dallas/Fort Worth, Delhi, Denpasar, Frankfurt, Geneva, Guam, Havana, Ho Chi Minh City, Hong Kong, Honolulu, Jakarta, Kuala Lumpur, Las Vegas, London, Los Angeles, Milan, Manila, Memphis, Mexico City, Moscow, Nagasaki, Nagoya, New York, Okinawa, Osaka, Paris, Pusan, Rome, Saipan, San Francisco, Sao Paulo, Sapporo, Seoul, Shanghai, Singapore, Sydney, Tokyo, Vancouver, Zürich.

Fleet

Fleet		Ordered
21 Boeing 767-200/300	3 Boeing 737-400	7 Boeing 747-400
40 Boeing 747-400	10 Boeing 777-200/300	5 Boeing 777
13 Boeing 747-300	14 McDonnell Douglas DC-10-40	
26 Boeing 747-100/200	10 (Boeing) McDonnell Douglas MD-11	

Boeing 777-289 JA-007D (Author's collection)

JAPAN AIR SYSTEM – JAS

JAS M1 Bldg., 5-1 Haneda kuko, 3-Chome, Ota-ku, Tokyo 144-0041, Japan, Tel. 3-57 564028, Fax. 3-57567020, www.jas.co.jp

Three- / Two- letter code	IATA No.	Reg'n prefix	ICAO callsign
JAS / JD	234	JA	Air System

Japan Air System (JAS) is the revised name adopted from 1st April 1988 by the former TOA-Domestic (TDA). Toa Domestic Airlines resulted from the amalgamation of Japan Domestic and TOA Airways on 15th May 1971; the latter was founded on 30th November 1953. Japan Domestic had been formed in March 1964 through the merger of North Japan Airlines, Nitto Aviation and Fuji Airlines. Toa Domestic operated NAMC YS-11s until the introduction of its first Douglas DC-9 jets in 1973; these were in turn phased out during a fleet modernisation during the 1990s

when various models of the MD-80 series were added. Airbus A300s have been in use since 1980 and form a significant part of the fleet. The change of name in 1988 was brought about by a change in legislation which allowed flights outside Japan to be undertaken. The first international flight was to Seoul in Korea. On 30th March 1988 JAS's first DC-10-30 was delivered, thus giving the airline the equipment to operate intercontinental flights for the first time; it was used for charter flights to Hawaii and Singapore. The delivery of new MD-90s from 1995 also saw the introduction of a

colourful new colour scheme, and re-equipment continued with Boeing 777s being added from early 1997. JAS is Japan's third largest airline, and has two major subsidiaries, Japan Air Commuter (see page 218) and Harlequin Air, established in 1998 with the stated long term aim of taking over all the international scheduled services. The airline's home base is at Tokyo's Narita airport, where it has extensive maintenance and training facilities.

Routes

Akita, Amami, Aomori, Asahikawa, Fukuoka, Guangzhou, Hiroshima, Hong Kong, Izumo, Kagoshima, Kita Kyushu, Kochi, Komatsu, Kumamoto, Kunming, Kushiro, Matsumoto, Matsuyama, Memambetsu, Misawa, Miyazaki, Morioka, Nagasaki, Nagoya, Nanki Shirahama, Niigata, Obihiro, Oita, Okayama, Okinawa, Osaka, Saga, Sapporo, Sendai, Seoul, Takamatsu, Tokunoshima, Tokushima, Tokyo, Yamagata, Xian.

Fleet

17 Airbus A300B4
18 Airbus A300-600
 7 Boeing 777-200
 2 McDonnell Douglas DC-10-30

17 McDonnell Douglas MD-81
 8 McDonnell Douglas MD-87
16 McDonnell Douglas MD-90

Boeing 747-246B JA 8155 (Author's collection)

JAPAN ASIA AIRWAYS

2-4-11-Higashi-Shinagawa, Shinagawa-ku, Tokyo 140-8637, Japan, Tel. 3-32842971, Fax. 3-32842945, www.japanasia.co.jp

Three- / Two- letter code	IATA No.	Reg'n prefix	ICAO callsign
JAA / EG	688	JA	Asia

Japan Asia Airways is a wholly-owned subsidiary of Japan Air Lines, having been established on 8th August 1975. The airline was set up for political considerations, as Japan Airlines wished to open up services to the People's Republic of China, but could only do so by giving up its services to Taiwan. However, as the Taiwan services were so lucrative and JAL did not wish to be forced to drop them, Japan Asia was created as a face-saving exercise and politicians in China and Japan were kept happy. Operations started on 15th September 1975, and in the first

years following its formation, JAA flew only to Taipei. The aircraft, at first DC-8s, but later DC-10s and Boeing 747s, were all supplied by the parent company, but painted in Japan Asia's colours (conveniently akin to those of JAL, to save major repaint work), and further aircraft were available from JAL as circumstances demanded. An expansion of services took place from the mid-1990s, with routes added to Kaohsiung on Taiwan, Bangkok and Hong Kong, but additionally within Japan as a low-fare operator for Japan Airlines. During 1997 and 1998 the first

Boeing 767-300s were introduced and older Boeing 747-100s retired. In addition to scheduled services, Japan Asia also operates charters to popular holiday destinations in the whole of the Asia-Pacific region. There is close co-operation with China Airlines.

Routes

Bangkok, Hong Kong, Kaohsiung, Nagoya, Okinawa, Osaka, Taipei, Tokyo.

Fleet

5 Boeing 747-200/300
4 Boeing 767-300

Boeing 737-3H9 YU-ANW (Albert Kuhbandner/Munich)

JAT – YUGOSLAV AIRLINES

Svetog Save1, Novi Beograd 11070, Yugoslavia
Tel. 11-4440022, Fax. 11-3442931,
www.jat.com

Three- / Two- letter code	IATA No.	Reg'n prefix	ICAO callsign
JAT / JU	115	YU	JAT

The predecessor of JAT was Aeroput, founded in 1927, but which was forced to quit operations at the outbreak of the Second World War. JAT was then founded on 1st April 1947 and began operations with the ubiquitous DC-3. The jet era arrived with the Caravelle in 1963 and marked an expansion of services in Europe especially; destinations such as Moscow, Amsterdam and Stockholm could now be reached non-stop. In 1969 the DC-9 was introduced and a year later the Boeing 707, allowing transatlantic service for the first time to the USA and Canada, plus additional destinations in the Far East and Australia. In 1974 the Caravelles were replaced for medium-length routes by the Boeing 727, and from 1978 the DC-10 succeeded the Boeing 707s for long-range work. A further fleet renewal began in 1985 with the acquisition of the Boeing 737-300. However on 31st May 1992 JAT was forced to give up its international flights as a result of United Nations sanctions because of the political situation in what was by then the former Yugoslavia and the ongoing civil war in Bosnia. The embargo was lifted and services resumed on 6th October 1994. To reflect the new situation, a new colour scheme was adopted and the 'Yugoslav Airlines' inscription added. Routes were flown from Belgrade to mainly European cities, but there was no demand for long-range routes and three DC-10s were sold; other aircraft in the formerly extensive fleet were leased out or stored. No new aircraft have been delivered since 1991, when ATR 72s were added. JAT suffered further problems in 1999, when from March NATO was bombing some parts of Yugoslavia; a fresh embargo was imposed, but lifted in March 2000. JAT is now trying to build up its former route network from its Belgrade base. JAT has a majority shareholding in Air Yugoslavia.

Routes

Amman, Amsterdam, Athens, Banjaluka, Barcelona, Beijing, Beirut, Belgrade, Bucharest, Cairo, Damascus, Düsseldorf, Frankfurt, Hamburg, Istanbul, Kiev, Kuwait, Larnaca, London, Milan, Moscow, Munich, Nis, Odessa, Ohrid, Paris, Podgorica, Skopje, Tel Aviv, Thessaloniki, Tivat, Tripoli, Tunis, Warsaw, Zürich.

Fleet

1 ATR 72	3 McDonnell Douglas DC-9-32
8 Boeing 727-200	
4 Boeing 737-300	
1 McDonnell Douglas DC-10-30	

De Havilland DHC-8-311 G-JEDA (Author's collection)

JERSEY EUROPEAN AIRWAYS

Terminal Building, Exeter Airport, EX5 2BD, Great Britain, Tel. 1392-366669, Fax. 1392-366151, www.jersey-european.co.uk

Three- / Two- letter code	IATA No.	Reg'n prefix	ICAO callsign
JEA / JY	267	G	Jersey

Jersey European Airways was formed on 1st November 1979 in order to take over the activities of two companies, Intra Airways and Express Air Services. Intra (Jersey) Airways goes back to 1969 when several BUA pilots decided to form their own airline. With a DC-3 they flew services from Jersey to the other Channel Islands, to northern France and later to Ostend in Belgium. For several years Intra flew passengers from Staverton to Jersey and other charter destinations followed, with up to six DC-3s in use. In 1974 a Britten-Norman Islander was acquired and a service to London Gatwick commenced.

Express Air Services had several Piper PA-31s which it used for passenger and courier flights. After acquisition by the Walker Group in 1983, the operations of both were brought together under the Jersey European name. Twin Otters and Embraer Bandeirantes ousted the smaller types and with the start of a new service to Birmingham, the first Fokker F.27 was introduced. 1989 saw the HS.748 also added for use on other UK domestic services such as Belfast to Birmingham. Further F.27s, Shorts 360s and the first jet type, the BAe 146 were added and formed the bulk of the fleet during the mid 1990s, when the route

network continued to expand, partly in close co-operation with Air France, with whom there are codeshare agreements. From 1999 new aircraft types, the DHC-8 and Canadair Regional Jet were introduced, allowing retirement of the F.27s. The airline has its headquarters and maintenance facility at Exeter, with major operating bases at Gatwick, Stansted and Birmingham. Reflecting its move away from its Jersey roots, it is changing its name to British European Airways in a process which is expected to be completed by early 2001.

Routes

Belfast, Birmingham, Blackpool, Bristol, Cork, Dublin, Edinburgh, Exeter, Glasgow, Guernsey, Isle of Man, Jersey, Leeds/Bradford, London-Gatwick, London-Stansted, Lyon, Paris, Shannon, Southampton, Toulouse. Charter flights within Europe and on behalf of the Post Office.

Fleet	Ordered
16 BAe 146-100/200/300	4 De Havilland DHC-8-400
9 De Havilland DHC-8	3 Canadair Regional Jet
1 Canadair Regional Jet	
2 Shorts SD-360	

Airbus A320-200 N503JB (Hans-Willi Mertens/Fort Lauderdale

JET BLUE AIRWAYS

90 Park Avenue, New York 10016, USA
Tel. 212-5576565,
www.jetblue.com

Three- / Two- letter code	IATA No.	Reg'n prefix	ICAO callsign
– / B6	–	N	Jetblue

David Neeleman, the founder of Jet Blue, is not unknown in airline circles, having over some years led Morris Air to such considerable success that it was bought out by its mighty competitor, Southwest Airlines. After his time at Morris Air, Neeleman went on to be a success at Southwest, building up a reservations system, and also helping the Canadian airline West Jet to set up their operation. However the notion of having his own airline stayed with him and in 1998 the idea became a reality. First it was necessary to find investors willing to come up with the sum of $130 million, an amount which had never before been raised for an airline start-up. Another feature of the plan was the aircraft choice; only factory-fresh aircraft were to be considered, and the choice fell in favour of Airbus. In April an order was placed for 82 A320s, all equipped with the latest 24-channel TV system, and leather seats. As an operating base and main departure point only New York's Kennedy Airport was on the agenda, since this was believed to offer the best market opportunities. Options were taken on 75 slots here. With the delivery of the first A320 in January 2000, Jet Blue was ready for the off, and on 11th February the first service took place, from New York to Fort Lauderdale. Days later, service to Buffalo was added. Tampa was added soon afterwards and as further aircraft are delivered, services are being built up, with the intention of having ten aircraft in the fleet and ten destinations in the first year.

Routes

From New York to Buffalo, Burlington, Fort Lauderdale, Oakland, Ontario, Rochester, Salt Lake City, Syracuse, Tampa.

Fleet	Ordered
9 Airbus A320	73 Airbus A320

Boeing 757-28A G-FCLI (Dieter Roth/Salzburg)

JMC AIR

Commonwealth Hse, Chicago Ave. Manchester Airport, M90 3FL, Great Britain, Tel. 161-4895757 Fax. 161-4895758, www.jmc-holidays.co.uk

Three- / Two- letter code	IATA No.	Reg'n prefix	ICAO callsign
JMC / MT	–	G	JMC

In 1995 the British tour operator Flying Colours Leisure Group (Sunset Holidays, Priority Holidays, Club 18-30) set up their own in-house airline, Flying Colours. Boeing 757s came into use, principally on routes to the popular Mediterranean destinations. During 1998 the Flying Colours Leisure Group was acquired by another UK tour operator, Sunworld, whose own airline, Airworld, was merged with Flying Colours. Sunworld was owned by Thomas Cook Holdings, one of the largest British tour companies, with worldwide interests. In a further bout of consolidation within the industry,

this was merged during 1998 with the Carlson Leisure Group, who had had Caledonian Airways as their own in-house airline since 1987, and were using Airbus A320s, Douglas DC-10s and Lockheed L-1011 TriStars. The new combined group took on the Thomas Cook name, but had two successful airlines under its umbrella, and so from the end of the 1999 summer season it was decided that they should be merged. However, as it was not clear that one name or the other should be continued, it was decided to adopt a completely new identity as JMC - being the initials of John Mason Cook, son of the founder of

Thomas Cook, with the airline element JMC Airlines Ltd, trading as JMC Air. The first aircraft appeared in the new colours in March 2000. The fleets are merged, and will be augmented from July 2001 by new Boeing 757-300s.

Routes

From London, Birmingham, Manchester and other airports to destinations in the Mediterranean, Canary Isles Northern Africa and the Caribbean .

Fleet	Ordered
10 Airbus A320-200	2 Boeing 757-300
16 Boeing 757-200	
2 McDonnell Douglas DC-10-30	

Boeing 737-4Q3 JA-8524 (Author's collection)

JTA – JAPAN TRANSOCEAN AIR

3-24 Yamashita-cho, Naha-shi, Okinawa 900
Japan
Tel. 98-8572112, Fax. 98-8589396

Three- / Two- letter code	IATA No.	Reg'n prefix	ICAO callsign
JTA / NU	353	JA	Jai Ocean

Southwest Airlines – SWAL was based at the airport at Naha, the capital of Okinawa, an island in the Ryukyu group which from 1945 until 1972 was under American control and administration. During the Second World War Okinawa had been occupied by the Americans. Occasional services had been provided by Air America, but for Japanese citizens there were certain restrictions. Thus on 22nd June 1967 a group of Okinawa business people set up their own airline. Support came from Japan Air Lines, who took a 51% shareholding, and a Convair 240 came into use from 1st July 1967. After a year a locally-produced NAMC YS-11 took over the services. The smaller islands in the archipelago were also served, using the de Havilland DHC-6 Twin Otter, which was able to cope with the short runways which were all that was available on some islands. At the beginning of the 1980s the first Boeing 737-200 came into service and was used to give service several times a day to Ishigaki, the most important route to the mainland. In July 1993 the airline's name was changed to Japan Trans Ocean Air. A year later JTA received the Boeing 737-400 as a more modern replacement for the older YS-11s. Ryukyu Air Commuter is a JTA subsidiary company, which uses de Havilland DHC-8s and Twin Otters to continue service to the smaller islands.

Routes

Aguni, Amami O Shima, Hateruma, Ishigaki, Kagoshima, Kerama, Kitadaito, Kochi, Komatsu, Kume Jima, Matsuyama, Minami Daito, Miyako Jima, Nahe, Okayama, Osaka, Taramajima, Tokyo, Yonaguni Jima, Yoronjima.

Fleet

5 Boeing 737-200
13 Boeing 737-400

Saab 340B VH-KDR (Uwe Gleisberg/Sydney)

KENDELL AIRLINES

86 Baylis Street OR,Wagga Wagga NSW 2650 Australia, Tel. 2-69220100, Fax. 2-69220116, www.kendell.com.au

Three- / Two- letter code	IATA No.	Reg'n prefix	ICAO callsign
KDA / KD	678	VH	Kendell

Set up in 1966 as a non-scheduled air carrier with the name PremiAir Aviation, the company initially flew a Piper Apache for air taxi work. The name was changed to Kendell Airlines (after founder Dan Kendell) in 1971. Regular scheduled flights from Wagga Wagga to Melbourne started on 18th October 1971 using a Piper Navajo. De Havilland Herons arrived in 1975, and Swearingen Metros by 1979. Merimbula was added as a destination in the 1970s and over the years Kendell developed in southern Australia into a regional airline flying to four federal states. In 1985 the Saab 340 was introduced. The TNT/News Corporation, owners of Ansett, increased its shareholding in Kendell over the years and in 1986 when Ansett closed down Airlines of South Australia, Kendell took over a number of its routes. Ansett is an important partner for Kendell, which flies feeder services from its hubs at Adelaide and Melbourne to smaller communities. Eventually Ansett Holdings came to own 100% of the shares and this was evidenced in the aircraft colour scheme, which became a variant of the Ansett livery. When Ansett reduced its Tasmanian services in 1999, Kendell moved to fill the void. Some flights are operated for Ansett under AN codes under franchise/codeshare arrangements. A fleet of Canadair Regional Jets is being introduced to supplement the mainstay Saab 340s.

Routes

Adelaide, Albury, Ballina, Brisbane, Broken Hill, Burnie, Canberra, Ceduna, Coffs Harbour, Coober Pedy, Devonport, Hobart, King Island, Kingscote, Launceston, Melbourne, Merimbula, Mildura, Mount Gambier, Olympic Dam, Port Lincoln, Portland, Rockhampton, Sydney, Wagga Wagga, Whyalla.

Fleet	Ordered
7 Canadair RJ-200ER	5 Canadair RJ-200ER
7 Fairchild Metro 23	
8 Saab 340 A	
8 Saab 340 B	

Boeing 737-3U8 5Y-KQD (Bastian Hilker/Harare)

KENYA AIRWAYS

Jomo Kenyatta Intl. Airport, P.O.Box 19002,
Nairobi, Kenya, Tel. 2-823000, Fax. 2-823488,
www.kenyaairways.co.uk

Three- / Two- letter code	IATA No.	Reg'n prefix	ICAO callsign
KQA / KQ	706	5Y	Kenya

Following the collapse of the multi-national airline East African Airways, the flag carrier for Kenya, Tanzania and Uganda in 1976, the Kenyan government was forced to set up its own airline. With the aid of British Midland Airways and using two leased Boeing 707s, services were begun from Nairobi to London, Frankfurt, Athens and Rome in February 1977, one month after the airline was formed on 22nd January 1977. The leased aircraft were replaced by the airline's own 707s, which in turn were replaced by more modern aircraft in the form of the Airbus A310 from 1986. Fokker 50s were introduced for shorter routes

from 1988. During the early 1990s the airline declined, earning a poor reputation for reliability and service, but the problem was tackled; reorganisation and rationalisation made and in 1996 the airline was partially privatised with the participation of KLM, which took a 26% shareholding. In April 1997 a daily service to Amsterdam was started, to feed into the KLM network, and this close co-operation continues. During 1998 a new colour scheme was adopted for the aircraft, and the Fokker 50s phased out. Further Boeing 737s were added, making the fleet all-jet. At the beginning of 2000 Kenya Airways

leased a Boeing 767, and this type, including the stretched -400ERX variant from 2004, is planned to replace the remaining A310s. New Boeing 737-700s are likewise to replace the older -200 series. Also in the early part of 2000, a subsidiary, Kenya Flamingo Airways, was set up to operate four Saab 340s on short range services. Both airlines are based at Nairobi's Jomo Kenyatta International Airport.

Routes

Abidjan, Addis Ababa, Amsterdam, Bujumbura, Cairo, Copenhagen, Dar-es-Salaam, Douala, Dubai, Eldoret, Entebbe/Kampala, Harare, Johannesburg, Karachi, Khartoum, Kigali, Kinshasa, Lagos, Lilongwe, London, Lusaka, Mahe, Malindi, Mombasa, Mumbai, Nairobi, Zanzibar.

Fleet	Ordered
3 Airbus A310-300	2 Boeing 737-700
2 Boeing 737-200	3 Boeing 767-300
4 Boeing 737-300	3 Boeing 767-400
1 Boeing 767-300	

Fokker 70 PH-KZC (Martin Bach/Berlin-TXL)

KLM-CITYHOPPER

Postbus 7700, 1117 ZL Schiphol Oost, the Netherlands, Tel. 20-6492227, Fax. 20-6488154, www.klm.com

Three- / Two- letter code	IATA No.	Reg'n prefix	ICAO callsign
KLC / KL	195	PH	City

The present KLM-Cityhopper is the successor in name to NLM Dutch Airlines, which was set up in 1966 and started scheduled flights between Amsterdam, Eindhoven and Maastricht on 29th August 1966, using the proven Fokker F.27 Friendship. Regional international schedules began in 1974. In 1976 the name of the airline was changed to NLM Cityhopper and KLM acquired a majority interest. Another independent Dutch operator, Netherlines, was set up in 1984 and on 8th January 1985 began operations with Jetstream 31s between Amsterdam and Luxembourg, with further routes opened up from 1985 and 1988. By 1987, Netherlines was owned by the Nedlloyd Group, who also owned Transavia. In 1988, KLM decided to buy Netherlines with the intention of asking NLM, which operated F.27s and F.28s, to merge the airlines together to form the new KLM-Cityhopper, a 100% KLM subsidiary. Saab 340s and Fokker 50s were introduced at the beginning of the 1990s, with the first Fokker 70 delivered in Spring 1996, but the planned total of this type was not reached as a result of Fokker's demise. The airline's base is at Amsterdam-Schiphol, where the whole KLM infrastructure is used.

KLM-Cityhopper flies under KLM flight numbers, providing service to smaller airports or on more poorly-supported routes.

Routes

Amsterdam, Basle, Berlin, Bologna, Bremen, Bristol, Brussels, Cardiff, Düsseldorf, Frankfurt, Hamburg, Kristiansand, London-Luton, Luxembourg, Lyon, Malmö, Munich, Nice, Oslo, Paris, Rotterdam, Toulouse, Turin, Venice, Verona.

Fleet

14 Fokker 70
13 Fokker 50

Boeing 767-306 PH-BZK (Dennis Wehrmann/Amsterdam)

KLM ROYAL DUTCH AIRLINES

P.O.Box 7700, 1117 ZL Amsterdam,
Airport Schiphol, Netherlands, Tel. 20-6499123,
Fax. 20-6493113, www.klm.com

Three- / Two- letter code	IATA No.	Reg'n prefix	ICAO callsign
KLM / KL	074	PH	KLM

Formed on 7th October 1919, KLM is one of the oldest operating airlines in the world. The first scheduled flights were Amsterdam to London on 17th May 1920. Mainly Fokker aircraft were used until the outbreak of war. In 1929 the route to Batavia (today called Jakarta) was opened, at that time the longest route. The first transatlantic link was to Curacao in 1934 and operations in the West Indies began in 1935. Douglas DC-2s were introduced in 1935, followed by DC-3s in 1936 and until 1940 KLM had one of the densest networks in Europe. After 1945, reconstruction commenced with DC-3s, with Convair 240s added from 1948; these were replaced by Convair 340s from 1953. The Vickers Viscount took over important routes in Europe from 1957 onwards, augmented by the Lockheed Electra from 1959. Overseas flights were initially flown by DC-4s, Lockheed Constellations, with DC-6s and DC-7s as the last of the propeller-driven aircraft. The first DC-8 was used to New York on 4th April 1960. Boeing 747s, introduced in 1971, and DC-10s took over the long-distance routes in the 1970s. For short and medium distances, KLM initially used DC-9s, which were then replaced by Boeing 737s (now in process of updating with new generation models) and augmented by Airbus A310s. KLM's present flagship is the Boeing 747-400 which has been used since May 1989. During 1993 KLM took a minority shareholding in Northwest Airlines and since then has worked closely with its US partner in the Wings Alliance. A merger with Alitalia was planned to take place during 1999, but was shelved with some acrimony, and during mid-2000, talks were being held with British Airways with a similar objective. KLM has interests in ALM-Antillean, buzz, Kenya Airways, KLM Alps, KLM UK, Martinair, Transavia and KLM-Cityhopper.

Routes

From its home base at Amsterdam-Schiphol, KLM serves an intensive European network and internationally connects over 165 cities on all continents.

Fleet

Fleet		Ordered
20 Boeing 747-400	19 Boeing 737-300	4 Boeing 737-800
3 Boeing 747-300	10 Boeing 737-800	4 Boeing 737-900
12 Boeing 747-200 (several SUD)	12 Boeing 767-300	4 Boeing 747-400
19 Boeing 737-400	10 (Boeing) McDonnell Douglas MD-11	

BAe 146-300 G-BSNS (Rainer Flath/ Brussels)

KLM UK

Endeavour House, London Stansted Airport, Essex CM24 1RS, Great Britain, Tel. 1279-660400, Fax. 1279-660330, www.klmuk.com

Three- / Two- letter code	IATA No.	Reg'n prefix	ICAO callsign
UKA / UK	130	G	Ukay

British Island Airways (formed July 1976), Air Anglia (formed August 1970) Air Wales (formed July 1977 and Air Westward (formed 1976) merged on 16th January 1980 to form the new joint airline, Air UK. The route networks were combined and the aircraft fleet co-ordinated. The carrier was a subsidiary of British Air Transport Holdings, in which British and Commonwealth Shipping Group had a 90% shareholding. The merged airline operated scheduled services to 21 airports in Britain and 10 points in Europe. Fokker F.27s were the main type in Air UK's fleet and by the mid-1980s it was Britain's third largest

airline. In 1987 KLM acquired a 14.9% stake, later increased to 45%. In April 1988 charter subsidiary UK Leisure was set up, but was autonomous and sold to Unijet, becoming Leisure International Airways. Older aircraft were retired with the delivery of Fokker 50s and 100s. There were codeshare agreements in place with KLM, with many services radiating from Amsterdam to the UK. In Autumn 1997, KLM took over the remaining shares, and after a reorganisation within the KLM group in 1998, Air UK became KLM UK, with a new colour scheme closely matching that of the parent company. BAe 146s and

Boeing 737s have also been added to the fleet, but these types have now been transferred to buzz, a low-cost division of KLM UK created late in 1999, and which commenced operations in January 2000, competing with other low-cost/low-fare operators from London's Stansted and Luton airports (see page 135).

Routes

Aberdeen, Amsterdam, Belfast, Bergen, Birmingham, Brussels, Düsseldorf, Edinburgh, Frankfurt, Glasgow, Guernsey, Humberside, Jersey, Leeds/Bradford, London, Milan, Manchester, Newcastle, Norwich, Paris, Rome, Sheffield, Southampton, Stavanger, Teesside.

Fleet

  5 ATR 72
  9 Fokker 50
17 Fokker 100

Tupolev Tu-204-100 RA-64016 (Albert Kuhbandner/Munich)

KMV - KAVKAZSKIE MINERALNYE VODY

Mineralnye Airport –5, Mineralnye Vody,
Stavropol 357310, Russia
Tel. 86533 56676, Fax. 86531 59637

Three- / Two- letter code	IATA No.	Reg'n prefix	ICAO callsign
MVD / KV	348	RA	Air Minvody

The provenance of KMV – Kavkazskie Mineralnye Vody, or Kavminvodyavia, as the airline is also known, is pretty much identical to that of other Russian airlines. After the disintegration of Aeroflot, a new organisation was formed in Mineralnye Vody called Mineralnye Vody C.A.P.O and Aeroflot Mineralnye Vody Product & Flying Unit. Several thousand people were seeking gainful employment and operations began using aircraft from the former local Aeroflot directorate. As well as scheduled services, charter work was also undertaken, notably to countries in the Persian Gulf, which are particularly attractive to Russians for their shopping opportunities. The Mineralnye Vody area is also attractive to tourists and because of its many mineral springs it is known for its curative qualities. Thus the region is slowly prospering. A new Tupolev 204, the first of the new generation of Russian airliners, was acquired in 1998, and this was used in 1999 to operate the airline's first scheduled service to the west, to Munich. A second Tu-204 was added in mid-2000.

Routes

Aleppo, Antalya, Athens, Chaborovsk, Chisinau, Chita, Dubai, Istanbul, Krasnoyarsk, Larnaca, Malta, Mineralnye Vody, Moscow, Munich, Murmansk, Nizhnevartovsk, Nizhny Novgorod, Nojabirsk, Norilsk, Novosibirsk, Omsk, Samara, St. Petersburg, Sharjah, Surgut, Tel Aviv, Thessaloniki, Tyumen, Ufa, Uljanovsk, Varna, Yekaterinburg.

Fleet

5 Tupolev Tu-134
14 Tupolev Tu-154
2 Tupolev Tu-204

Boeing 747-4B5 HL 7482 (Josef Krauthäuser/Los Angeles-LAX)

KOREAN AIR

C.P.O.Box 864, Seoul, Republic of Korea
Tel. 2-7517507, Fax. 2-7517386,
www.koreanair.com

Three- / Two- letter code	IATA No.	Reg'n prefix	ICAO callsign
KAL / KE	180	HL	Koreanair

The private company Hanjin Transport Group took over Korean Airlines, formed in 1962 and which had been state owned, and eight aircraft on 1st March 1969. Its international routes were to Hong Kong and Osaka. In 1973, KAL acquired its first Boeing 747, used from May 1973 for trans-Pacific services via Tokyo and Honolulu to Los Angeles. In the same year a weekly service to Paris started, the first destination in Europe, with Boeing 707s. The Airbus A300B4 came into service in 1975 and was used for the East Asian market; DC-10 deliveries also began in 1975. In 1984 the name Korean Air was introduced and the present colour scheme adopted. Korean Air developed to become one of the world's largest airlines, with services to all five continents, and a large fleet of dedicated freighters, including five passenger MD-11s converted in 1996/7. However, during the late 1990s, partly because of the Asian business crisis, and partly because of its own difficulties, KAL suffered a few turbulent years. Routes and fleet were reduced in order to contain losses, and a new management team was installed. By the first part of 2000 things were moving in the right direction and renewal and expansion of the fleet is in progress.The airline's base is at Seoul's Kimpo airport; with the opening of the new Inchon International Airport, Kimpo will be restricted to domestic services only.

Routes

Amsterdam, Anchorage, Atlanta, Auckland, Bangkok, Beijing, Boston, Brisbane, Brussels, Cairo, Cheju, Cheong Ju, Chicago, Chinju, Christchurch, Colombo, Copenhagen, Dallas/Fort Worth, Delhi, Dubai, Frankfurt, Fukuoka, Ho Chi Minh City, Hong Kong, Honolulu, Jakarta, Kangnung, Kuala Lumpur, Kunsan, Kwangju, London, Los Angeles, Manila, Moscow, Mumbai, Nagasaki, Nagoya, New York, Okayama, Osaka, Paris, Penang, Pohang, Portland, Pusan, Rome, San Francisco, Sao Paulo, Sapporo, Seoul, Shanghai, Shenyang, Singapore, Sydney, Tashkent, Taegu, Tianjin, Tokyo, Toronto, Ulaanbaatar, Vancouver, Vladivostok, Washington, Zürich.

Fleet

Fleet		Ordered
23 Airbus A300-600	8 Boeing 747-200F	4 Airbus A330-300
11 Airbus A330	2 Boeing 747-200	6 Boeing 737-700
3 Boeing 737-700	5 Boeing 777-200	5 Boeing 737-800
3 Boeing 737-800	4 Boeing 777-300	16 Boeing 737-900
25 Boeing 747-400	10 Fokker 100	3 Boeing 747-400
3 Boeing 747-400F	11 McDonnell Douglas MD-82/83	1 Boeing 777-200
2 Boeing 747-300	4 (Boeing) McDonnell Douglas MD-11F	2 Boeing 777-300

Boeing 777-269ER 9K-AOB (Dennis Wehrmann/Geneva)

KUWAIT AIRWAYS

P.O.Box 394, 13004 Safat,
Kuwait Tel. 4345555, Fax. 4314118
www.kuwait-airways.com

Three- / Two- letter code	IATA No.	Reg'n prefix	ICAO callsign
KAC / KU	229	9K	Kuwaiti

Kuwait Airways Corporation came into existence in 1953 as a national airline set up by local businessmen as Kuwait National Airways. Its first route was from Kuwait City to Basra, flown for the first time in 1954 with DC-3s. The present name was adopted in May 1958 when BOAC took over the management of the airline, which it continued until independence in 1962. Vickers Viscounts replaced the DC-3s and a de Havilland Comet 4C was used from 1964 on the routes to London, Paris and Frankfurt. The airline became wholly government-owned on 1st June 1963 and took over Trans Arabia. On 20th March 1966 the first of three HS Tridents was introduced; three Boeing 707s followed two years later and gradually took over all the routes. In 1978 Kuwait Airways acquired its first Boeing 747, and Airbus aircraft succeeded the Boeing 707s, with three Boeing 767s continuing the fleet renewal process from 1986. After the Iraqi occupation of Kuwait in Summer 1991 flights were discontinued; some aircraft were destroyed, some were seized by Iraq, while others were transferred abroad for lease. However, Kuwait Airways did manage to maintain a very restricted service, operating out of Cairo, and since the ending of the Gulf War, KAC has resumed its services and rebuilt its fleet, with a modestly updated colour scheme since 1993. By 1995 almost all of the fleet had been renewed, and the latest type to be added is the Boeing 777-200ER, the first of two of which was delivered in 1998. Services to Chicago and New York have also been commenced, routing via Amsterdam or London. Several Kuwait Airways aircraft are held at the disposal of the government for their flights. In partnership with Egypt Air, KAC has established Shorouk Air, in which it has a 49% shareholding.

Routes

Abu Dhabi, Alexandria, Amman, Amsterdam, Bahrain, Bangalore,Bangkok, Beirut, Cairo, Calcutta, Chennai, Chicago, Colombo, Damascus, Damman, Dacca, Delhi, Doha, Dubai, Frankfurt, Geneva, Islamabad, Istanbul, Jeddah, Karachi, Kuwait, Lahore, Larnaca, London, Luxor, Manila, Mumbai, Muscat, New York, Paris, Riyadh, Rome, Singapore, Teheran.

Fleet

5 Airbus A300-600	2 Boeing 747-200
2 Airbus A310-300	1 Boeing 747-400
3 Airbus A320-200	2 Boeing 777-200ER
4 Airbus A340-300	

Tupolev Tu-154 M EX-85718 (Author's collection/Frankfurt)

KYRGHYZSTAN AIRLINES

720062 Bishkek, Manus Airport,
Kyrghyzstan
Tel. 3312-257755, Fax. 3312-257162

Three- / Two- letter code	IATA No.	Reg'n prefix	ICAO callsign
KGA / K2	758	EX	Kyrgyz

Although independent since 1991, Kyrghyzstan has remained a member of the CIS. The former Aeroflot directorate was taken over to form the basis of the national airline and to develop future services. The transformed company was called Kyrgyzstan Aba Yoldoru National Airline, with Bishkek Air Enterprises as its major shareholder. It also has a subsidiary, Osch-Karakol Air Enterprises, located in the second major city in the country, Osch. Additionally the airline still works with Aeroflot for ticketing and marketing and as a codeshare partner. Furthermore, the company has responsibilities for government duties including ambulance and relief flights. Kyrghyzstan is one of the poorest states of the CIS; developing business relationships with neighbouring Kazakhstan, Uzbekistan and China bring an increased need for air services in this remote region. As well as scheduled services, charter flights are operated and efforts are made to fill aircraft with cargo.The first service to Western Europe, to Frankfurt, was inaugurated in Summer 1996. In 1998 the airline acquired its first new aircraft, an Airbus A319 which was used on international services, including the inauguration of a service to Birmingham, but the aircraft was returned to its lessor on cost grounds after only a few months.

Routes

Almaty, Baku, Beijing, Birmingham, Bishkek, Chisinau, Delhi, Frankfurt, Istanbul, Kaliningrad, Karachi, Karakol, Krasnoyarsk, Moscow, Novosibirsk, Omsk, Osch, Samara, Sharjah, St. Petersburg, Tashkent, Ufa and Yekaterinburg. Charters including to Irkutsk, Khabarovsk, Ulaanbaatar and Yumen.

Fleet

1 Antonov An-26
1 Ilyushin IL-76TD
12 Tupolev Tu-154
6 Tupolev Tu-134

23 Yakovlev Yak-40

Boeing 727-78 CP-1223 (Author's collection)

LAB – LLOYD AEREO BOLIVIANO

Casilla Correo 132, Cochabamba
Bolivia
Tel. 42-50736, Fax. 42-50766

Three- / Two- letter code	IATA No.	Reg'n prefix	ICAO callsign
LLB / LB	051	CP	Lloyd Aereo

LAB was set up by German immigrants on 15th September 1925, following an historic proving flight with an imported Junkers F-13 on 25th July from Cochabamba to Sucre as part of the centennial celebrations of Bolivia's independence. A regular service with the F-13 began a few months later on 24th December between Cochabamba and Santa Cruz. The Bolivian government had a stake in the airline, which however encountered financial difficulties in 1928. Shares were sold to the Junkers company, which supplied three further F-13s to the airline. The route network was steadily extended as far as the Brazilian and Argentinian borders. Over the years further Junkers types including W-34s and Ju-52 saw service with LAB. German influence disappeared in 1941 as a result of American pressure and the company was nationalised on 14th May 1941 and Lodestars were introduced after Panagra took an interest in operations. In 1948 Curtiss C-46s were added. The first DC-4s were used on the new route to Asuncion or Porto Vila, followed in 1961 by DC-6s. In the late 1960s LAB was reorganised and Fairchild FH227s were acquired for regional routes as well as Lockheed Electras for international services. In 1970 the change was made to Boeing 727s, with flights to Miami being operated for the first time from 1975. Further routes to Santiago and Caracas followed. Airbus A310-300s were introduced, the first in 1991 and a second in 1996. At the end of 1995 the Brazilian airline VASP took a 49% interest in LAB, one of the results of which was that the colour scheme was modified to resemble that of VASP. A boeing 737-300 was added on lease from mid-2000.

Routes

Arica, Asuncion, Bogota, Buenos Aires, Cancun, Caracas, Cobija, Cochabamba, Cordoba, Cuzco, Iquique, La Paz, Lima, Magdalena, Manaus, Mexico City, Miami, Montevideo, Panama, Riberalta, Rio de Janeiro, Salta, San Joaquim, Santiago, Santa Cruz de la Sierra, Sao Paulo, Sucre, Tarija, Trinidad, Tucuman.

Fleet

1 Airbus A310-300	1 Boeing 737-300
1 Boeing 707-320F	1 Fokker F.27
8 Boeing 727-100/200	
1 Boeing 737-200	

Boeing 737-2L9 N281LF (Josef Krauthäuser/Miami)

LACSA

Apartado 1531, San Jose 1000, Costa Rica
Tel. 2316064, Fax. 2329185,
www.erupotaca.com

Three- / Two- letter code	IATA No.	Reg'n prefix	ICAO callsign
LRC / LR	133	TI	Lacsa

Pan American set up Lineas Aereas Costarricenses SA in December 1945 with the support of the government of Costa Rica and private interests. Some domestic routes were flown from June 1946, and its designation as national flag carrier in 1949 presaged the introduction of service to Miami from 1950. In use were Convair CV-440s, Curtiss C-46s and Douglas DC-6s. In 1952 TACA de Costa Rica, their only competitor in the country, was bought up. In 1967 LACSA acquired its first jet type, the BAC One-Eleven 400; these were replaced by Boeing 727s in late 1970. The airline's domestic network was transferred in September 1979 to Servicios Aereos Nacionales (SANSA). A fleet acquisition programme for the 1990s saw the arrival of the first leased Airbus A320 at the end of 1990. TACA holds 10% of the shares, thus LACSA is a member of Grupo Taca. This became outwardly evident on the aircraft during 1999 when new colours were introduced in the group's style. Naturally there are co-operation agreements with the other members of the group, Aviateca, Nica, Taca and Avianca. The airline's base and major maintenance facility are at the airport at San Jose.

Routes

Bogota, Buenos Aires, Cancun, Caracas, El Salvador, Guatemala, Guayaquil, Havana, La Ceiba, Liberia, Los Angeles, Managua, Mexico City, Miami, New Orleans, New York, Orlando, Panama City, Quito, Rio de Janeiro, San Andres, San Jose, San Juan, San Pedro Sula, San Salvador, Santiago, Tegucigalpa, Toronto.

Fleet

5 Airbus A320
5 Boeing 737-200

Boeing 737-236 CC-CZN (Author's collection)

LADECO

Av. Bernado O'Higgins 107, Santiago, Chile
Tel. 2-6395053, Fax. 2-6397277,
www.lanchile.cl

Three- / Two- letter code	IATA No.	Reg'n prefix	ICAO callsign
LCO / UC	145	CC	Ladeco

Linea Aerea del Cobre Ltda., commonly abbreviated as Ladeco, was set up as a private company on 3rd September 1958 to serve the copper mining region of Northern Chile. Operations began on 1st November 1958, initially on the Santiago to El Salvador route. Ladeco took over the routes and DC-3 aircraft of Cinta-Ala. The DC-3s were equipped with the more powerful Twin Wasp engines in order to be able to tale off more easily from the high-altitude airport at Santiago. In 1965, larger Douglas DC-6s were added to the DC-3s and the network of routes was being expanded. In 1975 Ladeco acquired

its first Boeing 727-100; when the DC-6s were retired from service, two more aircraft of this type were added. Two Boeing 707s were bought for long-distance routes in 1978 and 1979 and these were used for services to New York and Miami. From 1992 there was evidence of a fleet renewal programme, with the acquisition of a Boeing 737-300 and two 757-200s, but these did not remain in the fleet for very long. During 1995 Lan-Chile took over Iberia's minority stake in Ladeco, and then in 1996 it acquired a majority shareholding. As a consequence, timetables have been harmonised and the routes divided

up. The Ladeco fleet has been rationalised to just one type, the Boeing 737-200, with a changed colour scheme. Ladeco is a participant in the Latin Pass Frequent Flyer Marketing Programmes and with Lan-Chile is linked to the Oneworld Alliance.

Routes

Antofagasta, Arica, Balmaceda, Calama, Concepcion, Iquique, La Serena, Mendoza, Osorno, Puerto Mott, Punta Arenas, Santiago, Termuco.

Fleet

10 Boeing 737-200

Boeing 767-200ER EI-CEM (Christofer Witt collection)

LAM

P.O.Box 2060, Maputo,
People's Republic of Mozambique
Tel. 1- 465026, Fax. 1-422936

Three- / Two- letter code	IATA No.	Reg'n prefix	ICAO callsign
LAM / TM	068	C9	Mozambique

DETA – Direccao de Exploracao dos Transportes Aereos – was set up in August 1936 as a department of the railways and harbours and airways administration in Laurenco Marques (now Maputo), the capital at that time of Mozambique, which was under Portuguese administration. An airfield was set up on the outskirts of the city for the first time and DETA's first flight was on 22nd December 1937 to Johannesburg with a Junkers 52. De Havilland Moths and Dragonflies were also used, as were further Ju 52s, but these were replaced after the end of the Second World War by Douglas DC-3s. July 1962 saw the first use of Fokker F.27s and the arrival of two Boeing 737s in December 1969 heralded the beginning of the jet age for DETA. During the revolution in the 1970s, flights practically came to a standstill, but after Mozambique's independence in June 1975 and reorganisation, the national airline was reinvigorated and received a new name: LAM-Lineas Aereas de Mocambique. In 1993 a leased Boeing 767 came into use alongside Boeing 737-300s, and all displayed a new colour scheme. TAP-Air Portugal is an important partner for LAM and the Lisbon to Maputo route is jointly operated. The other routes to Europe were abandoned in 1995 on cost grounds. The later part of the 1990s saw a slow improvement in business, partly due to the changes which have taken place in neighbouring South Africa. There are co-operation agreements (including technical and logistical assistance) in place with South African Airways and Air Zimbabwe.

Routes

Beira, Durban, Harare, Inhambane, Johannesburg, Lichinga, Lisbon, Luanda, Lusaka, Maputo, Manzini, Nampula, Pemba, Quelimane, Tete, Vilanculos.

Fleet

2 Boeing 737-200
1 Boeing 767-200ER
1 Beech 1900C
4 CASA 212-200
1 Fokker 100

Boeing 767-316ER CC-CZT (Björn Kannengiesser/Frankfurt)

LAN CHILE

Estado 10, Piso 21, Casilla 147-D,
Santiago de Chile, Chile
Tel. 2-6394411, Fax. 2-6383884, www.lanchile.cl

Three- / Two- letter code	IATA No.	Reg'n prefix	ICAO callsign
LAN / LA	045	CC	Lan

LAN Chile, Linea Aerea Nacional de Chile, is one of the oldest airlines in South America. Set up on 5th March 1929 as Linea Aeropostal Santiago-Africa under the command of the Chilean Air Force, it initially provided mail flights. The airline was nationalised in 1932 when the present name was adopted. Lockheed Lodestars were used in 1948 to open a service to Buenos Aires, and then DC-6s to Miami from 1958. The SE 210 Caravelle was LAN's first jet aircraft, delivered from March 1964. In 1967 the Boeing 707 followed and was used to start a route to the Easter Islands and on to Tahiti. In 1974 the South Pole route was opened to Australia, LAN being the first airline to link the two continents. Three DC-10s were acquired in 1980 and used for services to the USA and Europe. Boeing 767s were added from 1986 and later replaced the DC-10s. In September 1989 LAN Chile was privatised and the Cueto family became the principal shareholder. Regional and national flights were further improved and extended from 1990 with leased BAe 146s. In 1996 the Cueto family also acquired the majority shareholding in Ladeco and there has been a sharing out of routes. Since 1998 there has been a close co-operation with American Airlines, which has led to LAN Chile becoming a member of the Oneworld alliance. The airline introduced a new corporate identity during 1999 and has ordered 30 aircraft from Airbus to completely renew the short and medium haul fleet; deliveries of A319s and A320s are both due to commence towards the end of 2000. Also during 2000 a subsidiary, LAN-Peru, has been formed to allow expansion in the neighbouring country, but this has met with political obstacles in Peru.

Routes

Bogota, Buenos Aires, Cancun, Caracas, Cordoba, Frankfurt, Guayaquil, Havana, La Paz, Lima, Madrid, Mendoza, Mexico City, Miami, Montevideo, New York, Orlando, Papeete, Punta Cana, Rio de Janeiro, Rio Gallegos, Salta, San Salvador, Santa Cruz, Sao Paulo.

Fleet	Ordered
14 Boeing 737-200	11 Airbus A319
2 Boeing 767-300F	11 Airbus A320
13 Boeing 767-300	7 Airbus A340
1 McDonnell Douglas DC-8F	1 Boeing 767-300

Yunshuji Y-12 RDPL-34116 (Romano Germann/Luang Prabang)

LAO AVIATION

2, Rue Pang Kham, Vientiane,
People's Republic of Laos
Tel. 212057, Fax. 212056

Three- / Two- letter code	IATA No.	Reg'n prefix	ICAO callsign
LAO / QV	627	RDPL	Lao

As a consequence of the Vietnam War, in which what was then the Kingdom of Laos was also involved, there were three airlines which were active in Laos in the early1970s: Royal Air Lao, Lao Air Lines and Civil Aviation Co. The last of these was operated by the Pathet Lao movement for a free Laos, and this airline received help from North Vietnam. After the eventual takeover of power the remaining aircraft belonging to the airlines were brought together to form Lao Aviation, which was established on 19th January 1976 by the People's Republic of Laos and took over from Royal Air Lao as the national carrier.

The fleet consisted of Vickers Viscounts, Lockheed Hercules, Sikorsky S-58 helicopters, Douglas DC-3s and DC-4s. As there was no real need for domestic flights in Laos, and there was a lack of spare parts for their maintenance, these aircraft were sold or scrapped, and a new fleet built up favouring Soviet-built types. International flights between Vientiane and Bangkok and Hanoi were introduced and to Phnom-Penh, operated by Antonov An-24s. The present name of the airline was introduced in 1979. During the first part of the 1990s, Chinese-built aircraft came into favour, with the acquisition of small

fleets of 17-seat Yunshuji Y12s and 52-seat Y7s. After the government allowed foreign investors to take a stake in 1995, an ATR 72 and a Boeing 737 were acquired for international services, though the 737 was given up during the time of the Asian business downturn, the effects of which have constrained the development of the airline and pushed back expansion plans.

Routes

Bangkok, Chiang Mai, Hanoi, Ho Chi Minh City, Kunming, Luang Prabang, Pakse, Phnom Penh, Vientiane, Xieng Khouang, Yangon.

Fleet

1 Antonov An-24
1 ATR 72
6 Yunshuji Y12
4 Yunshuji Y7-100

Boeing 737-2T4 LV-WNB (Author's collection)

LAPA

Avenida Santa Fe 1970, Buenos Aires 1123
Argentina, Tel. 11-48196255,
Fax. 11-48196204, www.lapa.com.ar

Three- / Two- letter code	IATA No.	Reg'n prefix	ICAO callsign
LPR / MJ	069	LV	Lapa

Lineas Aereas Privadas Argentinas was formed in May 1978 by a group of business people in Buenos Aires. Two Shorts 330s began services in October 1979 from the Aeroparque Jorge Newbery in Buenos Aires. The provinces of Entre Rios and La Pampa had poor transport and were not served by other companies, so there was potential for passenger, freight and postal services to be developed. However the way ahead was impeded because of the business difficulties being experienced in Argentina. From 1986 new aircraft, Saab 340s were able to be taken on lease, and the arrival of these modern turboprops allowed the addition of new destinations. The first jet equipment came in 1993 – a Boeing 737, with further examples added during later years. 1998 was the year which showed the greatest growth in traffic, and a marked increase in the fleet, which from 1997 had become all-jet. LAPA offered services to more and more domestic destinations at prices more attractive than the competition, and this had its effect on passenger numbers. Also in 1997, service to the USA was offered for the first time, with a newly acquired Boeing 757 being used to Atlanta. Major fleet renewal began at the end of 1998 with the delivery of the first of the new Boeing 737-700s and by 2001 all the older 737-200s should have been retired. A Boeing 767-300 was added on lease in mid-1999.

Routes

Atlanta, Bahia Blanca, Buenos Aires, Catamarca, Comodoro Rivadavia, Cordoba, Corrientes, Formosa, General Roca, Iguacu, Jujuy, La Rioja, Mar del Plata, Mendoza, Montevideo, Neuquen, Posadas, Punta del Este, Resistencia, Rio Gallegos, Rio Grande, Salta, San Carlos de Bariloche, San Juan, San Luis, Trelew, Tucuman, Ushuaia, Villa Gesell, Villa Mercedes.

Fleet		Ordered
10 Boeing 737-200	1 Boeing 767-300	7 Boeing 737-700
8 Boeing 737-700		
2 Boeing 757-200		

Boeing 777-2Z9ER OE-LPA (Gerhard Schütz/Munich)

LAUDA AIR

Postfach 56, 1300 Flughafen Wien-Schwechat, Austria, Tel. 1-70000, Fax. 70074105, www.laudaair.com

Three- / Two- letter code	IATA No.	Reg'n prefix	ICAO callsign
LDA / NG	231	OE	Laudaair

Lauda Air was established in April 1979 when Niki Lauda, the former Formula One motor racing champion, took over a licence to operate non-scheduled flights from Alpair. Operations started on 24th May 1979 with two Fokker F.27s. After a phase of restructuring and conversion into a joint stock company, the airline leased two Rombac One-Elevens from Tarom in 1985. Boeing 737-200s and -300s were added and later used to replace the One Elevens. At that time Lauda Air was flying primarily to Greece and to Spain. In 1986 the airline applied for a licence to operate scheduled flights to Australia, which it finally obtained in 1988, and in this year also it took on its first Boeing 767-300ER; a second followed in November 1989. Scheduled services to Sydney, Hong Kong and Singapore were expanded. The first European scheduled routes were begun in late 1990, from Vienna to London-Gatwick, and in the same year licences were obtained for international services which had previously been reserved for Austrian Airlines. In the Autumn, Lufthansa acquired a 25% share in Lauda Air via Condor, and this was increased to 39.7% in 1994. As a result, there was co-operation between the two airlines with Lauda flying to Miami and on some European routes on behalf of the German airline. In 1993 an Italian subsidiary, Lauda Air SpA was formed, operating from Milan. In March 1997 Austrian Airlines acquired half of Lufthansa's shares, bringing Austrian's holding up to 36%. Lauda Air has thus become integrated into the AUA Group and from the beginning of 2000 is a member of the Star Alliance. The first Boeing 777 arrived in the fleet in Autumn 1997 and is used to Sydney and Miami; Boeing 737-700s are scheduled for delivery from April 2001.

Routes

Agadir, Bangkok, Barcelona, Cancun, Denpasar, Geneva, Graz, Innsbruck, Hamburg, Klagenfurt, Kuala Lumpur, Las Palmas, Linz, Lisbon, London, Madrid, Milan, Manchester, Melbourne, Miami, Munich, Nice, Phuket, Riga, Rome, Salzburg, Sofia, Split, Sydney, Tallinn, Tenerife, Timisoara, Verona, Vienna, Vilnius, Wroclaw.

Fleet		Ordered
2 Boeing 737-300	7 Boeing 767-300ER	2 Boeing 737-700
2 Boeing 737-400	2 Boeing 777-200	1 Boeing 767-300ER
2 Boeing 737-600	8 Canadair Regional Jet	2 Boeing 777-200ER
2 Boeing 737-800		

De Havilland DHC-8-103 V2-LEF (Christopher Witt/Antigua)

LIAT

P.O.Box 819 V.C.Bird Intl. Airport St.Johns, Antigua & Barbuda, Tel. 4620700, Fax. 4622682/4765, www.liat.com

Three- / Two- letter code	IATA No.	Reg'n prefix	ICAO callsign
LIA / LI	140	V2	Liat

Leeward Island Air Transport Services Ltd., LIAT for short, was set up in 1956 by two American businessmen, and started flights from Antigua to Montserrat with a Piper Apache. A year later LIAT became part of British West Indian Airways who took a 75% stake. Beech Bonanzas and de Havilland Herons were ideal aircraft for the short hops to other islands within the Virgin Islands. The first HS.748 was acquired on 1st February 1965. In November 1971 the British company Court Line Aviation took over the airline and introduced the BAC One-Eleven and Britten-Norman Islanders, but with the spectacular collapse of Court Line in August 1974, a rescue company was set up in November known as LIAT (1974) Ltd. Its participants were the governments of six Caribbean island states, with further states acquiring interests later on. The first de Havilland DHC-8s were bought in 1987, contributing to the expansion of the network. At the beginning of 1995 the last of the HS.748s left the fleet and in November 1995 the company was privatised. During 1996/97 further Dash 8-300s were added and the Twin Otters retired. The main operating and maintenance base is Antigua, and there are co-operation agreements with Winair and Carib Aviation. The airline is struggling financially with debt of over $30 million, and some form of reconstruction is being sought.

Routes

Anguilla, Antigua, Barbados, Barbuda, Beef Island, Caracas, Carriacou, Dominica, Fort de France, Georgetown, Grenada, Martinique, Montserrat, Nevis, San Juan, St.Croix, St. Kitts, St.Lucia, St.Maarten, St.Thomas, St.Vincent, Tobago, Tortola, Trinidad and Union Island.

Fleet

10 De Havilland DHC-8-100
3 De Havilland DHC-8-300

Airbus A320-231 EI-TLT (Dennis Wehrmann/Amsterdam)

LIBYAN ARAB AIRLINES

Haiti Street, P.O.Box 2555 Tripoli,
People's Republic of Libya
Tel. 21-602083, Fax. 21-30970

Three- / Two- letter code	IATA No.	Reg'n prefix	ICAO callsign
LAA / LN	148	5A	Libair

In September 1964 the merger of Libiavia and United Libyan Airlines resulted in the formation of the state-owned Kingdom of Libya Airlines. August 1965 saw the start of flights to Europe and North Africa as well as to the Middle East with two Caravelles. In 1969, Fokker F.27s were added to the fleet for domestic services and this year also saw political changes in the country following the September revolution, as a result of which the airline changed its name to Libyan Arab Airlines. Boeing 707s, 727s and later on, Airbus A310s were all added. However, political and trade sanctions meant that the western

built fleet could not be fully maintained and used and it was partly sold off. For this reason the fleet was expanded from 1990 onwards with soviet-built types, specifically the Tupolev Tu-154M. An independent division, Libyan Arab Cargo, was active in the freight business with Ilyushin IL-76s and Lockheed L-100 Hercules. From 15th April 1992, United Nations imposed sanctions meant that Libyan Arab Airlines no longer had any rights to fly abroad, and was unable to buy aircraft spares; thus it was reduced to a modest domestic service only. To combat their inability to buy parts, several aircraft

were reduced to spares donors. However, sanctions were lifted in 1999 and several former supporters of sanctions were looking for good business in the re-equipment of the airline. Libyan Arab used wet-leased Airbus A320s as replacements for the Boeing 727s to restart several routes in Europe, also taking the opportunity to introduce a new colour scheme for their aircraft.

Routes

Al Bayda, Al Kufra, Athens, Benghazi, Casablanca, Frankfurt, Ghadames, London, Milan, Mersa Brega, Rome, Sebha, Tobruk, Tripoli, Zürich.

Fleet

2 Airbus A320
3 Airbus A310
2 Fokker F.27
3 Fokker F.28

3 Boeing 727-200

Boeing 737-382 LY-BAG (Stefan Quanz/Frankfurt)

LITHUANIAN AIRLINES

A.Gustacio 4, Vilnius Airport, 2038 Vilnius, Lithuania, Tel. 2-306666, Fax. 2-306140, www.lal.lt

Three- / Two- letter code	IATA No.	Reg'n prefix	ICAO callsign
LIL / TE	874	LY	Lithuania

Lithuanian Airlines was the first airline to emerge in the Baltic republics which gained independence from the former Soviet Union; it started its own flights in 1991. The aircraft were taken over from the former local Aeroflot directorate. Lithuanian immediately turned its attentions towards western Europe and Scandinavia and started flights to these countries first. A leased Boeing 737 was first used to Copenhagen on 20th December 1991. The Hungarian airline Malev assisted in building up the airline and trained the pilots on 737s. In late 1992 Lithuanian was accepted into membership of IATA. With the delivery of further Boeing 737s, several Tupolev Tu-134s were sold and takers were also found for the Antonov 24s and Yakovlev 40s, thus rationalising the fleet. A new colour scheme was introduced in 1994. The final Tu-134s were taken out of service during 1997/98 when Saab 340s and 2000s were leased in. During 1999 the colour scheme was changed again. There are co-operation agreements with Air Baltic, Finnair and LOT.

Routes

Amsterdam, Berlin, Copenhagen, Frankfurt, Hamburg, Helsinki, Istanbul, Kiev, London, Moscow, Paris, Rome, Samara, St. Petersburg, Stockholm, Tallinn, Vilnius, Warsaw.

Fleet

2 Boeing 737-200	2 Saab SF 340
1 Boeing 737-300	2 Saab 2000
1 Boeing 737-500	8 Yakovlev Yak-42

Boeing 737-55D SP-LKE (Josef Krauthäuser/Frankfurt)

LOT – POLISH AIRLINES

Uliczka 17 Stycznia 39, 00906 Warsaw,
Poland, Tel. 6305621, Fax. 8300675,
www.lot.com

Three- / Two- letter code	IATA No.	Reg'n prefix	ICAO callsign
LOT / LO	080	SP	LOT

Aero Lloyd Warsaw (subsequently Aerolot) and Aero T2 were united to form the future state airline Polskie Linie Lotnicze-LOT on 1st January 1929 by order of the government. Aero Lloyd had begun regular flights in September 1922 and started international services in 1925, while Aero had been formed in 1922. LOT Junkers F-13s flew to Vienna, Berlin. Moscow and Helsinki. A fresh start was made after the war with Soviet-built aircraft in 1946. While the Ilyushin IL-14 was part of the fleet in the 1950s, western aircraft such as the Convair 240 and Vickers Viscount were also used. Tupolev Tu-134 and Tu-154 jets were the mainstay of the short and medium-range fleet, while the Ilyushin 62M was used for long hauls. A return to western-originated equipment was begun in 1989 with the acquisition of Boeing 767s. The fleet was to be brought up to western standards as quickly as possible, to enable LOT to compete effectively with other western operators. For regional routes ATR 72s were acquired from 1991, and Boeing 737s from 1993 to 1996 also signalling the departure of the last of the Russian-built jets. During 1997 LOT established Eurolot, a subsidiary for regional services and this operates ATR 72s and 42s. LOT had become a joint stock company in December 1992 as a first step towards privatisation and in 1997 the SAir Group took over 37% of the shares, with the rest remaining with the Polish state. Also in 1999 LOT took delivery of Embraer RJ-145s for use on European routes. The Boeing 737-800s on order are for delivery from January 2002.

Routes

Amsterdam, Athens, Bangkok, Barcelona, Berlin, Brussels, Budapest, Bydgoszcs, Chicago, Copenhagen, Düsseldorf, Frankfurt, Gdansk, Hamburg, Helsinki, Istanbul, Katowice, Kiev, Krakow, Larnaca, London, Lvov, Lyon, Madrid, Milan, Minsk, Moscow, Munich, New York, Nice, Oslo, Paris, Posen, Prague, Riga, Rome, Sofia, St. Petersburg, Stockholm, Szczecin, Tel Aviv, Vilnius, Warsaw, Vienna, Wroclaw, Zürich.

Fleet		Ordered
5 Boeing 767-200/300ER	7 Boeing 737-400	2 Boeing 737-800
2 Boeing 737-300	6 Embraer RJ-145	9 Embraer RJ 145
6 Boeing 737-500		

Airbus A320-232 D-ALTA (Patrick Lutz/Palma de Mallorca)

LTU INTERNATIONAL AIRWAYS

Halle 8, Flughafen, 40474 Düsseldorf, Germany, Tel. 0211-941808, Fax. 0211-9418881, www.ltu.de

Three- / Two- letter code	IATA No.	Reg'n prefix	ICAO callsign
LTU / LT	266	D	LTU

LTU was formed as Lufttransport Union on 20th October 1965 by an Englishman Mr. Dromgoole, but the major partner, soon to become sole owner was the Duisburg building contractor Conie; the present name was adopted in 1956. The first aircraft, Vickers Vikings were used until 1963. Also used were Bristol 170s, Fokker F.27s and DC-4s, until Caravelles began jet service in 1965. From 1969 LTU was one of the first charter airlines to use solely jets, with F.28 Fellowships joining the Caravelles from 1968. In 1973 came the first widebodies, Lockheed TriStars, and this type allowed LTU to make the breakthrough to become Germany's largest charter airline. Eleven TriStars were used and enabled the airline to serve faraway holiday destinations. In 1989 LTU applied for a licence to operate as a scheduled carrier, and permission was granted for some routes from Autumn 1990 onwards. The delivery of the first MD-11 late in 1991 set a fleet renewal in motion, which culminated in 1996 with the delivery of A330s as TriStar replacements, the last TriStar leaving the fleet in May 1996. In Spring 1996 LTU took over Rheinland Air Service and LTU-Süd was integrated into the parent company. The airline was not performing well financially and a restructuring announced in July 1997 meant that some long-haul routes were dropped and all the MD-11s taken out of service. The majority of the shares were acquired by the SAir Group which then again reorganised the whole LTU group, integrating LTE. Along with Sobelair, Air Europe and Balair, LTU forms a part of the leisure division of SAir. Because of overcapacity in the German holiday market, the airline has made crippling losses and so a deal has been struck with Rewe Touristik, reducing SAir's holding to 49.9% and allowing for a major restructuring to take place.

Routes

From most German airports to Agadir, Alicante, Almeria, Anchorage, Antalya, Araxos, Arrecife, Athens, Bangkok, Bodrum, Brindisi, Cagliari, Cancun, Capetown, Catania,Chongqing, Colombo, Corfu, Dalaman, Djerba, Faro, Fort Myers, Fuerteventura, Funchal, Genoa, Havana, Heraklion, Holguin, Hurghada, Ibiza, Istanbul, Izmir, Karpathos, Kavalla, Kos, Larnaca, Las Palmas, Lesbos, Lisbon, Los Angeles, Mahon, Malaga, Male, Malta, Miami, Mombasa, Monastir, Montego Bay, Naples, Olbia, Orlando, Palma de Mallorca, Porlamar, Puerto Plata, Punta Cana, Reykjavik, Rhodes, Rome, Salzburg, Samos, Sevilla, St. Cruz, Tenerife,Thessaloniki, Toronto, Varadero, Windhoek, Zakynthos.

Fleet

		Ordered
4 Airbus A320	6 Boeing 767-300ER	6 Airbus A320
6 Airbus A330-300		7 Airbus A330
12 Boeing 757-200		12 Airbus A321

Airbus A321-131 D-AIRD (Uwe Gleisberg/Munich)

LUFTHANSA

von Gablenz-Str 2-6, 50679 Köln,
Germany, Tel. 0221-826-0,
Fax. 0221-8263818, www.lufthansa.de

Three- / Two- letter code	IATA No.	Reg'n prefix	ICAO callsign
DLH / LH	220	D	Lufthansa

The 'old' Lufthansa, founded in 1926, was liquidated by the victorious powers in the Second World War. In early 1950 the German government made efforts to reassert its air sovereignty by having an independent national airline. To this end Luftag was set up in 1953, and renamed after the old Lufthansa in 1954. The first flight with a Convair 340 was on 1st April 1955, and the first international flight was to New York on 8th June 1955 with a Lockheed Constellation. From 1960 Lufthansa began using the Boeing 707 on transatlantic services; Boeing 720s were acquired for routes to Africa and the Middle East. Lufthansa was the first customer outside the USA for the Boeing 727 for medium-distance routes from April 1964, and was also the first to order the 737, delivered from 1967. The era of the widebody arrived with the Boeing 747 in March 1970, with DC-10s and Airbus A300s following during the mid-1970s. Lufthansa is well known for its ongoing fleet renewal policy. In 1988 the Boeing 747-400 and the Airbus A320 were introduced, in 1993 the Airbus A340, 1994 the A321 (as launch customer) and in 1996 the smaller Airbus A319. During 1997 Lufthansa was fully privatised, with a wide distribution of share ownership. In the same year, in co-operation with United, SAS, Air Canada and Thai International Lufthansa founded the Star Alliance, and in addition Lufthansa has direct shareholdings in the following airlines: Air Dolomiti, Condor Flugdienst, Lauda Air, Lufthansa Cargo, Lufthansa Cityline, Luxair, SAS. There are franchise arrangements with other airlines who fly as 'Team Lufthansa' on behalf of Lufthansa on German domestic and European routes:Air Littoral, Augsburg Airways, Cimber Air, Contact Air and Rheintalflug.

Routes

The Lufthansa route network stretches from Europe, North and South America to Asia and Africa. Nearly 200 destinations in some 100 countries are served. With its partners in the Star Alliance, there is service to just about every major airport in the world.

Fleet

20 Airbus A319
33 Airbus A320-200
22 Airbus A321-100
 5 Airbus A310-300
11 Airbus A300-600
24 Airbus A340-200/300

22 Boeing 737-200
46 Boeing 737-300
30 Boeing 737-500
 8 Boeing 747-200
26 Boeing 747-400

Ordered

14 Airbus A340-300
10 Airbus A340-600
 5 Airbus A321
 4 Boeing 747-400

(Boeing) McDonnell Douglas MD-11F D-ALCD (Oliver Köstinger/Sharjah)

LUFTHANSA CARGO

Postfach 1244, 65451 Kelsterbach, Germany, Tel. 6965437, Fax. 6966886, www.lhcargo.com

Three- / Two- letter code	IATA No.	Reg'n prefix	ICAO callsign
GEC / LH	020	D	Lufthansa Cargo

Lufthansa Cargo Aktiengesellschaft was established on 1st January 1995 as a 100% subsidiary of Lufthansa, to take over its worldwide freight activities. Its predecessor was Lufthansa Cargo Airlines, one of the many restructurings with Lufthansa, and German Cargo Services GmbH. The latter owed its existence to the withdrawal in 1977 of an anachronistic statute which had until then forbidden full-freight charter in the Federal Republic. The driving force behind this change was Lufthansa, who were losing tons of freight to neighbouring countries. Thus on 10th March 1977 German Cargo Services GmbH was founded in Frankfurt, making its first flight on 15th April 1975 with a Boeing 707 to Hong Kong. By mid-1979 four Boeing 707s were in use, such was the growth of the freight business. With the introduction of the Douglas DC-8, GCS's structure was altered, having until then been reliant on Lufthansa for the provision of crews and maintenance. It now employed its own pilots and had its own maintenance facility. German Cargo Services had four DC-8-73s in service, transporting everything which could travel by air and specialising particularly in services to Africa, South America and the Far East, as well as worldwide charters.

As a part of a reorganisation in 1994/95, the airline became Lufthansa Cargo. The first of the dedicated MD-11F freighters was delivered in mid 1998, and this type along with the Boeing 747-200F now forms the whole of the fleet.

Routes

Worldwide freight flights, both scheduled and charters.

Fleet

11 Boeing 747-200F
11 (Boeing) McDonnell Douglas MD-11F

Ordered

3 (Boeing) McDonnell Douglas MD-11F

Canadair RJ-100ER D-ACLD (Josef Krauthäuser/Munich)

LUFTHANSA CITYLINE

Heinrich Steinmann Str. 51147 Köln, Germany, Tel. 02203-5960, Fax. 02203-596801 www.lhcityline.de

Three- / Two- letter code	IATA No.	Reg'n prefix	ICAO callsign
CLH / CL	683	D	Hansaline

DLT-Deutsche Luftverkehrs-gesellschaft mbH was set up in 1974 as a successor to OLT-Ostfriesische Lufttransport GmbH. A German internal network was operated on behalf of Lufthansa using Shorts 330s, DHC-6 Twin Otters and Hawker Siddeley HS.748s. When the airline was short of its own aircraft, WDL with F.27s and other companies with the Fairchild Metro filled the breach. In 1987 Embraer EMB-120s were introduced, but soon proved to be too small, as DLT expanded. Fokker 50s were ordered after Lufthansa took a financial interest in DLT and the available capital was increased. By 1990 over a million passengers a year were being carried, and the rate was climbing. In March came the change of name to Lufthansa Cityline and following a reorganisation, another swift change of fleet to jet types. 50-seater Canadair Regional Jets were ordered, with the first being delivered in Autumn 1992. In 1994 Cityline received its first Avro RJ 85. Thus the airline was in a position to take over more routes from Lufthansa, which were not profitable for even their smallest jets. Lufthansa Cityline is today 100% owned by Lufthansa and participates in all marketing, ticketing and promotional programmes such as Miles & More. With a noteworthy initial order for 60 aircraft, and as a launch customer for this new generation of regional jet, the airline is committing to the development of the Fairchild Dornier 728JET, deliveries of which are expected to commence from Spring 2002. Cityline's main base is at the Cologne/Bonn airport, where it also has maintenance and repair facilities.

Routes

Lufthansa Cityline flies to about 80 destinations in Germany and Europe.

Fleet	Ordered
18 Avro RJ85	7 Canadair RJ-100
38 Canadair RJ-100ER	10 Canadair RJ-700
	60 Fairchild 728JET

Embraer RJ-145 LX-LGT (Pascal Mainzer/Luxembourg)

LUXAIR

Bp 2203, 2987 Luxembourg Airport,
Grand Duchy of Luxembourg
Tel. 4-7984281, Fax. 4-7984289, www.luxair.lu

Three- / Two- letter code	IATA No.	Reg'n prefix	ICAO callsign
LGL / LG	149	LX	Luxair

The Société Luxembourgeoise de Navigation Aérienne, or Luxair as it is usually known, was set up in 1961 as Luxembourg Airlines with the support of the government, of banks and Radio Luxembourg, and with technical assistance provided by KLM. Regular services began on 2nd April 1962 with a Fokker F.27 serving Amsterdam, Frankfurt and Paris. Luxair started using Vickers Viscounts in 1966 and SE 210 Caravelles in March 1970. These were replaced in 1977 by Boeing 737s. Leased Boeing 707s were added to the fleet in 1980 for long-haul services. A single Airbus A300B4 was also used, but only for

a short time as it proved too large for the airline's needs, and was exchanged for a Boeing 747SP which was then used on long-distance services, though these were abandoned from 1995. A fleet replacement programme began in 1989 with the delivery of the first Fokker 50s. Luxair Commuter is a subsidiary company, which served short-range destinations with Embraer 120s, but at the end of the 1990s this was integrated into Luxair. Embraer RJ-145s were introduced from 1998 as a long-term replacement for the Fokker 50. Luxair has a 24.5% holding in Cargolux, while Lufthansa holds

13% of Luxair. There is co-operation with both Lufthansa and Air France.

Routes

Athens, Amsterdam, Barcelona, Berlin, Copenhagen, Dublin, Florence, Frankfurt, Fuerteventura, Geneva, Hamburg, Innsbruck, Lanzarote, Las Palmas, Lisbon, London, Luxembourg, Madrid, Milan, Malaga, Manchester, Marseilles, Montpellier, Munich, Nice, Palma de Mallorca, Paris, Porto, Rome, Saarbrücken, Salzburg, Stockholm, Tenerife, Turin, Vienna, Zürich.

Fleet		Ordered
2 Boeing 737-400	4 Fokker 50	2 Embraer RJ-135
4 Boeing 737-500		
7 Embraer RJ-145		

Boeing 737-7L90 OY-MRE (Dennis Wehrmann/Billund)

MAERSK AIR

Copenhagen Airport South, 2791 Dragoer
Denmark, Tel. 32-314444, Fax. 32-314490,
www.maersk-air.com

Three- / Two- letter code	IATA No.	Reg'n prefix	ICAO callsign
DAN / DM	349	OY	Maerskair

The A.P. Moeller shipping company, owners of the Maersk shipping line, set up Maersk Air as a subsidiary in February 1969, intending it to operate purely as a charter business. Operations began in December 1969 with a Fokker F.27 and an HS.125. The young airline's urge to expand resulted in it taking over Falckair, a domestic airline, along with its routes to Odense and Aarhus in 1970. Air Business, another regional airline, was acquired in May 1983; it had been operating between Esbjerg and Stavanger. The route from Billund to Sonthad was opened with de Havilland DHC-7s and further

scheduled services connected Copenhagen with Billund and Ronne. As well as scheduled and charter flights, Maersk was doing increasing business in aircraft leasing. Thus several Boeing 737s were leased long-term to Deutsche BA. In July 1993 Maersk Air UK was founded to take over the activities of Birmingham European Airways; this has now become a British Airways franchise operation using principally Boeing 737s and Canadair Regional Jets supplied by the parent. A further subsidiary is Star Air in Denmark, and Maersk has close ties with Estonian, again with aircraft seconded. Maersk was one of the

first airlines to place order for the new Boeing 737-700, with the first arriving in March 1998, allowing older 737-300s to be phased out. Canadair Regional Jets were added from May 2000.

Routes

Scheduled services from Billund and Copenhagen to Aalborg, Amsterdam, Athens, Brussels, Dublin, Esbjerg, Faroe Islands, Frankfurt, Kristiansand, Lisbon, London, Nice, Odense, Paris, Ronne, Stockholm, Venice, Vojens. Seasonal charters to the Mediterranean or to the Alpine winter sports areas.

Fleet		Ordered
10 Boeing 737-500	2 Fokker 50	1 Boeing 737-700
7 Boeing 737-700		
2 Canadair RJ		

Boeing 777-2H6ER 9M-MRF (Uwe Gleisberg/Munich)

MALAYSIA AIRLINES

Jalan Sultan Ismail Bangunan MAS,
50250 Kuala Lumpur, Malaysia, Tel. 3-21610555,
Fax. 3-21613472, www.malaysia-airlines.com.my

Three- / Two- letter code	IATA No.	Reg'n prefix	ICAO callsign
MAS / MH	232	9M	Malaysian

Malaysian Airline System Berhad came into existence on 3rd April 1971 after the former MSA (Malaysia-Singapore Airlines) was split up. Using nine Fokker F.27s and three Britten-Norman Islanders, Malaysian domestic services were operated. From 1974 London was served on a weekly basis with a Boeing 707, with further services to Amsterdam, Zürich and Frankfurt following shortly afterwards. In 1976 the first DC-10-30 was delivered and in1982 two Boeing 747-200s were added; these were used to add service to destinations in the USA from 1995. On 15th October 1987

MAS introduced a new colour scheme and 'System' was dropped from the name, following the sale by the government of its shares. MAS continued to expand worldwide and invested heavily in new technology and aircraft. Airbus A330s began arriving in 1994 as DC-10 replacements, with MD-11s following in 1994 and 1995. The airline's own freight division, MAS Cargo, operates dedicated MD-11 and 747-200F freighters. Regional destinations are served with Fokker 50s and DHC-6 Twin Otters. In 1997 the company took delivery of its first Boeing 777; this type is replacing

older Boeing 747-100s and DC-10s on the long-range services. The Asian business crisis of the late 1990s affected Malaysia Airlines; as with other companies in the area, routes were suspended and aircraft either sold or returned to their lessors. However, by the beginning of 2000, things had stabilised and Malaysian was set to continue its expansion. Malaysian looks likely to become a member of the KLM/Northwest-led alliance.

Routes

About 35 domestic destinations, plus services to Australia, Japan, Korea, Hong Kong, Indonesia, Philippines, Thailand, Taiwan and the People's Republic of China. There are also services to the Middle East, South Africa, USA and Europe.

Fleet

		Ordered
10 Airbus A330-300	11 Boeing 777-200ER	5 Boeing 747-400
34 Boeing 737-400	5 De Havilland DHC-6	5 Boeing 777
4 Boeing 737-500	10 Fokker 50	
2 Boeing 747-200F	1 (Boeing) McDonnell Douglas MD-11F	
15 Boeing 747-400		

Boeing 737-3Q8 HA-LEJ (Martin Bach/London-LHR)

MALEV – HUNGARIAN AIRLINES

V, Roosevelt ter 2, 1051 Budapest, Hungary
Tel. 1-2353535, Fax. 1-2662759,
www.malev.hu

Three- / Two- letter code	IATA No.	Reg'n prefix	ICAO callsign
MAH / MA	182	HA	Malev

Malev was originally established on 26th April 1946 as a joint Hungarian/Soviet undertaking with the title Maszovlet, with a fleet of eleven Lisunov Li-2s and six Polikarpov Po-2s. Flight operations began on 15th October 1946 on domestic routes and international flights began in the next year. On 25th November 1954 the Hungarian government took complete control and the airline adopted the name Magyar Legiközlekedesi Vollat (MALEV). When Ilyushin IL-18s were delivered in May 1960, flights started to European destinations such as Amsterdam, Vienna and Moscow.

As Hungary's road system developed, the need for domestic services declined and the last such flights operated in 1969. The Tupolev Tu-134 was the first jet aircraft in 1968, followed by the Tu-154 in 1973. Replacement of Soviet-built aircraft with Boeing 737s started in 1989 with Malev being one of the first eastern bloc countries to obtain western equipment. Likewise Boeing was the source for new long-range equipment, with 767s arriving from the end of 1992. The airline became a public limited company from 30th June 1992. Alitalia acquired 30% of the capital and

started to work closely with Malev. During 1995 Malev received its first Fokker 70s for shorter European routes and several of the older Tupolevs were sold off, the remaining examples being used mostly for charter work. Ailing Alitalia was forced to sell its shares in 1998 and they were acquired by a consortium of Hungarian banks. There are co-operation and/or codeshare agreements with Air France, British Airways, CSA, Delta Air Lines, Moldavian, Swissair and Tarom. Malev's base is at Budapest-Ferihegy airport.

Routes

Amsterdam, Athens, Bangkok, Barcelona, Beijing, Berlin, Beirut, Bratislava, Brussels, Budapest, Bucharest, Cairo, Chisinau, Damascus, Debrecen, Dublin, Düsseldorf, Frankfurt, Hamburg, Helsinki, Istanbul, Kiev, Kosice, Larnaca, Ljubljana, London, Madrid, Moscow, Munich, New York, Paris, Prague, Rome, Sarajevo, Skopje, Sofia, St. Petersburg, Stockholm, Stuttgart, Tel Aviv, Thessaloniki, Tirana, Toronto, Tripoli, Warsaw, Vienna, Zagreb, Zürich.

Fleet

3 Boeing 737-200
4 Boeing 737-300
3 Boeing 737-400
2 Boeing 737-500

2 Boeing 767-200ER
6 Fokker 70
6 Tupolev Tu-154

Boeing 747-409 B-16801 (Dennis Wehrmann/Amsterdam)

MANDARIN AIRLINES

134 Minsheng East Road, Sector 3, Taipei 105
Republic of China, Tel. 2-27171188,
Fax. 2-27170716, www.mandarinair.com

Three- / Two- letter code	IATA No.	Reg'n prefix	ICAO callsign
MDA / AE	803	B	Mandarin Air

In June 1991 the Kuos Development Corporation and China Airlines founded a joint venture airline, Mandarin Airlines, with China Airlines taking over complete ownership late in 1992. Mandarin used Boeing 747SPs, Boeing 747-400s and MD-11s to fly to Canada, Europe and Australia. A private airline called Yun Shin Airlines was established in May 1966, which later changed name to Formosa Airlines and operated domestic services; Dornier 228s, Fokker 50s and Saab SF 340s were used to destinations which were not suited to jet service. China Airlines had a 42% holding in this company which was based at Taipei's Sung Shan city airport. In August 1999, Formosa Airlines and Mandarin Airlines were formally merged under the Mandarin Airlines identity. The long term plan is that all the domestic services of the China Airlines group should be conducted by Mandarin Airlines, and the necessary reorganisation within the group should be completed by the end of 2000. As well as scheduled services, Mandarin uses its 747s and MD-11s for charter work.

Routes

Brisbane, Chi Mei, Chiang Mai, Green Island, Hualien, Kaohsiung, Makung, Macau, Orchid Island, Sydney, Taichung, Taipei, Taitung, Vancouver, and Yangon are served on a scheduled basis. There are charter flights throughout South East Asia, and to the USA and Europe.

Fleet

1 Boeing 747-400	2 Fokker 100
2 (Boeing) McDonnell Douglas MD-11	2 Saab SF 340
3 Dornier 228	
7 Fokker 50	

BAe 146-200 G-MIMA (Dennis Wehrmann/Chambery)

MANX AIRLINES

Ronaldsway Airport, Ballasalla, Isle of Man
IM9 2JE, Great Britain, Tel. 1624-826000,
Fax. 1624-826001, www.manx-airlines.com

Three- / Two- letter code	IATA No.	Reg'n prefix	ICAO callsign
MNX / JE	916	G	Manx

Manx Air Charter was founded just after the Second World War, in 1947, but was bankrupt as soon as 1948 and was integrated into Silver City Airways. It was only in 1982 that the fine-sounding name of the airline was revived. Manx Airlines was founded on 1st November of that year, with British Midland Airways, who had a 75% stake, the balance being held by the British and Commonwealth Shipping Line, also a shareholder in Air UK. Flights started from Ronaldsway to London Heathrow using Fokker Friendships and Vickers Viscounts. The airline also acquired a Saab 340 and BAC One-Elevens plus a BAe 146 ,

replacing the Saab 340 in 1988. The Viscount 800 was replaced by BAe ATPs in 1989. British Midland assumed full control of the airline in 1988 and Manx became a member of the Airlines of Britain group, operating as Manx Airlines and Manx Airlines (Europe). In 1995 the latter became a British Airways franchise partner and in Summer 1996 BA's Scottish operations were also taken over, along with its aircraft. Thus Manx became the world's largest user of the ATP/Jetstream 61. The close alliance with BA did not sit entirely comfortably in the light of parent company British Midland's

competitive position with British Airways, and so the Airlines of Britain Group was dissolved and a new parent, British Regional Airlines was founded, a company traded on the London stock exchange. Thus Manx Airlines remains independent, even though it is much reduced in size and operates most routes on behalf of British Airways. Even the new colour scheme for their aircraft, introduced in November 1998, is similar to the British Airways tailfin artwork, though the airline's traditional green lower fuselage is retained.

Routes

Aberdeen, Birmingham, Cardiff, Cork, Dublin, Edinburgh, Glasgow, Isle of Man, Jersey, Leeds/Bradford, Liverpool, London, Manchester, Southampton.

Fleet

4 BAe ATP/Jetstream 61
1 BAe 146-200

(Boeing) McDonnell Douglas MD-11 PH-MCT (Dennis Wehrmann/Amsterdam)

MARTINAIR

Postbus 7507,1118 ZG Schiphol, Netherlands
Tel. 20-6011222, Fax. 20-6011303
www.martinair.com

Three- / Two- letter code	IATA No.	Reg'n prefix	ICAO callsign
MPH / MP	129	PH	Martinair

Martin Air Holland, or to be precise Martin's Luchtvervoer Maatschappij NV, was founded on 24th May 1958 by Martin Schröder with a single Douglas DC-3. The airline was first called Martins Air Charter until the present name was introduced in April 1968. Sightseeing and air taxi flights were provided. A smaller airline, Fairways Rotterdam, was taken over in January 1964. KLM acquired a 25% stake in the airline and further shares were sold to a shipping company, NedLloyd Reederei. Martinair acquired DC-7s, Lockheed Electras and DC-8s over time from KLM and used these types to go into the charter business in a

big way. The first widebody to join the fleet was the DC-10 in 1973, and this was followed by Airbus A310s in 1984 and the first Boeing 747, a combi version, in 1988. Further fleet renewal continued and the Boeing 767 replaced the Airbuses, and the first MD-11 convertible freighter arrived at the end of 1994; this type was to replace the DC-10s. The word 'Holland' was dropped from the title in 1995. Using a very modern fleet, Martinair continues to expand, and yet continues to undertake its traditional activities of aerial photography, survey, aerial advertising and air taxi work with a fleet of light aircraft, and is

particularly active in the airfreight world. A Fokker 70 is also maintained and flown on behalf of the Dutch royal family. On 1st July 1998 KLM acquired NedLloyd's shares in Martinair and is thus now the sole owner, though the airline continues to operate independently. In late 1999 Air Holland's Boeing 757s were taken over. Martinair's base and maintenance facility is at Amsterdam's Schiphol airport.

Routes

Amsterdam, Antwerp, Brussels, Cancun, Ciego de Avilla, Havana, Holguin, Los Angeles, Miami, Montego Bay, New York, Oakland, Orlando, Puerto Plata, Punta Cana, San Jose, San Juan, Santo Domingo, Varadero are all served on a regular basis, plus charter flights to holiday resorts in the Mediterranean, Caribbean, USA, Canada, and South East Asia.Freight flights worldwide.

Fleet

3 Boeing 747-200
3 Boeing 757-200
6 Boeing 767-300ER

6 (Boeing) McDonnell Douglas MD-11

Airbus A321-231 F-OHMQ (Albert Kuhbandner/Zürich)

MEA – MIDDLE EAST AIRLINES

P.O.Box 206, Beirut, Lebanon
Tel. 1-629250, Fax. 629260,
www.mea.com.lb

Three- / Two- letter code	IATA No.	Reg'n prefix	ICAO callsign
MEA / ME	076	OD	Cedar Jet

MEA, whose full title is Middle East Airline SA, was founded in May 1945 as a private company by a group of Lebanese businessmen and started a service with a de Havilland Dragon Rapide between Beirut and Nicosia on 20th November and to Baghdad on 15th February 1946. In 1949 Pan American acquired a stake, replacing the Rapide with a DC-3 in order to provide more cargo capacity. Pan American withdrew in 1955, its stake being acquired by BOAC. Scheduled services started on 2nd October 1955 to London using Vickers Viscounts; Karachi and Bombay followed. The first jet type was the de Havilland Comet

4B, used on the London route from 6th January 1961. Further expansion came in March 1963 when joint development was agreed with Air Liban, which was fully merged into MEA along with its DC-6s and SE 210 Caravelles in November 1965. Air France became a shareholder. Boeing 707s came into service in 1968 and in 1969 Lebanese International Airways (LIA) together with its fleet, routes and staff was taken over. This merger was government-inspired as several of LIA's and MEA's aircraft had been destroyed by an Israeli attack on Beirut airport in 1968. Operations were badly affected by the civil war

which went on for more than ten years, but MEA was the only airline to maintain links with the outside world despite every adversity. Two leased A310s replaced the Boeing 707s. To revive the fortunes of the airline, Air France and an investment company again took shares, and a fresh start was made, with new colours introduced at the beginning of 1997. The fleet and Beirut airport's infrastructure were renewed. Airbus A320s and A321s were delivered, the three Boeing 747s were sold and more A310s ordered, so that MEA has a very modern fleet and has built up a significant route network.

Routes

Abidjan, Abu Dhabi, Amman, Athens, Beirut, Cairo, Dammam, Dubai, Frankfurt, Geneva, Istanbul, Jeddah, Kano, Kuwait, Lagos, Larnaca, London, Paris, Riyadh, Rome, Teheran.

Fleet

2 Airbus A310-300
3 Airbus A310-200
3 Airbus A320-200
2 Airbus A321
4 Boeing 707-300

McDonnell Douglas MD-83 EI-CIW (Josef Krauthäuser/Düsseldorf)

MERIDIANA

193 Corso Umberto, Zona Industrialle A,
07026 Olbia, Italy, Tel. 0789-52600,
Fax. 0789-23661, www.meridiana.it

Three- / Two- letter code	IATA No.	Reg'n prefix	ICAO callsign
ISS / IG	191	I	Merair

Meridiana was the result of the strategic merger of the Italian airline Alisarda and the Spanish operator Universair in 1991. Until the Spanish airline Meridiana became bankrupt in late 1992, the two partners had co-ordinated their operations while remaining relatively independent. Alisarda was founded on 24th March 1963 in Olbia as an air taxi and general charter company using two Beech C-45s and began operations in that same year. Scheduled passenger services were added from 1st June 1966, initially with Nord 262s, later replaced by Fokker Friendships. Later, services took place to destinations in France, Switzerland and within Italy using DC-9s from 1975. Other destinations followed seasonally, such as Frankfurt or Munich, initially as charters but later as scheduled services. Two MD-82s were acquired in 1984 and the fleet of this type has gradually increased. A third-level operator, Avianova was established in 1986, but sold to the Alitalia group in 1991. On 1st September 1991 Alisarda changed its name to Meridiana and by 1992 it had become the largest privately-owned airline in Italy. Four BAe 146s were added in 1994. The main base is at Olbia and Florence is also being built up as a major hub in the network. Meridiana continues to expand strongly, with new routes and aircraft being added each year. As well as scheduled services, charters are also flown on behalf of various tour operators.

Routes

Amsterdam, Barcelona, Bologna, Cagliari, Catania, Florence, Frankfurt, Geneva, Genoa, London, Milan, Munich, Naples, Nice, Olbia, Palermo, Paris, Pisa, Rome, Turin, Verona, Zürich.

Fleet

4 BAe 146-200
6 McDonnell Douglas MD-83
11 McDonnell Douglas MD-82

Fokker F.27 Friendship PK-MFL (Björn Kannengiesser/Jakarta)

MERPATI

Jolan Angkasa 2, Kotak pos 323,
Jakarta 10720, Indonesia
Tel. 21-6546789, Fax. 21-6540620

Three- / Two- letter code	IATA No.	Reg'n prefix	ICAO callsign
MNA / MZ	621	PK	Merpati

The Indonesian government founded Merpati Nusantara Airlines on 6th September 1962 to take over the network of internal services developed by the Indonesian Air Force. Initial operations started on 11th September 1962 connecting Jakarta with domestic points. In 1964, Merpati took over the routes previously operated by KLM subsidiary de Kroonduif, which had been flown by Garuda since 1962. This predecessor had been particularly active in West Guinea. Merpati has used a variety of aircraft types: DC-3, HS-748, Vickers Viscount, Vickers Vanguard, NAMC YS-11, Dornier 28, and Pilatus Porter. Numerous CASA aircraft manufactured in Indonesia under licence are also used, such as IPTN 235s, replacing older equipment. On 28th October 1978 the airline was taken over by Garuda, though Merpati continues to operate independently as a part of the group. When the first DC-9s arrived in Autumn 1990, new, modern colours were introduced on the aircraft. The first Fokker 100 was introduced in 1993 and Boeing 737-200s taken on in 1994 as DC-9 replacements. Merpati has the densest route network in Indonesia and was on an expansion course until the 1998 political and economic crisis in the country. The general Asian crisis has also affected Indonesia especially badly, and there have been added problems with ethnic disputes and the plunge in the value of the currency, which is especially significant when leasing costs are to be paid in US dollars. Thus Merpati has been forced to return aircraft and drop routes. In 1999 there was discussion as to whether Garuda and Merpati should merge, but these ideas did not come to fruition.

Routes

Bandar Lampung, Bandung, Batam, Bengkulu, Biak, Bima, Denpasar, Jakarta, Jambi, Jayapura, Kuala Lumpur, Kupang, Mataram, Medan, Merauke, Padang, Palankarya, Palembang, Pekanbaru, Pontianak, Port Hedland, Sorong, Sumbawa, Surabaya, Tanjung Pinan, Ujung Padang.

Fleet		Ordered
3 Boeing 737-200	3 Fokker 100	15 ITPN-CN-235
7 De Havilland DHC-6 Twin Otter	14 ITPN-CN-235-10	
13 Fokker F.27	10 ITPN-212 AB4/CC4 Aviocar	
24 Fokker F.28	1 ITPN-C 235-200	

Boeing 737-287 N281AU (Josef Krauthäuser/St.Louis)

METROJET

23245 Crystal Drive, Arlington Virginia, USA
Tel. 888-6387653, Fax. 336-7446167,
www.flymetrojet.com

Three- / Two- letter code	IATA No.	Reg'n prefix	ICAO callsign
MET / US		N	

The advent of low-cost airlines and their entry into a lucrative marketplace has been a cause of concern amongst the established majors, whose costs are usually higher and who find it difficult to react quickly to changing market conditions. Some of the larger airlines set out to redress this competition: Continental set up Continental Lite, United Airlines created its Shuttle division and Delta Air Lines established Delta Express. A group of US Airways employees were tasked with setting up a low-cost division, to be called MetroJet, and this took to the air from 1st June 1998. Activities were concentrated on the lucrative East coast market and to holiday sunspots, as it was intended that the new division should attract the custom of new passengers who might formerly have chosen means of transport other than flying. Agreement was made with the pilots and cabin crew unions to allow the use of up to 50 aircraft from hubs at Philadelphia, Pittsburgh and Charlotte. As with other low-cost operators, flights are offered at high frequency between the various points served, on-board service is minimal, and ticketing and check-in procedures are simplified. Operations have been quickly expanded and more and more Boeing 737-200s, the standard aircraft for this service, seconded from US Airways, and painted in a predominantly red variant of the parent's colours. For the passengers, flying with a low-cost subsidiary of a major airline is particularly attractive, as frequent flier and similar benefits all still apply.

Routes

Albany, Atlanta, Baltimore, Boston, Chicago-Midway, Cleveland, Columbus, Fort Lauderdale, Hartford, Jacksonville, Manchester, Miami, Milwaukee, New Orleans, New York-La Guardia, Orlando, Providence, Raleigh/Durham, St. Louis, Syracuse, Tampa, Washington, West Palm Beach.

Fleet

45 Boeing 737-200

Fokker 100 XA-SGE (Stefan Schlick/Puerto Vallarta)

MEXICANA

Xola 535, Piso 30, Colonia de Valle 03100
Mexico City, Mexico, Tel. 5-4483096,
Fax. 5-4483096, www.mexicana.com

Three- / Two- letter code	IATA No.	Reg'n prefix	ICAO callsign
MXA / MX	132	XA	Mexicana

The Compania Mexicana de Aviacion is one of the world's oldest airlines. It was founded on 12th July 1921 initially to fly wages to the oilfields near Tampico, as transporting this money overland was no longer safe. The present name was adopted on 20th August 1924, and scheduled services began on 15th April 1928 between Mexico City and Tampico. From 1929 to 1968 Pan American had a majority interest in Mexicana. Aerovias Centrales was bought in 1935 and Transportes Aereos de Jalinco in 1955. In addition to DC-3s and DC-6s, Comet 4Cs were used on routes to Havana, Los Angeles and New York starting in 1960. The Boeing 727 was introduced in 1966 and the DC-10 in 1981. The Mexican government became the major shareholder in 1982, but on 22nd August 1989 it became a private company. A necessary reorganisation involved changes to flight operations and the route network. Mexicana's relatively old fleet was supplemented from mid 1991 with Airbus A320s and from 1992 by the smaller Fokker 100, and at this time a new colour scheme was introduced, with the tailfin of each aircraft being painted in a different hue. Mexicana has interests in various regional operators including Aerocaribe, Aerocozumel (both of which operate a feeder system on behalf of Aeromexico), Aeromonterrey and Turboreactores. In 1996 Mexicana was acquired by the Cintra Group, whose portfolio of other companies includes former competitor Aeromexico. Mexicana is a participant in the Latinpass frequent flyer scheme and since early 2000, a member of the Star Alliance.

Routes

Acapulco, Bogota, Buenos Aires, Cancun, Caracas, Chicago, Ciudad del Carmen, Cozumel, Denver, Durango, Guadalajara, Guatemala, Havana, Hermosilo, Huatulco, Ixtapa, Ixtepec, Las Vegas, Leon, Los Angeles, Managua, Manzanillo, Mazatlan, Merida, Miami, Mexicali, Mexico City, Montreal, Monterrey, Morelia, New York, Nuevo Laredo, Oakland, Oaxaca, Orlando, Panama City, Puerto Vallarta, Saltillo, San Antonio, San Francisco, San Jose, San Jose Cabo, San Juan, San Luis Potosi, San Salvador, Tampico, Toronto, Veracruz, Villahermosa, Zacatecas.

Fleet

16 Airbus A320-200
23 Boeing 727-200
 7 Boeing 757-200
12 Fokker 100

Ordered

8 Airbus A320-200

Airbus A310-304 F-OHPT (Josef Krauthäuser/Berlin-SXF)

MIAT – MONGOLIAN AIRLINES

PO Box 45, Buyant-Ukhaa 43, Ulaanbataar, People's Republic of Mongolia, Tel. 379935, Fax. 79226, www.miat.com.mn

Three- / Two- letter code	IATA No.	Reg'n prefix	ICAO callsign
MGL / OM	289	JU	Mongolair

The airline, founded in 1956, is known under a variety of names such as 'Mongolian Airlines', 'Mongoflot', or 'Air Mongol'. MIAT was built up with the aid of the USSR and Aeroflot. The first flight was on 7th July 1956 from Ulaanbaator to Irkutsk using an Antonov 24. Initially equipment including Lisunov Li-2s (Soviet-built versions of the Douglas DC-3) were supplied by the Soviet airline, and international routes were opened up to Irkutsk, to connect with Aeroflot's service to Moscow, and to Peking, though this was soon withdrawn for lack of demand. The bulk of the fleet built up since the 1980s consists of

Antonov twin turboprops, but Chinese Yunshuji Y-12s were used from 1992. As part of a co-operation and development agreement, MIAT received a Boeing 727 from Korean Airlines in 1992, with two more following, allowing the disposal of the former Tupolev Tu-154s. As well as scheduled and charter flights, MIAT is tasked with other state functions including agricultural flying and air ambulance work. A leased Airbus A310 was taken on in May 1998 and this has been used for flights to Europe, which are valuable as a means of earning foreign exchange. The revised colour scheme which has been applied to

the Airbus is an outward sign of MIAT's steps forward into the modern era.

Routes

From Ulaanbataar, Mongolian domestic destinations such as Darchan and Eerdenet are served. There are international services to Beijing, Berlin, Irkutsk, Moscow and Seoul, and charter flights to Korea, Japan, the Middle East and other destinations in China

Fleet

 1 Airbus A310-300
14 Antonov An-24/26
 3 Boeing 727-200

Boeing 737-76N N311ML (Josef Krauthäuser/Fort Lauderdale)

MIDWAY AIRLINES

300 West Morgan Street, Durham NC, 27701, USA, Tel. 800-4464392, Fax. 800-9568619, www.midwayair.com

Three- / Two- letter code	IATA No.	Reg'n prefix	ICAO callsign
MDW / JI	878	N	Midway

Created as Bader Express Service in 1983, operations began from Bader Field in Atlantic City with charter flights for casinos and air taxi work using a CASA 212. In 1985 plans were laid for a 'low-fare' service to Chicago-Midway, Los Angeles, Phoenix and New York and with this in mind the company was renamed as Jet Express. The hoped-for acquisition of three Boeing 727s failed for lack of capital. However, another CASA 212 was acquired in order to become a feeder carrier as a TWA-Partner. From 1992, with the Swearingen Metro III the company became a US Air-Express partner. In 1993 the group bought the name

Midway Airlines from the bankruptcy of a former airline, leased five Fokker 100s and began service from Chicago Midway to New York. The challenge of building a network from Chicago's second airport as a niche carrier as its predecessor had done proved to be more difficult, and after only six months, Midway was facing another closure. However, early in 1994 an investment company took over 90% of the shares, reorganised the company and installed new management. Early 1995 saw Midway take over the former American Airlines hub at Raleigh-Durham when the major drastically cut back its operations, and Midway

moved its headquarters there to concentrate on East Coast services. As well as more leased Fokker 100s, leased Airbus A320s were used for a while for holiday services to Las Vegas and Cancun, but returned. The rapid pace of early expansion turned to consolidation and service improvement. For less busy routes, Canadair Regional Jets were added from 1997 and in January 2000 Midway received its first Boeing 737-700; this type replaces the Fokker 100s.

Routes

Atlanta, Baltimore, Boston, Charleston, Chicago, Columbia, Columbus, Fort Lauderdale, Greenville, Hartford, Indianapolis, Jacksonville, Myrtle Beach, New Orleans, New York, Newburgh, Norfolk, Orlando, Philadelphia, Raleigh/Durham, Tampa, Washington, West Palm Beach, Wilmington.

Fleet	Ordered
2 Boeing 737-700	15 Boeing 737-300
23 Canadair Regional Jet 200ER	4 Canadair Regional Jet 200ER
8 Fokker 100	

McDonnell Douglas DC-9-32 N216ME (Dennis Wehrmann/Tampa)

MIDWEST EXPRESS

4915 South Howell Ave., Oak Creek,
Wisconsin 53154, USA, Tel. 414-7352030,
Fax. 414-7471499, www.midwestexpress.com

Three- / Two- letter code	IATA No.	Reg'n prefix	ICAO callsign
MEP / YX	453	N	Midex

Midwest Express was established after deregulation in November 1983 to provide passenger service in the Midwest and Southeast of the USA. The airline is a subsidiary of KC Aviation, which is itself the established aviation division of Kimberley-Clark, the major paper products company. The initial fleet was a DC-9 and Convair 580, but further DC-9s were soon added. Operations began on 29th April 1984 on the route Milwaukee-Boston. Over the following years a fleet of DC-9-10s and -32s was built up and routes extended to cover 20 cities including as far as Dallas and Los Angeles. During1994/95 capital was increased to allow further expansion, and in 1995 a revised colour scheme was introduced. This steady expansion has continued, and has included the establishment of a subsidiary, Skyway Airlines, which provides feeder services to Midwest at its Milwaukee and Omaha hubs. The fleet remains firmly fixed to the DC-9 and its developments, but more modern MD-80 series aircraft have supplanted some of the older DC-9s. The extended route network now reaches from Los Angeles to New York. There are alliances with American Eagle Airlines and Northwest Airlines.

Routes

Abilene, Alexandria, Amarillo, Appleton, Atlanta, Bakersfield, Baton Rouge, Beaumont, Boston, Carlsbad, Cincinatti, Cleveland, Columbus, Corpus Christi, Dallas/Fort Worth, Dayton, Denver, DesMoines, Fort Lauderdale, Fort Myers, Fort Smith, Fresno, Harlingen, Hartford, Houston, Indianapolis, Jackson, Kansas City, Lansing, Laredo, Las Vegas, Little Rock, Los Angeles, Milwaukee, Nashville, New York, Oklahoma City, Omaha, Orlando, Philadelphia, Phoenix, San Diego, San Francisco, St. Louis, Tampa, Toronto, Tulsa, Waco, Washington, Wichita.

Fleet

  8 Douglas DC-9-14/15
16 Douglas DC-9-32
11 McDonnell Douglas MD-81/82/88

Airbus A300-605R G-MAJS (Lutz Schönfeld/Arrecife)

MONARCH AIRLINES

Luton Airport, Luton Bedfordshire LU2 9NU
Great Britain, Tel. 1582-400000,
Fax. 1582-411000, www.monarch-airlines.com

Three- / Two- letter code	IATA No.	Reg'n prefix	ICAO callsign
MON / ZB	974	G	Monarch

Monarch Airlines, the well-known British charter company, was founded on 5th June 1967 by Cosmos Tours. Flight operations started on 5th April 1968 with a Bristol Britannia flying between Luton and Madrid. Its initial Luton-based fleet consisted of two Britannias and its destinations were principally Mediterranean holiday resorts. In 1971 the first jet aircraft was acquired, a Boeing 720. BAC One-Elevens followed in 1975, Boeing 707s in 1978 and the first Boeing 737 in 1980. Its first Boeing 757, the first in Europe, arrived in

1983. Licences to operate scheduled services from Luton to Mahon, Palma and Malaga were awarded in the mid-1980s and the first service to Mahon began on 5th July 1986. Long-haul charters to the USA were introduced from 1988. Apart from the charter business, Monarch has also been very active in aircraft leasing; for example, the entire Euroberlin fleet was leased from Monarch for some years. In 1990 Monarch received its first widebody, the Airbus A300-600, and the Boeing 737s were largely replaced by Airbus A320s from early

1993. Boeing 767s were acquired but leased to Alitalia. The first Airbus A321 was delivered in April 1997 and Airbus A330-200s in 1999 for long-range routes, for which a single DC-10 is also still used. The main operating and engineering base is at Luton, but operations are conducted also from Birmingham, Gatwick, Liverpool and Manchester.

Routes

Scheduled services to Alicante, Malaga, Menorca, Tenerife, Palma. Charters according to season to the Mediterranean, Alps, Caribbean, East Africa, Far East and USA.

Fleet

4 Airbus A300-600
5 Airbus A320-200
3 Airbus A321-200
2 Airbus A330-200

7 Boeing 757-200/200ER
1 McDonnell Douglas DC-10-30

Fokker F.27 Friendship OY-CCN (Josef Krauthäuser collection)

MYANMA AIRWAYS

123 Sule Pagoda Road, Yangon,
Myanmar
Tel. 1-80710, Fax. 1-89609

Three- / Two- letter code	IATA No.	Reg'n prefix	ICAO callsign
UBA / UB	209	XY	Unionair

Originally established in 1948 by the Burmese government as the Union of Burma Airways, the airline changed its name in December 1972 to Burma Airways Corporation and finally on 1st April 1989 to Myanma Airways, reflecting the change of name of Burma to Myanmar. In between lie 40 years of flight operations, which started in 1948 with de Havilland Doves. These were followed by DC-3s and Vickers Viscounts and the introduction of domestic and international services. The first Fokker F.27 was delivered in October 1963. In 1969 a Boeing 727 replaced the Viscount on international routes. From the time of the delivery of the the first Fokker F.28 in 1977 the airline has used exclusively Fokkers. In 1993 a co-operation agreement was concluded with Highsonics Enterprises of Singapore, under which international routes would be flown by a joint company, Myanmar Airways International, which has been active since early 1994 with leased Boeing 737-300s, leaving Myanma Airways to concentrate on domestic routes only. Myanma Airways also has a stake in Air Mandalay, which operates a pair of ATR 42s.

Routes

Akyab, Bhamo, Dawe, Heho, Kalemyo, Kawthaung, Kengtung, Khamti, Lashio, Loikaw, Mandalay, Maulmyne, Mong Hsat, Myeik, Myitkyina, Nyaung-u, Putao, Sittwe, Tachilek, Tandwe, Yangon.

Fleet

4 Fokker F.27
3 Fokker F.28

Boeing 757-236 N506NA (Josef Krauthäuser/Las Vegas)

NATIONAL AIRLINES

P.O.Box 19359 Las Vegas, NV 89132, USA,
Tel. 702 -944 2800, Fax 702 944 2947
www.nationalairlines.com

Three- / Two- letter code	IATA No.	Reg'n prefix	ICAO callsign
ROK / N7	007	N	Red Rock

Michael J Conway brought with him a good deal of airline experience when on 12th April 1995 he founded New Airline, but it was to take more years of preparation before an aircraft would fly for the new airline. Investors had to be found to back the new venture and as Conway had already decided that Las Vegas would be the starting point, these were to come from the casinos and hotels of this city. Harrah's Entertainment and Rio Hotels & Casinos were soon on board, and they were joined by Wexford Management and some private investors. Thus the start-up capital in excess of $50 million was secured. The final name was chosen for the airline on 31st July 1998, and was to be National Airlines, a name which already has a place in US airline history; the rights to the name were bought from the bankruptcy of the second incarnation of PanAm. On 12th February 1999 National Airlines took delivery of its first Boeing 757. This type was decided upon as it is suitable for flights from the US East Coast to Las Vegas in all weathers without restrictions. After the issue of an unrestricted airline licence on 20th May 1999, National began operations on 27th May, with a first flight from Las Vegas to Chicago-Midway and a second route to Los Angeles. Since then, as further 757s have been delivered, more new routes have been rapidly opened to San Francisco, New York, Dallas, Miami and Philadelphia. All routes are served several times a day. The development of the company plans for 40 aircraft and 50 destinations within the five year build-up phase. A co-operation agreement was concluded in mid-2000 with Virgin Atlantic.

Routes

Chicago-Midway, Dallas/Fort Worth, Denver, Detroit, Las Vegas, Los Angeles, Miami, Newark, New York JFK, Orlando, Philadelphia, San Diego, San Francisco, Seattle, Tampa, Washington.

Fleet	Ordered
13 Boeing 757-200	10 Boeing 757-200

Avro RJ 70 VH-NJT (Uwe Gleisberg/Leonora)

NATIONAL JET SYSTEMS

435 King William Street, Adelaide SA 5000, Australia, Tel. 8-83045600, Fax. 8-83045650, www.natjet.com.au

Three- / Two- letter code	IATA No.	Reg'n prefix	ICAO callsign
NJS / NC	–	VH	National Jet

Founded in Adelaide in 1990, this company is not strictly an airline, but specialises in the supply of aircraft and services packages. It all began with a Piper Navajo and an IAI Westwind. From 1992 expansion was the watchword with five BAe 146s delivered, flying scheduled services on behalf of Australian Airlink . For Australian Air Express freight flights were also undertaken and BAe 146QCs were added for use on the important overnight express package services. National Jet also operated on behalf of the Royal Australian Air Force, using specially equipped Learjets. An important sphere of activity has been, and still is, the leasing of aircraft. A complete service is offered, from the creation to the day-to-day operation of an airline. Since 1993 a specially modified de Havilland DHC-8 has been operated for the Australian government on coastal surveillance missions. Similarly, National Jet gives important support in the search for natural resources in inland areas; under contract to mineral companies, employees and materials are flown to airfield sites located close by the mines. On behalf of Qantas, some aircraft are used for their regional system. National Jet Italia started operations as a British Airways franchise in July 2000 using BAe 146-300s between Rome and Palermo. National Jet Systems is now a subsidiary of the UK-based Cobham Group, having been acquired early in 2000.

Routes

Christmas Island, Cocos Island, Darwin, Learmonth, McArthur River, and Perth are served on a scheduled basis. charter flights and ad hoc freight flights are also carried out.

Fleet

5 De Havilland DHC-8-100/200/300
17 BAe 146-100/200/300
2 Avro RJ 70

Boeing 727-95 ZS-NYY (Josef Krauthäuser collection via EAS)

NATIONWIDE AIRLINES

P.O.Box 422, Lanseria Airport, Gauteng 1748
Republic of South Africa Tel. 11 701 3330
Fax 11 701 3243 www.nationwideair.co.za

Three- / Two- letter code	IATA No.	Reg'n prefix	ICAO callsign
NTW / CE	567	ZS	Nationwide Air

As the political situation in South Africa was slowly altering at the beginning of the 1990s, so there also developed the opportunity for new airlines, as the practical monopoly position enjoyed by South African Airways was not especially welcomed by industry. For political reasons also there was a need for new formations, as many African countries were lifting their previous restrictions on flights by South African aircraft. Companies such as Nationwide Air Charter, which had since the 1970s operated business and air taxi services from Lanseria Airport with Beech aircraft, expanded their operations. In February 1994 a BAC One-Eleven was purchased and initially used on charter work. Business was good, and two further One-Elevens arrived in November 1994 in time for the beginning of the major travel season in South Africa. Flights to neighbouring countries, to Madagascar and to Mauritius were flown on behalf of several tour companies. The delivery of further One-Elevens allowed the commencement of scheduled services, at which point the airline's name was changed to Nationwide Airlines. From 1997 Boeing 727s strengthened the fleet, with Boeing 737s added from the end of 1998.

A codeshare agreement was made with Sabena and their name appears on most of Nationwide's aircraft. The company is not only active with scheduled and charter work, but in freight operations and in chartering aircraft to other companies.

Routes

From Johannesburg, schedules to Durban, George and Capetown. Charter flights to neighbouring countries Namibia, Zimbabwe, to Kenya, the Comores, Seychelles and Mauritius.

Fleet

11 BAe/BAC 1-11-400/500
 3 Boeing 737-200
 3 Boeing 727-100/200

Boeing 737-2T5 N501NG (Author's collection)

NICA AIRLINES

P.O.Box 6018 Managua,
Nicaragua
Tel. 2-631929, Fax. 2-631822

Three- / Two- letter code	IATA No.	Reg'n prefix	ICAO callsign
NIS / 6Y	930	YN	Nica

Following the collapse of Aeronica there was no longer an international airline active in the still politically unstable Nicaragua. Soon after the elections in 1992 a new company was established with the help of TACA – Nicaraguenses de Aviacion SA – or NICA for short. The TACA Group held 49% of the shares, the rest being with private investors and the Nicaraguan government. In July 1992 it was possible to open the first service to Miami, using a leased Boeing 737-200. The main base is Managua, from where an internal network was also run with a CASA 212. As well as scheduled passenger services, charters and freight services are also flown. NICA is a participant in the frequent flier programme of TACA, LACSA and Aviateca. These companies are building a marketing alliance and the dominance of the TACA group is to be seen in the livery of the aircraft, which apart from the name is essentially that of TACA.

Routes

Guatemala City, Managua, Miami, Panama City, Puerto Cabezas, San Jose, San Salvador.

Fleet

1 Boeing 737-200

Boeing 737-2F9 5N-AUB (Josef Krauthäuser collection via EAS)

NIGERIA AIRWAYS

P. O. B 21024, Ikeja,
Nigeria
Tel. 01-900476, Fax. 01-4936347

Three- / Two- letter code	IATA No.	Reg'n prefix	ICAO callsign
NGA / WT	087	5N	Nigeria

West African Airways Corporation started operations in the former British colony in West Africa in 1946. Nigeria Airways was established in 1958 to take over the Nigerian operations of WAAC, with the name of WAAC (Nigeria) Ltd. The Nigerian government assumed full ownership of the airline on 1st May 1959. Flight operations in the new independent state of Nigeria were started with the aid of BOAC using aircraft leased from the latter on 1st October 1958. Boeing 377 Stratocruisers were used to open a route from Lagos to London and from 1st April 1962 the de Havilland Comet 4B was used on this route. A Boeing 707 became the first aircraft to be owned by the airline, taking over the London route from an ex-BOAC VC-10 which had been introduced in 1969. The present title was formally adopted on 22nd January 1971, though it had been used for commercial purposes since 1958. With the arrival of the DC-10 in October 1976, Nigeria Airways had its first widebody in the fleet, with two Airbus A310s following in 1983 and 1984, principally for use on African routes. For several years Nigeria Airways has been in decline. Massive financial problems led to a reduction in routes, staff reductions and the disposal or long-term unserviceability of aircraft and generally unreliable service. British Airways took the company under its wing in 1999 and leased a Boeing 747 to operate the London route regularly. The 747, which is maintained by BA, has a special colour scheme which distinguishes it from the rest of the fleet. A further joint service, this time with South African Airways, commenced in Autumn 2000, flying Johannesburg-Lagos-New York.

Routes

Abuja, Calabar, Douala, Dubai, Jeddah, Jos, Kaduna, Kano, Kinshasa, Lagos, Libreville, London, Maiduguri, Malabo, Port Harcourt, Sokoto and Yola.

Fleet

1 Airbus A310-200
4 Boeing 737-200
1 Boeing 747-200
1 McDonnell Douglas DC-10-30

Boeing 757-28A N750NA (Albert Kuhbandner/Munich)

NORTH AMERICAN AIRLINES

Suite 250, Building 75, Jamaica, NY 11430
USA Tel. 718-6562650, Fax. 718-9953372
www.northamericanair.com

Three- / Two- letter code	IATA No.	Reg'n prefix	ICAO callsign
NAO / XG	455	N	Northamerican

Dan McKinnon, formerly in charge of the CAB - Civil Aeronautics Board of the USA, formed North American Airlines in 1989. A shareholder – officially with 25% – was El Al Israel Airlines. The initial objective of the new airline was to provide connecting services to El Al flights to New York and Montreal. Thus El Al could eliminate its expensive New York - Los Angeles sector which was unprofitable since no domestic passengers could be carried because of the lack of IATA fifth freedom rights. Operations began on 22nd January 1990 using a Boeing 757-200 from New York's J F Kennedy airport, where the airline's base had been established, to Los Angeles. From 1992 a McDonnell Douglas MD-83 was added to the fleet and from 1995 a further Boeing 757-200. As well as the New York to Los Angeles flights, charter operations were added on behalf of various tour operators. A further change to the fleet came with the delivery of Boeing 737-800s in August 1998 and February 1999, replacing the MD-83. Scheduled flights to Guyana were started in 1999 after Guyana Airways suspended its services including the connection to New York.

Routes

New York, Guyana as schedules; charter flights worldwide.

Fleet

2 Boeing 737-800
2 Boeing 757-200

Douglas DC-9-32 N3991C(Josef Krauthäuser/Kalamazoo)

NORTHWEST AIRLINES

5101 Northwest Drive, St. Paul, MN.55111-3034, USA, Tel. 320-7262331, Fax. 320-7263942, www.nwa.com

Three- / Two- letter code	IATA No.	Reg'n prefix	ICAO callsign
NWA / NW	012	N	Northwest

Founded on 1st August 1926 in Minneapolis/St.Paul as Northwest Airways, initial services were flown with a Stinson Post from Chicago to St.Paul. Regular passenger services began in 1933 with DC-3s. In 1934 Northern Air Transport was taken over and the name changed to Northwest Airlines. On 15th July 1947 the first polar route was opened with DC-4s; this was from Seattle via Anchorage to Tokyo and on to Manila and led to a change of name to Northwest Orient Airlines. Boeing Stratocruiser came into service for the South East Asia routes. Lockheed Constellations,

DC-6s, DC-7s and Lockheed Electras were the predominant types during the propliner era. Jets began to oust these from 1960, when the first DC-8s were delivered in 1960, for initial use from Seattle to Chicago. First widebody was the Boeing 747, from 30th April 1970, followed by the DC-10-40 late in 1972. In 1979 Northwest made the leap across the Atlantic, with service to Copenhagen and Stockholm, followed by London in 1980. Unlike many other companies, Northwest's growth was solely internal until 1986 when Republic was acquired. In 1988 the old name Northwest

Airlines was re-adopted and a re-structuring took place. With the delivery of the first Airbus A320s in late 1989, a new colour scheme was also adopted. Ten years later the smaller A319 was introduced, but Northwest has also acquired a large fleet of second-hand DC-9s and there has been emphasis on the refurbishment of older aircraft rather than wholesale re-equipment. There is close co-operation with KLM, and feeder and regional services are flown as Northwest Airlink by other airlines including Mesaba and Express Airlines I.

Routes

Northwest serves over 250 destinations in more than 20 countries, including over 120 in the USA. Feeder and regional services are flown in association with Northwest Airlink .

Fleet

		Ordered
17 Airbus A319	10 Douglas DC-9-41	54 Airbus A319
70 Airbus A320-200	35 Douglas DC-9-51	12 Airbus A320
31 Boeing 727-200	43 McDonnell Douglas DC-10-30/40	16 Airbus A330-300
31 Boeing 747-200	10 McDonnell Douglas DC-9-14/15	18 Boeing 757-200
14 Boeing 747-400	115 McDonnell Douglas DC-9-31/32	
55 Boeing 757-200	8 McDonnell Douglas MD-82	

McDonnell Douglas MD-83 EI-CGI (Andreas Witek/Graz)

NOUVELAIR TUNISIE

BP 66 Aéroport International H/B Monastir Monastir 5000, Tunisia, Tel. 3-520671, Fax. 3-520666, www.nouvelair.com

Three- / Two- letter code	IATA No.	Reg'n prefix	ICAO callsign
LBT / BJ	–	TS	Nouvelair

The French airline Air Liberté established a subsidiary of the same name in Tunisia in 1990 and it began regular charter flights from Monastir for the summer season with a MD-83 supplied by the parent company. Destinations in the former East Germany, newly part of the unified country, were especially served, since Tunisia proved to be a leading holiday destination from here. Additional aircraft were made available from Air Liberté to meet additional demand. The company showed satisfactory development and another MD-83 was added in 1991. However, financial crisis overtook the parent and things

looked black for the Tunisian arm until it was sold in 1996 to the Tunisian Travel Service Group, a semi-governmental organisation. There was to be increased co-operation with Tunisair and with Air Liberté until the latter was sold to British Airways. With the sale of shares Air Liberté Tunisie became a company under Tunisian law and a renaming as Nouvelair Tunisie followed in March 1996. Hand in hand with the new name came a new colour scheme for the aircraft. Two further MD-83s were added in 1997 before it was decided to adopt the Airbus A320 as the airline's future equipment. The first two

aircraft were delivered in December 1999 and March 2000 to Monastir, which is the company's base and the departure point for most of its flights.

Routes

Typical of the operations of such charter airlines, Nouvelair flies holidaymakers from many European countries to Tunisia. Tunis, Monastir and Djerba are regularly served.

Fleet

2 Airbus A320-200
3 McDonnell Douglas MD-82/83

Ordered

1 Airbus A320-200

Boeing 707-320F 5N-AOQ (Author's collection)

OKADA AIR

17 B Sapele Road, Benin City,
Nigeria
Tel. 019-241504

Three- / Two- letter code	IATA No.	Reg'n prefix	ICAO callsign
OKJ	–	5N	Okadaair

A consortium of companies led by Chief Gabriel Igbinedion founded Okada Air in 1983, in order to operate regional and international charter services. Operations began using BAC One-Elevens, followed by Douglas DC-8s and Boeing 707s. The first international destination was London, and occasional charters are also flown to other European cities including Frankfurt and Zürich. A network of domestic services was also built up, joining such cities as Lagos, Kano, Kaduna and Port Harcourt.Okada also flies subcharters for other airlines as well as cargo. With up to 20 BAC One-Elevens assembled over the years from various sources, Okada has the world's largest fleet of this British short/medium range jet on hand. During the 1990s however, larger Boeing 727s and a Boeing 747 were acquired, though the latter was only used for a short time before being disposed of. Political instability and business difficulties in Nigeria have made it necessary from time to time to partially or completely suspend services and re-equipment plans have thus faltered.

Routes

Charter flights in Nigeria and Africa, to Europe, the Middle East and ad hoc destinations.

Fleet

19 BAe BAC 1-11
 1 Boeing 727-200
 1 Boeing 707-300F

Airbus A300-605R SX-BEL (Josef Krauthäuser/Munich)

OLYMPIC AIRWAYS

96 Snygrou Ave. 11741 Athens, Greece
Tel. 1-9269111, Fax. 1-9267154,
www.olympic-airways.gr

Three- / Two- letter code	IATA No.	Reg'n prefix	ICAO callsign
OAL / OA	050	SX	Olympic

Olympic Airways was founded on 6th April 1957 by no less a person than Aristotle Onassis. The famous shipowner took over a state-owned airline called TAE Greek National Airlines which had been in existence since July 1951. By the time of the first oil crisis Onassis had turned Olympic into a modern airline, but the oil situation caused Olympic difficulties and it suspended operations for several months in 1974. In order to avoid complete bankruptcy, the Greek state intervened and took over Olympic from 1st January 1976. After a complete restructuring of the airline which involved the abandonment of unprofitable routes, things began to improve slowly. When flight operations began in April 1957, Olympic had a fleet of 13 DC-3s and a DC-4, with DC-6s added a year later. In 1960 leased de Havilland Comet 4Bs were added, with the Boeing 707 following in 1966. This type was used to start long-range services to New York, Johannesburg and Sydney. While still under the Onassis regime, the first Boeing 747 arrived. Under a fleet renewal plan, the Boeing 707s and 727s were replaced by 1992 with new Boeing 737-400s and Airbus A300-600s, and these new types were given an attractive new colour scheme. Olympic has been performing poorly and amassing huge losses, and in an effort to turn around this situation, British Airways was given the task of managing the airline, also with an eye to privatisation, for 30 months from 1999, but this was terminated in mid-2000. Airbus A340s replaced the 747s and from Spring 2000 Boeing 737-800s were added. Olympic has 100% shareholdings in Macedonian Airlines and Olympic Aviation (see page 279).

Routes

Amman, Amsterdam, Athens, Bangkok, Barcelona, Beirut, Berlin, Brussels, Cairo, Copenhagen, Dubai, Düsseldorf, Frankfurt, Geneva, Heraklion, Istanbul, Jeddah, Johannesburg, Karpathos, Kavala, Kerkyria, Kos, Kuwait, Larnaca, London, Milan, Manchester, Marseilles, Melbourne, Montreal, Moscow, Munich, Naples, New York, Paris, Rhodes, Riyadh, Rome, Strasbourg, Stuttgart, Sydney, Tel Aviv, Teheran, Thessaloniki, Tirana, Toronto, Vienna and Zürich.

Fleet

4 Airbus A340-300
2 Airbus A300B4
2 Airbus A300-600
2 Boeing 747-200

11 Boeing 737-200
13 Boeing 737-400
2 Boeing 737-800

Ordered

2 Airbus A340-300
11 Boeing 737-700
4 Boeing 737-800

Boeing 717-2K9 SX-BOA (Uwe Gleisberg/Munich)

OLYMPIC AVIATION

96 Snygrou Ave. Athens, Greece
Tel. 1-9362681, Fax. 1-9883009,
www.olav.gr

Three- / Two- letter code	IATA No.	Reg'n prefix	ICAO callsign
OLY / ML	898	SX	Olavia

Greece, with its numerous islands and its fragmented and mountainous mainland, is dependent not only on a dense network of ferry connections but also on properly functioning regional air services. In order to open up smaller islands to tourists and to save them having to endure long transfer times, Olympic Aviation was set up on 1st August 1971 with the objective of building up regional services. First of all, runways had to be laid, extended or repaired on many of the islands. As many runways did not have a hard surface, robust aircraft such as Shorts Skyvans and Dornier 228s were used. Initially the airline was privately-owned, but became government owned in 1974. Flights are operated to those places where parent company, Olympic Airways, cannot operate its larger aircraft, and in addition the airline operates as a feeder service to international flights at Athens. ATR 72s, introduced in 1992/93 are also used for charter services from European points directly to the Greek islands. The airline has been one of the first to take delivery of the new Boeing 717, in December 1999, and the acquisition of this type marks its increasing involvement in European scheduled services.

Routes

Olympic Aviation serves more than 45 points in Greece and some 15 international destinations in Europe.

Fleet

7 ATR 72
4 ATR 42
2 Boeing 717-200
6 Fairchild/Dornier Do228-200

Airbus A321-131 TC-ONI (Josef Krauthäuser/Düsseldorf)

ONUR AIR

Senlik Mah, Catal Sok. No.3, 34810 Istanbul, Turkey, Tel. 0212-6632300, Fax. 0212-6636054, www.onurair.de

Three- / Two- letter code	IATA No.	Reg'n prefix	ICAO callsign
OHY / 8Q	–	TC	Onur Air

Founded in 1992, this airline is a subsidiary of the Turkish tour operator TK Air Travel. Operations began with factory-fresh Airbus A320s on 14th May 1993. As well as the usual charter and inclusive tour work, the airline also wanted to operate scheduled services. During the high season, further A320s were leased in to augment its own fleet. From early in 1994 Ten Tours took over Onur Air and placed it on a more stable financial footing. Radiating from its base at Istanbul, a network of Turkish domestic services was built up during the 1990s. Airbus A300s were acquired from January 1996, with A321s following later in the same year. A change of fleet policy took effect from early 1997, with the acquisition of an MD-88, which was used for the first time for the 1997 summer season to destinations where there were fewer passengers. The international popularity of Turkish holiday resorts has also brought about an increase in the number of flights to Eastern Europe.

Routes

Amsterdam, Ankara, Antalya, Barcelona, Berlin, Billund, Birmingham, Bodrum, Bremen, Brussels, Cologne/Bonn, Copenhagen, Dalaman, Düsseldorf, Edinburgh, Frankfurt, Geneva, Istanbul, Izmir, Hamburg, Hanover, Helsinki, Leipzig, Linz, Liverpool, London, Liège, Milan, Manchester, Moscow, Munich, Münster/Osnabrück, Naples, Nuremberg, Paris, Prague, Rome, Salzburg, Sofia, Stuttgart, Tel Aviv, Warsaw, Vienna, Zürich.

Fleet

5 Airbus A320-200
2 Airbus A321-100
2 Airbus A300B4
5 McDonnell Douglas MD-88

Boeing 747-367 AP-BFY (Thomas Kim/Toronto-YYZ)

PAKISTAN INTERNATIONAL AIRLINES

PIA Building, Quaid-e-Azam Intl.Airport, Karachi 75200, Pakistan, Tel. 21-4572011, Fax. 21-4570419, www.fly-pia.com

Three- / Two- letter code	IATA No.	Reg'n prefix	ICAO callsign
PIA / PK	214	AP	Pakistan

Pakistan Airlines was set up by the government in 1951 and began Super Constellation services on 7th June 1954, providing a valuable connection between East and West Pakistan. International routes to Cairo and London followed from February 1955 and on 10th March 1955 the airline was reorganised after formal amalgamation with Orient Airways, which had been founded in 1946 prior to the partitioning of India. Convair 240s and DC-3s were used for domestic and regional services, to be replaced by Vickers Viscounts and later HS Tridents. In 1960, long-range flights were taken over by Boeing 707s, and in 1961 New York was served for the first time. The first widebody was the DC-10-30 in 1974. Two Boeing 747s were leased from TAP - Air Portugal in 1976 and later bought, with further 747s added during the 1980s. During 1971 many services had to be suspended due to the war situation and the secession of East Pakistan to become Bangladesh. After reorganisation, flight operations picked up again in late 1972 and abandoned routes including New York reinstated. The backbone of the fleet are Airbus A310s for long-range routes and A300B4s for high-density short and medium range routes. Regional services are looked after primarily by Fokker F.27s, the first of which was delivered as long ago as 1961. During 1999 PIA took on five Boeing 747-300s from Singapore Airlines, and a revised colour scheme was applied to these aircraft. The main base, with a large maintenance complex, is at Karachi, with important hubs at Islamabad, Lahore, Peshawar and Quetta.

Routes

Abu Dhabi, Al Ain, Amsterdam, Athens, Bahrain, Bangkok, Beijing, Birmingham, Colombo, Copenhagen, Dammam, Dacca, Delhi, Doha, Dubai, Frankfurt, Islamabad, Istanbul, Jeddah, Karachi, Kathmandu, Kuala Lumpur, Kuwait, London, Manchester, Manila, Mumbai, Muscat, New York, Oslo, Paris, Riyadh, Rome, Shannon, Sharjah, Singapore, Tashkent, Tokyo, Toronto and over 30 domestic destinations.

Fleet

6 Airbus A310-300	2 Boeing 707-300F
10 Airbus A300B4	6 Boeing 737-300
8 Boeing 747-200	2 De Havilland DHC-6
5 Boeing 747-300	13 Fokker F.27

Boeing 737-4Y0 TC-AFU (Uwe Gleisberg/Salzburg)

PEGASUS

Istasyon Caddeshi, TR-34800 Istanbul
Turkey
Tel. 212-6632931, Fax. 212-6635458

Three- / Two- letter code	IATA No.	Reg'n prefix	ICAO callsign
PGT / PG	–	TC	Pegasus

At a time when tourism to Turkey was at a low ebb as a result of the Gulf conflict, in December 1989, Pegasus was set up by Aer Lingus. The new holiday airline began operations in April 1990. Tour operators and their potential customers were offered the latest in technology, in the form of the Boeing 737-400. Originally it was planned to use three aircraft from the outset, but because of the political situation, this did not come about. Nevertheless, with help from the parent company, the first season was successfully negotiated, and in 1992 the tourists started to return to Turkey. A further 737-400 was added and Pegasus also leased in two Airbus A320s and other aircraft for a time to meet peak-season demand. Development of the company continued satisfactorily and further aircraft were acquired. In 1994 the Istanbul-based Yapi Kreditbank took over the ownership from Aer Lingus, and Pegasus became a purely Turkish enterprise. During the Winter months, Pegasus aircraft could be seen in the Caribbean or in Canada, where they were leased out as there was a shortage of work for them in Europe. The first of the new model Boeing 737-800s was delivered in March 1999.

Routes

Charter flights from Germany, Finland, France, Great Britain, Ireland, Israel, Italy, the Netherlands, Norway, Austria, Switzerland, Spain and other countries to Antalya, Dalaman, Izmir and Istanbul in Turkey.

Fleet

6 Boeing 737-400
2 Boeing 737-800

Embraer RJ-145EP CS-TPK (Uwe Gleisberg/Munich)

PGA – PORTUGALIA

Avenida Almirante Gago Coutinho 88, 1700 Lisbon, Portugal, Tel. 1-8425500, Fax. 1-8425623, www.pga.pt

Three- / Two- letter code	IATA No.	Reg'n prefix	ICAO callsign
PGA / NI	685	CS	Portugalia

Portugalia was founded as a regional airline on 25th July 1989 and nearly a year later, on 7th July 1990 it began operations with a Fokker 100. During the first two years, losses were made equivalent to about US$12 million, but 1993 showed a small profit. With the introduction of the sixth Fokker 100 in 1995 the colour scheme was slightly modified. Especially in holiday times, PGA is also active with charter work and serves Portuguese destinations, particularly Faro, from various European airports. In May 1997 PGA took delivery of its first Regional Jet from Embraer, an RJ-145 and put it into service on an expanded route network. During 1999 the SAir Group agreed to acquire from the 80% owner Espirito Santo a 42% shareholding in PGA and the airline's activities were realigned in anticipation of this being completed. However, the move was blocked in mid-2000 by the European Commission on competition grounds. There are co-operation agreements with Crossair and Regional Airlines and some routes are flown as codeshares. Portugalia has its operating and maintenance base in Lisbon.

Routes

Barcelona, Basle, Bilbao, Bordeaux, Brussels, Cologne/Bonn, Faro, Las Palmas, Lisbon, Lyon, Madrid, Milan, Manchester, Marseilles, Nice, Palma de Mallorca, Porto, Stuttgart, Tenerife, Toulouse, Turin, Valencia, Vigo.

Fleet

9 Embraer RJ-145
6 Fokker 100

Airbus A320-214 RP-C3224 (Author's collection)

PHILIPPINES

1, Legaspi Street, Makati, Metro Manila 1059, Philippines, Tel. 02-8171234, Fax. 02-8136715, www.philippineair.com

Three- / Two- letter code	IATA No.	Reg'n prefix	ICAO callsign
PAL/ PR	079	RP	Philippine

Philippine Air Lines was set up on 26th February 1941, but had to suspend operations at the end of the year as a result of the Japanese invasion. After liberation, PAL restarted services with five DC-3s on 14th February 1946. Far East Air Transport, which had routes to Hong Kong, Shanghai, Bangkok and Calcutta, was taken over with its five DC-4s in 1947. In the same year PAL began scheduled service to San Francisco, but in 1954 all international routes except Hong Kong were suspended. This allowed an expansion of domestic services to take place. In 1962, in co-operation with KLM, the San

Francisco route was re-opened. From May 1966 BAC One-Elevens were introduced, and from 1969 Douglas DC-8s were used to start Amsterdam, Frankfurt and Rome services. In 1974 Air Manila and Filipinas were bought, and in this same year the first leased DC-10-30 arrived as a DC-8 replacement. Boeing 747s and Airbus A300 B4s were introduced in 1979 and with the arrival of Fokker 50s from1988 the older HS-748s were retired. Likewise The BAC One-Elevens were replaced by Boeing 737-300s. The newest jet in the fleet is the Airbus A340-300, introduced in 1996 alongside the Boeing 747-400s for

long-range routes. Further re-equipment for the future was expected until 1998, when on 23rd September, Philippines was forced to cease operations, as a result of employees' strikes and the general Asian downturn. After a few weeks of difficult negotiations, service was restarted with a sharply reduced route network, fleet and staff. A programme of reorganisation and reconstruction is showing some success during 2000, and it seems that PAL is on its way out of its crisis.

Routes

Bacolod, Bangkok, Butuan, Cagayan, Cebu, Cotabato, Dammam, Davao, Dipolog, Fukuoka, Hong Kong, Honolulu, Jeddah, Legaspi, Los Angeles, Manila, Osaka, Puerto Princesa, Riyadh, Roxas, San Francisco, Seoul, Singapore, Tacloban, Tokyo, Xiamen, Zamboango.

Fleet

3 Airbus A320
8 Airbus A330
2 Airbus A340-300
8 Boeing 737-300

4 Boeing 747-400

Boeing 737-219 CX-VVT (Romano Germann/Buenos Aires-AEP)

PLUNA

Colonia 1013-1021, P.O.Box 1360 Montevideo, Uruguay, Tel. 2-980606, Fax. 2-921478, www.pluna.com.uy

Three- / Two- letter code	IATA No.	Reg'n prefix	ICAO callsign
PUA / PU	286	CX	Pluna

Primeras Lineas Uruguayas de Navigacion Aerea – PLUNA – was founded in September 1935 by the Marquez Vaeza brothers. Operations began on 20th November 1936 with two de Havilland DH.90 Dragonflies. The company expanded and ordered a DH.86B, but then operations had to be suspended on 15th March 1943. After the end of the Second World War, the government of Uruguay acquired 83% of the airline's shares and on 12th November 1951 the remaining shares were also transferred to the state. Douglas DC-3s were used to operate to neighbouring countries, and a domestic network was set up. In addition to the DC-3s, de Havilland Herons and Vickers Viscounts were used. In late 1967 PLUNA took over the route network and aircraft belonging to CAUSA. The airline took on its first jet, a Boeing 737-200, late in 1969. Pluna's sole overseas route was a weekly service from Montevideo to Madrid; Boeing 707s were used on this route from 1982, but Pluna entered into a co-operation agreement with Spanair in 1993, whereby the Spanish airline operated the route with its Boeing 767s, as Pluna had no suitable aircraft of its own. This situation altered late in 1994, when Brazilian airline VARIG bought 51% of the shares in Pluna, thus bringing about the anticipated privatisation. Flights to Spain were restarted with a Douglas DC-10-30, painted in a new colour scheme. During 1998 the colours were again modified to more closely match those of Varig.

Routes

Asuncion, Buenos Aires, Cordoba, Madrid, Montevideo, Porto Alegre, Punta de Este, Rio de Janeiro, Rosario, Salvador de Bahia, Santiago de Chile, Sao Paulo.

Fleet

5 Boeing 737-200
1 Boeing 767-200ER

Boeing 747-132F N857FT (Josef Krauthäuser/Los Angeles-LAX)

POLAR AIR CARGO

100 Oceangate Long Beach, California 90802, USA, Tel. 562-5287471, Fax. 562-4369333, www.polaraircargo.com

Three- / Two- letter code	IATA No.	Reg'n prefix	ICAO callsign
PAC / PO	403	N	Polar Tiger

Polar Air Cargo was established in January 1993 and began scheduled freight services to Anchorage, Honolulu and New York in May 1993. Two Boeing 747-100 freighters were brought into service initially, with two more added later in the year. On 7th July 1994 the Federal Aviation Administration gave permission for the airline to carry out its own maintenance at its main base in New York and during the year more Boeing 747s were added, so that by the end of the year there were 12 in the fleet. Since then the purely 747 fleet has continued to grow, and the first of five new 747-400Fs is expected to be delivered in

October 2000. Alongside FedEx and UPS, Polar is one of the fastest growing cargo airlines, with worldwide scheduled and charter operations. The airline works with cargo agencies worldwide and offers a dependable service. The scheduled services to Europe, India, Africa and the Middle East were augmented with further new destinations from the mid 1990s. There are co-operation agreements with Finnair and Air New Zealand.

Routes

Scheduled freight services to Amsterdam, Anchorage, Atlanta, Auckland, Cali, Chicago, Dubai, Gander, Glasgow, Helsinki, Hong Kong, Honolulu, Khabarovsk, London, Los Angeles, Manaus, Manchester, Manila, Melbourne, Miami, Nadi, New York, Santiago, Sao Paulo, Sapporo, Seoul, Singapore, Sydney, Taipei, Tokyo.

Fleet

13 Boeing 747-100F
5 Boeing 747-200F

Ordered

5 Boeing 747-400F

Boeing 737-3Q8 5W-ILF (Uwe Gleisberg/Sydney)

POLYNESIAN

Beach Road, P.O.Box 599 Apia, Samoa
Tel. 685-21261, Fax. 685-25315,
www.polynesianairlines.co.nz

Three- / Two- letter code	IATA No.	Reg'n prefix	ICAO callsign
PAO / PH	162	5W	Polynesian

After the collapse of its predecessor, Samoan Airlines, Polynesian Airlines Limited was founded on 7th May 1959. Its first service was from Apia to Pago Pago, using a Percival Prince. After the independence of Polynesia in 1962, further routes to the Cook Islands were opened on 5th July 1963 and a Douglas DC-3 was acquired. In 1968 Polynesian took on a Douglas DC-4 and from January 1972 onwards modern turboprops were acquired in the form of two HS.748s. Modernisation became possible after the state took a 70% stake in the airline and made more capital available. Polynesian entered the jet age in 1981 with the delivery of a Boeing 737, which in turn allowed the addition of new routes to Australia. Various smaller aircraft such as GAF Nomads, Britten-Norman Islanders and de Havilland Twin Otters were also used on regional routes. In the early 1990s Polynesian acquired the latest Boeing 737-300. A Boeing 767 leased from Air New Zealand followed in 1993; this was used for routes to the United States, but proved to be too large and was returned. There is close co-operation and a marketing alliance with Air New Zealand and long-range services are now operated by ANZ under a codeshare agreement.

Polynesian also co-operates with Qantas and Air Pacific. A new model Boeing 737-800 is on order, for delivery in November 2000.

Routes

Apia, Asau, Auckland, Maota Savail Island, Nadi, Nine, Pago Pago, Sydney, Tongatapu, Vila, Wellington.

Fleet	Ordered
1 Boeing 737-300	1 Boeing 737-800
1 Britten-Norman Islander	
2 De Havilland DHC-6 Twin Otter	

Airbus A300B4 OY-CNK (Patrick Lutz/Palma de Mallorca)

PREMIAIR

Hangar 276, Copenhagen Airport South,
2791 Dragoer, Denmark, Tel. 32-477200,
Fax. 32-451220, www.premiair.dk

Three- / Two- letter code	IATA No.	Reg'n prefix	ICAO callsign
VKG / DK	630	OY	Viking

1st January 1994 marked the inauguration of a new airline which represented the amalgamation of two well-known charter companies. Conair had been founded in 1964 as Consolidated Aircraft Corp. and from the 1965 summer season had flown exclusively for the Spies holiday concern. First it used DC-7s, later Boeing 720s and Airbus A300B4s. Scanair meanwhile was started on 30th June 1961; SAS had a 45% holding in the company and provided the aircraft. After a reconstruction it was passed over to the SAS participants, DNL, DDL and ABA. As well as leased DC-8s, Boeing 727s and later DC-10s were used. In 1993 the pressure of competition for charter companies in Europe indicated that a merger would be a good idea. Spies had become the owner of Conair and over the years had also acquired a stake in Scanair. The merger was decided in November 1993 and executed in January 1994, with the aircraft all receiving a new unified Premiair colour scheme. The joint owners were Spies Holdings and the Scandinavian Leisure Group, and the airline's main base was at Copenhagen, with major operating bases at Oslo and Stockholm. Independence did not last for all that long, as in 1996 Airtours acquired Spies and its airline, Premiair, which was brought into the Airtours Aviation Division.The aircraft were repainted into Airtours colours, with only the titling distinguishing them as Premiair aircraft, but this does allow for ease of interchange between the fleets to meet changing demand. During 1999 two Airbus A330s were added for long-range routes including the Caribbean and Asia. The DC-10s are shortly to transfer to Airtours.

Routes

Charter flights to the traditional Mediterranean holiday areas, the Canary Isles, Northern Africa, and Asia and to Alpine Winter sports resorts.

Fleet

3 Airbus A300B4
4 Airbus A320-200
2 Airbus A330-200
5 McDonnell Douglas DC-10-10

Boeing 737-49R N460PR (Author's collection)

PRO AIR

101 Elliott Avenue West, Suite 500 Seattle, WA 98119, USA, Tel. 206-6236612, Fax. 206-6236612, www.proair.com

Three- / Two- letter code	IATA No.	Reg'n prefix	ICAO callsign
PRH / P9	–	N	Prohawk

Unlike many start-up airlines, Pro Air started services with two factory fresh Boeing 737-400s, thus hopefully assuring a good public acceptance of the airline from the outset, especially when considered alongside its attractive ticket prices and simply structured fare system. Pro Air was founded in 1996 by Kevin Stamper, a young lawyer who had spent some years with Boeing and with West Air. Using his own resources and with assistance from investors, Pro Air was established as a low-cost airline, the first for 25 years which had started off with new aircraft. Detroit City Airport (DET) was chosen as the airline's base;

Pro Air is the only airline operator here and enjoys all the advantages of low airport costs, abundant parking and proximity to the city. The first flight took place on 4th July 1997 to Baltimore/Washington, followed by services to Newark, Indianapolis and Milwaukee. Pro Air has often learned from its mistakes, and consolidation and an assured market are more important than fast expansion. Thus the build-up of the network and fleet has been relatively slow. As well as its scheduled services, Pro Air also flies charters, especially at weekends, to make best use of its aircraft. Associate Pro Air Express flies a pair of Saab 2000s.

As this book went to press in September 2000, the Federal Aviation Agency had just grounded the airline for failure to correct maintenance, oversight, quality control and record-keeping deficiencies, but the airline was appealing against this decision. It had however already dropped some loss-making routes in June 2000 and laid off nearly 100 employees.

Routes

Atlanta, Baltimore/Washington, Chicago Midway, Detroit City, Indianapolis, Newark, New York La Guardia, Orlando, Philadelphia, Seattle.

Fleet

2 Boeing 737-300
3 Boeing 737-400

Tupolev Tu-154M RA-85800 (Albert Kuhbandner)

PULKOVO

18/4 Pilotov Ul.196210 St.Petersburg, Russia
Tel. 812-1043302, Fax. 812-1043702,
www.pulkovo.ru

Three- / Two- letter code	IATA No.	Reg'n prefix	ICAO callsign
PLK / Z8	195	RA	Pulkovo

The former Leningrad Division of Aeroflot, just as with other former Aeroflot directorates, was recast into individual airline companies after the break up of the Soviet Union. Lacking any particular form of organisation, a non-scheduled operation was continued as Aeroflot. Only with the new formation of Aeroflot Russian International Airlines ARIA was the former state aviation reorganised. Thus in 1992 the Pulkovo Aviation Concern was established in St. Petersburg (formerly Leningrad), taking its name from its home base airfield of Pulkovo. Initially it took over the aircraft of the former Aeroflot division and flew both domestic and international routes on behalf of ARIA. After the concern renamed itself in 1996 as Pulkovo Aviation Enterprise and painted the aircraft in its own distinctive colours, it undertook a pruning of routes which had been unprofitable. Pulkovo still has a strategic alliance with Aeroflot ARIA and flies some routes on its behalf, under a sort of codeshare arrangement. Several new routes have been established from St. Petersburg to Western Europe. Pulkovo is also active in the charter and freight businesses.

Routes

Adler/Sochi, Almaty, Amsterdam, Archangelansk,Baku, Barnaul, Berlin, Bishkek, Chelyabinsk, Copenhagen, Düsseldorf, Frankfurt, Gyandzha, Hamburg, Hanover, Helsinki, Irkutsk, Kaliningrad, Karaganda, Kiev, Krasnodar, Krasnoyarsk, Mineralnye Vody, Moscow, Munich, Murmansk, Norilsk, Novosibirsk, Omsk, Petropovlovsk, Prague, Rostov, Samara, St. Petersburg, Stockholm, Surgut, Tashkent, Tbilisi, Tel Aviv, Tyumen, Ufa, Vienna, Vladivostok, Volgograd, Yekaterinburg, Yerevan.

Fleet

3 Antonov An-12
9 Ilyushin IL-86
11 Tupolev Tu-134

21 Tupolev Tu-154

Boeing 767-238ER VH-EAJ (Uwe Gleisberg/Coolangatta)

QANTAS

Qantas Centre, 203 Coward Street, Sydney, NSW 2020, Australia, Tel. 2-96913636, Fax. 2-9693339, www.qantas.com.au

Three- / Two- letter code	IATA No.	Reg'n prefix	ICAO callsign
QFA / QF	081	VH	Qantas

Queensland and Northern Territory Aerial Service Ltd. – QANTAS for short – was formed on 16th November 1920. Two Avro 504s were stationed at Longreach; initially the airline operated sightseeing and air taxi flights, and the first route from Charleville to Cloncurry was flown in November 1922. Qantas aircraft were also used to set up the famous Flying Doctor Service in 1928 and in the same year began the first scheduled air service in Australia, covering the 80 miles from Brisbane to Toowoomba. In co-operation with Imperial Airways, Qantas served the London-Brisbane route, with Qantas flying the last leg from Singapore to Brisbane from 1934, using Short Empire flying boats to Sydney from 1938. The airline was known as Qantas Empire Airways from 1934 to 1967. During the war, flights in Australia were almost halted, but post-war, Lockheed Constellations, DC-3s and DC-4s were all acquired. In 1947 the Australian government acquired a controlling interest and in 1953 Qantas took over British Common-wealth Airlines with its aircraft and routes to the USA. Boeing 707s were delivered from 1959, Boeing 747s from August 1971 and Boeing 767s from 1985, the latter also bringing a new aircraft livery. Australian Airlines, also state-owned, was integrated into Qantas from 1st November 1993, giving the airline a new domestic dimension, having previously been responsible for international services only. Qantas has shareholdings in Airlink, Eastern Australian Airlines, Southern Australian Airlines and Sunstates Airlines; these airlines fly feeder services for the national carrier. British Airways took a 25% stake in Qantas in 1992, and there is close co-operation, and as a natural consequence Qantas is a founder member of the Oneworld Alliance.

Routes

Adelaide, Alice Springs, Atlanta, Auckland, Bangkok, Brisbane, Buenos Aires, Cairns, Canberra, Chicago, Christchurch, Coolangatta, Darwin, Denpasar, Frankfurt, Harare, Hobart, Hong Kong, Honolulu, Jakarta, Johannesburg, London, Los Angeles, Manila, Melbourne, Mumbai, Nadi, Nagoya, New York, Noumea, Osaka, Papeete, Paris, Perth, Port Moresby, Queenstown, Rome, Shanghai, Singapore, Sydney, Taipei, Tokyo, Townsville, Wellington.

Fleet

16 Boeing 737-300	24 Boeing 747-400
22 Boeing 737-400	31 Boeing 767-200/300ER
9 Boeing 747-200/300	2 Boeing 747SP

Airbus A300-622R A7-ABN (Uwe Gleisberg/Munich)

QATAR AIRWAYS

P.O.Box 22550, Doha, Qatar
Tel. 621717, Fax. 621533,
www.qatarairways.com

Three- / Two- letter code	IATA No.	Reg'n prefix	ICAO callsign
QTR / QR	157	A7	Qatari

The Qatar government, though a shareholder in the multi-national Gulf Air, decided that it would like to have its own flag carrier, and as a result Qatar Airways was brought into being. It was founded on the personal initiative of the Emir in 1993. At first an Airbus A310 was leased and services commenced in January 1994 with a route to London. The initial choice of aircraft was obviously not a good one, and the Airbus was returned to its lessor and replaced by a Boeing 747SP in 1995. Likewise the pricing and route policies were obviously causing some difficulty, and the performance of the airline lagged behind

expectations. Boeing 727-200s were bought for use on regional services, a market which the airline wished to enter. A change in the management of the company in early 1997 however brought a change of direction; Qatar Airways was repositioned in the market and set out to become a quality carrier. New examples of the most modern aircraft were acquired, Airbus A300-600s for the longer routes and A320s for short and medium distances. Since then Qatar has expanded slowly and cautiously in new markets. Munich was added as a second European destination from 1999, in addition to London, but

Qatar's concentration is however in the Middle East and Asia. There is a co-operation and codeshare agreement with Lufthansa.

Routes

Abu Dhabi, Amman, Bangkok, Beirut, Cairo, Colombo, Dacca, Dammam, Doha, Dubai, Jeddah, Karachi, Kathmandu, Khartoum, Kuwait, Lahore, London, Manila, Mumbai, Munich, Peshawar, Trivandrum.

Fleet	Ordered
3 Airbus A300-600	5 Airbus A320
5 Airbus A320	
2 Boeing 727-200	

Lockheed L-188A Electra N9744C (Romano Germann/Anchorage)

REEVE ALEUTIAN

4700 West Intl.Airport Road Anchorage, Alaska 99502-1091, USA , Tel. 907-2431112, Fax. 907-2492317, www.reeveair.com

Three- / Two- letter code	IATA No.	Reg'n prefix	ICAO callsign
RVV / RV	338	N	Reeve

The airline was founded at Valdez, Alaska on 25th August 1932 by Bob Reeve, a famous Alaskan pilot and airline pioneer who had flown for PanAm in South America and was ready to try his luck in Alaska. The airline flew initially under the name of Reeve Airways and operated charters for various firms using a single-engined Eaglerock biplane. Reeve's first owned aeroplane was a Fairchild 51 with which he busied himself as a bush pilot. During the war years, Reeve worked principally for the government and undertook support flights using a Boeing 80 and a Fairchild 71. In 1946 he bought a DC-3 for $20,000 and

established a 'real airline' in Anchorage. In 1948 the US government invited tenders for flights to the Aleutian Islands in the north-western extremity of the USA. Reeve obtained the licence in January 1948, initially for a five year period, on account of his experience on the 1,800 mile long route, and this was also the rationale behind the change of name from 1951 to Reeve Aleutian Airways. The DC-3 was the ideal aircraft for use on flights to these inhospitable and sparsely populated places. The arrival of DC-4s enabled the airline to open up the group of Pribilof Islands, and further new types

followed: DC-6s in 1962, Lockheed Electras from 1968 and Boeing 727s in 1983. The only route outside Alaska was the link with Seattle, flown as charters, but more recently there have been operations to neighbouring Siberia. As Reeve looks after the air transport need of the islands with passenger/freight combi aircraft, the passenger total is relatively low. Reeve undertakes charter work, including many anglers during the season. The airline's base and departure point for all those who would still like to fly as a passenger in a Lockheed Electra is the international airport at Anchorage.

Routes

Adak, Anchorage, Bethel, Cold Bay, Dillingham, Dutch Harbour, King Salmon, Petropavlovsk, Port Heiden, Sand Point, St. Paul Island and Yuzhno-Sachalinsk.

Fleet

2 Boeing 727-100C
3 Lockheed L-188 Electra

Embraer RJ-145EU F-GRGG (Josef Krauthäuser/Munich)

REGIONAL AIRLINES

Aéroport Nantes Atlantique, F-44345
Bouguenais Cedex, France, Tel. 2-40135300,
Fax. 2-40135313, www.regionalairlines.com

Three- / Two- letter code	IATA No.	Reg'n prefix	ICAO callsign
RGI / VM	982	F	Regional

The merger of Air Vendée and Airlec in 1992 brought a new airline, Regional Airlines, into being. Both constituent airlines were active regional operators in France, and operated between them Dornier 228s, Fairchild-Swearingen Metros and other smaller types. From Nantes, Rouen and Rennes Regional Airlines built up its network. Clermont-Ferrand is also an important hub for the company, providing good connecting services to other French cities. The fleet also grew steadily and was always kept relatively young; BAe Jetstream 31s in 1993, Saab 2000s from 1995 and Embraer Brasilias from 1997. In

1997 Regional acquired Deutsche BA's regional fleet of Saab 340s and Saab 2000s, as well as some routes. Regional was one of the first European customers for the new Embraer Regional Jet series. The first of these RJ 145s was brought into use in May 1997 between Clermont-Ferrand and Paris. The smaller RJ-135 arrived at the beginning of 2000 and replaced the Jetstreams, and the larger RJ 170 is on order for delivery from mid 2002.. Air France took a shareholding in Regional Airlines quite early in its life, and has increased it so that the national airline now owns 70%.

Routes

Amsterdam, Angers, Angoulème, Barcelona Basle, Biarritz, Bilbao, Birmingham, Bordeaux, Bourges, Brussels, Caen, Clermont-Ferrand, Copenhagen, Dijon, Düsseldorf, Geneva, La Rochelle, Le Havre, Limoges, Lisbon, London-City, Lyon, Madrid, Milan, Montpellier, Munich, Nantes, Nice, Paris, Pau, Poitiers, Porto, Rennes, Rouen, St. Etienne, Strasbourg, Stuttgart, Tours, Toulouse, Turin.

Fleet		Ordered
8 Embraer EMB-120 Brasilia	7 Saab 2000	11 Embraer RJ-170ER
4 Embraer RJ-135		
15 Embraer RJ-145		

De Havilland DHC-8-314Q OE-LSB (Albert Kuhbandner/Munich)

RHEINTALFLUG

Bahnhofstr. 10a, 6900 Bregenz, Austria
Tel. 5574-48800, Fax. 5574-4880076,
www2.vol.at/Rheintalflug/

Three- / Two- letter code	IATA No.	Reg'n prefix	ICAO callsign
RTL / WE	915	OE	Rheintal

Founded in 1977 as a non-scheduled airline, regular flights began in 1984 from Hohenems (Vorarlberg) to Vienna. Eventually, in 1988 it was possible to establish a second route, from the neighbouring airport of Altenrhein in Switzerland to Vienna using a Grumman Jetprop Commander 900, an unusual choice for airline operation. From Autumn 1989 Rheintalflug also connected Friedrichshafen to Vienna with a daily off-peak return service, using a de Havilland DHC-8-100. Further DHC-8s were acquired, and until recently formed the only type in the fleet. There is an agreement with Austrian Airlines for through traffic from Bregenz/Altenrhein to Vienna. Since 1998 Rheintalflug has also flown as a Lufthansa Team Partner. The first Embraer RJ-145 jet was delivered to the airline at the beginning of 2000, and this has been used especially on the Vienna route. At weekends Rheintalflug flies charters for various tour operators.

Routes

Altenrhein, Berlin, Cologne/Bonn, Elba, Friedrichshafen, Graz, Hamburg, Klagenfurt, Münster/Osnabrück, Olbia, Palma de Mallorca, Rotterdam, Stuttgart, Vienna, Zürich. Additionally charter and non-scheduled flights.

Fleet	Ordered
4 De Havilland DHC-8-300	1 Embraer RJ-145
2 Embraer RJ-145	

Boeing 737-5Y0 PT-SLN (Björn Kannengiesser/Rio de Janeiro)

RIO-SUL

Avenida Rio Branco 85, CEP 20040-004 Rio de Janeiro, Brazil, Tel. 21-2168591, Fax. 21-2532044, www.voeriosul.com.br

Three- / Two- letter code	IATA No.	Reg'n prefix	ICAO callsign
RSL / SL	293	PT	Riosul

On 12th November 1976 the Brazilian government decree number 76590 imposed a new order on regional air transport. Five companies were contracted, each to build up regional air services in their allocated territories. Varig acquired shares in Top Taxi Aereo and thus in December 1976 formed Rio-Sul Servicos Aereos Regionais SA. The airline was allocated the southern area of Brazil and began building a network using Embraer 110 Bandeirantes. The Piper Navajos which had been taken over from Top Taxi were also used. The company showed satisfactory

development and in 1988 was in a position to order new Embraer 120 Brasilias, and these were put into service in the same year. In1992 the government changed its policy and allowed companies to expand beyond the regional boundaries which had been laid down in the 1976 decree. This gave the opportunity for the acquisition of new aircraft; the routes were longer and because of the size of the country could only be served by jets. Rio Sul received its first Boeing 737-500 in October 1992, with more following in the next few years and these were used to expand the

previous network. During 1995 Nordeste was taken over and their Fokker 50s integrated into the fleet. With the introduction of the Embraer RJ 145 in 1998 Rio Sul is on track to operating a purely jet fleet in the near future, as the Fokker 50s are phased out. The airline is based at Sao Paulo Congonhas International Airport.

Routes

Araguaina, Belem, Belo Horizonte, Brasilia, Campinas, Campos, Carajas, Cascavel, Caxias du Sul, Chapeco, Criciuma, Curitiba, Florianopolis, Goiania, Iguacu Falls, Ilheus, Imperatiz, Joinville, Lages, Livramento, Londrina, Maraba, Maringa, Navegantes, Passo Fundo, Pelotas, Porto Alegre, Porto Seguro, Recife, Ribeirao Preto, Rio de Janeiro, Rio Grande, Santa Maria, Santo Angelo, Sao Jose do Rio Preto, Sao Jose dos Campos, Sao Paulo, Toledo, Uberaba, Uruguaiana, Vitoria.

Fleet

16 Boeing 737-500
8 Embraer EMB-120 Brasilia
15 Embraer RJ-145
1 Fokker 50

Boeing 737-4H6 9M-MMC (Romano Germann/Phnom Penh)

ROYAL AIR CAMBODGE

206A Nordodom Blvd., Phnom Penh, Cambodia
Tel. 23-428830, Fax. 23-428806

Three- / Two- letter code	IATA No.	Reg'n prefix	ICAO callsign
RAC / VJ	658	XU	Cambodge

The first Royal Air Cambodge was until 1970 known as the national airline of Cambodia; its beginnings could be traced to 1956, at a time when the country was French Indo-China. After the many years of war and political instability in the country, a new civil airline was established in 1994 – Air Cambodia – which however was only active for a few months before its licence was withdrawn. The Cambodian authorities had other plans and had already talked with MHS (the parent company of Malaysia Airlines) about setting up another airline. This was founded in December 1994, with

Malaysia Airlines taking a 40% shareholding; it was therefore a joint venture of the government with MHS. At the beginning of 1995 service was started with a route to Kuala Lumpur using a leased Boeing 737-400. Further destinations followed, especially with an eye to the tourist markets, and ATR 42s and Yunshuji Y-12s were acquired to carry passengers on domestic routes. The famous ruins at Angkor Wat are the destination of thousands of tourists, mostly travelling from Thailand. Naturally there is close co-operation with Malaysia Airlines and some

flights are operated as codeshares. A military coup in the country in mid 1997 cast doubt on the future of the airline, with the MAC-owned 737s being grounded in Kuala Lumpur for a while and international services suspended and the new government thought to want a new arrangement. However, this has not come about, and Royal Air Cambodge continues to operate, though with a somewhat reduced fleet.

Routes

Bangkok, Battambang, Guangzhou, Ho Chi Minh, Hong Kong, Koh Kong, Kuala Lumpur, Mundulkiri, Phnom Penh, Ratanankiri, Shanghai, Siem Reap, Sihanoukville, Singapore, Stung Treng.

Fleet

1 ATR 72
2 Boeing 737-400
1 Harbin Yunshuji Y-12-II

Boeing 747-2B6B CN-RME (Pascal Mainzer/Frankfurt)

ROYAL AIR MAROC

Aéroport Arifa, Casablanca, Morocco
Tel. 3-361620, Fax. 3-3600520
www.royalairmaroc.com

Three- / Two- letter code	IATA No.	Reg'n prefix	ICAO callsign
RAM / AT	147	CN	Royal Air Maroc

The name Royal Air Maroc was introduced on 28th June 1957, after Morocco had gained independence from Spain and France. The state-owned airline emerged from Société Air Atlas and Avia Maroc Aérienne, which together formed the Compagnie Chérifienne des Transports Aériens (CCTA) on 25th June 1953. At first there were only domestic services and some routes to France using Junkers Ju 52s but these were soon replaced by Douglas DC-3s. In 1957 a Lockheed Constellation came into use and was employed on the newly introduced international routes, including for example New York . In July 1958 Royal Air Maroc received its first Caravelle. Boeing 707s were bought in 1975 for long-distance services, and Boeing 727s were acquired from 1970 for regional and medium length routes. The next fleet replacement programme commenced in July 1986 with the delivery of the first Boeing 757, and the first of the ATR 42s arrived in March 1989 for use on domestic services. In 1993 RAM acquired a widebody, a Boeing 747-400, and also from Boeing in 1994 came the 737-400 to replace the 727s and older model 737s. The latest generation of Boeing 737 has also been ordered by Royal Air Maroc, with the first 737-700s and -800s both arriving during 1999. The government owns almost all of the shares, though Air France and Iberia have small stakes, and there is an intention that the government would like it to be 25% privatised. Air Algerie, Air France, Gulf Air, Iberia, Libyan Airlines, TAP Air Portugal, TWA and Tunis Air all co-operate with Royal Air Maroc.

Routes

Abidjan, Abu Dhabi, Agadir, Algiers, Al Hoceima, Amsterdam, Athens, Bahrain, Bamako, Barcelona, Basle, Bordeaux, Brussels, Cairo, Casablanca, Conakry, Constantine, Dakar, Dhaklia, Dubai, Errachidia, Essaouria, Fez, Frankfurt, Gaza, Geneva, Jeddah, Johannesburg, Las Palmas, Laayoune, Libreville, Lisbon, London, Los Angeles, Lyon, Madrid, Milan, Malaga, Marseilles, Marrakesh, Miami, Montreal, Nador, New York, Niamey, Nice, Nouakchott, Oran, Orlando, Paris, Quarzazate, Oujda, Rabat, Riyadh, Rome, Tangier, Tetuan, Toulouse, Tunis, Zürich.

Fleet		Ordered
2 ATR 72	5 Boeing 737-800	1 Boeing 737-700
6 Boeing 737-200	1 Boeing 747-200	1 Boeing 737-800
7 Boeing 737-400	1 Boeing 747-400	
6 Boeing 737-500	2 Boeing 757-200	
5 Boeing 737-700		

Boeing 757-236 C-GRYO (Albert Kuhbandner/Munich)

ROYAL AVIATION

655 Stuart Graham North, Dorval H4Y 1E4
Canada, Tel. 514-8289000,
Fax. 514-8289096, www.royalair.com

Three- / Two- letter code	IATA No.	Reg'n prefix	ICAO callsign
ROY / QN	498	C	Roy

Royal Airlines was founded in 1992, stemming from Conifair Aviation which had been set up in 1979. Operations began with a Boeing 727 in April 1992, initially confined to Canadian domestic services and to destinations in Florida; a further 727 was added for the Winter season. Lockheed L-1011 TriStars supplemented the 727s from 1993 and allowed the airline to undertake flights to the Caribbean, one of the leading destinations for sun-hungry Canadians. Royal expanded strongly during the following years and further TriStars were bought. As with other Canadian charter companies, the seasons are split,

with the Summer seeing flights predominantly to Europe and in Winter to the warmer climes of the Caribbean, though Las Vegas has a year-round appeal. The first Airbus A310 joined the fleet in 1997, during which year Royal also bought Can Air Cargo and took over their Boeing 737-200F. A new organisation was set up, whereby Conifair would be responsible for technical matters and Royal Cargo for freight, as individual profit centres. The stock exchange listed company changed its name to Royal Aviation and in addition formed Royal Handling, a ground handling company operating at several Canadian

airports. A further subsidiary is Royal Vacations, an in-house operator responsible for filling the aircraft. Boeing 757-200s strengthened the fleet from 1998 and the Boeing 727s sold. Royal Express was a further creation and is responsible for scheduled services from Montreal-Dorval, using aircraft provided by Royal Aviation. The older TriStars have also made way for more Airbus A310s, the last two having been leased out. Following the Air Canada takeover of Canadian, Royal is doubling its domestic schedules from September 2000, with five extra Boeing 737-200s being added.

Routes

Calgary, Edmonton, Halifax, Montreal, Ottawa, Toronto, Vancouver, Winnipeg as scheduled services. Charter flights to Europe, USA, Mexico and to more than 30 destinations in the Caribbean.

Fleet

4 Airbus A310-300
3 Boeing 757-200
5 Boeing 737-200
1 Boeing 727-200F

Boeing 767-33AER V8-RBJ (Frank Fielitz/Frankfurt)

ROYAL BRUNEI

P.O.Box 737 Bandar Seri Begawan BS 8671,
Sultanate of Brunei, Tel. 2-240500,
Fax. 2-244737, www.bruneiair.com

Three- / Two- letter code	IATA No.	Reg'n prefix	ICAO callsign
RBA / BI	672	V8	Brunei

Royal Brunei Airlines was founded on 18th November 1974 as the national airline of Brunei Negara Darussalam and began operations on the Bandar Seri Bagawan to Singapore route on 14th May 1975. A few Boeing 737-200s were the mainstay of the fleet until three Boeing 757s were acquired, the first on 6th May 1986. When this aircraft was delivered Royal Brunei adopted an attractive new colour scheme, principally in yellow and white. A service to London Gatwick was flown by the 757s, but in order to be able to serve long-distance destinations non-stop, a leased Boeing 767 was acquired in June 1990, with the airline's own 767-300ERs following from 1992. The 757s took over some of the routes previously flown by the 737s, which were disposed of. An Airbus A340 delivered in 1993, although it wears Royal Brunei colours, is operated as the personal transport of the Sultan of Brunei (said to be the world's richest man). More Boeing 767s were added during 1993 and 1994, and in 1996 two Fokker 100s were acquired for regional routes, but these have now been sold. The airline is owned by the small, but rich state, and yet was still adversely affected by the Asian business crisis of the late 1990s so that as bookings reduced, expansion plans were shelved and the fleet and routes sharply reduced. It seems that the first part of 2000 has seen the situation stabilising.

Routes

Abu Dhabi, Balikpapan, Bandar Seri Begawan, Bangkok, Brisbane, Calcutta, Darwin, Denpasar, Dubai, Frankfurt, Hong Kong, Jakarta, Jeddah, Kota Kinabalu, Kuala Lumpur, Kuching, London, Manila, Perth, Singapore, Surabaya, Taipei.

Fleet

2 Boeing 757-200
7 Boeing 767-300ER
2 Fokker 100

Airbus A320-212 F-OHGB (Dennis Wehrmann/Hamburg)

ROYAL JORDANIAN

P.O.Box 302 Amman 11118, Jordan
Tel. 6-5679178, Fax. 6-5672527,
www.rja.com.jo

Three- / Two- letter code	IATA No.	Reg'n prefix	ICAO callsign
RJA / RJ	512	JY	Jordanian

King Hussein declared the establishment of the Jordanian national airline Alia on 8th December 1963. It succeeded Jordan Airways, which itself had succeeded Air Jordan of the Holy Land two years previously. Alia (meaning high-flying) was named after King Hussein's daughter. Operations began from 15th December 1963 from Amman to Beirut, Cairo and Kuwait with two Handley Page Dart Heralds and a Douglas DC-7. In 1964 a second DC-7 was added to the fleet. With the introduction of the SE 210 Caravelle a European route to Rome was opened for the first time in 1965; Paris and London followed in 1966. The DC-7s were destroyed during the Israeli-Arab Six Day War and later replaced by Fokker F.27s. The Jordanian government assumed full control of the airline in 1968. In 1969 the network was expanded to include Munich, Istanbul and Teheran, followed by Frankfurt in 1970. In 1971 Alia acquired its first Boeing 707; the Caravelle was replaced in 1973 by Boeing 727s and in 1977 two Boeing 747s were bought. Flights to New York and Los Angeles began in 1984; Alia was the first of the Arab national carriers to fly schedules to the USA, using 747s. TriStars joined the fleet in 1981, and Airbus A310s in 1986, along with a new colour scheme and the new name, Royal Jordanian. During the Gulf War of 1990/91 the airline suffered severe losses, so some aircraft had to be leased. From 1992 Berlin, Jakarta and Aden were served, and Athens reinstated. The arrival of the third Airbus A320 in March 1996 saw the retirement of the last Boeing 727. Likewise, the last TriStar left the fleet in1999; the Airbus A340 had been envisaged as a replacement, but proved too large and so more A310s were acquired instead.

Routes

Abu Dhabi, Aden, Al Ain, Algiers, Amman, Amsterdam, Ankara, Aqaba, Athens, Bahrain, Bangkok, Beirut, Berlin, Brussels, Cairo, Casablanca, Chicago, Colombo, Damascus, Dammam, Delhi, Doha, Dubai, Frankfurt, Gaza, Geneva, Istanbul, Jakarta, Jeddah, Karachi, Kuala Lumpur, Kuwait, Larnaca, London, Madrid, Montreal, Mumbai, Muscat, New York, Paris, Riyadh, Rome, Sanaa, Shannon, Tel Aviv, Tripoli, Tunis, Vienna and Zürich.

Fleet

8 Airbus A310-300
2 Airbus A310-200
5 Airbus A320-200

2 Boeing 707F

De Havilland DHC-6 Twin Otter 300 9N-ABU (Romano Germann/Kathmandu)

ROYAL NEPAL AIRLINES

RNAC Building, P.O.Box 401 Kantipath Kathmandu, 711000 Nepal, Tel. 1-220757, Fax. 1-225348, www.royalnepal.com

Three- / Two- letter code	IATA No.	Reg'n prefix	ICAO callsign
RNA / RA	285	9N	Royal Nepal

Royal Nepal Airlines Corporation Limited was founded by the government on 1st July 1958, replacing Indian Airlines which had operated domestic services for some eight years on Nepal's behalf. External services to such points as Delhi and Calcutta continued to be operated by Indian Airlines until 1960 when Royal Nepal took over Douglas DC-3s and later, Fokker F.27 Friendships, ideal aircraft for the harsh conditions of Nepal because they are so undemanding. Three HS.748s came into use in 1970, and the first Boeing 727 in June 1972. However, the airfield at mountainous Kathmandu had to be extended by that time, which was a difficult business; even today it is not possible for very large aircraft to take off and land there. The Boeing 727 was used to open service to Delhi. The acquisition of de Havilland Twin Otters in 1971 improved services to remote mountain villages with short runways. The delivery of the first Boeing 757s in 1987 and 1988 marked both a fleet replacement plan and an expansion of services to Europe; Frankfurt and London were both served for the first time from the 1989/90 Winter timetable. As demand on these international services to India and Europe grew, further 757s were added. From 1996 services to Shanghai in China and Osaka in Japan were also added. Royal Nepal has plans to acquire Boeing 767s, and smaller jets to replace the HS.748.

Routes

Bangalore, Bangkok, Bharatpur, Biratnagar, Calcutta, Delhi, Dubai, Frankfurt, Hong Kong, Jomsom, Kathmandu, London, Lukla, Manang, Mumbai, Osaka, Paris, Pokhara, Shanghai, Singapore and to about ten further destinations in Nepal.

Fleet

4 Boeing 757-200
1 BAe HS.748
7 De Havilland DHC-6

Boeing 737-204 EI-CJE (Jörg Thiel/London-STN)

RYANAIR

Corporate Building Dublin Airport, Republic of Ireland, Tel. 1-8444489, Fax. 1-8444401, www.ryanair.com

Three- / Two- letter code	IATA No.	Reg'n prefix	ICAO callsign
RYR / FR)	224	EI	Ryanair

Founded in May 1985, Ryanair quickly became a competitor to Aer Lingus on its regional services and flights to Great Britain. No airline has served more points in Ireland, nine airports in all at one time, than Ryanair. It used ATR 42s and BAC/Rombac One-Elevens, and took over Aer Lingus routes from Dublin to Munich and Dublin to Liverpool. Dublin to Luton was also an important route in the early years. Starting from March 1994 the fleet was completely changed over from One-Elevens to Boeing 737-200s. Ryan Air UK was set up in 1995 as a wholly-owned subsidiary and operates from Stansted as a low-cost airline. It has put established British airlines under pressure and has been a pioneer in cheap flights to Europe, with particular expansion since 1997. Secondary airports in the general area of business centres are the main destinations; this helps to keep operating costs as low as possible, and allows the ticket prices to be particularly attractive to passengers. Some of Ryanair's aircraft have been painted as 'logojets', carrying colourful advertising for cars, beer, newspapers or telephone services. As well as its scheduled services, Ryanair also offers charters and flies to Mediterranean holiday resorts on behalf of various tour operators. Over the years the fleet of second-hand 737-200s has been built up, but a switch to factory fresh 737-800s began in March 1999.

Routes

Aarhus, Ancona, Biarritz, Birmingham, Bournemouth, Brescia, Bristol, Brussels (Charleroi), Carcassonne, Cardiff, Cork, Dinard, Dublin, Florence, Frankfurt (Hahn), Genoa, Glasgow, Kerry, Knock, Kristianstad, Lamezia Terme, Leeds/Bradford, Liverpool, London-Stansted, Londonderry, Lübeck, Malmo, Manchester, Nimes, Oslo, Paris (Beauvais), Perpignan, Rimini, St. Etienne, Stockholm, Teesside, Turin, Venice.

Fleet	Ordered
21 Boeing 737-200	15 Boeing 737-800
10 Boeing 737-800	

Airbus A320-200 G-BXKD (Stefan Schlick/Puerto Vallarta)

RYAN INTERNATIONAL AIRLINES

6800 West Kellogg, Wichita,KS 67209, USA
Tel. 316-9420141, Fax. 316-9427949,
www.ryanintl.com

Three- / Two- letter code	IATA No.	Reg'n prefix	ICAO callsign
RYN / HS		N	Ryan International

Ryan Aviation has been in existence since 1972 as an airline operating charter flights and began operations on 3rd March 1973 as DeBoer Aviation. Ryan International was a division of these operations until it was sold in 1985 to the PHH group. In February 1989 Ronald Ryan bought the company back and started an airfreight service from Indianapolis for the US Mail using eight DC-9s and nine Boeing 727s. The airline operates worldwide as a subcontractor for Emery Worldwide, using further Boeing 727s. Ryan sought to increase its activities in the Pacific, and a Boeing 727 is used to fly freshly caught fish from Saipan to Japan, and freight is flown between the islands of Micronesia. A Boeing 737-200 was made available to a tour operator for passenger flights from Cleveland and Cincinnati; this service was extended to Atlantic City in 1995 and switched to Airbus A320 operation. The fleet was also increased in that year by the acquisition of further Boeing 727s to meet demand. However, Ryan operates no aircraft in its own colours; all are painted in the colours of the particular client and only some small external lettering indicates the identity of the real operator. Aircraft are leased in and out as seasonal demand varies.

Routes

Numerous freight services on behalf of the US Postal Service, Emery Worldwide and other companies. Passenger charters on behalf of tour companies including Apple Vacations and Trans Global Tours.

Fleet

```
 9 Airbus A320
 2 Boeing 737-200
 3 Boeing 737-400
31 Boeing 727
```

Airbus A321-211 OO-SUC (Josef Krauthäuser/Munich)

SABENA WORLD AIRLINES

Avenue E. Mounier, 1200 Bruxelles/Brussels, Belgium, Tel. 2-7233111, Fax. 2-7238399, www.sabena.com

Three- / Two- letter code	IATA No.	Reg'n prefix	ICAO callsign
SAB / SN	082	OO	Sabena

The Société Anonyme Belge d´Exploitation de la Navigation Aérienne (SABENA) was founded on 23rd May 1923 to succeed SNETA, founded in 1919; revenue flights began on 1st April 1924 from Rotterdam to Strasbourg via Brussels. The carrier was a pioneer with many African services; flights to the Congo began in 1925. From May 1940 to October 1945 European services were suspended, but African operations continued. Post-war Sabena quickly built up its network. Douglas DC-3s were used in Europe, replaced in 1950 by Convair 240s. A route to New York was opened in 1947 with DC-4s and later DC-6s, and from Brussels to the Congo. The famous DC-7 'Seven Seas' followed in 1957. The independence of the Belgian Congo to become Zaire in 1960 had a significant effect on Sabena, as services there had to cease. The first Boeing 707s were added to the fleet in 1960 and were used for flights to the USA. SE 210 Caravelles were used for European routes, followed by Boeing 727s from 1967, with 737s added from 1973. Widebodies, DC-10s, were added in 1971 and Boeing 747s from 1974. A310-300s acquired from 1984 were for use on busy medium-range services. Sabena entered a phase of close partnership with Air France in 1993, with Air France taking a 49% stake, but this did not last; after a major restructuring during 1994, Swissair took a holding in 1995 instead. Since then Sabena has been a member of the Qualiflyer Group and did show profits for the first time in years, but recent performance is again disappointing. The fleet (in new colours) has been unified around principally Airbus types, the A319, A320, A321 and A330. Sabena itself has shareholdings in Delta Air Transport, Sobelair and City Bird.

Routes

The route network covers most major cities in Europe, with further destinations in Africa, the Far East and the USA.

Fleet		Ordered
12 Airbus A319	2 Boeing 737-200	16 Airbus A319
3 Airbus A320	6 Boeing 737-300	2 Airbus A320
3 Airbus A321	3 Boeing 737-400	
10 Airbus A330	6 Boeing 737-500	
4 Airbus A340-300		

Avro RJ 100 N505MM (Josef Krauthäuser collection via Manfred Turek/San Andres)

SAM COLOMBIA

Apartado Aereo 1085, Medellin
Columbia
Tel. 4-2515544, Fax. 4-2510711

Three- / Two- letter code	IATA No.	Reg'n prefix	ICAO callsign
Sam / MM	334	HK	Sam

In October 1945 the freight airline Sociedad Aeronautica de Medellin was founded in Medellin. It began flying from 1st September 1946 from Medellin to Miami, initially using Douglas DC-3s, which were also used to build up domestic services in Colombia. From 1950 larger Curtiss C-46 Commandos were added and these were used from 1955 to operate passenger flights also, under the name of Rutas Aereas de Columbia. KLM gave assistance in developing the airline with Douglas DC-4s and the flights to Rio de Janeiro were increased. However the end came for Rutas and SAM in 1962 when they were liquidated. The Avianca subsidiary company Aerotaxi SA took over the remains of the company in the same year however, and continued the business as Sociedad Aeronautica de Medellin Consolidata SA (SAM). Lockheed L-188 Electras took over the passenger services, leaving the DC-4s for freight work only. Medellin remained the base with Cali and Bogota as further hubs for both domestic and international services. Boeing 727s came into use as the first jets from 1982, but during 1994/95 the whole fleet was turned over to Avro RJ 100s. An MD-83 was acquired late in 1999, and the leased Avro RJ 100s are being returned. SAM continues to fly independently of its parent and has co-operation agreements with Avianca, Air Aruba and Copa.

Routes

Aruba, Bahia Solano, Barranquilla, Bogota, Capurgana,Cartagena, Caucasia, Cucuta, Letica, Medellin, Monteira, Nuqui, Panama City, Providencia, Quibido, San Andres.

Fleet

7 Avro RJ 100
2 De Havilland DHC-6 Twin Otter
1 McDonnell Douglas MD-83

Boeing 777-268 HZ-AKB (Uwe Gleisberg/Munich)

SAUDI ARABIAN AIRLINES

P.O.Box 620, CC181 Jeddah 21231, Saudi Arabia, Tel. 2-6860000, Fax. 2-6864552, www.saudiairlines.com

Three- / Two- letter code	IATA No.	Reg'n prefix	ICAO callsign
SVA / SV	065	HZ	Saudia

Saudi Arabian Airlines, the national carrier of the Kingdom of Saudi Arabia, was founded in late 1945 as the Saudi Arabian Airlines Corporation, but came to be known for most of its history as Saudia. Flights began from 14th March 1947 with Douglas DC-3s. In the early 1950s, five Bristol Freighter 21s, DC-4s and Convair 340s were used. The jet age began in April 1962 with the introduction of the Boeing 720B, which was used to start longer-distance services including Cairo, Karachi and Bombay, and in 1968 to London, Rome, Geneva and Frankfurt. In 1975 came the first widebody, the Lockheed TriStar,

with the Boeing 747 added from June 1977. The always cautious expansion policy has led Saudia to become the leading airline in the Arab world, and with about 11 million passengers a year, one of the world's largest international airlines. The fleet age is kept low and aircraft manufacturers in the USA and Europe are always looking for lucrative fleet renewal contracts. As soon as a massive new order for US aircraft had been announced at the beginning of 1996, a new corporate image was introduced and applied as the aircraft were delivered, and the name changed from Saudia to the present style.

Two new types were added from 1997, the McDonnell Douglas MD-90 and the MD-11 freighter, with Boeing 777s arriving from early 1998, replacing the last of the TriStars. Also operating in Saudi Arabian colours are the aircraft of the Saudi royal family and various government machines; these have their own VIP division. Saudi Arabian Airlines' base is at Jeddah, with further major operating bases at Riyadh and Dhahran.

Routes

Saudia Arabian Airlines flies from Jeddah, Dhahran and Riyadh to about 25 regional and over 50 international destinations in Europe, Africa, Asia and the USA.

Fleet		Ordered
11 Airbus A300-600	22 Boeing 777	3 Boeing 777
15 Boeing 737-200	4 (Boeing) McDonnell Douglas MD-11F	
1 Boeing 747SP	29 Mc Donnell Douglas MD-90	
20 Boeing 747-100/200/300		
5 Boeing 747-400		

Boeing 737-683 SE-DNM (Josef Krauthäuser/Munich)

SCANDINAVIAN – SAS

Fack, 19587 Stockholm-Bromma, Sweden
Tel. 8-7970000, Fax. 8-857980,
www.scandinavian.net

Three- / Two- letter code	IATA No.	Reg'n prefix	ICAO callsign
SAS / SK	117	SE/OY/LN	Scandinavian

SAS - Scandinavian Airlines came into existence on 1st August 1946 by the merger of DDL (Denmark), DNL (Norway) and ABA (Sweden), all of which were formed in the 1920s, except for DDL in 1918. The realisation that these three countries could not operate flights independently meant that old plans from 1940 were revived after the war. SAS started scheduled flights on 9th September 1946 with a DC-4 from Stockholm via Copenhagen to New York. A route to Buenos Aires was opened in 1946 and Bangkok from 1949. Johannesburg was added from 1953 with DC-6s. SAS's pioneering effort was to explore the polar routes to Los Angeles and Tokyo, which were opened on 15th November 1954 and 24th February 1957 respectively. In Europe, Saab Scandias and Convair 440s were used in addition to DC-3s. SAS's first jet was the SE 210 Caravelle, first used in 1959 from Copenhagen to Beirut. The DC-8 followed in 1960 for intercontinental routes, replacing DC-6s and DC-7s. In early 1971 came the first widebody, the Boeing 747; DC-10s and Airbus A300B4s were added in the late 1970s. Structural changes in the company and adjustment of capacity led to the sale of the 747s and Airbus A300s in the mid-1980s. MD-80s and Boeing 767s were ordered. A few MD-90s were also added in the mid-1990s but the main type for short and medium haul is now the Boeing 737, in various models, but principally the -600. The first of these was delivered in late 1998 and was the first aircraft to wear the new colour scheme. Current orders for future deliveries however favour Airbus. SAS is a member of the Star Alliance and has shareholdings in various other airlines including Air Baltic, Air Botnia, British Midland, Cimber Air, Groenlandsflyg, Skyways, Spanair and Wideroes. It took over and absorbed Linjeflyg in 1995.

Routes

Intensive network serving over 100 destinations in over 35 countries in Europe, North America, Africa and Asia.

Fleet / Ordered

Fleet		Ordered
30 Boeing 737-600	19 Douglas DC-9-41	6 Airbus A340
6 Boeing 737-700	51 McDonnell Douglas MD-81/82/83	4 Airbus A330
6 Boeing 737-800	16 McDonnell Douglas MD-87	12 Airbus A321
14 Boeing 767-300ER	8 McDonnell Douglas MD-90	9 Boeing 737-800
3 Douglas DC-9-21		

Boeing 767-36D B-2567 (Author's collection/Beijing)

SHANGHAI AIRLINES

212, Jiangning Road, 200040 Shanghai,
People's Republic of China, Tel. 21-62558888,
Fax. 21-62558107, www.shanghai-air.com

Three- / Two- letter code	IATA No.	Reg'n prefix	ICAO callsign
CSH / FM	774	B	Shanghaiair

As early as 1985 an airline was formed by the regional government of the Shanghai district. At that time it was not possible for aircraft to fly in their own colours, but it was the first airline in China to become independent from the all-embracing CAAC. Five Boeing 707s were used in CAAC livery on domestic services, but in 1988 one of these 707s appeared in Shanghai's own insignia. The airline's first Boeing 757 was delivered in August 1989 in the full colour scheme which is still in use today. Maintaining the all-Boeing fleet stance, 767s were introduced from 1994 and used for flights to Beijing and other major cities. Until 1997, Shanghai Airlines flew scheduled and charter flights only within the Peoples' Republic of China, but in that year it was given licences for international services, and began to fly to Bangkok, Hong Kong, Macau and Singapore. The fleet was further expanded and from 1998 the new generation Boeing 737-700 was added; further examples of this and of the 737-800 are on order for 2001 delivery, as are the first non-Boeing types, Canadair Regional Jets. The airline's base and home airport is Shanghai, and over 25% of its shares are privately-owned.

Routes

Beijing, Chengdu, Chongquing, Dalian, Fuzhou, Guangzhou, Guilin, Guiyang, Haiku, Harbin, Jinghong, Kaoshiung, Kunming, Macau, Ningbo, Shantou, Shenyang, Shenzen, Singapore, Wenzhou, Xiamen, Xian, Xining, Yantai, Yinchuan.

Fleet	Ordered
7 Boeing 757-200	3 Boeing 737-700
4 Boeing 767-300	3 Boeing 737-800
3 Boeing 737-700	3 Canadair RJ 200ER

Airbus A320-231 SU-RAB (Romano Germann/Paris-CDG)

SHOROUK AIR

2, El Shaheed Ismail Fahmy, P.O.Box 2684
Heliopolis-Cairo, Egypt
Tel. 2- 4172313, Fax. 2- 4172311

Three- / Two- letter code	IATA No.	Reg'n prefix	ICAO callsign
SHK(7Q	273	SU	Shorouk

Shorouk Air is a Cairo-based joint venture set up by Egypt Air and Kuwait Airways in 1992; the shares are held 51% and 49% respectively. Charter flights from Western Europe to Egypt were begun in the same year, as well as scheduled services in the Middle East, using a pair of new Airbus A320s. It was intended that Shorouk should operate cargo flights, particularly on behalf of Kuwait Airways, using Boeing 757-200PFs, but because of poor business results brought about by the effects of the Gulf War, the aircraft were not delivered. Similarly, Egyptian tourism has been badly affected by terrorist threats and attacks, causing visitors to stay away, and this has left Shorouk short of passengers. Thus the airline has turned its attentions to sub-charter work for other airlines including Air Sinai and Egyptair, especially at Hadj time, with many flights to Jeddah. A third A320 was however delivered to the airline at the end of 1999.

Routes

Scheduled services from Cairo to Beirut; charter flights from various points in Europe to Hurghada, Cairo and Luxor.

Fleet

3 Airbus A320-200

Tupolev Tu-154 M RA-85705 (Dennis Wehrmann/Hanover)

SIBERIA AIRLINES

Tolmachevo Airport, Ob-4, Novosibirsk 633115
Russia
Tel. 3832-599011, Fax. 3832-599064

Three- / Two- letter code	IATA No.	Reg'n prefix	ICAO callsign
SBI / S7	421	RA	Siberia Airlines

Aviakompania Sibir developed from the Tolmachevo State Enterprise, which was founded in 1992 in Ob, a town in the vicinity of Novosibirsk in Eastern Russia. As with most Russian airlines, its basis was in the former Aeroflot Novosibirsk division, from which it took over routes and aircraft. Moscow-Vnukovo and Novosibirsk-Tolmachevo were the two most important airports for the new airline, which also used the name Sibir and later Siberia Airlines. The company developed very positively, and alliances were set up with several other companies in Siberia including Chita Avia, Baikal and Novokuznetsk, with the intention that several smaller companies could be brought together under the Siberia Airlines name to mutual benefit and thus operate more profitably. As one of the more modern and well-organised airlines in the former Soviet Union Siberia is profitable and is able to finance the acquisition of new aircraft. The Tupolev Tu-204 was brought into use from December 1999 and the Tupolev Tu-154s and Ilyushin IL-86 have been modernised, as they are used on routes to Western Europe.

Routes

Adler/Sochi, Baku, Barnaul, Beijing, Bishkek, Blagoveschensk, Bratsk, Chita, Dubai, Dushanbe, Düsseldorf, Frankfurt, Hanover, Irkutsk, Kemerov, Krasnodar, Mineralnye Vody, Moscow, Novokuznetsk, Novosibirsk, Omsk, Orenburg, Petropavlovsk-Kamchats, Samara, Simferopol, St. Petersburg, Tashkent, Tel Aviv, Tianjin, Tomsk, Ufa, Urumqui, Vladivostok, Yakutsk, Yerevan.

Fleet

3 Antonov An-26/32
8 Ilyushin IL-86
1 Tupolev Tu-134

23 Tupolev Tu-154
1 Tupolev Tu-204

Airbus A320-232 B-2342 (Author's collection/Beijing)

SICHUAN AIRLINES

9 Nan Sanduan Yihuan Road, Chengdu 610041, People's Republic of China, Tel. 28-5551161, Fax. 28-5582641, www.hpis.com/sichuan/sichuan.htm

Three- / Two- letter code	IATA No.	Reg'n prefix	ICAO callsign
CSC / 3U	–	B	Chuanghang

In 1986 the regional government of the Sichuan province of China perceived a need for its own airline. After bureaucratic squabbles with the mighty CAAC, the new airline was in a position to commence services in July 1988 with Yunshuji Y-7s. The first and for a while only service was from Chengdu to Wanxian on the Yangtse River. More Y-7s were added in 1990 and the company's own colours were applied to the aircraft. At the end of 1991 Tupolev Tu-154Ms were acquired for use on a new service to Beijing. Western aircraft in the form of three Airbus A320s leased from ILFC appeared at the very end of 1995 and in early 1996, leading to a further expansion. In spite of this the airline is still only active within the confines of the Peoples' Republic of China, with no current plans for international routes. Late in 1997 the Xingxing alliance was formed, a co-operation between Sichuan Airlines, Hainan Airlines, Shandong Airlines, Shenzen Airlines, Wuhan Air and Zhongyuan Airlines. The delivery of new Airbus A320s and A321s during 1998 and 1999 has brought the fleet up to a modern standard, and Embraer Regional Jets are being added during the current year 2000.

Routes

Beijing, Chengdu, Chongqing, Daxian, Guangzhou, Guilin, Haikou, Harbin, Jian, Kunming, Luzhou, Nanchang, Nanjing, Shanghai, Shantou, Shenzen, Wanxian, Wenzhou, Wuhan, Xichang, Yibin, Zhengzhou.

Fleet	Ordered
5 Airbus A320	5 Embraer RJ 145LR
2 Airbus A321	
4 Tupolev Tu-154M	
5 Yunshiji Y-7-100	

Airbus A319-132 9V-SBB (Dennis Wehrmann/Hamburg)

SILKAIR

P.O. Box 501, Singapore 9181, Singapore,
Tel. 5428111, Fax. 5420023,
www.silkair.net

Three- / Two- letter code	IATA No.	Reg'n prefix	ICAO callsign
SLK / MI	629	9V	Silkair

Tradewinds Charters was founded in October 1976 as a subsidiary of Singapore Airlines to carry out its non-scheduled passenger flights. Its operations consisted of inclusive-tour work, oil-crew changes and ad hoc charters. Some flights were operated in the region from Seletar airport until 1988; it leased its aircraft from SIA as needed. Using MD-87s on scheduled flights to five destinations in Malaysia and Brunei, Tradewinds became Singapore's second scheduled airline operator. In 1991 the airline was renamed as Silkair. New routes were opened to Cebu, Medan, Phnom Penh and Ho Chi Minh City. Apart from scheduled flights, the airline continues with its charter work from its base at Singapore's Changi airport. In 1990 the fleet was augmented by the Boeing 737, and for a short while Airbus A310s seconded from the parent company were also in use. Two Fokker 70s were acquired in 1995 for short-haul work, but both these and the 737s were to be ousted by a complete changeover of the fleet to exclusively Airbus A320s (first delivered in Autumn 1998) and A319s (first arrival Autumn 1999).

Routes

Balikpapan, Cebu, Chiang Mai, Davao, Hat Yai, Jakarta, Kunming, Langkawi, Manado, Mataram, Medan, Padang, Pekanbaru, Phnom Penh, Phuket, Singapore, Solo City, Ujung Padan, Xiamen, Yangon.

Fleet	Ordered
3 Airbus A319	2 Airbus A319
4 Airbus A320	1 Airbus A320

Boeing 777-212 9V-SQF (Uwe Gleisberg/Perth)

SINGAPORE AIRLINES

P.O.Box 501, 25 Airline Road, Singapore
819829, Tel. 5423333, Fax. 5455034,
www.singaporeair.com

Three- / Two- letter code	IATA No.	Reg'n prefix	ICAO callsign
SIA / SQ	618	9V	Singapore

Singapore Airlines was formed on 28th January 1972 as the wholly government owned national airline to succeed the jointly-operated Malaysia-Singapore Airlines. Operations began on 1st October 1972, with Boeing 707s and 737s taken over from MSA, but in 1973 the changeover was quickly made to Boeing 747-200s. Since then Singapore Airlines has been one of those companies which is continually expanding. Concordes were used with British Airways on a joint London-Bahrain-Singapore route, but it was not a success and ended in 1980. More 747s were added, allowing expansion of routes to Australia, New Zealand, the USA and Europe. From 1979 there were daily flights via Honolulu to San Francisco. Airbus A310s were added from 1984 for Asian regional routes and Boeing 727s and 757s and DC-10s were also used, but the fleet was then rationalised around the 747 and A310. The first 747-400s were delivered in December 1988 and the first 747 freighter in 1989, with a new dedicated freight terminal opened at the new Changi airport in 1995. Famous for its good service and up-to-the-minute fleet, Singapore Airlines carries each year five times more passengers than the entire population of its home country. New Airbus A340s augmented the long-haul fleet , coming into service from Spring 1996; a year later the Boeing 777 was also introduced. With Swissair and Delta, Singapore built up the Quality Alliance, but in April 2000 joined the Star Alliance. Silkair (see page 313) is a 100% subsidiary company, and since 1999 Singapore Airlines has a 49% holding in Virgin Atlantic. The airline is based at Changi, where over 3,000 are employed at the airline's huge maintenance base.

Routes

Adelaide, Amsterdam, Anchorage, Athens, Auckland, Bandar Seri Begawan, Bangalore, Bangkok, Beijing, Beirut, Brussels, Cairns, Capetown, Chennai, Chicago, Christchurch, Colombo, Copenhagen, Dacca, Delhi, Denpasar, Durban,Dubai, Frankfurt, Fukuoka, Guangzhou, Hanoi, Hiroshima, Ho Chi Minh City, Hong Kong, Istanbul, Jakarta, Johannesburg, Kathmandu, Kuala Lumpur, Lahore, Los Angeles, London, Macau, Madrid, Manchester, Manila, Mauritius, Melbourne, Mumbai, Paris, Perth, Rome, San Francisco, Seoul, Shanghai, Sharjah, Singapore, Sydney, Taipei, Vancouver, Vienna and Zürich.

Fleet		Ordered
15 Airbus A310-300	5 Boeing 747-300	20 Boeing 777
15 Airbus A340-300	8 Boeing 747-400F	5 Boeing 747-400
38 Boeing 747-400	20 Boeing 777-200/300	

Airbus A330-322 C-FBUS (Josef Krauthäuser/Toronto)

SKYSERVICE AIRLINES

9785 Ryan Avenue, Dorval, Quebec H9P 1A2
Canada, Tel. 514-6361626, Fax. 514-6364855,
www.skyservice.com

Three- / Two- letter code	IATA No.	Reg'n prefix	ICAO callsign
SSV / 6J	884	C	Skytour

Skyservice was set up in 1994 as an air taxi and business flight company. Using several business jets, non-scheduled flights were operated in Canada and the United States. Charter flights for small groups were also undertaken, and for these a Jetstream 31 was available. From 1995 larger-scale seasonal charter flights were offered for the first time, and suitable aircraft leased in. The Airbus A320 was the favoured type, coming from ILFC and Monarch Airlines. Initially these activities were restricted to the Canadian wintertime, flying to the Caribbean and the warmer parts of the

southern United States. However, with the delivery of the airline's own first Airbus A330, this was all to change. The A330, the first of its type to be delivered to a North American operator, arrived in May 1997. During 1998 Airbus A320s were added to the airline's own fleet, which operated principally from Montreal and Toronto, and as demand dictated, further aircraft were leased in to provide additional capacity, including DC-10s from Airtours and A320s, again from Monarch. Skyservice operated its first charters to Europe from 1997. It also maintains a Boeing 727 for

Sports Hawks, and flies it on behalf of sports teams. In common with other Canadian independent operators, who have scrambled to establish scheduled services in the wake of the Air Canada takeover of Canadian, Skyservice is setting up a subsidiary called Rootsair to operate all business class services between eight Canadian cities from November 2000, using Airbus A320s and A330s.

Routes

Charter flights within Canada, to Europe, the Caribbean, Mexico and the USA.

Fleet

4 Airbus A320-200
1 Airbus A330
3 BAe Jetstream 31/32

Fokker 50 SE-LEB (Henning Landskerbsky/Stockholm-ARN)

SKYWAYS

Box 1537, 58115 Linköping, Sweden,
Tel. 13-375500, Fax. 13-375501,
www.skyways.se

Three- / Two- letter code	IATA No.	Reg'n prefix	ICAO callsign
SKX / JZ	752	SE	Skyexpress

Avia was founded in Visby, on the Swedish island of Gotland in the Baltic, as long ago as 1939, and during the 1980s used Beech and Cessna light aircraft to offer non-scheduled services, including operations to the mainland. Many Swedes like to go to Gotland during the Summer, which was Avia's high season. Larger aircraft, Shorts 330s and 360s were acquired. In 1991 Avia took over Salair, integrated their Saab SF340 fleet and became known as Avia & Salair AB. Using Salair's licence, activities were expanded markedly and the headquarters was moved to Norrköping. More Saab 340s were added to the fleet, which moved to a new base at Linköping in 1993. The year also marked the change of name to Skyways AB, with the company receiving its own licence in this new name. During 1995 the first Fokker 50 joined the fleet, and the Shorts 360s were ousted. Another smaller company, Highland Air, was acquired in 1997. SAS took a 25% shareholding in Skyways from 1998 and further shares are owned by Salenia AB, which is active in the leasing business. The latest type in the Skyways fleet is the Embraer 145, the first of which arrived in November 1998 for use on the longer routes.

Routes

Arvidsjaur, Bergen, Borlange, Brussels, Copenhagen, Galliväre, Gothenburg, Halmstad, Helsinki, Hemavan, Hultsfred, Kiruna, Kramfors, Linköping, Lulea, Lycksele, Malmö, Manchester, Mora, Norrköping, Orebro, Oskarshamm, Söderhamm, Stockholm, Sundsvall, Sveg, Trollhättan, Umea, Vaasa, Västeras, Växjo,Visby.

Fleet

5 Embraer RJ-145
13 Fokker 50
10 Saab 340

Embraer EMB-120ER Brasilia N236SW (Jörg Thiel/Las Vegas)

SKYWEST AIRLINES

444 South River Road, St.George Utah 84790 USA, Tel. 435- 6343000, Fax. 435-6343305, www.skywest.com

Three- / Two- letter code	IATA No.	Reg'n prefix	ICAO callsign
SKW / OO	302	N	Skywest

Skywest was established on 27th March 1972 in Salt Lake City, Utah, with services beginning just three months later with Swearingen Metros. After only a short time, routes were in place in the states of Arizona, Colorado, Idaho, California, Utah and Wyoming. A Californian competitor, Sun Aire was bought up in 1984. In 1986 new aircraft were acquired to meet new demands. During the mid-1980s the major US airlines were in the process of passing over the operation of regional services to smaller, established airlines. Thus Skywest became a partner for Delta Airlines, and introduced the modern 30-seater Embraer EMB-120 Brasilia turboprop. An extensive network was built up, radiating from Delta's important hub at Salt Lake City, and hand-in-hand with this was an expansion of the fleet with more Brasilias. The latter became the airline's standard type and had replaced the last of the Metros by 1989. The first Canadair Regional Jet joined the Skywest fleet at the beginning of 1994 and over time the whole fleet is being converted to this type. A further partnership agreement was concluded with United Airlines in 1997, covering a regional service as United Express with hubs at Los Angeles, San Francisco, Portland and Seattle/Tacoma. This service has been developed successfully, with aircraft flying either in Skywest colours or in those of United, and sometimes even in mixed livery.

Routes

Albuquerque, Arcata, Bakersfield, Bellingham, Billings, Boise, Bozeman, Butte, Calgary, Carlsbad, Casper, Cedar City, Chico, Cody, Colorado Springs, Crescent City, Elko, Eugene, Fresno, Grand Junction, Helena, Idaho Falls, Imperial, Inyokern, Jackson, Las Vegas, Los Angeles, Medford, Merced, Missoula, Modesto, Monterey, Omaha, Ontario, Oxnard, Palm Springs, Pasco, Pocatello, Portland, Rapid City, Redding, Redmond, Reno, Sacramento, Salt Lake City, San Diego, San Francisco, San Jose, San Luis Obispo, Santa Ana, Santa Maria, Santa Rosa, Seattle, Spokane, St.George, Sun Valley, Twin Falls, Vancouver, Vernal, West Yellowstone, Yakima, Yuma.

Fleet	Ordered
11 Canadair RJ 100	49 Canadair RJ 200
6 Canadair RJ 200	
98 Embraer EMB-120 Brasilia	

Boeing 767-33AER OO-SBY (B.I. Hengi/Zürich)

SOBELAIR

Building 117A Airport, 1930 Zaventem, Belgium
Tel. 2-7541211, Fax. 2-7541288,
www.sobelair.be

Three- / Two- letter code	IATA No.	Reg'n prefix	ICAO callsign
SLR / S3	–	OO	Sobelair

Société Belge de Transports par Air SA was established on 30th July 1946 and operations began in the following year with a Douglas DC-3. The intention was to provide charter flights, mainly to the Belgian Congo, with DC-4s. In 1948 Sabena acquired a controlling interest in Sobelair. From 1957 to 1962 a domestic network of routes was set up using Cessna 310s on behalf of Sabena within the Congo to supplement the main services operated by the Belgian national carrier. As well as a DC-6, Sobelair also acquired ex-Sabena SE 210 Caravelles as its first jet aircraft. Up to 1960 the major activity had involved schedules between Belgium and the Congo (now Zaire) but from then on, the airline has been operating mainly charter flights for holidaymakers to the Mediterranean. After the last Boeing 707 was sold in 1988, Sobelair used only Boeing 737s. When Sabena introduced a new colour scheme in Spring 1993, Sobelair's aircraft adopted a similar livery. The first of two Boeing 767-300ERs was delivered to Sobelair in 1994, with the second in Spring 1996, thus allowing long-range services to be flown. As requirements change seasonally, Sobelair leases aircraft in from Sabena and other carriers.

Within the SAir Group, Sobelair forms part of a so-called Leisure Alliance, along with Air Europe, Balair, LTU and Volare. The base is at Brussels-National.

Routes

To destinations in the Mediterranean, Canary Isles, Northern Africa, Caribbean and various other charters and subcharters.

Fleet

3 Boeing 737-300
3 Boeing 737-400
2 Boeing 767-300ER

Ordered

2 Boeing 767-300

Boeing 737-376 VH-TJB (Uwe Gleisberg/Sydney)

SOLOMONS

P.O.Box 23, Honiara, Solomon Islands
Tel. 677-20031, Fax. 677-23992,
www.solomonairlines.com.au

Three- / Two- letter code	IATA No.	Reg'n prefix	ICAO callsign
SOL / IE	193	H4	Solomon

Solair, a subsidiary of Macair (Melanesian Airline Charter Company) was founded on 1st May 1968. This had been preceded by the takeover of Megapode Airways' routes; the latter was an airline serving the Solomon Islands capital Honiara from Papua New Guinea since 1963. Solair's first flight took place on 1st June 1968. In September 1975 Solair was bought by Talair, also an airline from New Guinea, as a consequence of Talair's acquisition of Macair. It was only a while later that Solair became the property of the island administration, which acquired 49% of the shares in April 1979 and the balance in stages by 1985. In the mid-1980s a Brisbane service from the Solomon Islands was introduced in association with Air Pacific. The present name was introduced in early 1990. With a Boeing 737 added to the fleet, direct services to Nadi and Cairns started in 1993. The airline co-operates with Air Caledonie, Air Pacific, Air Nauru, Air Niugini, Air Vanuatu and Qantas, the latter also providing technical support.

Routes

Aulei, Arvavu, Ballalae, Barakona, Bellona, Brisbane, Choiswul Bay, Fera, Gizo, Honaira, Kirakiva, Marabu, Moro, Nadi, Noumea, Parasi, Port Moresby, Port Vila, Ramata, Rennell, Santa Ana, Santa Cruz, Segla, Suavanao, Sydney, Yandina.

Fleet

1 Boeing 737-300
3 De Havilland DHC-6
3 Britten-Norman BN-2 Islander

Airbus A300B2 ZS-SDD (Jörg D. Zmich/Johannesburg)

SOUTH AFRICAN AIRWAYS

SAA Towers, P.O.Box 7778, Johannesburg 2000, Republic of South Africa, Tel. 11-9781111, Fax. 11-9704387, www.saa.co.za

Three- / Two- letter code	IATA No.	Reg'n prefix	ICAO callsign
SAA / SA	083	ZS	Springbok

South African Airways was founded on 1st February 1934 when Union Airways passed into government ownership. Operations started the same day with a fleet of single-engined Junkers F-13s, later supplemented by a large number of Ju 52s and Ju 86s. Numerous routes were operated, including to Nairobi, until the outbreak of the Second World War. November 1945 saw the start of the 'Springbok' service to London, using DC-4s, DC-7s and Lockheed Constellations. The latter were also used to open a route to Perth in Australia in November 1957, and with the introduction of the

Boeing 707 from 1960 this was extended to Sydney. A further long-range route was opened to Rio de Janeiro in 1969. For political reasons, SAA was obliged to restrict its European services to a few points only; many African nations refused flyover rights. In order to be able to operate direct flights, Boeing 747SPs and later 747-300s with extreme long ranges were ordered. Airbus A300s and Boeing 737s were acquired for regional and domestic routes, replacing Vickers Viscounts and other older types. The first Airbus A320 was delivered to SAA in 1991 and in the same year the Boeing 747-400. After

the 1994 elections and change of political regime, the situation changed markedly for SAA; sanctions were lifted and it became possible to fly to any country, which resulted in new routes. Aircraft were painted in a new livery, based on the new national flag. A partial privatisation took place in 1999, with the SAir group taking 20% of SAA's capital. The latest type to join the fleet is the Boeing 737-800; deliveries commenced in May 2000. SAA has financial stakes in regional airlines SA Alliance Air, SA Airlink and SA Express. Its main bases are in Johannesburg, Durban and Capetown.

Routes

Abidjan, Accra, Atlanta, Bangkok, Blantyre, Buenos Aires, Bulawayo, Cairo, Capetown, Dar es Salaam, Durban, East London, Fort Lauderdale, Frankfurt, Harare, Hong Kong, Johannesburg, Kinshasa, Lagos, Lilongwe, Lome, London, Luanda, Lusaka, Maputo, Mauritius, Mumbai, Nairobi, Nelspruit, New York, Paris, Perth, Port Elizabeth, Sao Paulo, Sal, Singapore, Sydney, Windhoek, Zürich.

Fleet

Fleet		Ordered
8 Airbus A300	3 Boeing 747SP	12 Boeing 737-800
7 Airbus A320-200	4 Boeing 747-300	2 Boeing 777
1 Airbus A300F	8 Boeing 747-400	
12 Boeing 737-200	3 Boeing 767-200ER	
4 Boeing 737-800		
5 Boeing 747-200		

Boeing 737-3H4 N609SW 'California One' (Josef Krauthäuser/Las Vegas)

SOUTHWEST AIRLINES

PO Box 36611 Love Field, Dallas,TX 75235-1611
USA, Tel. 972 904 4000, Fax. 972 904 5097,
www.southwest.com

Three- / Two- letter code	IATA No.	Reg'n prefix	ICAO callsign
SWA / WN	526	N	Southwest

This famous low-cost pioneer came on the scene on 15th March 1967 under the name of Air Southwest, but it was some time before operations actually began. The established airlines tried their utmost to prevent the troublesome newcomer from taking to the air, as the airline intended to rock the boat by setting up a 'one class service' with particularly low fares. Major legal controversy for many years concerned Southwest's use of Love Field airport in Dallas; other airlines and some local officials tried to force the carrier to use the more distant Dallas-Fort Worth Regional Airport, which was then quite small. In March 1971 the airline's name was changed to Southwest Airlines, and in June 1971 service was begun from Dallas to Houston and San Antonio. The airline acquired Muse Air on 25th June 1985, renaming it TranStar in 1986, but operations of the subsidiary ceased due to losses in 1987. After deregulation in the United States, Southwest's fortunes soared. Expanding from initial operations restricted to the state of Texas only, it covers a wide swathe of the continental USA, with a massive, unified fleet composed entirely of the Boeing 737 in various models, and carrying ever more passengers to more destinations year on year. Utah-based Morris Air was acquired in December 1993 and completely integrated in 1995, and the long-neglected area in the South-East of the USA and Florida was brought into the network from 1996. Fleet renewal is in full flow with Boeing 737-700s being delivered from December 1997, and the East Coast area service is being strengthened, with a hub on Long Island. Southwest made a huge commitment for the new generation Boeing 737 in June 2000, for up to 290 737-700s worth $4.5 billion for delivery between 2003 and 2006, in addition to existing orders.

Routes

Albuquerque, Amarillo, Austin, Baltimore, Birmingham, Boise, Burbank, Chicago, Cleveland, Columbus, Corpus Christi, Dallas, Detroit, El Paso, Fort Lauderdale, Harlingen, Hartford, Houston, Indianapolis, Jackson, Jacksonville, Kansas City, Las Vegas, Little Rock, Long Island McArthur, Los Angeles, Louisville, Lubbock, Manchester, Midland/Odessa, Nashville, New Orleans, Oakland, Oklahoma City, Omaha, Ontario, Orlando, Phoenix, Portland, Providence, Raleigh/Durham, Reno, Sacramento, Salt Lake City, San Antonio, San Diego, San Francisco, San Jose, Santa Ana, Seattle, Spokane, St. Louis, Tampa, Tucson, Tulsa.

Fleet		Ordered
35 Boeing 737-200	73 Boeing 737-700	72 Boeing 737-700
195 Boeing 737-300		
25 Boeing 737-500		

McDonnell Douglas MD-83 EC-GBA (Albert Kuhbandner/Munich)

SPANAIR

Airport P.O.Box 50086, Palma de Mallorca
07000, Spain, Tel. 971-745020,
Fax. 971-492553, www.spanair.com

Three- / Two- letter code	IATA No.	Reg'n prefix	ICAO callsign
JKK / JK	680	EC	Spanair

The tour operators Vingresor AB and Scandinavia & Viajes Marsoms SA founded their own charter airline by the name of Spanair in 1987. It is based on the holiday island of Majorca. Operations commenced during March 1988 and a fleet of new MD-83s were leased from Irish Aerospace and Guinness Peat Aviation, primarily flying Scandinavian holidaymakers to the sunny beaches of Spain. Spanair also flies from UK and German airports and from Zürich and Salzburg and has increased its European coverage, and its fleet of MD-80 derivatives. When Boeing 767-300ERs were acquired in 1992 flights were also added to destinations in the USA, Mexico and the Caribbean. In addition to its basic charter business, from 1994 Spanair went into the scheduled service market from Madrid, Barcelona and other major cities and this part of the operation has seen steady growth. In order to provide the additional capacity for these services, the fleet has required expansion; new aircraft, Airbus A320s and A321s have been ordered for delivery from the later part of 2000.

Routes

Alicante, Arrecife, Asturias, Barcelona, Bilbao, Buenos Aires, Copenhagen, Frankfurt, Fuerteventura, Havana, Las Palmas, Lisbon, London, Madrid, Malabo, Malaga, Menorca, Palma de Mallorca, Rio de Janeiro, Santiago de Compostela, Sao Paulo, Seville, Stockholm, Tenerife, Valencia, Vigo and Washington as scheduled services, plus many charter destinations.

Fleet	Ordered
1 Boeing 757-200	10 Airbus A320
2 Boeing 767-300ER	4 Airbus A321
32 McDonnell Douglas MD-82/83	
3 McDonnell Douglas MD-87	

McDonnell Douglas MD-82 N801NK (Josef Krauthäuser/Fort Lauderdale)

SPIRIT AIRLINES

2800 Executive Way, Miramar, Florida 33025
USA, Tel. 954-4477965, Fax. 954-4477979,
www.spiritair.com

Three- / Two- letter code	IATA No.	Reg'n prefix	ICAO callsign
NKS / NK	487	N	Spirit Wings

Tour operator Charter One was set up in 1980 and organised day and weekend trips to the gambling and entertainment paradise of Atlantic City from Chicago, Boston, Detroit and Providence. From 1984 the company also specialised in short trips to the Bahamas. Success led the tour operator to offer accompanied Caribbean tours from 1987 and the addition of Las Vegas to the programme. Aircraft were leased from various different companies for these operations. In 1990 Charter One bought a pair of Convair 580s and applied for a scheduled service licence, which

was granted on 8th September, allowing flights to Atlantic City to be started. In 1992 four DC-9-32s were leased and the name changed to Spirit Airlines. Florida was the declared objective and so services were offered from Boston, Chicago and Detroit to Miami, Fort Lauderdale, Fort Myers and Tampa. As the number of new services grew, so did the fleet and further DC-9-41 were added. The base was at Detroit and within a few months a move was made into larger premises at this airport. During 1996 services from Cleveland and Newark were added. The important New

York market was tapped for the first time in 1998, and further Florida destinations were added at Myrtle Beach, Melbourne and Orlando. MD-80s were also used for the first time, as the market for suitable used DC-9s was exhausted. Additional aircraft are also leased in on a seasonal basis. During 1999 Spirit also began flights from Detroit to Los Angeles, and a new headquarters was established at Miramar, Florida.

Routes

Atlantic City, Cleveland, Detroit, Fort Lauderdale, Fort Myers, Long Island MacArthur, Los Angeles, Melbourne, Myrtle Beach, New York, Orlando, Tampa, West Palm Beach.

Fleet

11 Douglas DC-9-30/40
13 McDonnell Douglas MD-81/82
 2 McDonnell Douglas MD-87

Airbus A340-312 4R-ADD (Stefan Quanz/Frankfurt)

SRILANKAN

37, York Street, Colombo, Sri Lanka
Tel. 1-735555, Fax. 1-735122,
www.airlanka.com

Three- / Two- letter code	IATA No.	Reg'n prefix	ICAO callsign
ALK / UL	603	4R	Airlanka

Air Lanka was set up on 10th January 1979 in order to continue the business of Air Ceylon, which had ceased operations in 1978. The airline was then 60% owned by the Sri Lankan government and 40% by local businesses. Management and technical assistance was supplied by Singapore Airlines. Operations started on 1st September 1979 with two Boeing 707s leased from SIA. The first TriStar owned by the airline flew from Colombo to Paris on 2nd November 1990; Zürich, Frankfurt and London soon followed. For a while a leased Boeing 747 was used to London Gatwick, but because of an unstable political situation in Sri

Lanka, passenger numbers were insufficient. The Boeing 737 was acquired for regional flights to India and the Maldives. A planned renewal of the long-distance fleet had to be postponed in 1993 as financing for the planned Airbus A340s was not initially possible. However this was in time arranged through an international banking consortium and in Autumn 1994 the first two A340s joined the fleet. Further examples followed in 1995 and 1995, replacing the TriStars. During 1999 Emirates took a shareholding in Air Lanka, which was restructured. The airline changed its name to SriLankan, at

the same time adopting a whole new corporate identity and aircraft colours. With the delivery of new Airbus A330s from 2000 new destinations including Berlin, Stockholm and Sydney have been added, and other routes are now flown in codeshare with Emirates.

Routes

Regional network from Colombo, and international service to Abu Dhabi, Amman, Bahrain, Bangkok, Berlin, Dhahran, Doha, Dubai, Frankfurt, Hong Kong, Karachi, Kuwait, Kuala Lumpur, London, Male, Mumbai, Muscat, Paris, Riyadh, Rome, Singapore, Stockholm, Sydney, Tokyo, Trivandrum and Zürich.

Fleet	Ordered
2 Airbus A320-200	4 Airbus A330
5 Airbus A330-300	
4 Airbus A340-300	
2 Lockheed L-1011-500	

Boeing 737-85H OY-SEH (Stefan Schlick/Arrecife)

STERLING EUROPEAN AIRLINES

Copenhagen Airport South, 2791 Dragoer
Denmark
Tel. 32-890000, Fax. 32-451412

Three- / Two- letter code	IATA No.	Reg'n prefix	ICAO callsign
SNB / NB	373	OY	Sterling

The name of Sterling has a certain resonance in the world of aviation, having originally been started as a charter company in Denmark in 1962 by an evangelical pastor for his tour company Tjaereborg, which offered Mediterranean holidays at attractive prices to many sections of the population, but especially to families. However, after thirty years of operation, the familiar airline failed in September 1993, when all rescue attempts failed and bankruptcy became inevitable. A new business took over the company mantle, including the name, which still had a competitive value. Operations recommenced in 1994 as Sterling European Airlines with several Boeing 727s, though flying exclusively on behalf of freight operator TNT. In 1996 the company was granted a passenger licence for the 727 and began flying holidaymakers again. During 1998, after new investors had taken shareholdings, this part of the business was strongly rebuilt. Boeing 737-300s and -500s as well as the new generation -800s (from June 1998) were leased in and flown under the marketing name of Sterling. The aircraft are painted in an attractive, colourful livery with a beach-ball logo on the fin and using different base colours for each aircraft, thus creating the holiday mood at the airport. The freight operations on behalf of TNT have also been built up, and these now operate from the TNT hub at Liège in Belgium, with these aircraft painted in TNT colours.

Routes

Charter flights from Aarhus, Billund, Copenhagen and Esbjerg to the Mediterranean, Northern Africa and the Canary Isles, and other ad hoc destinations. Scheduled freight flights for TNT from Liège.

Fleet	Ordered
7 Boeing 727-200F	1 Boeing 737-800
2 Boeing 737-300	
5 Boeing 737-800	

Boeing 707-3J8C ST-AFB (Oliver Köstinger/Sharjah)

SUDAN AIRWAYS

P.O.Box 253, Amarat Khartoum,
Sudan
Tel. 11-47953, Fax. 11-47978

Three- / Two- letter code	IATA No.	Reg'n prefix	ICAO callsign
SUD / SD	200	ST	Sudanair

Sudan Airways was founded in February 1946 by the Sudanese government as a subsidiary of Sudan Railways System and a contract was signed for technical and operational assistance from the British company Airwork. Domestic services began in July 1947 with a fleet of four de Havilland Doves. In November 1954, the first international service was the route to Cairo, which was served with Douglas DC-3s. On 8th June 1959 a scheduled service was opened via Cairo, Athens and Rome to London using Vickers Viscounts, and Comet 4Cs from 1962 onwards. The first Fokker F.27 was delivered in 1962

and the first de Havilland Comet on 13th November 1962. The second jet generation was introduced in 1972 in the form of the Boeing 707, which was used for regular flights to Europe. For domestic services mainly F.27s were used, replaced in Spring 1990 by modern Fokker 50s. Sudan Airways is also responsible for agricultural flying and other government work, and the small aircraft used for these duties and for training can sometimes also be used for short domestic routes. Civil unrest in the Sudan has had an effect on air traffic; however new aircraft have been introduced to the fleet, the Airbus A320, A310 and

A300-600 from 1993. These have been used on the sharply reduced international network. As Sudan has become more politically marginalised, services have declined and some aircraft were returned to their lessors at the end of the 1990s.

Routes

Abu Dhabi, Amman, Bangui, Cairo, Damascus, Dharan, Doha, Dongala, Dubai, El Fasher, El Obeid, Jeddah, Juba, Kano, London, Merowe, Nyala, Port Sudan, Riyadh, Sanaa, Sharjah, Tripoli, Wadi Halfar.

Fleet

3 Airbus A300-600
3 Boeing 707-300
1 Boeing 737-200
1 Fokker F.27-600

Boeing 727-282 N281SC (Josef Krauthäuser/Las Vegas)

SUN COUNTRY AIRLINES

2520 Pilot Knob Road, Mendota Heights, MN 55120, USA, Tel. 651-6813900, Fax. 651-6813972, www.suncountry.com

Three- / Two- letter code	IATA No.	Reg'n prefix	ICAO callsign
SCX / SY	337	N	Sun Country

Sun Country was set up in Minneapolis on 1st July 1982 by a group of former employees of Braniff International Airlines, which had gone spectacularly bankrupt on 12th May 1982. After the issue of a licence as a charter operator in January 1993, flights were begun on 20th January with Boeing 727s and operating for MLT Tours. This organisation held 51% of the share capital, but this was given up in 1988 when the company underwent a fundamental reorganisation. In 1984 a scheduled service licence was issued and a route inaugurated between Minneapolis and Las Vegas. Further Boeing 727s were added to the fleet over the years as the company made good progress and flights were undertaken to Florida, Mexico and the Caribbean. In 1986 Sun Country took on its first widebody, a DC-10, and from 1994 the airline went into international charter services in a much bigger way, giving up its scheduled operations. From this time also the aircraft were painted into a new colour scheme. Additionally, aircraft were leased out to other operators from time to time, and thus Sun Country aircraft can be seen worldwide at various times. A further change of policy came in 1999, with a reorientation towards scheduled services again, but this time as a low-cost, low-fares operator, with various routes on offer from its Minneapolis base. The bulk of the fleet is made up of Boeing 727s, though some of these are 'Super 27' re-engined quiet versions, and Boeing 737-800s are on order for delivery from January 2001.

Routes

Aruba, Boston, Bullhead City, Dallas/Fort Worth, Detroit, Fort Lauderdale, Fort Myers, Harlingen, Houston, Las Vegas, Los Angeles, Miami, Milwaukee, Minneapolis/St. Paul, New York, Orlando, Phoenix, San Antonio, San Diego, San Francisco, Sarasota/Bradenton, Seattle, St. Petersburg, Washington.

Fleet	Ordered
12 Boeing 727-200 4 Douglas DC-10-15	6 Boeing 737-800

Boeing 737-3Y0 TC-SUN (Josef Krauthäuser/Munich)

SUN EXPRESS

Fener Mahallesi Sinanoglu Cad, Oktay Airport, 07100 Antalya, Turkey Tel. 3234047, Fax. 3234057 www.sunexpress.com.tr

Three- / Two- letter code	IATA No.	Reg'n prefix	ICAO callsign
SXS / XQ	564	TC	Sun Express

On 11th September 1989 Lufthansa (40% of the shares), Turkish Airlines (40%) and Turkish investors (20%) set up the airline Sun Express with its headquarters in Antalya. Operations started with a leased Boeing 737-300 on 4th April 1990; the first flight was from Nuremberg to Antalya. Two further leased Boeing 737-300s were added for 1991, and additional aircraft were available from Lufthansa or Turkish as required. Because of the Gulf War, Turkish tourism came almost to a standstill in 1991, and the planned additional destinations could not be taken on. However, tourists returned to the Turkish market in the following years and the fleet of 737s has been expanded, with series 400s used, though the fleet for 2000 consists mostly of the new series 800s, of which the first was delivered in January 2000. Sun Express is a typical niche carrier of the type to be found developing charter services to Turkey from Europe's smaller airports.

Routes

Charter services from airports in Germany, Czech Republic, Austria, Switzerland, Holland, England and other European countries to Antalya, Bodrum, Dalaman, Izmir and other Turkish holiday destinations.

Fleet

1 Boeing 737-300
4 Boeing 737-800

Douglas DC-9-51 N54642 (now PZ-TCK) ((Christofer Witt collection)

SURINAM AIRWAYS

P.O.Box 2029, Coppenamestraat 136,
Paramaribo, Surinam
Tel. 433273 Fax. 491213, www.slm.firm.sr

Three- / Two- letter code	IATA No.	Reg'n prefix	ICAO callsign
SLM / PY	192	PZ	Surinam

Surinaamse Luchtvaart Maatschappij NV was established in January 1955 with the objective of providing service from the capital, Paramaribo, to the little developed hinterland of Surinam. Initial service commenced with DC-3s and was at first scanty, but from 1964 routes to neighbouring countries – to Georgetown, Port of Spain and Curacao – were begun with the help of KLM as a pool partner. With Surinam's independence from the Netherlands in 1975 came the introduction of a service to Amsterdam, for which leased Douglas DC-8s were brought into use. In 1980 service was also begun to Miami. For short-range services, two 20-seater de Havilland Twin Otter 300s were acquired in 1979, and these have remained in the fleet ever since. At the beginning of 1993 the Amsterdam route was passed over to KLM, as Surinam Airways had no aircraft suitable for this long-distance route. Since then the airline has concentrated on regional services, for which a DHC-8 (in 1993) and an MD-87 (in 1996) were acquired. At the end of 1999 the MD-87 was replaced in the fleet by a DC-9-50 and the Dash 8 has also been returned to its lessor. KLM remains an important partner and there is a codeshare agreement in place for the important tourist route to Amsterdam. ALM also participates in this co-operation.

Routes

Aruba, Barbados, Belem, Cayenne, Curacao, Georgetown, Miami, Paramaribo, Port au Prince, Port of Spain.

Fleet

2 De Havilland DHC-6 Twin Otter
1 Douglas DC-9-51

Airbus A330-223 HB-IQC (Dieter Roth/Munich)

SWISSAIR

Postfach, 8058 Zürich-Flughafen, Switzerland
Tel. 1-8121212, Fax. 1-8129000,
www.swissair.com

Three- / Two- letter code	IATA No.	Reg'n prefix	ICAO callsign
SWR / SR	085	HB	Swissair

On 26th March 1931 Basler Luftverkehr (Balair) and Ad Astra Aero AG merged to form Schweizer-ischen Luftverkehrs AG. The company traded as Swissair and continued the routes of its predecessors, using Fokker F VIIbs and the famous Lockheed Orion on the Zürich-Munich route. In 1935 Swissair acquired Douglas DC-2s, and DC-3s in 1937; these were used on the London route. Post-war came DC-4s, Convair 240s and later, Convair 440s. In 1947 Alpair Berne was taken over and from then on Swissair became the Swiss flag carrier. DC-6Bs and DC-7s were the last of the propliners, before DC-8s

and Caravelles were introduced from 1960. Convair 990 Coronados were used for Far East services from September 1961. The first DC-9 was delivered on 20th July 1966. Swissair's first widebody was a Boeing 747 in January 1971, followed by the DC-10 a year later. Airbus A310s were also added from 1978, Swissair being a launch customer. The first MD-11s were acquired in early 1991. During 1995 Swissair acquired a 49% holding in Sabena and on 25th January took delivery of its first A321, followed on 1st June by the first A320, replacing MD-81s. 1995 also brought major restructuring, with subsidiary

Balair/CTA being integrated into Swissair and Crossair. In 1996 the A319 was added, making Swissair the first operator of all three models in the A320 family. The Airbus A330 was added to the long range fleet and the Boeing 747s withdrawn by mid-1999. Swissair has in recent years invested in many other airlines including Air Europe, Air Littoral, Air One, AOM, Cargolux, LOT, LTU, SAA, TAP-Air Portugal, Ukraine Intl. and Volare. Swissair founded the Qualiflyer Group and has co-operation agreements with various other airlines. Co-operation with Delta ended on 6th August 2000, in favour of codeshares with American.

Routes

Swissair connects Switzerland with over 150 destinations in North and South America, Asia, Africa, the Middle and Far East and Europe.

Fleet

9 Airbus A319-100
20 Airbus A320-200
12 Airbus A321-100
13 Airbus A330-200

19 (Boeing) McDonnell Douglas MD-11

Ordered

8 Airbus A320
5 Airbus A330
9 Airbus A340-600

Airbus A320-232 YK-AKA (Gerhard Schütz/Munich)

SYRIANAIR

P.O.Box 417, Damascus,
Syria
Tel. 2220700, Fax. 2214923

Three- / Two- letter code	IATA No.	Reg'n prefix	ICAO callsign
SYR / RB	070	YK	Syrianair

The Syrian national airline was founded in October 1961 by the government after its predecessor Syrian Airways (founded on 21st December 1946) had united with Misrair to form United Arab Airlines. However, this union lasted for less than two years. Egyptian carrier Misrair had been renamed as UAA in February 1958 and Syrian Airways merged with it from 23rd December 1958. After Syria's break with Egypt, Syrian Arab Airlines, to give the airline its full name, took back its fleet and routes from UAA. Syrian Airways had operated domestic and regional routes from Damascus; Syrian Arab inherited these and

started operating into Europe with Douglas DC-6Bs, serving Paris and London from 1964 and also flying east to Karachi and Delhi. Depending on the political orientation of the government from time to time, both Western and Soviet-built aircraft were used. SE 210 Caravelles were introduced from 1965 and Boeing 747SPs in 1976. The first Boeing 727 was delivered in March 1976 to supplement the Caravelles, the latter only being retired at the beginning of 1996. During the early 1980s Tupolev Tu-134s were acquired, followed by Tu-154s. A well overdue fleet renewal was started in the later

part of 1998 and early 1999 when Airbus A320s were delivered, in a new colour scheme for the airline, to replace the Boeing 727s by mid-2000. In addition to the airline's 'proper' fleet, the Syrian Air Force operates a selection of Yak 40s, Antonov 26s and Ilyushin 76s in full Syrianair colours.

Routes

Abu Dhabi, Aleppo, Algiers, Amsterdam, Athens, Bahrain, Beirut, Berlin, Bucharest, Budapest, Cairo, Damascus, Deirezzor, Delhi, Dharan, Doha, Dubai, Frankfurt, Istanbul, Jeddah, Kameshli, Karachi, Khartoum, Kuwait, Larnaca, Latakia, London, Madrid, Moscow, Mumbai, Munich, Muscat, Paris, Riyadh, Rome, Sanaa, Sharjah, Stockholm, Teheran, Tunis.

Fleet

6 Airbus A320-200	4 Ilyushin IL-76M
1 Antonov An-24	5 Tupolev Tu-134B
5 Antonov An-26	3 Tupolev Tu-154M
2 Boeing 747SP	6 Yakovlev Yak-40
2 Boeing 727-200	

Boeing 747-312 Combi D2-TEA (Pascal Mainzer/Paris-CDG)

TAAG ANGOLA AIRLINES

R. da Missao, C P 3010, Luanda,
People's Republic of Angola
Tel. 2-332485, Fax. 2-393548

Three- / Two- letter code	IATA No.	Reg'n prefix	ICAO callsign
DTA / DT	118	D2	DTA

Direccao de Exploracao dos Transportes Aeros (DTA) was established by order of the Portuguese government in September 1938. However, it was not possible to begin operations until 1940 because of a lack of infrastructure. With an initial fleet of three de Havilland Dragon Rapides, scheduled services were started on 17th July 1940 on domestic routes, and additionally on an international route between Luanda and Pointe Noire in the Congo Republic (then French Equatorial Africa), where connections were available to various European destinations. The name was changed also in this year to DTA - Linhas Aereas de Angola, in which form it remained until 1973. For political reasons operations, with a few exceptions, were suspended between late 1974 and the country's independence from Portugal in November 1975. When the airline was renamed TAAG - Linhas Aereas de Angola, it became the flag carrier of the new people's republic. Boeing 707s and 737s were acquired in the late 1970s and early 1980s, with Fokker F.27s forming the basis of the domestic fleet, though Soviet-built types were also acquired. A TriStar was leased from TAP from 1990 for long-range services, and a Boeing 747-300 was acquired for routes to South America and Europe. From the late 1990s there has been co-operation with Air Namibia and SAA-South African Airways. Angola Air Charter and Aviacao Ligeira are subsidiaries for freight and regional services respectively.

Routes

Benguela, Cabinda, Catumbela, Dundo, Harare, Huambo, Johannesburg, Kinshasa, Kuito, Lisbon, Luanda, Lubango, Lusaka, Malange, Menongue, Moscow, Paris, Pointe Noire, Rio de Janeiro, Sal, Sao Tome, Soyo, Windhoek.

Fleet

1 Boeing 707-300	2 Ilyushin IL-62M
5 Boeing 737-200	
2 Boeing 747-300	
4 Fokker F.27	

Airbus A320-233 N458TA (Dennis Wehrmann/Miami)

TACA INTERNATIONAL AIRLINES

Edifico Altos 2 Piso, San Salvador, El Salvador
Tel. 2678888, Fax. 2233757,
www.grupotaca.com

Three- / Two- letter code	IATA No.	Reg'n prefix	ICAO callsign
TAI / TA	202	YS	Taca

TACA International Airlines was founded in November 1939 in El Salvador as TACA El Salvador, at that time a division of TACA-Airways SA, a powerful multi-national organisation in Central America. The well-known airline pioneer Lowell Yerex had formed TACA originally in Honduras in 1931. Operations began on the Salvador-Tegucigalpa-Managua-San Jose trunk route. In 1942 flights started with DC-3s to Bilbao in the Panama Canal Zone and a year later to Havana. TACA International succeeded TACA El Salvador in 1950 and acquired all remaining assets of the original TACA Corporation in 1960. The airline used Douglas DC-4s and DC-6s and Vickers Viscounts until the first jet aircraft, a BAC One-Eleven, entered service in 1966. Twenty years later TACA added its first widebody, a Boeing 767. Investment in other airlines has become a feature, and the following airlines are all members of the TACA group, though with differing shareholdings: Aviateca, Islena Airlines, LACSA, NICA and TACA Peru. From 1998 a new marketing alliance was instituted within the group, evidenced externally by a new unified set of colour schemes for the aircraft. Co-operation within the group bring synergies and possibilities for savings, for instance in a group order of new equipment from Airbus. Fleet renewal began with the delivery of the first A320 in 1997, with the smaller A319 being delivered from Summer 1999. Aircraft are moved around within the group to meet changing demands.

Routes

Belize, Cuzco, Flores, Guatemala, Houston, Iquitos, La Ceiba, Lima, Los Angeles, Managua, Mexico City, Miami, Montego Bay, New Orleans, New York, Panama, San Francisco, San Jose, San Pedro Sula, San Salvador, Tegucigalpa, Washington.

Fleet	Ordered
4 Airbus A319	17 Airbus A319
14 Airbus A320	11 Airbus A320
9 Boeing 737-300	
2 Boeing 767	

Tupolev Tu-154M EY-85651 (Uwe Gleisberg/Munich)

TAJIKISTAN AIRLINES

31/2 Titov, Dushanbe Airport 734006
Tajikistan
Tel. 372-212195, Fax. 372-510091

Three- / Two- letter code	IATA No.	Reg'n prefix	ICAO callsign
TZK / 7J	502	EY	Tajikistan

Also known as Tajik Air or Tjikair, the former Aeroflot regional directorate was taken over from the state in 1990 and reorganised. It was anticipated that the airline would operate schedules, cargo and charter flights, and provide special services for members of the government. Mil-8 helicopters are used to provide passenger and emergency service in inaccessible mountain areas, where they are often the only means of speedy connection with a major town. There is an alliance with Tajikistan International Airlines, which has no aircraft of its own, and thus relies on Tajikistan Airlines for its operations.

In 1998 all the other airlines were merged into Tajikistan Airlines. Because the country has economic problems and a shortage of foreign exchange, part of its extensive but ageing fleet is either unserviceable or has been sold, and new services are seldom added, but Munich was added on a weekly basis from the Summer of 1999.

Routes

Almaty, Beijing, Delhi, Dubai, Frankfurt, London, Mumbai, and Munich are international destinations and about 20 regional points are served .

Fleet

3 Antonov An-28
8 Antonov An-24/26
6 Tupolev Tu-134A
10 Tupolev Tu-154B/M
10 Yakovlev Yak-40

Airbus A330-223 PT-MVD (C.W. Krauthäuser/Miami)

TAM

Rue Monsenhor Antonio Pepe 94, CEP
04357080 Sao Paulo, Brazil, Tel. 11-55828685,
Fax. 11-55828155, www.tam.com.br

Three- / Two- letter code	IATA No.	Reg'n prefix	ICAO callsign
TAM / KK	877	PT	TAM

TAM was set up by VASP and Taxi Aereo Marila on 12th May 1976 as Transportes Aereos Regionais to operate scheduled services in the interior of Sao Paulo state in Brazil. Operations began on 12th July 1976 with Fokker F.27s from Sao Paulo (Congonhas). For less well frequented routes, Brazilian-built, Embraer 110 Bandeirantes have been used. In October 1990 the first jet aircraft, Fokker 100s entered service. The airline continued its network expansion with a mix of Fokker F.27s, Fokker 50s and 100s, but following the demise of Fokker, a number of aircraft whose delivery had been anticipated would not now be built, and an alternative fleet plan had to be made. The decision went in favour of Airbus, and so A319s, A320s and even A330s were ordered. Though in 1999 the airline had been active almost exclusively within Brazil, this was to change from 28th June 1999 with the delivery of the first A330, at the same time as two A320s. A daily service to Miami was instituted late in 1999, and European services are also envisaged. TAM, together with regional companies TAM-Meridonal and TAM-Express, is developing into Brazil's largest airline. It is based at Sao Paulo's Congonhas airport.

Routes

Dense domestic network in Brazil from hubs at Sao Paulo, Brasilia and Rio de Janeiro. Miami is served daily.

Fleet		Ordered
11 Airbus A319-100	48 Fokker 100	13 Airbus A319
11 Airbus A320-200		7 Airbus A320
5 Airbus A330		
4 Fokker F.27		
4 Fokker 50		

Boeing 727-2T3 HC-BHM (Hans-Willi Mertens/Miami)

TAME - LINEA AEREA DEL ECUADOR

Avenida Amazonas 1354, Quito, Ecuador
Tel. 509375, Fax. 509594,
www.pub4.ecua.net.ec/tame

Three- / Two- letter code	IATA No.	Reg'n prefix	ICAO callsign
TAE / EQ	269	HC	Tame

In 1962 the Ecuadorian Air Force set up an air transport service to try to improve the poor infrastructure within the country. Using two DC-3s Transportes Aereos Militares began its first routes from Quito and Guayaquil to the more isolated regions of Ecuador, which were not served by commercially-run airlines. Included were the Galapagos Islands in the Pacific, which would receive a TAM aircraft once or twice a month. Until the DC-6 took over this route, it was served by Douglas DC-3s fitted with additional fuel tankage. Some of the DC-3s were replaced from 1970 by more modern HS.748 turboprops, but others remained in service until the beginning of the 1990s. In 1970 the military partially withdrew and TAME was reconstituted as a joint stock company. Two years later TAME took over Compania Ecuatoriana de Aviacion and their regional route network. Further aircraft including Lockheed L-188 Electras and Douglas DC-7s came into use. The first jet came in 1980 with the Boeing 727-300, followed by a 737-200 in 1981. Further second hand 727s were added during 1984 and 1985. During the 1990s TAME has acted as a feeder airline for Lufthansa and Air France from Caracas, and has provided services to Havana and Miami. A Boeing 757 was used briefly in 1999, and the name has been demilitarised as Transportes Aéreos Mercantiles Ecuatorianas SA, though several of the aircraft retain their dual civil registrations and FAE military serials which they have worn for some years.

Routes

Bogota, Cuenca,Guayaquil, Havana, Lago Agrio, Machala, Macara, Manta, Miami, Quito, Santiago, Tulcan.

Fleet

3 Boeing 727-100	2 Fokker F.28-4000
5 Boeing 727-200	3 De Havilland DHC-6 Twin Otter
2 BAe HS-748	

Airbus A310-304 CS-TEJ (B.I. Hengi/Zürich)

TAP AIR PORTUGAL

Edifico 25, Aeroporto Lisboa 1704 Lisboa, Portugal, Tel. 01-8415000, Fax. 01-8415881, www.tap-airportugal.pt

Three- / Two- letter code	IATA No.	Reg'n prefix	ICAO callsign
TAP / TP	047	CS	Air Portugal

Transportes Aereos Portugueses - TAP was established on 14th March 1945 by the Portuguese government. Operations began on 19th September 1946 with a converted C-47 (DC-3) from Lisbon to Madrid, and Casablanca was served with a Lockheed Lodestar. Routes were opened to Luanda and Laurenco Marques in Mozambique on 31st December 1946, followed in 1947 by London and Paris. All these were operated with Douglas DC-4s. TAP became a joint stock company, partly with private shareholders from 1st June 1953. Lockheed L-1049 Constellations were used for long-distance routes. When Caravelles

were commissioned in 1962, followed by Boeing 707s in 1966 as well as Boeing 727s a year later, this provided TAP with an all jet fleet. In 1972 TAP took on its first widebody, a Boeing 747. The turmoil of the revolution in Portugal in 1975 brought most TAP services to a standstill, but in 1977 after reorganisation it was possible to return flights to their full extent. The present name and colour scheme and logo were adopted in 1979. Two new types were integrated in 1984: the Lockheed L-1011 TriStar for long-range and the Boeing 737 for short and medium-haul. The first Airbus A320-200 arrived in 1992 and

the TriStars were sold off during 1994/95 following the arrival of the Airbus A340 as a replacement. Airbus A319s commenced delivery from December 1997, ousting the remaining Boeing 737s. Larger A321s are on order for delivery from September 2000. TAP has holdings in Air Macau and Air Sao Tome, and ATA-Aerocondor flies Shorts 360s from Madeira on inter-island services under TAP flight numbers. In April 1999 the SAir Group took a 20% holding in TAP, which is now a member of the Qualiflyer Group.

Routes

Abidjan, Amsterdam, Barcelona, Bissau, Bologna, Boston, Brussels, Caracas, Copenhagen, Dakar, Faro, Fortaleza, Frankfurt, Funchal, Geneva, Horta, Johannesburg, Lisbon, London, Luanda, Luxembourg, Lyon, Milan, Madrid, Maputo, Munich, Natal, New York, Nice, Paris, Ponta Delgada, Porto, Porto Santo, Punta Cana, Recife, Rio de Janeiro, Rome, Sal, Salvador, Sao Paulo, Sao Thome, Stockholm, Terceira, Varadero, Vienna, Zürich.

Fleet		Ordered
16 Airbus A319-100	4 Airbus A340-300	3 Airbus A320
8 Airbus A320-200	1 Boeing 737-300	2 Airbus A321
5 Airbus A310-300		

ATR 42-500 YR-ATF (Uwe Gleisberg/Munich)

TAROM

OTP A/P SOS Bucuresti Ploesti km 16,5
R-11181 Bucharest, Romania, Tel. 1-2014000,
Fax. 1-2014770, www.tarom.digiro.net

Three- / Two- letter code	IATA No.	Reg'n prefix	ICAO callsign
ROT / RO	281	YR	Tarom

Transporturile Aeriene Romana Sovietica (TARS) was established as a Romanian-Soviet airline in 1946 to succeed the pre-war state airline LARES. Operations began with a fleet of Lisunov Li-2s provided by the Russian partner. The Romanian state acquired the shares in 1954 and it was renamed as TAROM (Transporturile Aeriene Romane). Tarom flew Ilyushin IL-14s from 1958 to destinations in eastern and western Europe and the first IL-18s entered service in 1963. In 1968 Tarom took on its first BAC One-Eleven, a type which was later built under licence in Romania. Ilyushin IL-62s and Boeing 707s were commissioned in 1973 and 1974, the latter used to open a New York route. The IL-62s allowed extension of services to Africa and the Far East. Two Airbus A310s for long-distance routes were delivered late in 1992, with five Boeing 737-300s arriving in late 1993 and 1994. The intention was to bring the whole fleet up to 'western' standard by the mid-1990s, but this aim has been hindered by Romania's poor economic progress. Some of the older Soviet-built types which are more or less unsaleable have simply been mothballed. A planned privatisation has also faltered and could only take place after further modernisation. ATR 42s replaced older Antonov 24s from 1997, with improved ATR 42-500s in use from 1998 and new generation Boeing 737s are on order for delivery from around the turn of the year 2000/01. The new aircraft have allowed the network to be further developed. Tarom co-operates with Alitalia, Austrian, Iberia, LOT, Malev, Sahara and Swissair.

Routes

Abu Dhabi, Amman, Amsterdam, Athens, Barcelona, Beijing, Beirut, Berlin, Brussels, Budapest, Bucharest, Cairo, Chicago, Chisinau, Copenhagen, Damascus, Dubai, Dublin, Düsseldorf, Frankfurt, Gaza, Istanbul, Kuwait, Larnaca, Lisbon, London, Madrid, Milan, Montreal, Moscow, Munich, New York, Paris, Prague, Riyadh, Rome, Satu Mare, Sibiu, Sofia, Stuttgart, Tel Aviv, Thessaloniki, Timisoara, Tripoli, Warsaw, Vienna.

Fleet		Ordered
2 Airbus A310-300	1 Boeing 737-500	2 ATR 42-500
2 Antonov An-24	3 RomBAC 1-11	4 Boeing 737-700
7 ATR 42-500	4 Tupolev Tu-154	4 Boeing 737-800
2 Boeing 707-300F		
7 Boeing 737-300		

Airbus A330-321 HS-TEG (Uwe Gleisberg/Perth)

THAI AIRWAYS INTERNATIONAL

89 Vibhavachi Rangit Road, Bangkok 10900, Thailand, Tel. 02-5130121, Fax. 02-5130203, www.thaiair.com

Three- / Two- letter code	IATA No.	Reg'n prefix	ICAO callsign
THA / TG	217	HS	Thai

Thai Airways celebrated 40 years of service in May 2000. It was established in August 1959 as a joint venture between SAS (30%) and the Thai Airways Company (70%), which operated regionally, to take over Thai's international routes. Flights started in May 1960 to neighbouring countries, to Hong Kong and Tokyo, using three DC-6Bs. The change to jets came in 1963 with the SE 210 Caravelle, replaced from 1969 by DC-9-41s. When DC-8-33s arrived Thai expanded its network to Australia in April 1971, Copenhagen from June 1972, and Frankfurt from 1973. In May 1975, when the DC-10-30 was delivered, Thai introduced a new colour scheme. The airline has been in state ownership since April 1977 when SAS gave up its holding. Fleet expansion and updating has continued, with Airbus A300s in 1975 and Boeing 747s from 1979, allowing services to the USA to start from 1980. On 1st April 1980 Thai International and Thai Airways merged in preparation for a privatisation, which proved to be a long drawn out process. The older DC-10s were replaced during 1991/92 with new MD-11s and from 1995 the first Airbus A330 was added, with the first Boeing 777 arriving in the following Spring. As ever, Thai maintains a modern fleet and carried some 16.6 million passengers in 1999. The airline's headquarters and maintenance base are at Bangkok's Don Muang Airport. In May 1997 Thai International became a founder member of the Star Alliance.

Routes

Thai Airways International serves around 80 destinations in 35 countries worldwide.

Fleet

1 Airbus A310-200
21 Airbus A300-600
12 Airbus A330-300
2 ATR 72-200
11 Boeing 737-400

2 Boeing 747-300
14 Boeing 747-400
12 Boeing 777-200/300
4 (Boeing) McDonnell Douglas MD-11

Ordered

4 Boeing 777

BAe 146 G-GNTB (Author's collection)

TNT AIRWAYS

Aéroport de Liège, B-4460 Grace-Hollogne, Belgium , Tel.4 239 5000, Fax. 4 239 5939, www.tntew.com

Three- / Two- letter code	IATA No.	Reg'n prefix	ICAO callsign
TAY / 3V		Various	Quality

TNT, which originated in Australia in 1968, is one of the world's largest cargo organisations. TNT came to Europe in 1984 and in 1987 the European airfreight system was established with a special version of the BAe 146, the QT (or 'quiet trader'). This particularly quiet jet is not subject to night-flight restrictions and can therefore be used for overnight parcel services. TNT did not operate its own aircraft but chartered them to partners such as Air Foyle, Mistral Air, Sterling, Channel Express, Pan Air Lineas Aereas and Hunting Cargo. Until 1998 the hub was at Cologne/Bonn and cargoes were flown here from around 30 points in Europe for distribution, sorting and transfer, before being flown out to its destinations later in that same night. A similar hub was set up at Manila in1993 to cover the Far East region, in conjunction with Pacific East Asia Cargo Airlines (formerly Air Philippines). Because of German environmental restrictions and a lack of space for long term growth, the European hub was moved in 1998 to a new superhub at Liège in Belgium, and at the same time the nature of the airline operation was changed. Previously the flying had been contracted out to various airlines by UK-based TNT International Aviation Services, who owned most of the mainly British-registered aircraft, but it was decided to establish TNT's own airline, TNT Airways, which now operates some of its own aircraft, transferred to the Belgian register and using the callsign 'Quality' instead of the previous 'Nitro'. Panair, Sterling and Channel Express also continue as contractors however. Airbus 300Fs have increased capacity, and a new colour scheme has been adopted.

Routes

TNT flies from its main hub in Liège to over 40 destinations within Europe.

Fleet	Ordered
19 BAe 146-200/300 QT	3 Airbus A300F
4 Boeing 727-200F	
4 Airbus A300F	

Boeing 747-130 N603FF (Hans-Willi Mertens/ Miami)

TOWER AIR

Hangar 17, JFK Internatl. Airport, Jamaica, New York 11430, USA, Tel. 718-5534300, Fax. 718-5534312, www.towerair.com

Three- / Two- letter code	IATA No.	Reg'n prefix	ICAO callsign
TOW / FF	305	N	Tee Air

Tower Air was founded as a pure charter airline in August 1982. Flights to Europe and Israel were marketed without the airline possessing its own aircraft; the flights were carried out by Metro International Airways on Tower's behalf. By Spring 1983, Tower became the general sales agent for Metro International's scheduled services and on 1st November 1983 Tower Air took over from Metro on the New York-Brussels-Tel Aviv route with its first Boeing 747-100. A year later the airline entered the American domestic scheduled business as a 'low-fare operator'. It entered into competition with PeoplExpress with flights between New York and Los Angeles, but with little success, so these loss-making schedules were dropped in 1984. Two more Boeing 747s were delivered in 1985 and a fourth in 1988. During the rest of the 1980s charters were flown between the USA and a number of European destinations. In 1992 scheduled flights to Cologne/Bonn were offered for the first time. During an expansion phase at the end of 1995 and early 1996 further Boeing 747-200s were added and charter work further increased. Special contract and troop charters for the US military have also been flown on a regular basis, either in support of exercises, or to war zones such as Yugoslavia and the Gulf. In February 2000 Tower Air sought Chapter 11 bankruptcy protection, though continued flying with a reduced fleet, some aircraft being returned to their lessors or sold.

Routes

Amsterdam, Athens, Berlin, Bombay, Buenos Aires, Hong Kong, Los Angeles, Milan, Miami, New York, Paris, Rome, Sao Paulo, San Juan, Tel Aviv are served regularly, plus military and ad hoc charters.

Fleet

6 Boeing 747-100
8 Boeing 747-200

Airbus A320-231 EI-TLI (Dieter Roth/Salzburg)

TRANSAER INTERNATIONAL AIRLINES

Transaer House, Dublin Airport, Ireland
Tel. 1-8080800, Fax. 1-8080801,
www.transaer.ie

Three- / Two- letter code	IATA No.	Reg'n prefix	ICAO callsign
TLA	839	EI	Translift

Founded in October 1991 as Translift, this airline began charter operations five months afterwards, initially using a Douglas DC-8-71 for both passenger and freight work. From the outset, Translift specialised in sub-charter work and this proved very successful, though scheduled services from Dublin and Shannon to Los Angeles were also offered on its own account. Further DC-8-71s augmented the fleet, with a total of five being used. In 1994 the business moved its headquarters from Shannon to Dublin and the fleet policy was radically changed. The leased DC-8s were returned and the first Airbus A320 acquired.

By the end of 1994 four more of this type had been added to the fleet, but were leased out to a newly-formed airline. The demand for larger aircraft and more capacity brought about the purchase of the Airbus A300B4. Between 1995 and 1998 a total of six examples were leased, and further A320s were also acquired. To meet the particular needs of a client company, a Boeing 727-200 was also hired in. Charter flights were operated for tour companies from Irish and other European airports. In 1997 the company changed its name to Transaer. For 1998 a subsidiary Transaer Cologne was established

to operate from Germany, but this was dropped after only one season, and the airline retrenched to concentrate on its core activity. In a switch from the previous Airbus loyalty, Boeing 737-800s are on order for delivery from 2001.

Routes

Scheduled and charter flights on a wet-lease basis for tour operators and other airlines in Europe, USA, Africa and the Caribbean.

Fleet	Ordered
5 Airbus A300B4	2 Airbus A300-600
11 Airbus A320-200	3 Airbus A320-200
	4 Boeing 737-800

Boeing 737-7K9 N100UN (Lutz Schönfeld/Berlin-SXF)

TRANSAERO AIRLINES

GosNII GA, Sheremetyevo 1 Airport, Moscow 103340, Russia, Tel. 095 5785038, Fax. 095 5788688, www.transaero.ru

Three- / Two- letter code	IATA No.	Reg'n prefix	ICAO callsign
TSO / UN	670	RA	Transaero

Transaero was founded in late 1991 as one of the first private joint stock companies in Russia and the first non-Aeroflot airline approved for scheduled passenger services in Russia. The shareholders are Aeroflot and aircraft manufacturers Ilyushin and Yakovlev. Operations commenced in early 1992, using Tupolev Tu-154s. Thousands of emigrants were flown from Russia to Israel in a spectacular action which caught the attention of the media and gave the young airline publicity. Two Boeing 737-200s were leased in late 1992 and two Ilyushin IL-86s acquired, as well as IL-76s for cargo work. In April 1994 Transaero took

delivery of its first Boeing 757, and was admitted as a member of IATA. Further 757s were added during 1995, allowing more routes to be opened up. In 1996 the first routes to the United States in competition with Aeroflot were started. Leased ex-American Airlines DC-10s were used for the Moscow-Los Angeles route, with a further route to Orlando being added in the Autumn. More international services were added, and in 1997 the airline took a 30% stake in Latvian airline Riga Air, with whom some joint services were flown. However, Russia's mounting economic problems at the end of the 1990s had their effect on

Transaero; passenger numbers dropped dramatically and far from implementing further expansion, the airline was forced to drop routes, including those to the USA, and return the DC-10s and 757s to their lessors. Two new Boeing 737-700s were however added on lease from mid-1998 and an Airbus A310-300 from September 2000. Tupolev Tu-204s and Tu-214s are on order for delivery from 2001; these are to be leased from Ilyushin Finance. There is co-operation with Azerbaijan Airlines on the Baku route.

Routes

Almaty, Astana, Baku, Berlin, Frankfurt, Irkutsk, Karaganda, Karlovy Vary, Kiev, Krasnoyarsk, London, Nizhnvartovsk, Norilsk, Novosibirsk, Odessa, Omsk, Orel, Riga, St. Petersburg, Tashkent, Tel Aviv, Vladivostok, Yekaterinburg, Yuzhno Sakhal.

Fleet	Ordered
1 Airbus A310-300	6 Tupolev Tu-204-100
5 Boeing 737-200	4 Tupolev Tu-214
2 Boeing 737-700	
1 Ilyushin IL-86	

Airbus A321-131 F-WQGL (now B-22606) (Dennis Wehrmann/Hamburg)

TRANSASIA AIRWAYS

139 Cheng Chou Road, Taipei, Republic of China, Tel. 5575767, Fax. 5580240, www.tna.com.tw

Three- / Two- letter code	IATA No.	Reg'n prefix	ICAO callsign
TNA / GE	170	B	Foshing

Foshing Airlines, founded in 1951, experienced more downs than ups in its lifetime, and surrendered its operating licence in 1965. However, it was reactivated in 1990 by the Gold Sun Group and since then has made rapid progress. It was renamed as Transasia Airways in 1992 in order to better reflect the airline's ambitions with regard to an international network. The first jet aircraft was the Airbus A320, which was delivered in August 1992. In this same year international services were opened to Cambodia and the Philippines. The fast-growing company took delivery of more A320s in 1995 as well as the first of six larger A321s. Shorter-range services were flown by a fleet of ATR 42s introduced in 1989, but now replaced by ATR 72s, the first of which was delivered in November 1990.The company's main operating bases are at Taipei-Sung Shan and Kaoshiung. As well as scheduled flights, Transasia is also active in the holiday business with flights to Thailand and the Philippines.

Routes

Chiayi, Hualien, Kaoshiung, Kinmen, Kota Kinabalu, Macau, Makung, Pingtung, Phnom Penh, Tainan, Taipei, Taitung.

Fleet

6 ATR 72-500
4 Airbus A320-200
6 Airbus A321-100

Boeing 737-8K2 PH-HZD (Dennis Wehrmann/Amsterdam)

TRANSAVIA AIRLINES

Postbus 7777, 1118 ZM Schiphol, Netherlands
Tel. 020-6046555, Fax. 020-6484637
www.transavia.nl

Three- / Two- letter code	IATA No.	Reg'n prefix	ICAO callsign
TRA / HV	979	PH	Transavia

Transavia Airlines, which was originally formed as Transavia Limburg in 1965 and changed its name to Transavia Holland in 1967 before becoming Transavia Airlines in 1986, has been in operation since 16th November 1966 when it carried out a charter to Naples. Initially flights to the Mediterranean were offered with three Douglas DC-6s. The airline acquired its first jet, a Boeing 707, followed by an SE 210 Caravelle in 1969; the Caravelles were replaced by the Boeing 737 in 1974. A scheduled service from Amsterdam to London was introduced on 26th October 1986 and there were also schedules to Spain, but by far the major activity was charter work, particularly a large share of the Dutch holiday market, and the leasing out to other airlines of some of its not insubstantial fleet of Boeing 737s and from early 1993, 757s. Since 1991, Schiphol-based Transavia has been a subsidiary of KLM, which has an 80% holding. The current colour scheme was adopted during the Summer of 1995. The first of the new Boeing 737-800s were received from June 1998, but as replacements for older model 737s rather than to increase the size of the fleet.

Routes

Alicante, Amsterdam, Barcelona, Casablanca, Chambery, Djerba, Faro, Funchal, Heraklion, Innsbruck, Izmir, Kathmandu, Las Palmas, Lisbon, London, Malaga, Malta, Nice, Palma de Mallorca, Rhodes, Rotterdam, Salzburg, Seville, Sharjah, Tenerife.

Fleet	Ordered
9 Boeing 737-300	2 Boeing 737-800
10 Boeing 737-800	
4 Boeing 757-200	

Boeing 737-3K9 PP-TEU (Author's collection)

TRANSBRASIL

Rua General Panteleao Telles 40, CEP 04355-040, Sao Paulo, Brazil, Tel. 11-5324600, Fax. 11-5334983, www.transbrasil.com.br

Three- / Two- letter code	IATA No.	Reg'n prefix	ICAO callsign
TBA / TR	653	PT/PP	Transbrasil

The Brazilian meat wholesaler Sadia started flight operations as Sadia SA Transportes Aereos on 5th January 1955 with a Douglas DC-3, primarily to transport freight from Concordia to Sao Paulo. The airline entered the passenger business on 16th March 1956 and then proceeded to develop routes in Brazil's south east. Close co-operation with REAL and Transportes Aereos Salvador began in 1957; the latter was taken over by Sadia in 1962 after the collapse of REAL, and services were expanded into north-eastern Brazil. The aircraft used were Handley Page Dart Heralds and, from 1970, BAC One-Elevens; Boeing 727s were used from 1974 onwards. Sadia changed its name to Transbrasil in June 1972 and moved its headquarters to Brasilia. Fleet replacement began in July 1983 with the purchase of Boeing 767s; the Boeing 727s were replaced by Boeing 737-300s and -400s from 1987. The airline divides its scheduled and charter routes up with Varig. In 1994 a new regional subsidiary, Interbrasil Star was set up, operating Embraer Brasilias. With bases at Sao Paulo and Brasilia it has suitable departure points for unlimited internal services, though international schedules depart from Sao Paulo-Guarulhos.

In co-operation with Varig and VASP, an 'air bridge' is operated between the city airports of Rio de Janeiro and Sao Paulo in a pool arrangement. 1999 was noteworthy for the introduction of a new colour scheme, though some routes were also withdrawn for economic reasons.

Routes

Aracaju, Belem, Belo Horizonte, Brasilia, Buenos Aires, Cascavel, Chapeco, Cuiaba, Curitiba, Florianopolis, Fortaleza, Goiania, Igacu Falls, Joao Pessoa, Joinville, Lisbon, Londrina, Maceio, Manaus, Maringa, Natal, Navegantes, Porto Alegre, Porto Velho, Recife, Rio de Janeiro, Salvador, Santiago, Sao Luiz, Sao Paulo.

Fleet

12 Boeing 737-300
 4 Boeing 737-400
 3 Boeing 767-200
 3 Boeing 767-300ER

Boeing 757-2Q8 D4-CBG (Albert Kuhbandner/Munich)

TRANSPORTES AEREOS DE CABO VERDE

Caixa Postal 1, Praia,
Republic of Cape Verde
Tel. 613215, Fax. 613585

Three- / Two- letter code	IATA No.	Reg'n prefix	ICAO callsign
TCV / VR	696	D4	Transverde

Transportes Aereos de Cabo Verde (TACV) was founded on 27th December 1958 to succeed a local flying club which had provided some domestic air services from May 1955 using de Havilland Doves until its bankruptcy in 1958. TACV began operations in January 1959. In 1971 the first of three Britten-Norman Islanders was commissioned. Operations were suspended for a while in 1967, while re-organisation took place with the help of the Portuguese airline TAP. After the country gained independence from Portugal on 5th July 1975, TACV became the flag carrier of the newly established republic. With the acquisition of a BAe HS.748 in 1973, a weekly service to Dakar in Senegal was set up; this was to remain TACV's sole international route for several years. In association with TAP Air Portugal there was a direct service to Lisbon under a TCV flight number, but operated by a TAP Airbus. As a more modern supplement to the HS.748, two ATR 42s were delivered at the end of 1994, and the arrival in March 1996 of the airline's own Boeing 757-200 allowed the route to Lisbon, and new routes to Frankfurt and Amsterdam, to be flown by TACV aircraft. A third ATR 42 was delivered in 1997, allowing the retirement of the HS.748. The Cape Verde Islands are slowly developing as a tourist destination and so from 1998 further European airports were added to TACV's network, at the expense of some African services, which were dropped.

Routes

Amsterdam, Boa Vista, Bologna, Dakar, Las Palmas, Lisbon, Madrid, Maio, Mosteiros, Munich, Paris, Praia, Rome, Sal, Santo Antao, Sao Filipe, Sao Nicolau, Sao Vicente, Vienna, Zürich.

Fleet

3 ATR 42-300
1 Boeing 757-200
1 De Havilland DHC-6 Twin Otter

Embraer RJ-145ER N805HK (Author's collection)

TRANS STATES AIRLINES

9275 Genaire Drive, St.Louis MO 63134-1912 USA, Tel. 573-8958700, Fax. 573-8951040, www.transstates.net

Three- / Two- letter code	IATA No.	Reg'n prefix	ICAO callsign
LOF / 9N	414	N	Waterski

In May 1982 Resort Air was founded in St.Louis and it began operations in April 1983 with Fairchild-Swearingen Metros, serving regional destinations in the states of Illinois and Missouri. An agreement was reached with Trans World in 1985 for the TWA Express feeder service to be built up. In 1986 there was a change of ownership at Resort Air, but the airline remained in private hands and the current name of Trans States Airlines was adopted from 1989. Air Midwest also flew Metros on feeder services for TWA, and after this company encountered financial difficulties, Trans States took it over in 1991. At that time the most suitable aircraft for Trans States Airlines' services was the British Aerospace Jetstream 32, and a large fleet of this type was brought into use from 1990. Later, the fleet was augmented with ATR 42s and its larger brother the ATR 72, as well as the Jetstream 41. From 1993 co-operation with other major airlines – US Air, Northwest and Alaska Airlines – brought further work. Summer 1998 saw the delivery to Trans States of the first of their Embraer RJ-145 regional jets. During early 2000 the airline closed its California operation for US Airways, Northwest and Alaska, and is to cease its Delta Connection operations from early 2001, launching instead a Pittsburgh-based operation for US Airways. It still operates for TWA at St.Louis.

Routes

Albany, Baltimore, Birmingham, Bloomington/Normal, Boston, Burlington, Champaign, Chattanooga, Chicago, Cleveland, Columbia, Decatur, Detroit, Evansville, Fayetteville, Fort Wayne, Grand Rapids, Hartford, Joplin, Lexington, Madison, Memphis, Moline, New York, Norfolk, Peoria, Philadelphia, Pittsburgh, Raleigh/Durham, Sioux City, South Bend, Springfield, St. Louis, Washington, Waterloo.

Fleet

5 ATR 42
3 ATR 72
23 BAe Jetstream 32

25 BAe Jetstream 41
8 Embraer RJ-145

Boeing 757-2Q8 N702TW (Josef Krauthäuser/St.Louis)

TRANS WORLD AIRLINES

One City Centre, 515 North 6th Street, St. Louis, MO 63101, USA, Tel. 573-5893000, Fax. 573-5893129, www.twa.com

Three- / Two- letter code	IATA No.	Reg'n prefix	ICAO callsign
TWA / TW	015	N	TWA

Founded on 1st October 1930 as Transcontinental and Western Air, TWA was a leading US airline for many years. It was the first with scheduled US coast-to-coast service, it opened up air traffic in California and was joint initiator of such famous aircraft as the DC-1/2 and the DC-3. Howard Hughes, who had a controlling interest in TWA, ordered the Lockheed Constellation in 1939 and it entered service in 1944. TWA's first overseas service was Washington-Paris on 5th December 1945. On 21st May 1950 the name changed to Trans World Airlines, and in September services began to London and Frankfurt. On international flights the Constellation was used and in the USA DC-3s and Martin 404s. The first jet, a Boeing 707 entered service in March 1960 and from August 1969 a round-the-world service began. TWA acquired its first Boeing 747 in December 1969, with the Lockheed TriStar added from 1972. Ozark Airlines was taken over in 1986. In the mid 1990s the Boeing 767 was acquired for international services. Following deregulation, TWA hit hard times and was reduced to a shadow of its former self, slimming down fleet, staff and routes, including the sale of all London routes to American Airlines in 1991. It was forced to seek Chapter 11 bankruptcy protection, but emerged on 23rd August 1995 after reconstruction, now 30% employee-owned. The opportunity was taken to introduce a new corporate identity and colours. The largest fleet restructuring in TWA's history began in 1996; 747s, TriStars and older DC-9s and 727s were all retired and replaced with Boeing 757s and 767s. TWA was the launch customer for the Boeing 717, the first of 50 being delivered early in 2000. Airbus A318s and 319s are also on order for delivery from 2003. However TWA continues to incur heavy losses with an operating loss of $133 million for 1999.

Routes

TWA's major US hubs are St. Louis and New York. Including routes operated by TWA Express, over 125 points are served, including destinations in Europe, the Middle East and the Caribbean

Fleet		Ordered
10 Boeing 727-200	12 Boeing 717-200	25 Airbus A318
17 Boeing 767-200/300ER	29 Douglas DC-9-31/32/33	25 Airbus A319
27 Boeing 757-200	102 McDonnell Douglas MD-80	38 Boeing 717-200

Boeing 737-5H3 TS-IOI (Albert Kuhbandner/Munich)

TUNISAIR

Boulevard 7 Novembre, 1012 Tunis, Tunisia
Tel. 700100, Fax. 700897,
www.tunisair.com.tn

Three- / Two- letter code	IATA No.	Reg'n prefix	ICAO callsign
TAR / TU	199	TS	Tunair

Tunisair was established in 1948 as a subsidiary of Air France by agreement with the Tunisian government. Operations began in 1949 with Douglas DC-3s, initially from Tunis to Corsica and Algiers. In 1954 Tunisair acquired its first Douglas DC-4 for services to Paris. By 1957 the government had acquired a controlling 51% interest; Air France's shareholding has gradually reduced. In 1961 the airline entered the jet era with the beginning of services with SE 210 Caravelles. As no successor to the Caravelle was available from a French manufacturer, the airline decided to acquire Boeing 727s and the first of these was added to the fleet in 1972, with the type giving long service into the 1990s. After the Caravelles had been taken out of service in late 1977, the Boeing 737-200 arrived in 1979. A swing back into favour for European aircraft manufacturers came in 1982 with the single Airbus A300, and the first A320 in 1990, the latter delivery prompting the introduction of the present, modern colour scheme. More A320s were added in 1994/95, with Boeing 737-500s between 1992 and 1995. New model 737-600s replaced some of the old 727s during 1999, and from February 2000 two Airbus A300-600Rs were added on lease. The Tunisian government now holds 45.2% of the shares and Air France 5.2%, with the rest in private hands. Tunisair has a shareholding in Tuninter, which operates domestic services and like Tunisair, is based at Tunis-Carthage. There is close co-operation with Air Algerie, Royal Air Maroc and Air France.

Routes

Algiers, Amman, Amsterdam, Athens, Barcelona, Beirut, Berlin, Bilbao, Bordeaux, Bratislava, Brussels, Budapest, Cairo, Casablanca, Copenhagen, Damascus, Dakar, Djerba, Düsseldorf, Frankfurt, Geneva, Graz, Hamburg, Istanbul, Jeddah, Lille, Lisbon, London, Luxembourg, Lyon, Madrid, Malta, Marseilles, Milan, Monastir, Moscow, Munich, Nice, Nouakchott, Palermo, Paris, Prague, Rome, Salzburg, Sfax, Stockholm, Tabarka, Toulouse, Tozeur, Tunis, Warsaw, Vienna, Zürich

Fleet

		Ordered
1 Airbus A300B4	4 Boeing 727-200	1 Airbus A319
2 Airbus A300-600R	4 Boeing 737-200	1 Airbus A320
2 Airbus A319	4 Boeing 737-500	
11 Airbus A320	6 Boeing 737-600	

Boeing 737-8F2 TC-JFF (Albert Kuhbandner/Amsterdam)

TURKISH AIRLINES

Genel Yönetim Binsai,Atatürk Hava Limani, 34830
Yesilköy Istanbul, Turkey, Tel. 212-6636300
Fax. 212-6634744, www.turkishairlines.com

Three- / Two- letter code	IATA No.	Reg'n prefix	ICAO callsign
THY / TK	235	TC	Turkair

THY stems from Turkiye Devlet Hava Yollari (DHY), founded in 1933 and taken over by the state in 1956, along with its aircraft including Douglas DC-3s. The first new acquisition, the Vickers Viscount, was delivered from January 1958. In 1960 the first services to western Europe were started, including Frankfurt. The first Douglas DC-9 was delivered in August 1967 and the first widebody, the DC-10 on 1st December 1972. For regional services the Fokker F.27 and F.28 were used. Boeing 727-200s were taken on from 1974 and from 1984

the first Airbus A310. For a long time THY concentrated on the development of domestic rather than international services; only from the late 1960s were services to the major European cities to become a feature, no doubt influenced by the need to provide for the travel needs of the many expatriate Turkish workers. The first Airbus A310 was brought into service from 1985, and in 1990 came the first overseas destination, New York. In this year also, a new colour scheme was adopted for THY's aircraft. Capacity continued to be increased, with the Airbus A340

arriving in 1993, along with further Boeing 737s. Also from 1994 the Avro RJ100 was introduced for short and medium range services, replacing older DC-9s and Fokker F.28s; the latest model 737-800 was introduced from October 1998. THY has shareholdings in Sun Express and Kibris Cyprus Turkish Airlines and is also quite active in the charter and freight business. It became a member of the Qualiflyer alliance in March 1998. The airline made one of the largest losses in the air transport industry for 1999: $257 million.

Routes

THY flies to over 35 Turkish domestic destinations, and to Abu Dhabi, Algiers, Almaty, Amman, Amsterdam, Ashgabat, Athens, Bahrain, Baku, Bangkok, Barcelona, Basle, Beirut, Berlin, Bishkek, Brussels, Bucharest, Cairo, Cologne, Copenhagen, Dubai, Düsseldorf, Frankfurt, Geneva, Hamburg, Hanover, Jeddah, Kuwait, London, Lyon, Madrid, Milan, Munich, New York, Nice, Nuremberg, Osaka, Paris, Riyadh, Rome, Singapore, Stockholm, Stuttgart, Tashkent, Teheran, Tel Aviv, Tokyo, Tunis, Vienna and Zürich.

Fleet		Ordered
13 Airbus A310-200/300	20 Boeing 737-400	8 Boeing 737-800
7 Airbus A340-300	2 Boeing 737-500	
13 Avro RJ 70/100	20 Boeing 737-800	
2 Boeing 727-200F		

Canadair Regional Jet 200LR OE-LCK (Dieter Roth/Salzburg)

TYROLEAN AIRWAYS

Postfach 81 Flughafen, 6026 Innsbruck, Austria, Tel. 22221220, Fax. 22229005, www.tyrolean.at

Three- / Two- letter code	IATA No.	Reg'n prefix	ICAO callsign
TYR / VO	734	OE	Tyrolean

Founded in 1958 as Aircraft Innsbruck, the airline operated non-scheduled services until 1980, when it acquired the rights to operate scheduled services from Innsbruck to Vienna. In preparation for these operations which began in April 1980, using de Havilland Canada DHC-7s, the company changed its name during 1979 to Tyrolean Airways. Also in 1980 further routes were opened to Zürich and Frankfurt. In 1994 the domestic arm of Austrian Airlines, Austrian Air Services, was integrated with Tyrolean following the acquisition by Austrian Airlines of a 43% stake in Tyrolean Airways (Tiroler Luftfahrt AG). Since then Tyrolean has expanded strongly. New aircraft have been introduced: Fokker 70s from May 1995 and Canadair Regional Jets from May 1996 supplementing the previously all de Havilland Canada fleet of DHC-7s and DHC-8s. As well as scheduled services, Tyrolean operates charter flights quite extensively, some in connection with tour operators bringing holidaymakers to the Tyrol. Through its close association with Austrian Airlines, the airline has been linked into the Star Alliance since March 2000.

Routes

Amsterdam, Banja Luka, Berlin, Berne, Birmingham, Bologna, Bozen, Bremen, Brussels, Budapest, Chisinau, Cork, Dresden, Dublin, Düsseldorf, East Midlands, Edinburgh, Elba, Florence, Frankfurt, Gothenburg, Graz, Hanover, Helsinki, Innsbruck, Katowice, Klagenfurt, Kosice, Krakow, Leipzig, Linz, Ljubljana, Luxembourg, Lyon, Mostar, Munich, Nuremberg, Olbia, Oslo, Paris, Prague, Pristina, Rome, Salzburg, Strasbourg, Venice, Zagreb, Zürich.

Fleet	Ordered
10 Canadair Regional Jet	6 Canadair Regional Jet
18 De Havilland DHC-8-100/300/400	6 De Havilland DH-8-400
6 Fokker 70	

Boeing 737-247 UR-GAC (Josef Krauthäuser/Brussels)

UKRAINE INTERNATIONAL AIRLINES

Prospekt Peremogy 14, 252135 Kiev, Ukraine
Tel. 44-2218135, Fax. 44-2167994,
www.uia.ukrpack.net

Three- / Two- letter code	IATA No.	Reg'n prefix	ICAO callsign
AUI / PS	566	UR	Ukraineinternational

This airline was formed in October 1992 as Air Ukraine International, a subsidiary company of Air Ukraine (which operates extensive domestic services with a large fleet of Soviet-built types) to operate international services. The newly-independent state of Ukraine took a 90% shareholding. Flights were started to Western Europe with a leased Boeing 737-400. In contrast with Air Ukraine, it was decided to operate modern aircraft which would appeal to western business travellers. However, the 737-400 proved to be expensive in leasing costs and was returned to its lessor in late 1994, being replaced with an older 737-200, with a further 737-200 added in early 1995. The early hopes for the airline failed to be met and so the company, which was renamed as Ukraine International Airlines in 1995, has developed only slowly, but the fleet has grown with the addition of Boeing 737-300s. Austrian Airlines, Guinness Peat Aviation and Swissair have all taken shareholdings. The airline is based at Kiev's Borispol airport, where it shares a maintenance facility with Air Ukraine.

Routes

Amsterdam, Barcelona, Berlin, Brussels, Donetsk, Frankfurt, Kiev, Larnaca, London, Luxembourg, Lvov, Odessa, Paris, Riga, Rome, Simferopol, Vienna, Zürich.

Fleet

2 Boeing 737-200
3 Boeing 737-300

Boeing 777-222 N783UA (Martin Bach/London-LHR)

UNITED AIRLINES

P.O.Box 66100 Chicago, IL 60666, USA
Tel. 847-7004000, Fax. 847-7007345,
www.ual.com

Three- / Two- letter code	IATA No.	Reg'n prefix	ICAO callsign
UAL / UA	016	N	United

United Airlines Inc. of Chicago was founded on 1st July 1931 as the new holding company of the former Boeing Air Transport, Varney Air Lines, National Air Transport and Pacific Air Transport. All four of these had started their operations in either 1926 or 1927. United flew with Boeing 247s initially but decided to buy Douglas DC-3s, using over 100 during the 1940s. After the end of the Second World War Douglas DC-4s and DC-6s were used, notably on the airline's route from New York to Chicago. In 1947 Hawaii was served for the first time and in 1959 the airline's first jet aircraft, a Douglas DC-8, was accepted into the fleet. United was the only US airline to order the French SE 210 Caravelle, with 20 for short and medium range routes. There were no follow-up orders however, and Boeing 727s were acquired. On 1st June 1961 Capital Airlines, one of America's largest airlines at the time, was taken over, putting United into the position of being the largest airline in the free world, a position which was only bettered by American Airlines in the late 1980s. The

Boeing 747 joined the United fleet from June 1970. In 1986 the rights to various routes in the Pacific and the Lockheed TriStars with which to operate them were acquired from a struggling Pan Am. At the same time new aircraft were bought from Boeing in order to renew the fleet; 737-300s and 767s have taken a major role since then, with the 757, the first of which was delivered in August 1989, increasing in numbers during the 1990s. The Douglas DC-10 first appeared in United colours in 1972, with acquisitions up until 1987 forming a modest fleet. Not insignificantly, United, with its strong Boeing associations, also ordered large numbers of the Airbus A320s and then A319s. It is also remarkable in view of its size and significance, that United only began European services from 1990; from Autumn 1993 it entered into a partnership with Lufthansa, which ultimately formed the basis of the worldwide Star Alliance, of which both airlines were founder members in May 1997. The current aircraft colour scheme was introduced in early 1994, in which year also UAL

employees became the majority shareholders in the holding company with over 55%; not only is this motivational to providing good service, but it also allows them to have a say in how the company is run and its future. United was the launch customer for the Boeing 777, introduced on services to Europe in June 1995. In response to competition from low-cost airlines such as Southwest, United has created a Shuttle by United division which operates on the US west coast and in other markets, as an 'airline within an airline' and offers attractive fares; around 60 Boeing 737-300s and -500s are earmarked for these 'no frills' services. United Express feeder services are operated on behalf of United and in their colours by Atlantic Coast Airlines, Great Lakes Aviation, Sky West, Air Wisconsin and Trans States Airlines. Thus United offers a blanket coverage of air services in the USA. United flew over 87 million passengers during 1999, with group sales of $18 billion.

United Shuttle Boeing 737-322 N392UA (Author's collection)

United Express Embraer EMB-120 Brasilia N250YV owned and operated by Skywest (Patrick Lutz/San Francisco)

Routes

Major hubs are San Francisco, Chicago, Denver and Washington-Dulles with services to over 200 US destinations; international services to Amsterdam, Auckland, Bangkok, Beijing, Brussels, Buenos Aires, Calgary, Düsseldorf, Frankfurt, Guatemala, Hong Kong, Lima, London, Milan, Manila, Melbourne, Mexico City, Montevideo, Munich, Nagoya, Osaka, Paris, Rio de Janeiro, San Jose, San Salvador, Santiago, Sao Paulo, Seoul, Shanghai, Singapore, Sydney, Taipei, Tokyo, Toronto, Vancouver, Winnipeg.

Fleet		Ordered
30 Airbus A319	43 Boeing 747-400	18 Airbus A319
62 Airbus A320	98 Boeing 757-200	29 Airbus A320
75 Boeing 727-200	34 Boeing 767-300	1 Boeing 747-400
24 Boeing 737-200	19 Boeing 767-200	2 Boeing 767-300
101 Boeing 737-300	47 Boeing 777-200	17 Boeing 777-200
57 Boeing 737-500	16 McDonnell Douglas DC-10-10/30	
4 Boeing 747-200		

Boeing 747-100 N674UP (Author's collection)

UPS AIRLINES

1400 North Hurstbourne Parkway, Louisville Kentucky 40223, USA, Tel. 502-3296500, Fax. 502-3296550, www.ups.com

Three- / Two- letter code	IATA No.	Reg'n prefix	ICAO callsign
UPS / 5X	406	N	UPS

UPS – United Parcel Service was founded as long ago as 1907, and today is the largest company in the world in its sphere of business. In 1953 the two-day 'UPS-Air' service was set up. In 1982 UPS entered the overnight small package market and now serves more US points than any other carrier. It was only in 1987 that UPS established its own flight operations; up until then other airlines had been commissioned to carry out flights for UPS (even today a large number of outside companies still operate on its behalf). There are also regular flights to the European hub at Cologne, and there are further hubs in Hong

Kong, Singapore, Miami and Montreal, with the main US centre of operations in Louisville. Dedicated DC-8 freighters were initially the mainstay of the long-haul fleet and many are still in service today, but there is also a major fleet of Boeing 747 freighters which has been built up since 1984. UPS induced Boeing to build a cargo version of their 757-200 and was the first customer to receive the -200PF from 1987. Older Boeing 727s have been re-equipped with new, more powerful and more environmentally friendly Rolls-Royce Tay engines; these modified aircraft were first used in 1993, primarily to Europe where environmental

regulations are more stringent. Some of the 727s are set up to be able to fly passenger charters at weekends, with palletised, easily-installable seating. As with the 757PF, UPS was also the launch customer for the Boeing 767-300F, the first of 30 of which was delivered in October 1995. During 1999 UPS bought the South American routes of Challenge Air Cargo, in order to provide expansion in this market. The first of 30 new-build Airbus A300-600F freighters was delivered in July 2000.

Routes

Regular cargo services to around 400 US domestic and 220 international airports.

Fleet

2 Airbus A300-600F
16 Boeing 747-100/200F
59 Boeing 727-100/200F
75 Boeing 757-200F
30 Boeing 767-300F

49 McDonnell Douglas DC-8-70

Ordered

28 Airbus A300-600F

Boeing 757-225 N603AU (Josef Krauthäuser/Fort Lauderdale)

US AIRWAYS

2345 Crystal Drive,Arlington Virginia 22227, USA, Tel. 540 872 7000, Fax. 540 872 5437, www.usairways.com

Three- / Two- letter code	IATA No.	Reg'n prefix	ICAO callsign
USA / US	037	N	US Air

All-American Aviation was set up on 5th March 1937 to provide postal services over a network of routes from Pittsburgh. Postal services were discontinued in 1949 and the concern changed its name to All American Airways on 7th March 1949 to coincide with the start of passenger services from Pittsburgh via Washington to Atlantic City using Douglas DC-3s. Martin 2-0-2s and Convair 340/440s replaced the DC-3s, the name was changed again to Allegheny Airlines and new routes were opened, especially in the eastern United States. Lake Central Airlines was taken over on 1st July 1968 and on 7th April 1972 Mohawk

Airlines followed, with its large route network and BAC One-Eleven aircraft. After deregulation, Pacific Southwest Airlines and the much larger Piedmont Airlines were also both taken over. US Air was adopted as the new, less parochial, name from 28th October 1979. Its first services to London were in 1988, followed in 1990 by Frankfurt, Paris and Zürich. Fokker 100s were introduced in 1989, providing a breakthrough in the American market for the Dutch jet. US Air took over the shuttle service from New York to Washington and Boston from Trump and shareholdings were taken in various US Air Express

partner airlines. In January 1993 British Airways made a $400 million investment and operated joint transatlantic services, but the partnership became acrimonious and BA sold its holding in early 1997, at which time the airline took on the new identity of US Airways and new colours. Rome and Munich were added to the network in 1995 and 1996. Major fleet renewal, mostly courtesy of Airbus Industrie, began from 1998 with the introduction of A319s and A320s, with the A330 following in Spring 2000 and A321s scheduled to follow from mid-2001.

Routes

US Airways' major hubs are at Pittsburgh, Philadelphia and Charlotte, with service to over 130 destinations in the USA, Caribbean and Europe.

Fleet

		Ordered
46 Airbus A319-100	34 Boeing 757-200	4 Airbus A330-300
15 Airbus A320-200	12 Boeing 767-200ER	35 Airbus A319-100
5 Airbus A330-300	40 Fokker 100	32 Airbus A320-200
64 Boeing 737-200	42 McDonnell Douglas DC-9-30	34 Airbus A321-200
82 Boeing 737-300	31 McDonnell Douglas MD-80	
54 Boeing 737-400		

Boeing 767-33PER VP-BUZ (Stefan Quanz/Frankfurt)

UZBEKISTAN AIRWAYS

Ulitsa Proletarskaya 41,700100 Tashkent, Uzbekistan, Tel. 3712-911490, Fax. 3712-327371, www.uzbekistan-airways.com

Three- / Two- letter code	IATA No.	Reg'n prefix	ICAO callsign
UZB / HY	250	UK	Uzbek

In 1992 the government of the newly independent state of Uzbekistan took responsibility for its air services. The aircraft of the former Aeroflot Tashkent directorate became the property of Uzbekistan, and were passed to Uzbekistan Airways, which was formed as the national airline. Some of the routes previously operated by Aeroflot were taken over and continued. Particular attention was paid to the new routes from western Europe via Tashkent to the Indian subcontinent and Far East and it was here that the airline with its particularly low priced tariffs entered into competition with established airlines. In order to be in a position to meet the higher expectations of Western travellers, Uzbekistan leased two Airbus A310-300s and concluded an agreement with Lufthansa for technical support. The first of these arrived in Tashkent in July 1993 and services started to London and Middle Eastern cities. In 1995 Kuala Lumpur and New Delhi were added as destinations, and in 1996 Jeddah and Tel Aviv came on line. As well as the schedules, there are numerous charters to Arab countries. Modernisation and re-equipment with western aircraft started with the delivery in early 1997 of two leased Boeing 767-300s, and three Avro RJ 85s later in the year, with Boeing 757s added from September 1999. Uzbekistan is by far the largest airline operating in the country and has additional responsibilities for government tasks including patrol and agricultural work for which helicopters such as the Mil-8 are used.

Routes

Almaty, Amsterdam, Ashgabad Athens, Bahrain, Baku, Bangkok, Beijing, Birmingham, Bishkek, Bukhara, Chelyabinsk, Delhi, Dacca, Frankfurt, Istanbul, Jeddah, Kazan, Kiev, Krasnodar, Krasnoyarsk, Kuala Lumpur, London, Mineralnye Vody, Moscow, New York, Novosibirsk, Nukus, Omsk, Paris, Riyadh, Rostov, Samara, Samarkand, Seoul, Sharjah, Simferopol, St. Petersburg, Tashkent, Tel Aviv, Termez, Tyumen, Ufa, Urgench, Yekaterinburg.

Fleet

3 Airbus A310-300
12 Antonov An-24
3 Avro RJ 85
3 Boeing 757-200
2 Boeing 767-300ER
8 Ilyushin IL-62

10 Ilyushin IL-76
8 Ilyushin IL-86
2 Ilyushin IL-114
17 Tupolev Tu-154
16 Yakovlev Yak 40

Ordered

5 Ilyushin IL-114

Boeing 737-222 N219US (Josef Krauthäuser/Dallas-DFW)

VANGUARD AIRLINES

533 Mexico Avenue, Kansas City, Missouri, 64153, USA, Tel. 816-2432100, Fax. 816-2432937, www.flyvanguard.com

Three- / Two- letter code	IATA No.	Reg'n prefix	ICAO callsign
VGD / NJ	311	N	Vanguard Air

Vanguard Airlines is one of several United States airlines which have sought out a niche market and who have been able to exploit this with good marketing activities. Set up in 1994, Vanguard began its services on 2nd December of that year from its home base at Kansas City in Missouri. For many years at this airport there had been little in the way of competition for TWA, who thus had market control. By offering flights at attractive prices, Vanguard Airlines soon gained in importance and was able to expand its activities. As well as scheduled services, the airline offers charters for groups, associations and for tour operators. The well-proven Boeing 737-200 was chosen as the airline's equipment on grounds of operating cost, and the fleet has grown continually with further acquisition or leases. Likewise the route network has expanded as new aircraft have been added. In1998 Vanguard Airlines took an 8% shareholding in Denver-based Frontier Airlines. Future expansion is planned, with the intention that the fleet should total 25 aircraft by 2002.

Routes

Atlanta, Buffalo, Chicago-Midway, Cincinatti, Dallas/Fort Worth, Denver, Kansas City, Minneapolis/St. Paul, Myrtle Beach, Pittsburgh.

Fleet

13 Boeing 737-200

Boeing 737-76N PP-VQB (Author's collection)

VARIG BRASIL

Avenida Almirante Silvio de Noronha 365, CEP 20021-10 Rio de Janeiro, Brazil, Tel. 21-8145644, Fax. 21-8145718, www.varig.com.br

Three- / Two- letter code	IATA No.	Reg'n prefix	ICAO callsign
VRG / RG	042	PP	Varig

Founded on 7th May 1927 by German immigrant Otto Ernst Meyer, Varig developed initially in the south of Brazil. The first aircraft was a Dornier Wal flying-boat which operated the first service on 3rd February 1928. First international service was in 1942 to Montevideo and Lockheed 10As were introduced in 1943. After the Second World War, Varig acquired 35 C-47/DC-3s and built up its network. In 1951 Aero Geral with its routes to Buenos Aires and Montevideo were taken over. Scheduled service to New York started in August 1955; from

October 1959 the Caravelle was substituted and from late 1960 Boeing 707s took over the route. REAL, a much larger airline, was taken over in 1961 and thus under its famous president Ruben Berta, Varig acquired new aircraft such as the CV 990, Lockheed L-188, C-46 and an extensive route network. The international network was also expanded in 1965 when it took over Panair do Brasil by government order. DC-10-30s came into service in May 1971. A further airline, Cruzeiro do Sol, was bought in 1975 (and integrated in 1993) and in 1981

Airbus A300s and Boeing 747-200s were acquired. Boeing 767s, 747-400s and MD-11s were all added later, with the current colour scheme being adopted from 1998. Varig has majority shareholdings in Rio Sul and Nordeste Linhas Aereas. South America's largest and most modern overhaul base is owned by Varig at Rio de Janeiro, the airline's main base. A dedicated cargo airline called Varig Log is being created in the latter part of 2000 to take on all Varig's cargo assets and services. Varig has been a member of the Star Alliance since October 1997.

Routes

Aracaju, Asuncion, Belem, Belo Horizonte, Boa Vista, Bogota, Brasilia, Buenos Aires, Campo Grande, Cancun, Caracas, Copenhagen, Cordoba, Cuiaba, Curitiba, Florianopolis, Fortaleza, Frankfurt, Goiania, Iguacu Falls, Joao Pessoa, Joinville, La Paz, Lima, Lisbon, London, Londrina, Los Angeles, Macapa, Maceio, Madrid, Manaus, Mexico City, Miami, Montevideo, Nagoya, Natal, New York, Paris, Porto Allegre, Porto Seguro, Porto Velho, Recife, Rio Branco, Rio de Janeiro, Rome, Rosario, Salvador, Santa Cruz, Santiago, Sao Luiz, Sao Paulo, Tabatinga, Tefe, Teresina, Tokyo, Vitoria.

Fleet

		Ordered
12 Boeing 737-200	2 Boeing 747-300	2 Boeing 737-700
31 Boeing 737-300	12 Boeing 767-200/300ER	8 Boeing 737-800
7 Boeing 737-700	2 McDonnell Douglas DC-10-30F	5 Boeing 767-300
2 Boeing 737-800	14 (Boeing) McDonnell Douglas MD-11	4 Boeing 777-200
5 Boeing 727-100F		

McDonnell Douglas MD-11 PP-SFA (Josef Krauthäuser/Toronto-YYZ)

VASP

Praca Cte. Lineu Gomes sn, Ed. Sede VASP Congonhas Airport, Sao Paulo CEP 04695, Brazil, Tel. 11-5311949, Fax. 11-5437227, www.vasp.com.br

Three- / Two- letter code	IATA No.	Reg'n prefix	ICAO callsign
VSP / VP	343	PP	Vasp

Viacao Aerea Sao Paulo SA was founded on 4th November 1933 by the regional government of Sao Paulo and the municipal bank, with operations beginning on 16th April 1934. In 1935 two Junkers Ju 52/3s were acquired and scheduled service opened between Rio de Janeiro and Sao Paulo. The takeover of the Brazilian-German Aerolloyd Iguacu in 1939 added many routes. VASP used six Saab Scanias from 1950, and later all the aircraft of this type ever built, eighteen, were used until retired in 1966. Vickers Viscounts were used

from 1958. Two more airlines, Loide Aero Nacional and Navegaceo Aerea Brasileiro were taken over as part of a general rationalisation of Brazilian air service in 1962. The first jet, the BAC One-Eleven arrived in December 1967, and eight NAMC YS-11s were acquired in late 1968; these replaced the Viscounts and DC-4s. VASP evolved over the years to become Brazil's second largest airline, continually modernising its fleet. The first four Boeing 737s were introduced in July 1969 and in the late 1970s the Brazilian-built Embraer Bandeirante regional

aircraft came into service briefly, until the airline became all-jet. Boeing 727s and Airbus A300s then formed the fleet, until MD-11s were added in 1992. During the late 1990s VASP took shareholdings in long-established South American carriers Ecuatoriana and Lloyd Aereo Boliviano, but early in 2000 VASP itself entered a period of financial difficulty. A reorganisation took place, and some aircraft returned to their lessors, with a consequent reduction in activity; all European services were dropped.

Routes

Aracaju, Belem, Brasilia, Buenos Aires, Campinas, Campo-Grande, Culaba, Curitiba, Florianopolis, Fortaleza, Goiania, Guayaquil, Iguacu, Ilheus, Joao Pessoa, Londrina, Macapa, Maceio, Manaus, Miami, Natal, New York, Porto Allegre, Porto Seguro, Porto Velho, Quito, Recife, Ribeirao Preto, Rio de Janeiro, Salvador, Sao Jose do Porto Preto, Sao Luiz, Sao Paulo, Teresina, Toronto, Uberlandia.

Fleet

3 Airbus A300
5 Boeing 727-200F
22 Boeing 737-200
7 Boeing 737-300

1 McDonnell Douglas DC-10-30
5 (Boeing) McDonnell Douglas MD-11

Fokker 70 VN-A504 (Romano Germann/Vientiane)

VIETNAM AIRLINES

Gialem Airport, Hanoi 1000, Vietnam
Tel. 4-8732732, Fax. 4-8272291,
www.vietnamair.com.vn

Three- / Two- letter code	IATA No.	Reg'n prefix	ICAO callsign
HVN / VN	738	VN	Vietnam Airlines

After the ending of the Vietnam war and the coming together of North and South Vietnam, a new airline also came into existence in 1976: Hang Khong Vietnam. It took over the aircraft and staff of the former CAAV in the north and partly those of Air Vietnam. Air Vietnam had been 92.75% owned by the old southern government in 1975, shortly before the fall of Vietnam; it had been formed to take over the services of Air France in the area. Hang Khong Vietnam's fleet was very quickly changed over to Soviet standard as spare parts could not be obtained for the western-built aircraft and in the early and mid-1980s, Tupolev

Tu-134As operated several weekly services from Hanoi to Ho Chi Minh City (formerly Saigon), Phnom Penh, Bangkok and Vientiane. It was only when the country opened up politically towards the West and towards the USA that it was possible in 1990 to place an order for western aircraft. As a replacement for Ilyushin IL-18s, two ATR 72s were ordered. A slow expansion of the route network was planned for the 1990s. In 1990 some Tu-134s were bought from surplus Interflug stocks, the name was changed to Vietnam Airlines and new colours were introduced. Political change also made it possible for Air France

to acquire a stake in the airline and to provide Airbus A320s from late 1993 for international flights as well as providing training and other support. As part of a plan to replace the Russian types, further western aircraft, Boeing 767s and Fokker 70s were acquired to meet increased demand for services to this aspiring country. Routes to Australia and Europe have been introduced.

Routes

Bangkok, Ban Me Throut, Da Nang, Dalat, Dien Bien Phu, Dubai, Guangzhou, Haiphong, Hanoi, Ho Chi Minh City, Hong Kong, Hue, Kaoshiung, Kuala Lumpur, Manila, Melbourne, Na Trang, Osaka, Paris, Phnom Pen, Phuquoq, Pleiku, Quinhon, Rachgia, Siem Reap, Singapore, Son La, Sydney, Taipei, Vientiane, Vinh City.

Fleet

10 Airbus A320-200	2 Tupolev Tu-134
5 ATR 72	
4 Boeing 767-300ER	
2 Fokker 70	

Boeing 747-4Q8 G-VFAB (Thomas Kim/Los Angeles-LAX)

VIRGIN ATLANTIC

The Office, Crawley Business Quarter RH10 1DQ, Great Britain, Tel. 1293-562345, Fax. 1293-561721, www.virgin-atlantic.com

Three- / Two- letter code	IATA No.	Reg'n prefix	ICAO callsign
VIR / VS	932	G	Virgin

Virgin Atlantic has its origins in British Atlantic Airways founded in 1982, but which the CAA declined to licence. Richard Branson thus set up Virgin Atlantic through the Virgin Group. The collapsed Laker Airways was used by Branson as a model as there was an obvious demand for a 'cheap airline' to operate from London. Virgin Atlantic was granted a licence for London to New York (Newark) and the first flight was on 22nd June 1984. In November a daily connecting flight to Maastricht, Holland using BAC One-Elevens was started: this was later operated by Viscounts but ceased in 1990. With imaginative advertising and

marketing the airline offering only cheap flights, attracted more sophisticated passengers. In 1986 another 747 was added, with four more in 1989 and further routes including Miami, New York JFK and Tokyo via Moscow were started. The Airbus A340 was introduced in late 1993 and used for routes to Hong Kong and Australia. An A320 was also used for a feeder service to Athens, and this has recently been replaced by an A321. During 1996 the Belgian airline EBA was bought and used as the basis for a European network under the Virgin Express name (see page 364). Also in 1996 the Johannesburg route was

finally established. In 1998 Virgin was given authority to carry military personnel between London and Washington. In 1999 a Manchester-based charter airline was set up as Virgin Sun (see page 365). Plans were also made for an Australian low-cost airline, and this came to fruition in mid-2000 as Virgin Blue. Virgin gained the strength of Singapore Airlines as a partner in December 1999 when SIA took a 49% holding in Virgin. Also in 1999 the current 'Silver Dream' colour scheme was introduced for Virgin's fleet. Airbus A340-600s are on order for delivery from 2002.

Routes

Antigua, Athens, Barbados, Boston, Chicago, Hong Kong, Johannesburg, Las Vegas, Los Angeles, Manchester, Miami, Moscow, New York JFK, New York/Newark, Orlando, San Francisco, Shanghai, St. Lucia, Tokyo, Washington.

Fleet	Ordered
1 Airbus A321-200	12 Boeing 747-400
10 Airbus A340-300	6 Airbus A340-600
11 Boeing 747-200	
6 Boeing 747-400	

Boeing 737-3M8 OO-LTM (Frank Fielitz/Frankfurt)

VIRGIN EXPRESS

Building 116 Airport, B-1820 Melsbroek, Belgium
Tel. 2-7520511, Fax. 2-7520506,
www.virgin-exp.com

Three- / Two- letter code	IATA No.	Reg'n prefix	ICAO callsign
VEX / TV	665	OO	Virgin Express

In November 1991 EuroBelgian Airlines was set up by the City Hotels Group and it began operations from 1st April 1992 with Boeing 737-300s as a general European charter airline, partly in the expectation of providing some of the capacity which would be needed in the wake of the collapse of Air Europe. Richard Branson, founder and head of the British airline Virgin Atlantic took over EBA in April 1996 to form a basis for his European expansion plans, renamed it as Virgin Express and set about building a low-cost airline operating scheduled services within Europe. Until that time, 'low-cost' in Europe

had been equated with the use of old, less reliable aircraft, but Virgin Express took over EBA's modern Boeing 737-300s and augmented them with further examples. Likewise, EBA's existing network formed a good basis, with some modifications, and its charter operations were also continued. Rather than enter into head on competition, a strong partnership was quickly established with Sabena and the national airline's London service taken over, flown by Virgin Express aircraft on a codeshare basis, several times a day. The first brand new Boeing 737-300 for Virgin – painted in an

unmistakable red colour scheme complementary to that of Virgin Atlantic – was delivered at the end of 1996. In 1997 49% of Virgin Express shares were sold via the stock market: the balance remains with Branson. From 1998 a sister company Virgin Express (Ireland) was created in Dublin, with aircraft seconded from Belgium, as they have been for the newly launched Australian operation, Virgin Blue, launched in July 2000. Virgin Express now concentrates on scheduled operations which have been extended in 2000 to include Berlin. Boeing 737-700s are on order for delivery from July 2001.

Routes

Barcelona, Berlin, Brussels, Copenhagen, London-Gatwick, London-Heathrow, London-Stansted, Madrid, Milan, Nice, Rome, Shannon.

Fleet	Ordered
9 Boeing 737-300	11 Boeing 737-700
4 Boeing 737-400	4 Boeing 737-800

Airbus A320-214 G-VTAN (Dieter Roth/Salzburg)

VIRGIN SUN

The Galleria,Station Road, Crawley W.-Sussex
RH10 1WW, Great Britain, Tel. 1293-444616,
Fax. 1293-5533555, www.virginholidays.com

Three- / Two- letter code	IATA No.	Reg'n prefix	ICAO callsign
VIR / V2	–	G	Virgin Sun

Tour operator Virgin Holidays is a part of the Virgin conglomerate, and was set up in 1985 primarily to fill seats on Virgin Atlantic aircraft, by offering inclusive tours and packages based on all of Virgin Atlantic's services. However, as these are almost exclusively long-range, Virgin Holidays, in offering packages to attractive European destinations, was forced to rely on the services of other airlines. It was therefore inevitable that sooner or later it would make sense for its own airline operation to be set up for this market, and this came to pass in 1998 with Virgin Sun. New Airbus A320s direct from the production line began the airline's operations from 1st May 1999, flying from London-Gatwick and Manchester. The aircraft are painted in a bright red and yellow, holiday-like, variant of Virgin's colours, and as is traditional with Virgin, the aircraft carry appropriate names; in the example illustrated it is 'Sunshine Girl', painted in a way which puts a 'smile' on the face of the aircraft. A third Airbus A320 was added during 1999, followed by the first A321 for the 2000 summer season. Also for 2000, operations are carried out from other airports including East Midlands and Newcastle.

Routes

Charters on behalf of the Virgin Group's own tour operator Virgin Holidays to destinations in the Mediterranean, Northern Africa and the Canary Isles. In Winter to the Alpine ski resorts.

Fleet

3 Airbus A320-200
1 Airbus A321-200

Fokker 50 PH-VLM (Stefan Schlick/Saarbrücken)

VLM

Luchthaven, Gebouw B50 Antwerp Airport
B-2100 Deurne, Belgium, Tel.3-2856868,
Fax. 3-2813200, www.vlm-air.com

Three- / Two- letter code	IATA No.	Reg'n prefix	ICAO callsign
VLM / VG	978	OO	Rubens

Vlaamse Luchttransportmaatschappij NV was set up in Antwerp, the main city and business centre of Flanders, in February 1992. It took fifteen months for operations to get under way on 15th May 1993 with the first scheduled flight from Antwerp to London City Airport. VLM is a typical niche carrier, offering services from smaller airports. Thus it flies from Rotterdam and from Mönchengladbach, which now has retitled itself with the somewhat more fancy name of Düsseldorf-Express-Airport. For a while the London City service was extended with a British domestic leg to Liverpool, but this experiment was not a success and was dropped. The fleet has been expanded with the acquisition of further Fokker 50s, the airline's standard type, and the airline has expanded carefully in new markets. It also flies subcharters for other airlines. The original aircraft was acquired from the Norwegian operator Busy Bee, and retained their basic yellow and white colours, but in 1998 a new dark blue and white scheme was adopted, with the Flanders lion in gold on the fin. New seasonal routes to Guernsey and Jersey were introduced, and Manchester and Hanover were also added to the network. VLM is now Antwerp's leading operator with over 150 departures a week. There is co-operation with KLM UK, Lufthansa, Luxair and Sabena.

Routes

Antwerp, Düsseldorf Express, Geneva, Guernsey, Hanover, Jersey, London City, Luxembourg, Manchester, Rotterdam.

Fleet

8 Fokker 50

Tupolev Tu-154 M RA-85628 (Dennis Wehrmann/Hanover)

VNUKOVO AIRLINES

B 121 Reysovaya, Vnukovo AP,
Moscow 103027, Russia,
Tel. 095-4367995, Fax. 095-4362626

Three- / Two- letter code	IATA No.	Reg'n prefix	ICAO callsign
VKO / V5	442	RA	Vnukovo

Vnukovo is Moscow's third airport, and this airline was founded here in 1993 as Vnukovskie Avialinii. The former Aeroflot Vnukovo Production and Central Test Division provided material and personnel. Vnukovo soon developed to be a leading airline, run to Western standards; punctuality and quality of service are outstanding compared with some other airlines from the former Soviet Union. Likewise, the fleet. though all Soviet-built, is relatively young and well cared-for. Routes are flown from Moscow to destinations in the south of the CIS and the airline is also active with worldwide charters. In 1993 the airline received the first example of Russia's new-generation aircraft production, the Tupolev Tu-204, which it used for extensive testing under normal airline operating conditions. Two further aircraft were used initially as freighters and then converted for passenger use when so licensed. Before the testing had been completed, the airline had placed an order for 20 of the 210-seaters.

Routes

Anapa, Aktau, Antalya, Athens, Barcelona, Dunai, Hurghada, Igarka, Istanbul, Kaliningrad, Kambala, Kemerovo, Krasnodar, Moscow, Nadym, Novosibirsk, Norilsk, Novo Urengoy, Odessa, Samarkand, Sochi, Tblisi, Ulan Ude, Vladikavkaz,Yerevan.

Fleet	Ordered
22 Ilyushin IL-86	20 Tupolev Tu-204
19 Tupolev Tu-154	
7 Tupolev Tu-204	

Airbus A320-212 F-GJVX (Stefan Schlick/Arrecife)

VOLARE AIRLINES

Corso Garibaldi 186, 36016 Tiene (VI)
Italy
Tel. 0445-800100, Fax. 0445-800101

Three- / Two- letter code	IATA No.	Reg'n prefix	ICAO callsign
VLE / 8D	–	I	Revola

Volare Airlines was established in 1997 by a group of people from the travel industry. A leased Airbus A320 was used to begin services in April 1998 for the summer season from airports in the North of Italy including Bergamo, Milan and Verona. Two more A320s were added during 1998 and scheduled services were also begun from Milan to Olbia. The SAir Group took a 34% shareholding in the young airline from September 1998. During 1999 more scheduled services were added, including to Rome, and more A320s were added. There is naturally now co-operation with the other members of the SAir Group, particularly fellow Italian Air Europe and Swissair is responsible for aircraft technical matters. The growth has continued into the new millennium and more destinations and increased frequencies are being added; there is also a boom in the Italian charter market. In 1999 Volare carried about 700,000 passengers, and it became a member of the Qualiflyer Group from January 2000. SAir intends to merge the airline into the same holding company as Air Europe (see page 50), but continue independent operation

Routes

Alghero, Antalya, Bergamo, Cagliari, Istanbul, Las Palmas, Milan, Olbia, Palma de Mallorca, Rome.

Fleet	Ordered
9 Airbus A320	1 Airbus A320

BAe 146-100 D-AWDL (Albert Kuhbandner/Munich)

WDL AVIATION

Postfach 980267, 51130 Köln-Flughafen
Germany
Tel. 02203-9670, Fax. 02203-967105

Three- / Two- letter code	IATA No.	Reg'n prefix	ICAO callsign
WDL	–	D	WDL

Westdeutsche Luftwerbung WDL was established in 1955, with the objective of aerial advertising, be it with banners towed by aircraft, or with airships operating as flying billboards. The firm's headquarters was at the Essen-Mülheim airport. Charter and sightseeing flights were also offered and proved very popular at weekends. From this developed non-scheduled services, for which four to six-seater aircraft were used. The step to larger aircraft came in 1974 with the first Fokker F.27, and this type was used for both freight and passenger work. WDL-Flugdienst GmbH was created in 1991 for the operation of the larger aircraft and took over all the F.27s. DLT was building up a regional network on behalf of Lufthansa, and WDL helped with this. Aircraft and crews were provided for several years for the network of this predecessor of Lufthansa Cityline. As the F.27 fleet continued to grow, so the company acquired new contracts. The new package companies such as TNT and UPS often contracted national companies to fly regional services from their central hubs, and Cologne/Bonn's airport is one of these hub airports. In 1991 the newly-formed1991 WDL Aviation GmbH moved its headquarters and base to this airport and provided German and European distribution for these freight companies. In 1998 WDL took on its first BAe 146 jet, a series 100 which was used for passenger charter work; two more of the type, a 200 and a 300, have been added since. A decision about the successor to the F.27 will have to be made in the next couple of years.

Routes

Regular freight flights on behalf of UPS and others within Germany and Europe. Passenger flights as charters or ad hoc for Eurowings and other companies.

Fleet

3 BAe 146
15 Fokker F.27

Boeing 737-281 C-GQWJ (Author's collection)

WESTJET AIRLINES

35 McTavish Place NE, Calgary, Alberta T2E 7J7, Canada, Tel. 403-7352600, Fax. 403-5714649
www.westjet.com

Three- / Two- letter code	IATA No.	Reg'n prefix	ICAO callsign
WJW / M3	–	C	Westjet

The notion of a low-cost airline for the West of Canada was mooted in 1994 by a group of businessmen in Calgary and set out in a master plan for interested investors. Thus Westjet was set up in June 1995 after the successful model of US companies Morris Air and Southwest Airlines. David Neeleman, who had been a leading light at both Morris Air and Southwest, and was founder of Jet Blue Airlines, was an adviser. Services began on 29th February 1996 with two Boeing·737-200s from Calgary, at first serving Edmonton, Kelowna, Vancouver and Winnipeg. During 1996 two further 737-200s

were added to the fleet, which continued to grow steadily in the following three years. 1999 was a year of considerable change on the Canadian airline scene, after Canadian was taken over by Air Canada, and Westjet seized the newly-offered opportunities to expand its services into the east of the country, with services to Thunder Bay and Moncton. Also in 1999 a share offering was made in order to increase the capital base, in turn allowing the building of a new headquarters and hangars in Calgary as well as further fleet expansion. From early 2000 Hamilton was established as a hub

for services in Eastern Canada, with flights to Halifax, Montreal and Ottawa following. By 2002 Westjet intends to have doubled the size of its aircraft fleet and its number of routes, with expansion into the USA envisaged. The fleet plan calls for up to 24 Boeing 737-700s to be on delivery from 2003.

Routes

Abbotsford, Calgary, Edmonton, Grande Prairie, Halifax, Hamilton, Kelowna, Moncton, Montreal, Ottawa, Prince George, Regina, Saskatoon, Thunder Bay, Vancouver, Victoria, Winnipeg.

Fleet

18 Boeing 737-200

De Havilland DHC-8-311 LN-WFC (Author's collection)

WIDEROE

P.O.Box 247, Langstranda 6, 8001 Bodo, Norway, Tel. 51-513500, Fax. 51-513582, www.wideroe.no

Three- / Two- letter code	IATA No.	Reg'n prefix	ICAO callsign
WIF / WF	701	LN	Wideroe

Viggo Wideroe founded his Wideroe's Flyveselskap A/S on 19th February 1934. First he obtained a licence to open a route from Oslo to Haugesund. On behalf of DNL, the established Norwegian airline of the time and one of the predecessors of SAS, he opened a postal service in 1936 to Kirkenes in the north of Norway. After the Second World War, Wideroe started charter and supply flights again. It took over the Narvik-based Polarfly in 1950 and made a particular contribution to the opening up of the north of Norway. The first de Havilland DHC-6 Twin Otters were received in 1968 and used to open scheduled services on local routes. With government support a network from Bodo and Tromso was built up and this was extended over the years to around 30 to 40 smaller airfields, all of them standardised with similar landing aids and a runway of between 800 and 1,000 metres. In this way the necessary infrastructure was created in this inaccessible area criss-crossed with fjords. Towns such as Kirkenes and Hammerfest had only been accessible by ship until the air services began. From 1993 to 1996 almost the entire fleet, including the DHC-7s which had served for some years, was replaced by modern DHC-8s and international service was opened for the first time to Sumburgh in the Shetland Islands and to Copenhagen. Wideroe also undertakes charter work. Other airlines, Fred Olsen, SAS and Braathens S.A.F.E. all had shares in Wideroe but in the late 1990s SAS took over the majority holding and Wideroe has since then been more closely involved and co-ordinated with SAS.

Routes

Aberdeen, Alta, Andenes, Batsfjord, Bergen, Bervelag, Bodo, Bromnoysund, Copenhagen, Fagernes, Floro, Forde, Gothenberg, Hammerfest, Hasvik, Honningsvag, Kirkenes, Leknes, Maloy, Moirana, Mosjoen, Murmansk, Namsos, Narvik, Oslo, Roervik, Rost, Sandane, Skolvaer, Sorkjosen, Sogndal, Stavanger, Stockholm, Stokmarknes, Sumburgh, Tromso, Trondheim, Vadso, Vardo.

Fleet

1 De Havilland DHC-6
26 De Havilland DHC-8

(Boeing) McDonnell Douglas MD-11 N271WA (Author's collection)

WORLD AIRWAYS

13873 Park Center Road, Herndon, VA 20171, USA, Tel. 703-8349200, Fax. 703-8349212, www.worldair.com

Three- / Two- letter code	IATA No.	Reg'n prefix	ICAO callsign
WOA / WO	468	N	World

World Airways was founded on 29th March 1948 and began charter flights with a Boeing 314 flying boat from the US east coast. A year later flights moved from water to land; two Curtiss C-46s were used. Edward Daly acquired an 81% interest in the airline and made it into a large and well-known supplemental charter airline. From 1960 World took over an increasing number of flights for the USAF's Military Airlift Command, and DC-4s, DC-6s and Lockheed 1049 Constellations were bought or leased. The first Boeing 707s were acquired in 1963 and regular flights to Europe were introduced using

these aircraft, as well as services to the Caribbean and South America. In May 1973 charter flights to London began from Oakland, using Boeing 747s. World linked Newark and Baltimore/Washington with Los Angeles and Oakland from April 1979. Scheduled flights were further expanded with the introduction of DC-10s, and the Hawaii-Los Angeles-Baltimore-London-Frankfurt flights were the lowest priced charters to these destinations for many years. After restructuring in 1988 World abruptly withdrew from scheduled services. Malaysian Helicopter took over 25% of the shares in 1994 and invested in the

company. From 1993, passenger services were restarted to Israel and charters were resumed under the airline's own name to Great Britain and other European destinations. However, yet again these were withdrawn after the 1996 summer season, and the airline was to concentrate in future on ad hoc charters and freight flights. The airline has moved towards a specialisation in wet-leasing their aircraft out, with World Airways aircraft thus flying in other airlines' colours.

Routes

Charter and freight flights worldwide.

Fleet

3 McDonnell Douglas DC-10-30
6 (Boeing) McDonnell Douglas MD-11

Boeing 737-225C B-2524 (Author's collection/Beijing)

XIAMEN AIRLINES

Gaoqi Airport 361009 Xiamen,Fujian
People's Republic of China
Tel. 592-6022961, Fax. 592-6028263

Three- / Two- letter code	IATA No.	Reg'n prefix	ICAO callsign
CXA / MF	731	B	Xiamen Airlines

Xiamen Airlines was founded in 1991 by China Southern Airlines (with 60% of the shares) and the regional governments of Xiamen and Fujian, and is virtually a subsidiary of CSA but with its own fleet and operating area. Operations began in 1992 with a leased Boeing 737-200. More 737s have been added, including -500 series from 1992 onwards, and Boeing 757s were added to the fleet with deliveries from August 1992 to February 1996. There are services to the South and East of the People's Republic. In late 1992 a route to Hong Kong was opened, the first international destination. During

1998 Xiamen Airlines received four Boeing 737-700s to replace the older -200s. The airline is based at Xiamen, where maintenance also takes place, and works closely with the companies in the China Southern group.

Routes

Anqing, Beijing, Changchun, Changsha, Chengdu, Chongqing, Dalian, Fuzhou, Guangzhou, Guilin, Guiyang, Haikou, Hangzhou, Harbin, Hefei, Jinan, Jinjiang, Kunming, Lanzhou, Macau, Nanchang, Nanjing, Nanning, Nantong, Ningbo, Qingdao, Shanghai, Shantou, Shenyang, Shenzen, Shijiazhuang, Tianjin, Wenzhou, Wuhan, Wuyshan, Xian, Xiamen, Zhengzhou, Zhousan.

Fleet		Ordered
5 Boeing 737-200	5 Boeing 757-200	2 Boeing 737-700
6 Boeing 737-500		
4 Boeing 737-700		

Boeing 727-2N8 7O-ACY (Uwe Gleisberg/Munich)

YEMENIA

P.O.Box 1183, Sanaa, Republic of Yemen
Tel. 232380, Fax. 252963,
www.yemenia.com.ye

Three- / Two- letter code	IATA No.	Reg'n prefix	ICAO callsign
IYE / IY	635	7O	Yemeni

The 'new' Yemenia is the result of the amalgamation of the former Alyemen and Yemenia, respectively the two national airlines of the North and South Yemen, now merged into one nation again. Saudi Arabian Airlines is a 40% shareholder in the new airline. The two precursors were completely dissolved, bringing aircraft, routes, handling etc all completely into the new airline. The original Yemenia can be traced back to 1961 when it was established as Yemen Airlines, whilst Alyemen was set up soon after the split of the country into North and South in 1971. Several aircraft are also used for transport roles by the country's air force. The mixed fleet arising from the merger includes two DHC-7s delivered in 1996 to augment two earlier examples, and two Airbus A310s leased from Spring 1997 to give a modern image to international routes. An alliance was formed with Daallo Airlines in 1998, and some flights are operated under a codeshare arrangement.

Routes

Abu Dhabi, Addis Ababa, Aden, Albuq, Al Gaydah, Amman, Asmara, Ataq, Bahrain, Cairo, Damascus, Djibouti, Doha, Dubai, Frankfurt, Hodeidah, Jeddah, Karachi, Khartoum, Larnaca, London, Moroni, Mumbai, Nairobi, Paris, Riyadh, Rome, Sanaa, Seiyun, Sharjah, Taiz.

Fleet

3 Airbus A310-300
3 Boeing 737-200
5 Boeing 727-200
2 de Havilland DHC-6 Twin Otter

4 de Havilland DHC-7
2 Lockheed L-382 Hercules
1 Ilyushin IL-76TD

Boeing 737-37K B-2935 (Romano Germann/Beijing)

ZHONGYUAN AIRLINES

No.106 Jinshua Rd.Zhengzhou,
Henan 450003, People's Republic of China
Tel. 371-6222542, Fax. 371-62222542

Three- / Two- letter code	IATA No.	Reg'n prefix	ICAO callsign
CYN / Z2	–	B	Zhongyuan

Zhongyuan Airlines was formed in 1991 in the Chinese province of Henan, and began operations in that same year with two Yunshuji Y7s, Chinese licence-built versions of the proven Antonov 24, though with some improvements over the Russian original. Initially the two Y7s served 15 destinations. As propeller driven types were taking too long to fly some of the longer routes, a Boeing 737-300 was acquired in April 1994. Some airports were also not allowing the use of propeller aircraft on safety grounds, and so the airlines were being influenced to acquire modern jets. Later in 1994 more 737-300s arrived and expansion has continued by the acquisition of further examples in 1999. Zhongyuan built up an alliance with Hainan Airlines, Shandong Airlines, Shenzen Airlines, Sichuan Airlines and Wuhan Air Lines to compete with China's larger airlines, but in mid-2000 was acquired by China Southern as an early move under the great new Chinese airline consolidation plan. It will however continue to operate under its own identity.

Routes

Beijing, Changsha, Chengdu, Chongging, Guilin, Guiyang, Haikou, Harbin, Huangyan, Jingdezhen, Kunming, Nanjing, Ningbo, Shanghai, Shenyang, Shenzen, Wenzhou, Wuhan, Xiamen, Yantai.

Fleet

2 Yunshuji Y7-100
5 Boeing 737-300

International Aircraft Registration Prefixes

By Prefix

Prefix	Country	Prefix	Country	Prefix	Country	Prefix	Country
AP	Pakistan	HR	Honduras	TT	Chad	4R	Sri Lanka
A2	Botswana	HS	Thailand	TU	Ivory Coast	4X	Israel
A3	Tonga	HZ	Saudi Arabia	TY	Benin	5A	Libya
A4O	Oman	H4	Solomon Islands	TZ	Mali	5B	Cyprus
A5	Bhutan	I	Italy	T2	Tuvalu	5H	Tanzania
A6	United Arab Emirates	JA	Japan	T3	Kiribati	5N	Nigeria
A7	Qatar	JU	Mongolia	T7	San Marino	5R	Madagascar
A9C	Bahrain	JY	Jordan	T8A	Palau	5T	Mauritania
B	People's Republic of China	J2	Djibouti	T9	Bosnia-Herzegovina	5U	Niger
B-H	Hong Kong	J3	Grenada			5V	Togo
B-M	Macau	J5	Guinea Bissau	UK	Uzbekistan	5W	West-Samoa
B	Republic of China (Taiwan)	J6	St. Lucia	UN	Kazakstan	5X	Uganda
C	Canada	J7	Dominica	UR	Ukraine	5Y	Kenya
CC	Chile	J8	St. Vincent and Grenadines	VH	Australia	6O	Somalia
CCCP	former Soviet Union	LN	Norway	VN	Vietnam	6V	Senegal
CN	Morocco	LV	Argentina	VP-A	Anguilla	6Y	Jamaica
CP	Bolivia	LX	Luxembourg	VP-B	Bermuda	7O	Yemen
CS	Portugal	LY	Lithuania	VP-C	Cayman Islands	7P	Lesotho
CU	Cuba	LZ	Bulgaria	VP-F	Falkland Islands	7Q	Malawi
CX	Uruguay	N	USA	VP-G	Gibraltar	7T	Algeria
C2	Nauru	OB	Peru	VP-L	British Virgin Islands	8P	Barbados
C3	Andorra	OD	Lebanon			8Q	Maldives
C5	Gambia	OE	Austria	VP-M	Montserrat	8R	Guyana
C6	Bahamas	OH	Finland	VQ-T	Turks & Caicos	9A	Croatia
C9	Mozambique	OK	Czech Republic	VT	India	9G	Ghana
D	Germany	OM	Slovakia	V2	Antigua and Barbuda	9H	Malta
DQ	Fiji	OO	Belgium	V3	Belize	9J	Zambia
D2	Angola	OY	Denmark	V4	St. Kitts and Nevis Islands	9K	Kuwait
D4	Cape Verde Islands	P	North Korea	V5	Namibia	9L	Sierra Leone
D6	Comores Islands	PH	Netherlands	V6	Micronesia	9M	Malaysia
EC	Spain	PJ	Netherlands Antilles	V7	Marshall Islands	9N	Nepal
EI	Ireland	PK	Indonesia	V8	Sultanate of Brunei	9Q	Congo (ex-Zaire)
EK	Armenia	PP	Brazil	XA,XB,XC	Mexico	9U	Burundi
EL	Liberia	PT	Brazil	XT	Burkina Faso	9V	Singapore
EP	Iran	PZ	Surinam	XU	Cambodia	9XR	Rwanda
ER	Moldavia	P2	Papua New Guinea	XY	Myanmar	9Y	Trinidad and Tobago
ES	Estonia	P4	Aruba	YA	Afghanistan		
ET	Ethiopia	RA	Russia	YI	Iraq		
EW	Belarus	RDPL	Laos	YJ	Vanuatu		
EX	Kyrgyzstan	RP	Philippines	YK	Syria		
EY	Tajikistan	SE	Sweden	YL	Latvia		
EZ	Turkmenistan	SP	Poland	YN	Nicaragua		
E3	Eritrea	ST	Sudan	YR	Romania		
F	France	SU	Egypt	YS	El Salvador		
G	Great Britain	SX	Greece	YU	Yugoslavia		
HA	Hungary	S2	Bangladesh	YV	Venezuela		
HB	Switzerland (including Lichtenstein)	S5	Slovenia	Z	Zimbabwe		
HC	Ecuador	S7	Seychelles	ZA	Albania		
HH	Haiti	S9	Sao Tomé & Principe	ZK	New Zealand		
HI	Dominican Republic	TC	Turkey	ZP	Paraguay		
HK	Columbia	TF	Iceland	ZS, ZU	South Africa		
HL	South Korea	TG	Guatemala	Z3	Macedonia		
HP	Panama	TI	Costa Rica	3A	Monaco		
		TJ	Cameroon	3B	Mauritius		
		TL	Central African Republic	3C	Equatorial Guinea		
		TN	Congo	3D	Swaziland		
		TR	Gabon	3X	Guinea		
		TS	Tunisia	4K	Azerbaijan		
				4L	Georgia		

By Country

Country	Prefix
Afghanistan	YA
Albania	ZA
Algeria	7T
Andorra	C3
Angola	D2
Anguilla	VP-A
Antigua & Barbuda	V2
Argentina	LV
Armenia	EK
Aruba	P4
Azerbaijan	4K
Australia	VH
Bahamas	A9C
Bangladesh	S2
Barbados	8P
Barbuba	V2
Belgium	OO
Belize	V3
Benin	TY
Bermuda	VP-B
Bhutan	A5
Bolivia	CP
Bosnia-Herzegovina	T9
Botswana	A2
Brazil	PP/PT
British Virgin Islands	VP-L
Brunei	V8
Bulgaria	LZ
Burkina Faso	XT
Burundi	9U
Cayman Islands	VP-C
Chile	CC
China, People's Republic	B
China, Republic (Taiwan)	B
Costa Rica	TI
Denmark	OY
Germany	D
Djibouti	J2
Dominica	J7
Dominican Republic	HI
Ecuador	HC
Ivory Coast	TU
El Salvador	YS
Equatorial Guinea	3C
Eritrea	E3
Estonia	ES
Ethiopia	ET
Falkland Islands	VP-F
Fiji	DQ
Finland	OH
France	F
Gabon	TR
Gambia	C5
Georgia	4L
Ghana	9G
Gibraltar	VP-G
Grenada	J3
Greece	SX
Great Britain	G
Guam	N
Guinea	3X
Guinea Bissau	J5
Guyana	8R
Haiti	HH
Honduras	HR
Hong Kong	B-H
India	VT
Indonesia	PK
Iraq	YI
Iran	EP
Iceland	TF
Israel	4X
Italy	I
Jamaica	6Y
Japan	JA
Jordan	JY
Kazakstan	UN
Kenya	5Y
Kyrgyzstan	EX
Kiribati	T3
Korea, North	P
Korea, South	HL
Kuwait	9K
Laos	RDPL
Latvia	YL
Lesotho	7P
Lebanon	OD
Liberia	EL
Libya	5A
Liechtenstein	HB
Lithuania	LY
Luxembourg	LX
Macau	B-M
Macedonia	Z3
Madagascar	5R
Malawi	7Q
Malaysia	9M
Maldives	8Q
Mali	TZ
Malta	9H
Morocco	CN
Marshall Islands	V7
Mauritania	5T
Mauritius	3B
Mexico	XA
Micronesia	V6
Moldavia	ER
Monaco	3A
Mongolia	JU
Montserrat	VP-M
Mozambique	C9
Myanmar	XY
Namibia	V5
Nauru	C2
Nepal	9N
Netherlands	PH
Netherlands Antilles	PJ
New Zealand	ZK
Nicaragua	YN
Niger	5U
Nigeria	5N
Norway	LN
Oman	A40
Pakistan	AP
Palau	T8A
Panama	HP
Papua New Guinea	P2
Paraguay	ZP
Peru	OB
Philippines	RP
Poland	SP
Portugal	CS
Puerto Rico	N
Qatar	A7
Romania	YR
Russia	RA
Rwanda	9XR
Samoa	5W
San Marino	T7
Sao Tomé & Principe	S9
Saudi Arabia	HZ
Senegal	6V
Seychelles	S7
Sierra Leone	9L
Singapore	9V
Slovakia	OM
Slovenia	S5
Solomon Islands	H4
Somalia	6O
Spain	EC
Sri Lanka	4R
St. Kitts & Nevis	V4
St. Lucia	J6
St. Vincent and Grenadines	J8
Sudan	ST
South Africa	ZS
Surinam	PZ
Swaziland	3D
Sweden	SE
Switzerland	HB
Syria	YK
Taiwan	B
Tajikistan	EY
Tanzania	5H
Thailand	HS
Togo	5V
Tonga	A3
Trinidad/Tobago	9Y
Tunisia	TS
Turkey	TC
Turkmenistan	EZ
Turks and Caicos Islands	VQ-T
Tuvalu	T2
Uganda	5X
Ukraine	UR
United Arab Emirates	A6
United States	N
Uruguay	CX
Uzbekistan	UK
Vanuatu	YJ
Venezuela	YV
Vietnam	VN
Western Samoa	5W
Yemen	7O
Yugoslavia	YU
Zambia	9J
Zimbabwe	Z

Airline Three-letter codes (IATA codes in parentheses)

AAA	Ansett (AN)	AIG	Air Inter Gabon	ARN	Air Nova (QK)
AAA	Ansett, NZ (ZQ)	AIH	Airtours International (VZ)	ARP	L'Aeroposte
AAG	Atlantic Airways (KI)	AIJ	Air Jet (BC)	ARU	Air Aruba (FQ)
AAH	Aloha Airlines (AQ)	AIN	African International Airways	ASA	Alaska Airlines (AS)
AAL	American Airlines (AA)	AIP	Alpine Air (5A)	ASD	Air Sinai (4D)
AAR	Asiana (OZ)	AIX	Aircruising Australia	ASE	ASA-Delta Connection (EV)
ABB	Air Belgium (AJ)	AIZ	Arkia (IZ)	ASF	Air Schefferville
ABD	Air Atlanta Iceland (CC)	AJI	Ameristar Jet Charter	ASH	Mesa Airlines (YU)
ABG	Abakan-Avia	AJM	Air Jamaica (JM)	ASJ	Air Satellite
ABL	Air BC (ZX)	AJO	Aeroexo (SX)	ASM	Air Saint Martin (S6
ABO	APSA Colombia	AJT	Amerijet (JH)	ASU	Aerosur
ABR	Air Contractors (AG)	AKA	Air Korea	ASW	Air Southwest
ABS	Athabaska Airways (9T)	AKC	Arca Colombia (ZU)	ATC	Air Tanzania (TC)
ABW	Albanian Airlines (7Y)	AKH	Turkmenistan/AKHAL Air-	ATK	Aerotaca Colombia
ABX	Airborne Express (GB)		company (T5)	ATN	Air Transport International
ACA	Air Canada (AC)	AKK	Aklak Air (6L)		(8C)
ACD	Academy Airlines	AKL	Air Kilroy	ATT	Aer Turas Teoranta
ACF	Air Charter (SF)	AKN	Alkan Air	AUA	Austrian Airlines (OS)
ACI	Air Caledonie Intl. (SB)	AKT	Karat (2U)	AUB	Augsburg Airways (IQ)
ACO	Air Colombia	AKZ	Aerokuznetsk	AUI	Ukraine International Airlines
ACQ	Aerocontinente (N6)	ALG	Air Logistics		(PS)
ACX	Air Charters	ALK	Srilankan (UL)	AUL	AVL (5N)
ADB	Antonov Airlines	ALM	ALM Antillean Airlines (LM)	AUR	Aurigny Air Services (GR)
ADH	Air One (AP)	ALO	Allegheny Airlines (US)	AVA	Avianca Columbia (AV)
ADK	ADC Airlines	ALX	CAL-Congo (EO)	AVE	Avensa (VE)
ADO	Air Hokkaido Intl. (HD)	AMC	Air Malta (KM)	AVN	Air Vanuatu (NF)
ADR	Adria Airways (JP)	AMF	Ameriflight	AVZ	Aeroservice Kazakstan
ADZ	Aviosarda Airlines (DF)	AMI	Air Maldives (L6)	AWC	Titan Airways
AEA	Air Europe (UX)	AMK	Amerer Air	AWE	America West Airlines (HP)
AEE	Aegean Aviation	AML	Air Malawi (QM)	AWI	Air Wisconsin-United
AEF	Aero Lloyd (YP)	AMM	Air 2000 (DP)		Express
AEL	Air Europe (PE)	AMO	Air Montreal (F8)	AWS	Arab Wings
AER	Alaska Central Express (KO)	AMT	American Trans Air (TZ)	AWT	Air West
AES	ACES Colombia (VX)	AMU	Air Macau (NX)	AXF	Asian Express Airlines (HJ)
AEW	Aerosweet Airlines (VV)	AMC	Aeromexico (AM)	AXL	KLM Exel (4X)
AEY	Aero Lyon (4Q)	AMV	AMC Aviation	AXM	Air Asia (AK)
AFE	Airfast Indonesia	AMW	Air Midwest (ZV)	AXX	Avioimpex (M4)
AFG	Ariana Afghan Airlines (FG)	AMX	Aeromexico (AM)	AYZ	Atlant Soyuz Airlines (3G)
AFJ	SA Alliance (Y2)	ANA	ANA-All Nippon Airways (NH)	AZA	Alitalia (AZ)
AFL	Aeroflot Russian Airlines (SU)	ANG	Air Niugini (PX)	AZI	Azzurraair (ZS)
AFM	Affretair (ZL)	ANI	Air Atlantic Cargo	AZL	Air Zanzibar
AFO	Aero Empresa Mexicana	ANK	Air Nippon (EL)	AZM	Aerocozumel (AZ)
AFP	TAM	ANO	Air North Regional (TL)	AZW	Air Zimbabwe (UM)
AFR	Air France (AF)	ANS	Air Nostrum (YW)	BAG	Deutsche BA (DI)
AGJ	Air Greece (JG)	ANT	Air North (4N)	BAL	Britannia Airways (BY)
AGL	Air Angouleme	ANZ	Air New Zealand (NZ)	BAW	British Airways (BA)
AGN	Air Gabon (GN)	AOD	Aero Vodochody	BBC	Biman Bangladesh (BG)
AGO	Angola Air Charter (C3)	AOK	Aeroatlantico	BBR	Santa Barbara Airlines (BJ)
AGU	Air Guadeloupe (OG)	AOM	AOM French Airlines (IW)	BCS	European Air Transport (QY)
AGV	Air Glaciers (GB)	AOO	AS Aviakompania	BCY	City Jet (WX)
AGX	Aviogenex (JJ)	APB	Air Atlantique (KI)	BER	Air Berlin (AB)
AHA	Air Alpha	APC	Airpac Airlines (LQ)	BES	Aero Services Executive (W4)
AHC	Azerbaijan Airlines	APO	Aeropro	BFC	Basler Airlines
AHG	Aerochaga Airlines	APP	Aeroperlas (WL)	BFF	Air Nunavut
AHK	Air Hong Kong (LD)	APR	Air Provence International	BFL	Buffalo Airways (J4)
AHL	Air Hanson	APT	LAP Colombia	BGA	Airbus Transport
AHR	Air Holland (GG)	APW	Arrow Air (JW)		International
AHY	Azerbaijan Airlines (J2)	ARB	Avia Air (8R)	BGM	Tatarstan Air Enterprise
AIC	Air India (AI)	ARE	Aires Colombia (4C)	BHO	Bhoja Airlines (B4)
AID	Alti Air Company	ARG	Aerolineas Argentinas (AR)	BHS	Bahamasair (UP)
AIE	Air Inuit (3H)	ARK	Ararat Avia (4A)	BIE	Air Mediterranee

BIM	Binter Mediterraneo (AX)	CFE	City Flyer Express (FD)	CWC	Challenge Air Cargo (WE)
BKL	Baikal Airlines (X3)	CFG	Condor (DE)	CWU	Wuhan Air Lines (WU)
BKP	Bangkok Airways (PG)	CFJ	Fujian Airlines (IV)	CXA	Xiamen Airlines (MF)
BKU	Bykovo Avia	CFZ	Zhongfei Airlines	CXH	China Xinhua Airlines (X2)
BLC	TAM-Express (JJ)	CGH	Air Guizhou	CXI	Shanxi Aviation (BC)
BLI	Belair	CGT	CNG Transavia	CXJ	China Xinjiang Airlines (XO)
BLL	Baltic Airlines	CGW	Air Great Wall (G8)	CXN	China Southwest Airl. (SZ)
BLR	Atlantic Coast Airlines (DH)	CHB	Chelyabinsk Air Enterprise	CXP	Casino Express (XP)
BLS	Bearskin Airlines (JV)		(H6)	CXT	Coastal Air Transport (DQ)
BLV	Bellview Airlines (B3)	CHH	Hainan Airlines (H4)	CYH	China Yunnan Airlines (3Q)
BLX	Britannia Airways (6B)	CHJ	Chaika Aircompany	CYN	Zhongyuan Airlines (Z2)
BMA	British Midland (BD)	CHP	Aviacsa (6A)	CYP	Cyprus Airways (CY)
BOA	Boniair	CHQ	Chautauqua Airlines (US)	DAG	Daghestan Airlines
BOI	Aboitiz Air	CIB	Condor-Berlin	DAH	Air Algerie (AH)
BON	Air Bosna (JA)	CIC	ICC Air Cargo Canada	DAL	Delta Air Lines (DL)
BOT	Air Botswana (BP)	CIM	Cimber Air (QI)	DAN	Maersk Air (DM)
BOU	Bouraq Indonesia (BO)	CIR	Artic Circle Air Service	DAO	Daallo Airlines (D3)
BPA	Blue Panorama (9S)	CKS	Kalitta American International	DAT	DAT Delta Air Transport
BRA	Braathens (BU)		Airways (CB)	DAZ	DAS Air Cargo
BRD	Brock Air Service	CLC	Classic Air	DBY	Britannia Airways (BN)
BRG	Bering Air (8E)	CLG	Chalair (M6)	DHL	DHL Airways (ER)
BRO	Base Airlines (5E)	CLH	Lufthansa Cityline (CL)	DHX	DHL Aviation (ES)
BRT	British Regional Airlines (TH)	CLT	Air Caribbean (XC)	DJU	Air Djibouti (DY)
BRU	Belavia (B2)	CLX	Cargolux (CV)	DLA	Air Dolomiti (EN)
BRY	Brymon European Airw. (BC)	CMI	Continental Micronesia (GS)	DLH	Lufthansa (LH)
BRZ	Samara Airlines (E5)	CMM	Canada 3000 (2T)	DMO	Domodedovo Airlines (E3)
BSK	Miami Air (GL)	CMP	Copa Panama (CM)	DNM	Denim Air (3D)
BSY	Big Sky Airlines (GQ)	CNA	Centennial Airlines (BE)	DNV	Donavia (D9)
BTA	Continental Express (CO)	CNJ	Nanjing Airlines (3W)	DOA	Dominicana de Aviacion
BTC	BAL-Bashkirski (V9)	CNK	Sunwest International		(DO)
BTH	Air Saint Barthelmy (OJ)	CNM	Canarias Regional (FW)	DOB	Dobrolet Airlines
BTI	Air Baltic (BT)	CNW	China Northwest Airl. (WH)	DRG	Italair (B8)
BUK	Buckley Air	COA	Continental Airlines (CO)	DRK	Druk Air (KB)
BVT	Berjaya Air (J8)	COM	Comair (OH)	DSB	Air Senegal (DS)
BVU	Bellview Airlines	CPA	Cathay Pacific (CX)	DSR	DAS Air Cargo (SE)
BWA	BWIA International (BW)	CPI	Cebu Pacific Air (5J)	DTA	TAAG Angola Airlines (DT)
BWL	British World Airlines (VF)	CRC	Conair Aviation	DTR	Danish Air Transport (DX)
BZH	Brit Air (DB)	CRF	Crimea Air (OR)	EAA	TAAN
CAG	CNAC-Zhejiang Airlines (F6)	CRG	City Link Airlines	EAQ	Eastern Australia Airlines
CAL	China Airlines (CI)	CRL	Corse Air (SS)	EAT	Air Transport Europe
CAM	Camai Air (R9)	CRN	Aero Caribbean	EAV	Eagle Airlines (ZN)
CAV	Calm Air (MO)	CRQ	Air Creebec (YN)	ECA	Eurocypria Airlines (UI)
CAW	Comair (MN)	CRX	Crossair (LX)	ECC	Crossair Europe (QE)
CAY	Cayman Airways (KX)	CSA	CSA (OK)	EDW	Edelweiss Air
CBB	Air Caribbean (C2)	CSB	Air Commerce	EEA	Ecuatoriana (EU)
CBE	Aerocaribe (QA)	CSC	Sichuan Airlines (3U)	EEU	Eurofly Service
CBF	China Northern Airlines (CJ)	CSH	Shanghai Airlines (FM)	EEX	Avanti Air
CBJ	Caribjet	CSN	China Southern Airl. (CZ)	EEZ	Eurofly (GJ)
CCA	Air China (CA)	CSO	Casino Airlines	EGF	American Eagle Airlines
CCI	Capital Cargo International	CSZ	Shenzhen Airlines (4G)	EIA	Evergreen Intl.Airlines (EZ)
	(PT)	CTB	City Bird (H2)	EIN	Aer Lingus (EI)
CCM	Compagnie Corse	CTH	China General Aviation (GP)	ELG	Alpi Eagles (E8)
	Mediterranee (XK)	CTN	Croatia Airlines (OU)	ELK	Elk Airways (S8)
CCP	Champion Air (MG	CTP	Tapo Avia (PQ)	ELL	Estonian Air (OV)
CDG	Shandong Airlines (SC)	CTZ	CATA-Lineas Aerea	ELO	Eurolot
CDL	CC Air (ED)	CUA	China United Airlines (HR)	ELP	Aerolineas Ejecutivas
CDN	Canadian (CP)	CUB	Cubana (CU)	ELV	TANS
CDP	Aero Condor (P2)	CUS	Cronus Airlines (X5)	ELY	EL AL Israel Airlines (LY)
CDS	Central District Airlines	CUT	Court Air	ENI	Enimex
CES	China Eastern Airlines (MU)	CVA	Air Chathams (CV)	ENW	Airnor
CET	Centralafrican Airlines (GC)	CVU	Grand Canyon Airlines	EQA	Eagle Aviation (Y4)

EQL	Air Sao Tomé & Principe (KY)	GOE	GO Fly (OG)	JTA	Japan Transocean Air
ERG	Aviaenergo	GRL	Groenlandsfly (GL)	JUS	USA Jet Airlines
ERH	ERA Aviation (7H)	GRO	Allegro Air	KAC	Kuwait Airways (KU)
ERT	Red Sea Air	GTI	Atlas Air (5Y)	KAL	Korean Air (KE)
ESL	East Line Airlines (P7)	GTV	Aerogaviota	KBA	Ken Borek Airlines (4K)
ETH	Ethiopian Airlines (ET)	GUG	Aviateca (GU)	KDA	Kendell Airlines (KD)
EUA	ERA (E5)	GYA	Guyana Airways (GY)	KFA	Kelowna Flightcraft
EUL	Euralair (RN)	GZP	Gazpromavia	KFB	Air Botnia (KF)
EVA	Eva Air (BR)	HAL	Hawaiian Air (HA)	KGA	Kyrghyzstan Airlines (K2)
EWG	Eurowings (EW)	HAR	Harbour Airlines (HB)	KHA	Kitty Hawk Air Cargo (KR)
EWW	Emery Worldwide (GJ)	HCB	Helenair	KHB	Dalavia (H8)
EXS	Channel Express (LS)	HDA	Dragonair (KA)	KIL	Kuban Airlines (GW)
EXT	Night Express Luftverkehr	HHI	Hamburg International	KIS	Contact Air (3T)
EXY	South African Express	HHN	Hahn Air	KJC	Kras Air
	Airways	HJA	Air Haiti	KKB	Air South (WV)
EZS	Easyjet Switzerland (BH)	HLA	Heavylift Cargo Airlines (NP)	KLA	Air Lithuania (TT)
EZY	Easyjet Airline (U2)	HLF	Hapag-Lloyd Flug (HF)	KLC	KLM Cityhopper (HN)
FAB	First Air (7F)	HLQ	Harlequin Air	KLM	KLM Royal Dutch Airl. (KL)
FAJ	Air Fiji (PC)	HMS	Hemus Air (DU)	KLN	Kaliningrad Avia (K8)
FAO	Falcon Air Express (F2)	HRH	Royal Tongan Airlines (WR)	KOR	Air Koryo (JS)
FAT	Farner Air Transport	HTT	Air Tchad	KQA	Kenya Airways (KQ)
FBF	Fine Air (FB)	HVN	Vietnam Airlines (VN)	KRE	Aerosucre
FCN	Falcon Aviation (IH)	HZL	Hazelton Airlines (ZL)	KSM	Kosmos Aviakompania
FDE	Federico II Airways (2D)	IAC	Indian Airlines (IC)	KYV	Kibris Turkish Airlines (YK)
FDX	Fed Ex (FX)	IAW	Iraqi Airways (IA)	KZK	Air Kazakhstan
FEA	Far Eastern Air Transp. (EF)	IBB	Binter Canarias (NT)	LAA	Libyan Arab Airlines (LN)
FFR	Fischer Air (8F)	IBE	Iberia (IB)	LAJ	British Mediterranean (KJ)
FFT	Frontier Airlines (F9)	ICB	Islandsflug (HH)	LAL	Air Labrador (WJ)
FIN	Finnair (AY)	ICE	Icelandair (FI)	LAM	Linhas Aereas Mocambique
FJI	Air Pacific (FJ)	ICL	CAL Cargo Air Lines		(TM)
FLI	Atlantic Airways (RC)	ILM	Inter Air (D6)	LAN	LAN Chile (LA)
FOM	Freedom Air Intl.	IMX	Zimex Aviation (MF)	LAO	Lao Aviation (QV)
FRN	Tulip Air Charter	INI	Benair	LAP	TAM Paraguayas (PZ)
FRS	Flandre Air (IX)	IRA	Iran Air (IR)	LAV	Aeropostal (VH)
FSC	Four Star Aviation (HK)	IRB	Iran Airtours	LAZ	Balkan Airlines (LZ)
FTI	Fly FTI	IRC	Iran Aseman Airlines	LBC	Albanian Airlines (7Y)
FUA	Futura Intl.Airways (FH)	IRK	Kish Air (KN)	LBT	Nouvelair Tunisie
FWI	Air Guadeloupe (TX)	IRM	Mahan Air	LCI	Lufthansa Hinduja Cargo
FWL	Florida West Airlines (RF)	ISR	Israir		India (LF)
FWQ	Flight West Airlines (YC)	ISS	Meridiana (IG)	LCO	Ladeco (UC)
FXI	Flugfelag Islands (NY)	IST	Istanbul Airlines (IL)	LDA	Lauda Air (NG)
GAA	Bex-Delta Connection (HQ)	ISV	Islenia Airlines	LDE	LADE (LD)
GAP	Air Philippines (2P)	IWD	Iberworld (TY)	LDI	Lauda Air SpA (L4)
GAW	Gambia Airways	IYE	Yemenia Airways (IY)	LFA	Alfa Hava Yollari (H7)
GBL	GB Airways (GT)	JAA	Japan Asia Airways (EG)	LGL	Luxair (LG)
GBU	Air Bissau (YZ)	JAC	Japan Air Commuter (JN)	LGW	Luftfahrtgesellschaft Walther
GCO	Gemini Air Cargo (GR)	JAI	Jet Airways Ltd. (9W)		(HE)
GDI	Grandair (8L)	JAK	Jana Arka	LHN	Express One Intl. (EO)
GEC	Lufthansa Cargo (LH)	JAL	Japan Airlines (JL)	LIA	Liat Caribbean Airlines (LI)
GFA	Gulf Air (GF)	JAS	Japan Air System (JD)	LIB	Air Liberte (VD)
GFT	Gulfstream International (3M)	JAT	JAT-Yugoslav Airlines (JU)	LIL	Lithuanian Airlines (TE)
GHA	Ghana Airways (GH)	JAZ	Japan Air Charter (JZ)	LIT	Air Littoral (FU)
GIA	Garuda Indonesia (GA)	JEA	Jersey European Airways	LKR	Laker Airways (6F)
GIB	Air Guinee (GI)		(JY)	LLB	Lloyd Aereo Boliviano (LB)
GIL	Gill Airways (9C)	JEM	Emerald Airways (G3)	LOF	Trans States Airlines (9N)
GIO	Regionair (RH)	JEX	JAL Express (JC)	LOG	Loganair (LC)
GLA	Great Lakes Airlines (ZK)	JKK	Spanair (JK)	LOT	LOT Polish Airlines (LO)
GLB	Trans Global	JLH	Jet Link Holland	LPR	LAPA (MJ)
GMI	Germania Fluggesellschaft	JMC	JMC Airlines	LRC	Lacsa (LR)
	(ST)	JMX	Air Jamaica Express	LTP	Latpass Airlines (QI)
GNT	British Midland Commuter	JSC	Airstan	LTU	LTU Intl. Airways (LT)

LYC	Lynden Air Cargo (L2)	
MAA	MAS Air Cargo (MY)	
MAH	Malev Hungarian Airl. (MA)	
MAK	MAT-Macedonian Airlines (M7)	
MAS	Malaysia Airlines (MH)	
MAU	Air Mauritius (MK)	
MDG	Air Madagascar (MD)	
MDJ	JARO International (JT)	
MDL	Mandala Airlines (RI)	
MDS	MED Airlines (M8)	
MDV	Moldavian Airlines (2M)	
MDW	Midway Airlines (JI)	
MEA	Middle East Airlines (ME)	
MEP	Midwest Express (YK)	
MES	Mesaba (XJ)	
MFZ	Mofaz Air	
MGL	Miat Mongolian Airl. (OM)	
MKA	MK Airlines (7G)	
MLD	Air Moldova (9U)	
MLI	Air Mali (L9)	
MLV	Air Modova Intl. (3R)	
MNA	Merpati (MZ)	
MNB	MNG Cargo Airlines (MB)	
MNX	Manx Airlines (JG)	
MON	Monarch Airlines (ZB)	
MPD	Air Plus Comet (2Z)	
MPH	Martinair Holland (MP)	
MRS	Air Marshall Islands (CW)	
MRT	Air Mauritanie (MR)	
MSK	Maersk Air(VB)	
MSR	Egypt Air (MS)	
MTL	RAF Avia	
MTM	MTM Aviation	
MUK	MUK Air (ZR)	
MVD	KMV (KV)	
MWT	Midwest Aviation	
MXA	Mexicana (MX)	
MZS	Mahfooz Aviation (M2)	
NAC	Northern Air Cargo (HU)	
NAO	North American Airl. (XG)	
NCA	Nippon Cargo Airlines (KZ)	
NGA	Nigeria Airways (WT)	
NIS	Nica (6Y)	
NJS	National Jet Systems (NC)	
NKS	Spirit Airlines (NK)	
NMB	Air Namibia (SW)	
NRX	Filder Air Service	
NTS	Cirrus Air	
NTW	Nationwide Airlines (CE)	
NWA	Northwest Airlines (NW)	
NZM	Mount Cook Airline (NM)	
OAC	Oriental Airways	
OAE	Omni Air (X9)	
OAL	Olympic Airways (OA)	
OCA	Aserca Airlines (R7)	
ODS	Odessa Airlines (5K)	
OEA	Orient Thai Airlines (OX)	
OHY	Onur Air (8Q)	
OIR	Slov Air	
OKJ	Okada Air (9H)	

OLT	Ostfriesische Lufttransport (OL)	
OLY	Olympic Aviation (7U)	
OMA	Oman Air	
OMS	Omsk Avia	
ONT	Air Ontario (GX)	
ORB	Orenburg Airlines	
PAA	Pan Am	
PAC	Polar Air Cargo (PO)	
PAL	Philippines (PR)	
PAO	Polynesian Airlines (PH)	
PAR	Spair Air Transport (S4)	
PAS	Pelita Air Service (EP)	
PAV	VIP Avia	
PAX	Pan Air	
PBU	Air Burundi (PB)	
PCO	Pacific Coastal (8P)	
PEG	Pelangi Air (9P)	
PFC	Pacific Intl. Airlines	
PGA	PGA-Portugalia (NI)	
PGP	Perm Airlines	
PGT	Pegasus Airlines	
PIA	Pakistan Intl.Airlines (PK)	
PLA	Polynesian Airways (PH)	
PLK	Pulkovo Aviation (Z8)	
PMI	Air Europe Express	
PNW	Palestinian Airlines (PF)	
PRH	Pro Air (P9)	
PTB	Passaredo (Y8)	
PTN	Pantanal (P8)	
PUA	Pluna (PU)	
QFA	Qantas (QF)	
QNK	Kabo Air (9H)	
QSC	ASA African Safari	
QTR	Qatar Airways Co. (Q7)	
QXE	Horizon Air (QX)	
RAM	Royal Air Maroc (AT)	
RBA	Royal Brunei (BI)	
RDN	Dinar (D7)	
RGI	Regional Airlines (VM)	
RIT	Asian Spirit	
RJA	Royal Jordanian (RJ)	
RKA	Air Afrique (RK)	
RLD	RAS-Flug (RW)	
RME	Armenian Airlines (R3)	
RMV	Romavia (VQ)	
RNA	Royal Nepal Airlines (RA)	
ROM	Aeromar Airlines (BQ)	
RON	Air Nauru (ON)	
ROT	Tarom (RO)	
RPB	Aerorepublica (P5)	
RQX	Air Engadina/ KLM Alps (RQ)	
RSL	Rio Sul (SL)	
RSN	Royal Swazi Natl. Airways	
RTL	Rheintalflug (WG)	
RUS	Cirrus Airlines (C9)	
RVV	Reeve Aleutian Airways (RV)	
RWD	Alliance Air Express	
RYN	Ryan International Airlines	
RYR	Ryanair (FR)	
RZO	SATA International (S4)	

SAA	South African Airways (SA)	
SAB	Sabena (SN)	
SAI	Shaheen International (NL)	
SAM	Sam Columbia (MM)	
SAS	Scandinavian (SK)	
SAT	Sata Air Acores (SP)	
SAY	Scott Airways (CB)	
SBE	Sabre Airwys (TJ)	
SBI	Sibir Airlines (S7)	
SBY	Tempelhof Express (FC)	
SBZ	Scibe Airlift Zaire (ZM)	
SCH	Schreiner Airways (AW)	
SCI	Special Cargo Airways (C7)	
SCW	Braathens Malmö Aviation (BU)	
SCX	Sun Country Airlines (SY)	
SER	Aero California (JR)	
SEU	Star Airlines (2R)	
SEY	Air Seychelles (HM)	
SFB	Air Sofia (CT)	
SFR	Safeair (FA)	
SGL	Senegal Air	
SHK	Shoruk Air (7Q)	
SIA	Singapore Airlines (SQ)	
SIB	Sibaviatrans (5M)	
SIC	Air Sicilia (BM)	
SKW	Skywest-Delta Connection (OO)	
SKY	Skymark Airlines (BC)	
SLK	Silkair (MI)	
SLL	Slovak Airlines (6Q)	
SLM	Surinam Airways (PY)	
SLR	Sobelair (S3)	
SNB	Sterling European Airlines (NB)	
SNZ	Santa Cruz Imperial	
SOL	Solomon Airlines (IE)	
SPA	Sierra Pacific Airlines (SI)	
STU	STAF (FS)	
SUD	Sudan Airways (SD)	
SUF	Sunflower Airlines (PI)	
SUZ	Premiair Charter	
SVA	Saudia (SV)	
SVR	Ural Airlines (U6)	
SVV	Servivensa (VC)	
SWA	Southwest Airlines (WN)	
SWD	Southern Winds (A4)	
SWL	SAE Swe Aviation	
SWR	Swissair (SR)	
SXS	Sunexpress (XQ)	
SYR	Syrianair (RB)	
TAB	Taba (TT)	
TAE	Tame (EQ)	
TAI	TACA Intl. Airlines (TA)	
TAJ	Tunisavia	
TAM	TAM Brasil (KK)	
TAO	Aeromar Airlines (VW)	
TAP	TAP Air Portugal (TP)	
TAR	Tunis Air (TU)	
TAS	Lotus Air	
TAY	TNT Airways (3V)	

TBA	Transbrasil (TR)	
TCF	Shuttle America (S5)	
TCV	TACV Cabo Verde (VR)	
TEP	Transeuropean Airlines (UE)	
THA	Thai Airways Intl. (TG)	
THT	Air Tahiti Nui (TN)	
THY	Turkish Airlines (TK)	
TII	ATI Aircompany	
TLA	Transaer Intl.	
TMA	TMA of Lebanon (TL)	
TOW	Tower Air (FF)	
TPA	TAMPA Columbia (QT)	
TPC	Air Caledonie (TY)	
TRA	Transavia Airlines (HV)	
TRJ	AJT Air International (E9)	
TRS	Air Tran Airways (FL)	
TRZ	Transmeridian Airlines (T9)	
TSC	Air Transat (TS)	
TSO	Trans Aero (4J)	
TTA	TTA	
TTR	Tatra Air (QS)	
TUI	Tuninter (UG)	
TUL	Tulpar Av. Company
TVS	Travel Service Airlines
TWA	Trans World Airlines (TW)
TYM	Tyumen Airlines
TYR	Tyrolean Airways (VO)
TZK	Tajikistan Airlines (7J)
UAE	Emirates (EK)
UAL	United Airlines (UA)
UBA	Myanma Airways (UB)
UCA	USAir Express-Commutair
UGA	Uganda Airlines (QU)
UKA	KLM UK
UKR	Air Ukraine (GU)
UPA	Air Foyle (GS)
UPS	UPS Airlines (5X)
USA	US Airways (US)
USS	USAir Shuttle (TB)
UYA	Yute Air Alaska (4Y)
UYC	Cameroon Airlines (UY)
UZB	Uzbekistan Airways (HY)
VAT	Avant Airlines (OT)
VBW	Air Burkina (VH)
VDA	Volga Dnepr Cargo Airlines (VI)
VGD	Vanguard Airlines (NJ)
VIM	VIA (VL)
VIR	Virgin Atlantic Airways (VS)
VKG	Premiair (DK)
VKO	Vnukovo Airlines (V5)
VLE	Volare Airlines (8D)
VLM	VLM (V4)
VRG	Varig (RG)
VSP	VASP (VP)
VTA	Air Tahiti (VT)
VTR	Air Ostrava (8K)
VUN	Air Ivoire (VU)
WDL	WDL Aviation
WDY	Chicago Express Airlines (C8)
WIF	Wideroe (WF)
WOA	World Airways (WO)
XST	Skyteam
YRR	Scenic Airlines (YR)

The World's Largest Airlines 1999

By Total Passengers

1: Delta Air Lines . . . . 105 Million
2: United Airlines . . . . 87 Million
3: American Airlines . . . . 84 Million
4: US Airways . . . . 58 Million
5: Southwest Airlines . . . . 57 Million
6: Northwest Airlines . . . . 56 Million
7: Continental Airlines . . . . 45 Million
8: All Nippon Airways ANA . . . . 42 Million
9: Lufthansa . . . . 39 Million
10: British Airways . . . . 36 Million

By Revenue Passenger Kilometre (RPK)

1: United Airlines
2: American Airlines
3: Delta Air Lines
4: Northwest Airlines
5: British Airways
6: Continental Airlines
7: Air France
8: Japan Airlines
9: Lufthansa
10: US Airways

Related titles from Midland

WRECKS & RELICS
17th Edition

Ken Ellis

Now in its 39th year of publication, this standard reference work takes the reader on a county-by-county and province-by-province journey through the fascinating world of museums, military stores and dumps, 'geriatric' airliners awaiting the axe, restoration workshops, technical schools, treasures in garages and barns and much more. Within the wealth of detailed information supplied on thousands of aircraft can be found commentary, items to raise the eyebrow and myriad 'I never knew that', expressions!

Fully revised and updated, this latest edition has an array of appendices to take the subject further and the usual extensive indexing and cross-referencing.

In full colour for the first time for this edition, the 64 page photographic section is packed with fascinating and obscure subjects and is as wide-ranging and comprehensive as ever.

Hardback
210 x 148mm, 320 pages
192 colour photographs
Published May 2000
1 85780 100 8
£14.95

AIRLINERS
WORLDWIDE

Tom Singfield

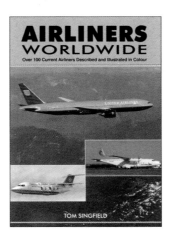

Interest in the airliners of the world continues to grow and with it demands for better reference material. Now, following on from the highly popular full colour format of *Airlines Worldwide,* comes a companion volume, devoted to the wide variety of types that ply the world's airways.

The author, an air traffic controller, has scoured the world for the illustrations for this book and provided an informative but highly readable reference to each aircraft. From Anglo-French Concorde to DHC Twin Otter, Airbus A340 to Beech 1900D, Douglas Dakota to Boeing 777 – the details of the airliner workhorses of the late 1990s are all there.

Ranging from the humble 15-seat feederliner to the huge Boeing 747-400, the book provides full colour illustrations of the major types, and roams the planet for rare and colourful examples. Detail given includes development, conversions and sub-series, number built and number in service. Also included is a listing of the airlines using each type.

Softback,
240 x 170 mm, 128 pages
135 full colour photographs
1 85780 056 7
Published August 1997
UK £11.95 / US $19.95

CLASSIC
AIRLINERS

Tom Singfield

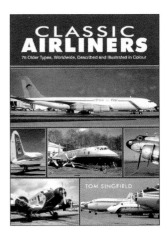

This companion volume to *Airliners Worldwide, Airlines Worldwide* and Airlines Remembered, reviews the specifications, histories and operations of 76 airliner types from the last half century.

The book is illustrated with over 200 outstanding full colour photographs from all around the world, showing the aircraft both in airline service and examples which have been preserved and can still be seen today.

Included are fondly remembered types such as the Lockheed Constellation, Douglas DC-3 and Vickers Viscount, plus some less well-known yet significant types, for instance the Dassault Mercure, Breguet Deux Ponts, Saab Scandia, and VFW-614.

Of course, all the appropriate types from the major manufacturers including Boeing, Douglas, Antonov, Lockheed, Ilyushin, and Tupolev also appear in the book . Classic Airliners offers a wealth of aviation nostalgia for all of those interested in the rapidly changing world of civil aviation.

Softback
240 x 170 mm, 160 pages
234 colour photographs
1 85780 098 2
Published May 2000
UK £13.95 / US $23.95

Related titles from Midland

AIRLINE TAIL COLOURS
550 colour illustrations to aid in the
quick recognition of airlines (2nd edn)

B I Hengi

With the continued growth in air travel,
interest in airliners, their liveries and
operations has never been higher. This
second edition contains 590 colour
illustrations showing the tail markings
of about 570 of the world's leading
airlines. Primarily intended as a basic
aid to the recognition of those individual
airlines, this pocket guide covers much
more. Each entry contains additional
information in a concise and easy-to-
use format to provide the airline's
three-letter code (used for flight
numbers); radio call-sign; international
registration prefix; ITU country code (its
main operating base); and aircraft types
used. Helpful de-code tables to ensure
that this indispensable companion is
user friendly and easily understood.

Softback
150 x 105mm, 160 pages
590 colour photographs
1 85780 104 0
Published July 2000
UK £7.95 / US $14.95

**AIRLINES
REMEMBERED**

B I Hengi

In the same format as the enormously
popular *Airlines Worldwide* and *Airliners
Worldwide,* this new companion
volume reviews the histories and
operations of over 200 airlines from the
last 30 years of aviation history, which
are no longer with us.

Each is illustrated with a full colour
photo showing at least one of their
aircraft in the colour scheme of that era.
Operators such as BEA, CP Air,
Eastern, Jet 24, Laker , Fred Olsen,
PeoplExpress and Valujet are examples
of the extensive and varied coverage
which this book provides.

In the rapidly changing world of civil
aviation, once familiar operators and
liveries frequently change or vanish
almost overnight. This book is a
wonderful wallow in aviation nostalgia
which will appeal to all interested in this
fascinating international business over
recent decades.

It will also provide inspiration for
aviation modellers and encourage them
to recreate these forgotten liveries on
their models.

Softback
240 x 170 mm, 224 pages
252 colour photographs
1 85780 091 5
Published April 2000
UK £14.95 / US $24.95

We hope you enjoyed this book . . .

Midland Publishing titles are edited by
an experienced and enthusiastic team
of specialists.

Further titles are in preparation though
we welcome ideas from authors or
readers for books they would like to
see published.

In addition, our associate company,
Midland Counties Publications, offers
an exceptionally wide range of aviation,
spaceflight, astronomy, military, naval
and transport books and videos for sale
by mail-order around the world.

For a copy of the appropriate catalogue,
or to order further copies of this book,
or the titles featured on the following
pages, please write, telephone, fax or
e-mail to:

Midland Counties Publications
Unit 3 Maizefield, Hinckley, Leics.,
LE10 1YF, England
Tel: (+44) 01455 233 747
Fax: (+44) 01455 233 737
E-mail:
midlandbooks@compuserve.com

US distribution by **Specialty Press** -
details on page 2